Collecting Modern First Editions

Collecting
Modern First Editions

Joseph Connolly

Studio Vista
London

For Patricia

A Studio Vista book published by
Cassell & Collier Macmillan Publishers Ltd
35 Red Lion Square, London WC1R 4SG
and at Sydney, Auckland, Toronto, Johannesburg
an affiliate of
Macmillan Publishing Co., Inc.
New York

First published 1977
ISBN 0 289 70790 0
Designed by Anthony Cohen and Brooke Snell
Photography by Ken Randall
Filmset and printed in Great Britain by
BAS Printers Limited, Over Wallop, Hampshire

Acknowledgments

Where possible, I have attempted to go back to source in order to compile the checklists contained in this volume, and I am indebted to the National Book League for the constant and uncomplaining help which they have given throughout the writing of this work. I also thank the University College Library and the American Library, and Miss Fiona McKenzie for her editing work, and helpful suggestions.

I am very grateful to the following publishers, listed in alphabetical order, for kindly granting permission for their dust-wrapper designs to be reproduced in this book:

Agenda Publications Ltd
W. H. Allen & Co. Ltd
George Allen & Unwin (Publishers) Ltd
Associated Book Publishers Ltd
Barrie & Jenkins Ltd
Jonathan Cape Ltd
Chatto and Windus Ltd
William Collins Sons and Co. Ltd
J. M. Dent & Sons Ltd
Doubleday & Company Inc.
Faber and Faber Ltd
Samuel French Ltd
Victor Gollancz Ltd
Hamish Hamilton Ltd
Hart-Davis MacGibbon Ltd
William Heinemann Ltd
Hodder & Stoughton Ltd
The Hogarth Press Ltd
The Hutchinson Publishing Group Ltd
Michael Joseph Ltd
Alfred A. Knopf Inc.
Longman Group Ltd
Macmillan Publishers Ltd
John Murray (Publishers) Ltd
Observer/Transworld
Penguin Books Ltd
Martin Secker & Warburg Ltd

All the books illustrated are from the author's personal collection.

Why collect First Editions?

'Why do you collect first editions? I mean, isn't the print the same in the second or third or fiftieth editions?'

'Well, yes, but . . .'

Already the sceptic has gained an advantage, for by now the collector is looking at his shoes—or, worse, polishing them on the backs of his trousers.

'Well why then?' Relentless.

'It's difficult to explain . . .'

'I see.'

'. . . but basically, you see, it is very exciting to possess the book in its original state—the state that it first reached a rapturous public and awe-stricken critics, possibly even the very copy handled by the author himself— particularly if it is signed, for this is proof, as it were. The *first* is the most difficult to find, usually—yes, this is an advantage, as it makes eventual acquisition trebly satisfying.'

'I see.' He does not see.

'Yes, that's it all right. And, of course, they appreciate in value, unlike subsequent editions.'

'I see.' And this time, he does.

'Of course, that is not the chief aim. The aesthetics appeal more than the aspect of investment, although it is vastly pleasing when one can pick up an item at a fraction of its true value, or merely watch one's carefully chosen library become more valuable. But really, it is the thrill of the chase, the completing of sets, the final tracking down of that one elusive volume, the occasional sense of—yes, connoisseurship . . .'

The manic collector has once more descended into abstract sentiments, and the sceptic is no longer listening.

Introduction

This is the book I needed about ten years ago, when I began to be interested in the subject of modern first editions. There was no such book then, and despite the phenomenal growth in general enthusiasm, there has been no such book since. All Modern First collectors are familiar with the grudging few pages slipped in at the end of every book on collecting, telling one that Dylan Thomas's first book, *18 Poems,* is now very hard to come by, and worth £100. The chapter might then continue to say that some modern books have been illustrated by desperately famous artists, and issued in limited editions of around 17 copies; these, the chapter will inform you, are rare. Having thus covered the whole subject pretty adequately, there might be a rounding-off to the effect that John Berryman and Ted Hughes, or similar, are promising young talents that might be worth looking out for; as both have been keenly collected for many years, this information does not help, or inspire. Such general books on book-collecting are usually very adequate on other branches, but when it comes to modern firsts, one always feels a few have been included merely for the sake of completeness, and not from any desire to inform, or indeed treat the subject with any seriousness at all.

To provide absolutely everything, of course, would be impossible in less than twenty volumes—complete bibliographies, with points, of every contemporary author, would easily run to this—but I hope that the information in this book will be more than adequate for reference in the field, and to help the beginner carve out a path, for many, I know, are uncertain of what is available, and which way to go.

Collecting modern first editions is fun. It is exciting and compulsive, and although one needs hard facts as one's ammunition, it is not a dreary, bookish pursuit, doggedly followed by the status-conscious rich, as some critics would have one believe. It is vital, concerned wholly with the pursuit of current literature, in fine, original editions,

and the deep, dark points, and the scrupulously detailed knowledge that the more 'Clique-conscious' dealers will tell you is fundamental, are not so difficult to acquire, nor is the information available only to these dealers. I sell books myself, for a living, but I get far more pleasure from collecting them—although it must be admitted that the two together form an almost ideal partnership. There are dealers, however, who do not welcome such books as this, which they see as being too explicit to be good for the trade. This might be so, in some way, but I believe it is time for at least some of the mystique to be removed, and to provide more information for the people who actually *collect*, without whom the dealer would begin to look rather silly. Make no mistake, though: just as the plethora of books on, say, English porcelain has not made everyone an expert, so this book provides merely the bones, nothing being a substitute for a collector's 'feel', that indefinable sense that is the only true mystique in the book world.

There are two factors to be taken into account when deciding what to collect: taste and financial stability. This may seem obvious, but many stunted collections exist which have been governed either by the god Fashion, or by a very low maximum price allowed for each book. I think it is unwise to be too unbending with regard to price, for there are many examples in this book where all an author's output may be obtained for a very small outlay, save one—usually the first; it would be a great pity if the collector were content to leave the collection lacking this item—although such an instance is almost inconceivable within my experience. Much more likely is the collector who pursues only the authors of the moment; this can only lead to higher and higher prices, and if the choice of author was not initially governed by the collector's own personal taste, then eventually he might come to sell the books at a substantially reduced price, once the craze has faded.

Taste and pocket taken into account, the

collector's choice is limitless. Some collect a very few authors' entire output, some pursue only 'highlights'—the accepted greats—and then some are interested only in one decade, or an imprint, or a genre—or even those books illustrated, or with dust-wrappers by, a certain artist. The disadvantage of collecting an imprint—say the Hogarth Press, or an illustrator—say Ardizzone or Sendak—is that one is almost certain to acquire a number of books that are uninteresting—for, contrary to popular belief, most modern first collectors do *read* their acquisitions, and usually possess a good knowledge of current literature. On the other hand, such narrow collections can have the unchallenged advantage of completeness, something that a collection of highlights cannot have, in a strict interpretation of the word, for such definition once more reverts to taste, as much as does the very arrangement of books on the shelves—a telling form of literary criticism. My personal view is that the most satisfying and representative collection would take the form of the collector's few favourite authors in their entirety, together with as many highlights as the collector's taste demands. It is a sound idea also to restrict one's collection to only poetry, or drama, or novels, though this can be frustrating, for one is constantly tempted to cross boundaries, and although a collector must, to a certain extent, remain within his field—in order to preserve both his solvency and his sanity—collecting is not about self-denial or repression. Many collectors are after books of cartoons, lately, by such artists as Giles, Thelwell, Charles Addams and Steinberg, to name a few. This is a relatively unexploited field, and one favoured by the young—as is the field of novels and plays that have been filmed, both interests reflecting the current more easygoing and all-embracing attitudes to collecting. Much of the enthusiasm for such work is, I believe, attributable to the fact that it is truly contemporary, and the feeling of relevancy and excitement might be similar to that of being young in the thirties, for I am

told that the thrill of buying and reading the new Auden, while the whole new wave was going on all around, has yet to be equalled.

I have hinted several times already at what this book might be expected to do for the beginner and for the established collector, but I should now like to be more specific as to the precise contents. I have not split the subject-matter into sections, such as novels, plays, poetry, as so many authors diversify; it was thought better to keep an author's work together, and so they appear alphabetically— a list of those included is to be found at the end of this essay—in most cases with a checklist of their works, including publishers, dates and other relevant information. There are a few authors whose output was so huge that I have been able to give only a selection—and this is also true of some who have either been previously very well documented, or else are responsible for only a few key books. Within the confines of space, as much information as possible will be given; if there is a standard biography or bibliography, it is recorded, and, as a rule, any films that have been made from an author's work, together with the maker of the film, and its date. Also included is a price estimate for every book; this is a guide only, and must be used with discretion, though later I shall discuss more fully prices and values.

With a very few exceptions, the books are post-1900, and in the English language, with particular accent, of course, on British and American writers of the 1930–1970s period. The term 'Moderns' does not any more mean authors such as Galsworthy, Maugham and Wells, as it did during the book-collecting boom of the thirties, but rather the writers *since* then, and it is on these that I shall dwell. This does not imply criticism of those named, but this book, it must be remembered, is for the collector, and enough has been written about the former greats, and very little about our contemporary writers, in whom there is currently the most interest. Although I do not believe I have omitted any twentieth-century literary giant, I do not apologize for including, sometimes lengthily, those authors who have come to be termed 'light' or 'recreational', such as P. G. Wodehouse or Agatha Christie, for although many collect these authors, many also smile nervously on having admitted it. No excuses are necessary, I feel. Entertaining authors, and entertaining books, are possibly the greatest thing the world has left.

And now, the thing itself: the pursuit of books.

How to obtain First Editions

Well, in secondhand and antiquarian bookshops, most obviously, but not only those that specialize in the subject, though these can be very valuable—particularly for their catalogues, or that single, sought-after book. Small, general shops are always worth investigation, for here the finds are to be made on the Fiction, Plays and Poetry shelves, and it is sometimes true that the first-edition section of such shops is half as interesting, and twice as expensive. Bookshops selling new books are not to be neglected either, being mainly useful, of course, for the latest works of collected authors, as they are published. It is folly to wait too long, by the way, for a sudden second impression can mean a chase all over the country to find a bookseller who has not moved his stock quite so quickly. Energy may thus be conserved by having relevant publishers' six-monthly catalogues sent to you, to keep abreast of what is due. Bookshops selling review copies can also be useful in these days of heavy prices, but one would advise only copies in first-class condition—and once more, do not wait overlong in the hope that the shop may obtain a copy. Such shops do not by any means get *all* the new books, but certainly if you see a good copy of a new book at a reduced price, it makes good sense to buy. But do buy—do not go away and think about it, for it will be gone; but this, as collectors know, is true of all books. The only regrets a collector ever has are the books he did not buy. This prompt-action rule is especially applicable to postal lists—phone or write immediately. Collectors are very familiar with the feelings of elation, or else a sense of having been cheated, after such early-morning phone calls.

Identifying First Editions

This, of course, can pose problems, for as one would expect there is no hard and fast rule. It is true that *most* will state 'First Published . . .' or 'First Printing . . .', followed by the date, but by no means all. Some merely have a date, which changed with each edition in a new year. Some publishers, though less often today, leave the verso of the title-page completely blank. I once offered a 1st of Colin Wilson's *The Outsider* to a collector, who first favoured me with a demonic stare that such people reserve for shyster dealers, and then backed out of the shop, stumbling only once. All this because nowhere on the book did it *say* it was the 1st; I didn't argue. A generally safe rule, though, is that if the book bears no information to the contrary, it probably is a 1st. To try and make this a little more clear, if there are details of a second or third impression, then obviously one is handling a reprint. Similarly, if the words 'This edition . . .' appear, the book is most likely not the first appearance. Such books are referred to in trade catalogues as '1st Thus', a most misleading term, which means simply that the book is the first edition *in this form*—e.g. with these illustrations, from this publisher, in this anthology. In short, '1st Thus' means not a 1st. Incidentally, the 1st edition of an anthology need not mean, and generally does not, that any or all of the contents is printed for the first time, but the list of acknowledgments will usually determine this. Sometimes a first edition will have subsequent issues, as distinct from impressions. A second impression is as good as a fiftieth to the collector, but the second issue can be quite acceptable. It usually means that a number of the original impression were held back and issued later, sometimes in a variant binding, which is the only means of identification; however, such identification is not possible without consulting a bibliography.

The other two important factors in identifying a 1st are binding and dust-wrapper. One wants the publisher's original cloth (or pitted paper more commonly used today), which can usually be identified by the presence of the colophon at the foot of the spine, not present when a book has been recased by a library. Some books are remaindered in sheets, though, and then bound by the purchaser. In this case, the colophon might well be present, but the binding would be inferior to the original; this does not happen often with modern 1sts, though a recent example is Durrell's *Sauve Qui Peut*. It should also be remembered that even the most exquisite hand-tooled, deep-banded walrus-skin, or whatever, binding is second best on a modern first.

The question of dust-wrappers is a very important one. First—should there be one? Almost always for post-1920 books, the answer is yes, though sometimes laminated or decorated boards substitute. Dust-wrappers are really essential for a complete 1st, and usually of some interest in themselves, either in the artwork, or in the biographical or bibliographical information they provide. The artist is occasionally of equal—or superior—stature to the author, and of course where the author is the dust-wrapper artist as well—as, for instance, in the cases of Mervyn Peake and some of Evelyn Waugh—the importance becomes evident. One will come across later dust-wrappers married to 1sts, from time to time—presumably in order to enhance their value to the unsuspecting—but there are a few giveaways, such as reviews of the book quoted on the rear or flaps—providing they are not, say, American reviews of an American book, now published in Britain—and lists or reviews of the author's work subsequent to the book being examined.

From the point of view of design, modern first collectors owe a special debt to Faber's artwork over the decades, though they too are now succumbing to photography and lamination, and have virtually dropped their very distinctive Albertus typeface. Many other publishers recently seem to be swinging back to artwork, however, and the white, laminated dust-wrapper of the sixties, bearing the Technicolor sub-Aldridge doodle, is thankfully not quite so predominant today.

Condition

Condition, of course, is important in all fields of book collecting, but particularly so with modern firsts, for generally speaking I think the more recent a book, the more perfect it should be. By perfection, the collector usually means in a state precisely as published, and the most common disfigurement, together with the absence of the dust-wrapper, discussed above, is some sort of inscription on the front endpaper—other than that of the author, which is mentioned later. Many collectors do not object to the name of the last owner neatly inscribed, particularly if it is accompanied by a date contemporary with the book, but sometimes one comes across a book with the first name rudely crossed out, and another in its place—or, worse still, a gift inscription. I sold a book quite recently with the following carved in blue felt-pen *all over* the endpaper: 'For Lovely Flossie, in memory of that immemorable [*sic*] week in Ramsgate. Gordon.' As I say, I sold it, so there are people impervious to the grotesque. I hasten to add, however, that this deface-ment was in a book of no consequence, and if either Flossie or Gordon is offended, I am sorry. In all seriousness, though, it is up to the collector whether an even less extreme inscription is preferable to a new endpaper, though substitution ought to be carried out with great care, preferably by an expert, and only, in my opinion, when absolutely necessary.

Boots Circulating Library stickers are a common eyesore on books of this period, and

I think it is true to say that they can never be removed totally without trace. Items bearing these things really ought not to be considered, unless one is desperate.

No page or plate should ever be missing from a collector's book, and although the price falls dramatically if such is the case, such a book ought not to be bought, unless extremely scarce, and then grudgingly. If the title-page is missing, then of course the book may safely be thrown away.

A word on booksellers' descriptions of books. It is very difficult to translate the terms unless one knows the criteria of the bookseller in question from past experience, but from my own research over the years, 'mint' almost never exists, 'fine' means pretty near brand-new condition, 'very good' means less than fine—an average, secondhand book—'nice' is slightly silly, and probably means the same as 'very good'. 'Good' means not very good. 'Fair', 'poor', 'reading copy' and 'working copy' can generally be taken to mean appalling.

Autographs and MSS

Manuscripts and typescripts are coveted by many as being the true 'originals'. This, of course, is true, but it does not make a very practical proposition for the collector. There are very few MSS around, and they are very expensive. Signed copies of books and autograph letters are more plentiful, and both are very desirable. The authors who are known to sign very little, of course, are more sought after, and more expensive, but generally speaking, any price estimate in this book may safely be doubled if the book is signed. With some authors—e.g. Ezra Pound, Virginia Woolf—the value of the book could rise four or five times, but this is not usual unless the inscription is to someone relevant, thus making the item an Association Copy. The bare name, or initials, are of less interest, though they still command a fair price. I have been asked how to identify a signature as real, but I do not think there is any way, a comparison with the original proving very

little. I believe it is true, however, that there is very little, if any, forgery in the book world, but one ought to buy from a reputable dealer.

Beware how far the desire for association material takes you, though. I received a list of autograph items for sale recently, and among them was a *typed* postcard from Mrs Nabokov, explaining that sorry, no, her husband didn't sign anything.

Legendary Firsts

One hears of legendary 1sts quite a lot. These are the 1sts no-one has for sale, but once upon a time every dealer in the world had, and sold for a pittance. Worse than this, there exists quite a number of dealers who have every legendary 1st in their cellars, it's just that they are a bit difficult to get at. Legendary 1sts to the collector are the ones he has been searching for all his adult life, and the dealer sold yesterday. Legendary 1sts are a fact of life. There *are* legendary 1sts, though. Ask your book dealer if he has any 1sts of Edgar Allen Poe, or the true (recalled) 1st of *Alice in Wonderland*, or Auden's *Poems* (1928). He might laugh, he might twitch nervously, or he might faint. What he will *not* do is reach under the counter and produce them—but of course he always might, you never know with books. If he does, then depending on your character, you might consider asking him whether he is trying to be funny.

Other interests

There are a few areas of interest for the collector outside the strict confines of Modern First Editions, the main one being that of proof copies. Interest in these has grown lately, for as it is true that they precede the first edition, collectors maintain they become 'pre-1sts'. There is also the rarity value to consider, for it is unusual for more than 50 to be printed, and as all are the property of the publisher, and not intended to be sold, relatively few come onto the market. Against this, critics say that they are ugly in their plain wrappers (true), they are commonly full of errors (true), and they are more expensive than the 1st (true). It can be desirable to have *both,* however, particularly so when notable changes have been made—in the title, for instance—between proof stage and publication. Sometimes they are sent out to reviewers in a special proof dust-wrapper, an apt example of this being John Fowles' first book *The Collector.*

First paperback appearances of books are also collected nowadays, and the first editions of very early Penguins are collected in their own right—the very first Penguin, André Maurois' *Ariel,* having been recently catalogued by Quaritch at £65.

Magazine and periodical contributions are collected by some, though usually only if the collector is concentrating solely upon one or two authors; otherwise one's study is in danger of resembling the warehouse of Messrs W. H. Smith & Son—a grim prospect. Other than the 'little magazines', such as Cyril Connolly's *Horizon* or John Lehmann's *London Magazine* (dealt with under the respective authors), periodicals are often unsightly, and difficult to store. It is perhaps partly for this reason that there are many examples of works which first appeared in periodical form fetching far *less* than the 1st book form which shortly followed. Notable examples of this are the Sherlock Holmes stories in *The Strand Magazine*—which, although very undervalued at present, will never approach the prices of the 1st book forms—and P. G. Wodehouse's school stories in *The Captain,* bound volumes of which may be acquired at a figure way below those commanded for the subsequent books.

Prices and values

The value of a certain book to a collector—apart from its literary wealth—is the figure he is willing to pay for it. The price charged by a dealer is usually the generally agreed current figure—assuming that the dealer knows the value of what he is selling, not always the case, and it is not as arbitrary as sometimes it might seem. Most dealers stick to the norm, some pitch below, and some—through either ignorance or greed—pitch above, constantly. Word gets around about such dealers, though, such being the world of book collecting, and the incomprehensible grapevine that supports it. Rest assured, if you have just discovered a wonderful/lousy, very cheap/extortionate shop, whoever you tell will already know about it—indeed, have been going there/avoiding it for years.

Eventually, though, the way in which a dealer prices a book will be unique to him. Some go by what they paid for a book, and in this way a bargain gets passed on. Some are very much influenced by the title itself—deliberately marking up a much-loved book, half-hoping no-one will buy it, and pricing some unfavoured work very, very cheaply in the knowledge that soon they will be rid of it. I know one bookseller in the South of England who goes farther than that: he removes all dust-wrappers from his stock and throws them away for, he claims, they give the shop an untidy look. Modern poetry, and in particular modern American poetry, he refuses to buy, but if any is discovered in a lot, it joins the wrappers in the bin. If you specialize in current verse and are searching for fine copies, I should give this place a miss.

It should also be remembered that, contrary to what a few might tell you, no bookseller knows everything. If you are a specialist in one particular field, your knowledge in this particular area will probably be greater than that of a general dealer, and this, obviously, can be very useful. It is therefore quite possible that a bookseller may make a mistake in pricing a book—after all, he prices hundreds in a week—or he may, in haste, mistake a later impression for a first. In such a case, most will be ready to rectify the error, but not many dealers relish the occasional customer who will offer three pounds for a book correctly priced at six, for contrary to wide-held belief, dealers do *buy* books, and rent premises, and pay for taxes and rates, not to mention tea and other necessities of life, such as tobacco and Sellotape.

The major factor influencing the sudden steep increase in the price of a book is, of course, demand, or fashion. The god Fashion can raise a humble hardback and hurl it to unimagined heights—and the more fashionable people who want the book, the higher it will go. This does not mean that one should avoid fashionable literature—it is sometimes quite good—but certainly one's collection ought not to be governed by it. Taste is the thing, acquired by reading. Many think that the books of Sylvia Plath and those illustrated by Arthur Rackham are reaching ultra-fashionable prices, but many more are searching for them, willing to pay. Thus the spiral ascends. Only the collector's wallet, discretion and taste can resolve this issue, but we might look back to the boom of the thirties again. No-one wanted the young writers of the time—Auden, Isherwood, Eliot, Woolf, Lawrence—but unbelievably high prices were being reached for Galsworthy and the others; many Galsworthy items sold at twenty pounds forty years ago would be lucky to fetch four pounds today—because of fashionable taste, of course; the books themselves have not altered.

Care and preservation

Having acquired first editions in the finest possible state, then, the collector is anxious to keep them that way. He also wants to read them. It is here that we reach another club with which the collector is often bashed: the man who expends large amounts of money on rare books so that he can salt them away and spend the rest of his life looking at the spines is on a par with one who would purchase the Mona Lisa in order to deposit it with Coutts. Well, yes probably, but the modern first collector really does enjoy reading literature, you know . . . It is no good. The sceptic has stopped listening again. But the collector knows it is true, and one *can* read a book without harming it in any way. With a much-loved and a read title,

though, a paperback as well would not be a bad idea, so long as you do not try and explain to an outsider why you have a book too good to read. Some sensible precautions, though, are to store books well away from damp and radiators—both arch-enemies—and not to insert letters or programmes within the covers, which may become warped as a result, or the binding sprung. *Non-adhesive* Libra-film is a very good protection for dust-wrappers; it eliminates the possibility of tearing or fingermarks, and actually enhances the appearance of the book. Do not leave books angled or sloping, as they are in danger of remaining so—though this is an unlikely action for a true collector, he being more likely to commit the other don't: don't cram too many onto a shelf; but sometimes, with bookcases in all but the most intimate places, it seems the only way to make space, so that yet more books may be acquired. The collector will understand this; in the eyes of the sceptic, one more nail in the coffin has just been driven home.

Book Books

There have been some first-class books about book-collecting in general, and I append a list of a few of the best—some available, and some sadly out-of-print. Such books almost always become sought-after in their own right, and can become very difficult to find. Look after this book.

1. P. H. Muir *Book-Collecting as a Hobby* (Gramol; out of print).
2. A. Edward Newton *This Book-Collecting Game* (Routledge 1930)
   This I consider to be the best, most lively and entertaining book on the subject, as well as being enormously informative. It is, as one would expect, out-of-print.
3. John Carter *Taste and Technique in Book-Collecting* (CUP 1948)
4. John Carter *ABC for Book Collectors* (Hart-Davis 1952)
   This really is essential. It explains absolutely every term and abbreviation, and it is in print.

Bookseller Directories

1. *A Directory of Dealers in Secondhand and Antiquarian Books in the British Isles* (Sheppard Press; published every three years)
2. *Book Dealers in North America and Canada* (Sheppard Press)
3. *The Clique Annual Directory of Booksellers* (The Clique. An annual, and hence the most reliable)
4. Roy Harley Lewis *The Book Browser's Guide* (David & Charles 1975)
   Chatty and readable. The most up to date, but not comprehensive.

A phone call is always advisable before a trip to a bookshop, as in recent years shops have come and gone with alarming frequency. Booksellers are also prone to this: the infamous 'Back in Five Minutes' signs have been known to be displayed in windows for days, or else until the sticky tape yellows, and the notice drops off in disgust.

List of authors

Abse, Dannie
Adams, Richard
Albee, Edward
Aldington, Richard
Aldiss, Brian W.
Amis, Kingsley
Asimov, Isaac
Auden, W. H.

Bainbridge, Beryl
Ballard, J. G.
Banks, Lynne Reid
Barker, George
Barnes, Djuna
Barstow, Stan
Beckett, Samuel
Beerbohm, Max
Behan, Brendan
Bellow, Saul
Benchley, Peter
Bennett, Alan
Bentley, E. C.
Berryman, John
Betjeman, John
Bolt, Robert
Bond, Edward
Bowen, Elizabeth
Bradbury, Malcolm
Bradbury, Ray
Braine, John
Braithwaite, E. R.
Bramah, Ernest
Brautigan, Richard
Brenan, Gerald
Brooke, Rupert
Bunting, Basil
Burgess, Anthony
Burroughs, Edgar Rice
Burroughs, William S.

Camus, Albert
Capote, Truman
Chandler, Raymond
Charteris, Leslie
Chesterton, G. K.
Christie, Agatha
Clarke, Arthur C.
Connolly, Cyril
Corvo, Baron

Crompton, Richmal
cummings, e. e.

Dahl, Roald
Davies, W. H.
Day-Lewis, C.
Deighton, Len
de la Mare, Walter
Delaney, Shelagh
Donleavy, J. P.
Douglas, Keith
Doyle, Arthur Conan
Drabble, Margaret
du Maurier, Daphne
Dunn, Nell
Durrell, Lawrence
Dyer, Charles

Eliot, T. S.

Faulkner, William
Feiffer, Jules
Ferlinghetti, Lawrence
Firbank, Ronald
Fitzgerald, F. Scott
FitzGibbon, Constantine
Fleming, Ian
Forester, C. S.
Forster, E. M.
Forsyth, Frederick
Fowles, John
Francis, Dick
Frayn, Michael
Frost, Robert

Gardner, Erle Stanley
Gibbons, Stella
Ginsberg, Allen
Golding, William
Grahame, Kenneth
Grass, Günter
Graves, Robert
Gray, Simon
Green, Henry
Greene, Graham
Greenwood, Walter
Grigson, Geoffrey
Grossmith, George and Weedon
Gunn, Thom

Hall, Radclyffe
Hammett, Dashiell
Hardy, Thomas
Hartley, L. P.
Heaney, Seamus
Heath-Stubbs, John
Heller, Joseph
Hemmingway, Ernest
Hesse, Hermann
Highsmith, Patricia
Hill, Susan
Hilton, James
Household, Geoffrey
Howard, Elizabeth Jane
Hughes, Richard
Hughes, Ted
Hume, Fergus
Huxley, Aldous

Isherwood, Christopher

Jarrell, Randall
Jellicoe, Ann
Jennings, Elizabeth
Jerome, Jerome K.
Johns, W. E.
Jones, David
Joyce, James

Kästner, Erich
Kazantzakis, Nikos
Kerouac, Jack
Kesey, Ken
Koestler, Arthur

Lancaster, Osbert
Larkin, Philip
Lawrence, D. H.
Lawrence, T. E.
Leacock, Stephen
le Carré, John
Lee, Laurie
Lehmann, John
Lennon, John
Lessing, Doris
Levi, Peter
Levin, Bernard
Lewis, C. S.
Lewis, P. Wyndham
Lofting, Hugh

London, Jack
Loos, Anita
Lovercraft, H. P.
Lowell, Robert

McCarthy, Mary
MacDiarmid, Hugh
Mackenzie, Compton
MacLean, Alistair
MacNeice, Louis
Mailer, Norman
Mansfield, Katherine
Marcus, Frank
Marsh, Ngaio
Masefield, John
Maugham, W. Somerset
Miller, Arthur
Miller, Henry
Milne, A. A.
Mitchell, Margaret
Mitford, Nancy
Monsarrat, Nicholas
Moore, Marianne
Mortimer, Penelope
Muir, Edwin
Murdoch, Iris

Nabokov, Vladimir
Naipaul, V. S.
Nash, Ogden
Naughton, Bill
Nichols, Peter

O'Brien, Edna
O'Brien, Flann
O'Casey, Sean
Orton, Joe
Orwell, George
Osborne, John
Owen, Wilfred

Parkinson, C. Northcote
Pasternak, Boris
Patten, Brian
Peake, Mervyn
Perelman, S. J.
Pinter, Harold

Plath, Sylvia
Plomer, William
Pound, Ezra
Powell, Anthony
Powys, J. C.
Powys, Llewelyn
Powys, T. F.
Priestley, J. B.
Pritchett, V. S.
Puzo, Mario

Raine, Kathleen
Ransome, Arthur
Raven, Simon
Read, Herbert
Rhys, Jean
Richards, Frank
Rohmer, Sax
Rosenberg, Isaac
Roth, Philip
Runyon, Damon
Russell, Bertrand

Sackville-West, Vita
Sagan, Françoise
Sandford, Jeremy
Sapper
Sassoon, Siegfried
Sayers, Dorothy L.
Searle, Ronald
Shaffer, Peter
Shaw, George Bernard
Sillitoe, Alan
Simenon, Georges
Sitwell, Edith
Sitwell, Osbert
Sitwell, Sacheverell
Smith, Stevie
Snow, C. P.
Solzhenitsyn, Alexander
Spark, Muriel
Spender, Stephen
Stevens, Wallace
Stewart, J. I. M.
Stoppard, Tom
Storey, David

Story, Jack Trevor
Stout, Rex
Strachey, Lytton
Symons, Julian

Taylor, Elizabeth
Thomas, Dylan
Thomas, Edward
Thomas, R. S.
Thurber, James
Tolkien, J. R. R.
Travers, P. L.

Uris, Leon

Vidal, Gore
Vonnegut Jnr, Kurt

Wain, John
Waley, Arthur
Wallace, Edgar
Waterhouse, Keith
Watkins, Vernon
Waugh, Evelyn
Webb, Mary
Welch, Denton
Wells, H. G.
Wesker, Arnold
Wheatley, Dennis
White, Patrick
White, T. H.
Wilde, Oscar
Williams, Charles
Williams, Tennessee
Williamson, Henry
Wilson, Angus
Wilson, Colin
Wodehouse, P. G.
Woolf, Leonard
Woolf, Virginia
Wyndham, John

Yates, Dornford
Yeats, W. B.
Yevtushenko, Yevgeny

Scale of values

Grade A up to approx. £3 ($5)
Grade B up to approx. £5 ($8)
Grade C up to approx. £10 ($16)
Grade D up to approx. £15 ($24)
Grade E up to approx. £20 ($32)
Grade F up to approx. £25 ($40)
Grade G up to approx. £30 ($48)
Grade H up to approx. £35 ($56)
Grade I up to approx. £40 ($64)
Grade J up to approx. £45 ($72)
Grade K up to approx. £50 ($80)
Grade L up to approx. £60 ($96)
Grade M up to approx. £70 ($112)
Grade N up to approx. £80 ($128)
Grade O up to approx. £90 ($144)
Grade P up to approx. £100 ($160)
Grade Q up to approx. £200 ($320)
Grade R over £200 ($320)

Values within Grades Q and R are given more specifically.

Please bear in mind that this scale is intended as a guide only, and that many factors must be considered when pricing any given item. This fact is stressed throughout the book.

ABSE, Dannie
Born in Cardiff 1923.

1. *After Every Green Thing* (verse) Hutchinson 1949
2. *Walking Under Water* (verse) Hutchinson 1952
3. *Ash on a Young Man's Sleeve* (novel) Hutchinson 1954
4. *Some Corner of an English Field* (novel) Hutchinson 1956
5. *Fire in Heaven* (play) Hutchinson 1956
6. *Tenants of the House* (verse) Hutchinson 1957
7. *Poems, Golders Green* (verse) Hutchinson 1962
8. *Dannie Abse: A Selection* (verse) Studio Vista 1963
9. *Medicine on Trial* (non-fiction) Aldus 1967
10. *Three Questor Plays* Scorpion Press 1967 (cont.: *House of Cowards, Gone, In the Cage. In the Cage* is revised version of 5)
11. *A Small Desperation* (verse) Hutchinson 1968
12. *Demo* (verse) Sceptre Press 1969
13. *Selected Poems* Hutchinson 1970
14. *O. Jones, O. Jones* (novel) Hutchinson 1970
15. *Funland and Other Poems* Hutchinson 1973
16. *The Dogs of Pavlov* (play) Vallentine Mitchell 1973
17. *A Poet in the Family* (autobiog.) Hutchinson 1974
18. *Collected Poems 1948–1976* Hutchinson 1977

Abse has edited several publications, the most notable being: *European Verse* (Studio Vista 1964) and *Corgi Modern Poets in Focus* Nos 1, 3 and 5 (Corgi 1971, 1972, 1973). His first publication is scarce, and would be Grade C, as might be 10 and 12, being private presses. All the others, however, should be Grade B, the most recent even Grade A. Abse is growing in popularity among collectors, and is, according to many, underrated as a poet.

ADAMS, Richard
Born in Berkshire 1920.

1. *Watership Down* Collings 1972; 1st Amer. Macmillan 1974
2. *Shardik* Lane 1974; 1st Amer. Simon & Schuster 1975
3. *Nature Through the Seasons* Kestrel 1975; 1st Amer. Simon & Schuster 1975
4. *The Tyger Voyage* Cape 1976; 1st Amer. Knopf 1976

A very recent phenomenon. The 1st of *Watership Down* is of legendary rarity, very few collectors or dealers ever having seen it. The author is said to have several copies in a vault, which gives a fairly accurate idea of its value—it could easily reach Grade K, or even higher. The original d/w is beige, decorated with line drawings, and not the later laminated photographic one. The first Puffin edition is also desirable, for although published in 1973, it has run through countless impressions, been promoted to Penguin, and had a cover change. Nonetheless, a 1st Puffin is very much Grade A.
None of the others should be much over Grade B, but they are probably worth getting while this situation remains.

ALBEE, Edward
Born in Washington D.C. 1928

1. *The Zoo Story, The Death of Bessie Smith, The Sandbox: Three Plays* Coward McCann NY 1960
2. *The Zoo Story* in *Evergreen Review* March–April 1960
3. *Fam and Yam* Dramatists Play Service NY 1961
4. *The American Dream* Coward McCann NY 1961
5. *Who's Afraid of Virginia Woolf?* Atheneum NY 1962; 1st Eng. Cape 1964
6. *The Zoo Story and Other Plays* (same as 1) Cape 1962
7. *The Ballad of the Sad Cafe* Atheneum 1963; 1st Eng. Cape 1965
8. *Tiny Alice* Atheneum 1965; 1st Eng. Cape 1966
9. *Malcolm* Atheneum 1966; 1st Eng. Cape 1967
10. *A Delicate Balance* Atheneum 1966; 1st Eng. Cape 1968
11. *Box* and *Quotations from Chairman Mao Tse-*

Tung Atheneum 1969; 1st Eng. Cape 1970

12. *All Over* Atheneum 1971; 1st Eng. Cape 1972

Film:
Who's Afraid of Virginia Woolf? Warner Bros 1965

Bibliography:
Richard E. Amacher and Margaret Rule *Edward Albee at Home and Abroad: A Bibliography 1958–June 1968* (AMS Press NY 1970)
All the above publications are plays. Nos 1, 3, 4 and 5 in the American editions would be Grade C, or even D in the case of *The Zoo Story*. Cape editions are Grade A, or at most B, although, like many plays, they can be difficult to find in good condition.

ALDINGTON, Richard
Born 1892. Died 1962.
Aldington published poetry, criticism and biographies, in addition to the novels for which he is best known. He also published many limited, signed editions—too numerous to mention within the confines of this work. Unfortunately, one must confine oneself to the few works that collectors seem most interested in: *Death of a Hero* (1929)—this, with the d/w by Paul Nash, can reach Grade D—*The Colonel's Daughter* (1931) and *All Men Are Enemies* (1963) (all Chatto & Windus, and Doubleday in America). These should not go above Grade C, unless exceptional copies.
His *Portrait of a Genius, But* . . .(Heinemann 1950) also merits a mention. This biography of D. H. Lawrence is generally wanted more by Lawrence collectors than by those of Aldington. Grade B.

Film:
All Men Are Enemies 20th Century Fox 1934

ALDISS, Brian W.
Born in Norfolk, England 1925.

1. *The Brightfount Diaries* (novel) Faber 1955

2. *Space, Time and Nathaniel* (stories) Faber 1957
3. *Non-Stop* (novel) Faber 1958
4. *Starship* (same as 3) Criterion NY 1959
5. *Vanguard from Alpha* (novel) Ace NY 1959
6. *No Time Like Tomorrow* (stories) NAL NY 1959
7. *The Canopy of Time* (stories) Faber 1959
8. *Bow Down to Nul* (novel) Ace 1960
9. *Galaxies Like Grains of Sand* (novel) NAL 1960
10. *Equator* (novel) Digit 1961
11. *The Interpreter* (novel) Digit 1961
12. *The Male Response* (novel) Beacon Press, Boston 1961; 1st Eng. Dobson 1963
13. *The Primal Urge* (novel) Ballantine NY 1961; 1st Eng. Sphere 1967
14. *Hothouse* (novel) Faber 1962
15. *The Long Aftermath of Earth* (same as 14) NAL 1962
16. *The Airs of Earth* (stories) Faber 1963
17. *Starswarm* (stories) NAL 1964
18. *The Dark Light Years* (novel) Faber/NAL 1964
19. *Greybeard* (novel) Faber/Harcourt Brace 1964
20. *Best SF Stories of Brian Aldiss* Faber 1965 (rev. ed. 1971)
21. *Earthworks* (novel) Faber 1965; 1st Amer. Doubleday 1966
22. *Who Can Replace a Man?* (same as 20) Harcourt Brace 1966
23. *The Saliva Tree and Other Strange Growths* (stories) Faber 1966
24. *Cities and Stones: A Traveller's Jugoslavia* (non-fiction) Faber 1966
25. *An Age* (novel) Faber 1967
26. *Cryptozoic* (same as 25) Doubleday 1968
27. *Report on Probability A* (novel) Faber/Doubleday 1968
28. *A Brian Aldiss Omnibus* (stories) Sidgwick & Jackson 1969
29. *Intangibles Inc. and Other Stories* Faber 1969
30. *Barefoot in the Head* (novel) Faber 1969; 1st Amer. Doubleday 1970
31. *Neanderthal Planet* (stories) Avon NY 1970
32. *The Shape of Further Things* (non-fiction) Faber 1970; 1st Amer. Doubleday 1971
33. *The Hand-Reared Boy* (novel) Weidenfeld/McCall NY 1970

34. *A Soldier Erect* (novel) Weidenfeld/McCann NY 1971
35. *The Moment of Eclipse* (stories) Faber/Doubleday 1971
36. *Brian Aldiss Omnibus 2* Sidgwick & Jackson 1971
37. *The Comic Inferno* (stories) Daw Books NY 1972; 1st Eng. NEL 1973
38. *Frankenstein Unbound* (novel) Cape 1973; 1st Amer. Random House 1974
39. *Billion Year Spree: The History of Science Fiction* Weidenfeld/Doubleday 1973
40. *The Eighty Minute Hour* (novel) Cape/Random House 1974
41. *The Malacia Tapestry* (novel) Cape 1976

Aldiss has also edited many volumes of SF stories for Faber, Penguin and Weidenfeld, as well as Sphere. These can be found cheaply, though *Farewell, Fantastic Venus!* (Macdonald 1968; published as *All About Venus* in America by Dell 1968), which he edited with Harry Harrison, would be Grade A.

No. 1 could reach Grade D, whereas Nos 2–12 would be Grade C at the maximum. The rest should be A–B, but many of the more recent can be bought for a pound or two.

Aldiss is, of course, avidly collected by SF enthusiasts, though less so by collectors of novels, possibly because there is no discernible highlight. Some say that in the duet 33 and 34 Aldiss reached a climax.

AMIS, Kingsley

Born London 1922 and educated at Oxford, Amis was later a Fellow at Cambridge. Forerunner of the so-called 'Angry Young Men' of the fifties, his novel *Lucky Jim* immediately established him as a writer, and it won the Somerset Maugham Award. By the time his second novel was published, two years later, *Lucky Jim* was in its 12th impression. The novel remains a very fine and very funny work, rivalled only by *Ending Up*. Amis—never really very angry—seems even less so today, as might possibly be seen by looking at his Fabian Society pamphlet (see below) and his later work for the Conservative Political Centre.

He is married to Elizabeth Jane Howard (q.v.) and his son Martin Amis has published *The Rachel Papers* (1974)—winner of that year's Somerset Maugham Award—and *Dead Babies* (1975).

1. *Bright November* (verse) Fortune Press 1947
   Mint copy should be unopened and in d/w. Copies with grey boards are apparently of later issue. Very scarce. Grade H.
2. *A Frame of Mind* (verse) Reading School of Art 1953
   Early and privately printed—hence very scarce. Grade G—only 150 copies.
3. *Lucky Jim* (novel) Gollancz 1953; 1st Amer. Doubleday 1954
   Very scarce, and a keystone to any collection of fiction. Green boards with yellow Gollancz house-style d/w. Grade E.
4. *Fantasy Poets* No. 22 (verse) Fantasy Press 1954
   A fairly fragile item, and hard to find. Grade E.
5. *That Uncertain Feeling* (novel) Gollancz 1955; 1st Amer. Harcourt Brace 1956
   Red boards, house-style d/w. Grade B.
6. *A Case of Samples: Poems 1946–1956* Gollancz 1956; 1st Amer. Harcourt Brace 1957
   In print a very short time, surprisingly never reissued, and always a very difficult book to find. Grade E.
7. *Socialism and the Intellectuals* Fabian Society 1957
   Fabian Tract No. 304. A very interesting, but ephemeral, item. As it is just a 13-page pamphlet, there are very few remaining in a condition acceptable to collectors, hence Grade C–D.
8. *I Like It Here* (novel) Gollancz 1958; 1st Amer. Harcourt Brace 1958
   Standard Gollancz production. Grade B.
9. *Take a Girl Like You* (novel) Gollancz 1960; 1st Amer. Harcourt Brace 1961
   Standard Gollancz production. Grade B.
10. *New Maps of Hell: A Survey of Science Fiction* Harcourt Brace 1960; 1st Eng. Gollancz 1961
    According to the d/w of Gollancz edition, the American edition preceded for 'technical

reasons'. This is the only Amis to be published in America first. Both editions are scarce. Grade B.

11. *My Enemy's Enemy* (stories) Gollancz 1962; 1st Amer. Harcourt Brace 1963
    Usual Gollancz production, but never as easy to find as the novels of this period. Grade B–C.

12. *The Evans Country* (verse) Fantasy Press 1962
    Grey wraps, lettered in black and red. A slim pamphlet, and scarce. Grade C.

13. *One Fat Englishman* (novel) Gollancz 1963; 1st Amer. Harcourt Brace 1964
    Standard Gollancz production. Not difficult. Grade A.

14. *The Egyptologists* (novel) Cape 1965; 1st Amer. Random House 1966 (with Robert Conquest)
    The beginning of Amis's association with Cape, and his first photographic, laminated d/w! Not too difficult. Grade B.

15. *The James Bond Dossier* Cape 1965; 1st Amer. NAL 1965
    Appropriately, the d/w reproduces excerpts of Richard Chopping's Bond wrappers, and the book is published by Fleming's own publishers. Not very difficult, despite being sought by both Amis and Fleming collectors. Grade A.

16. *The Anti-Death League* (novel) Gollancz 1966; 1st Amer. Harcourt Brace 1966
    Although the first Gollancz Amis to break with house style, the last Amis for Gollancz. Photographic d/w much like Raymond Hawkey's designs for the early Deightons (q.v.). Not too difficult. Grade A–B.

17. *A Look Round the Estate: Poems 1957–1967* Cape 1967; 1st Amer. Harcourt Brace 1968
    Green boards with white spine. Green, black and white d/w. This slim volume was reprinted soon after publication, and the 1st is quite difficult. Grade B.

18. *Colonel Sun: A James Bond Adventure* Cape 1968; 1st Amer. Harper 1968
    By 'Robert Markham'—the most un-secret pseudonym in the world. See essay in 22. A similar situation to 15, this—a novel wanted by Amis and Fleming collectors, this time with a 'Choppingesque' d/w, but quite easy to find. Grade A, but only 50p if, perchance, the vendor does not know of Markham's true identity.

19. *Lucky Jim's Politics* Conservative Centre 1968
    A scarce, ephemeral item, but a pretty counterpart to 7. Grade B.

20. *I Want It Now* (novel) Cape 1968; 1st Amer. Harcourt Brace 1969
    Blue boards, laminated, photographic d/w. Quite easy. Grade A.

21. *The Green Man* (novel) Cape 1969; 1st Amer. Harcourt Brace 1970
    Blue boards, laminated, photographic d/w. Quite easy. Grade A.

22. *What Became of Jane Austen? and Other Questions* Cape 1970; 1st Amer. Harcourt Brace 1971
    Amis's only book of essays. Not too difficult. Grade B.

23. *Girl, 20* (novel) Cape 1971; 1st Amer. Harcourt Brace 1972
    Black boards, laminated, photographic d/w. A pushover. Grade A.

24. *On Drink* Cape 1972; 1st Amer. Harcourt Brace 1973
    Boards, aptly, are wine-coloured. Laminated, photographic d/w featuring Kingsley tippling. Was reprinted very quickly. Grade B.

25. *Dear Illusion* (story) Covent Garden Press 1972
    Mustard wrpps. Limited edition of 600—100 numbered and signed. Quite difficult now. Signed: Grade C. Unsigned: Grade B.

26. *The Riverside Villas Murder* (novel) Cape 1973; 1st Amer. Harcourt Brace 1973
    Green boards, laminated, photographic d/w. Easy. Grade A.

27. *Ending Up* (novel) Cape 1974; 1st Amer. Harcourt Brace 1974
    Easy to find at present, but destined to become a highlight of his work. Grade A.

28. *Rudyard Kipling and His World* (biog.) Thames & Hudson 1975; 1st Amer. Scribner 1975
    One of the well-known series. Easy. Grade B.

29. *The Alteration* (novel) Cape 1976; 1st Amer. Viking Press 1976

Bibliography:
Jack Benoit Gohn *Kingsley Amis: A Checklist* (Kent State University Press 1976)
Kingsley Amis has also edited a number of publications, most notably the *Spectrum* volumes, with Robert Conquest. The first was published by Gollancz in 1961 (Harcourt Brace 1962) and should be Grade B. The subsequent volumes are Grade A, except perhaps *Spectrum IV,* which contains a discussion between Amis, Brian Aldiss and C. S. Lewis. Amis has also edited *G. K. Chesterton: Selected Stories* (Faber 1972) and *Tennyson* (Penguin 1973). Both should be Grade A.
Also worth having are his contributions to *Penguin Modern Poets 2* (Penguin 1962)—difficult now, but Grade A—*G. K. Chesterton: A Centenary Appraisal* (Elek 1974) and *Bookmarks* (Cape 1975)—containing a short essay on Amis's reading tastes.

Films:
Lucky Jim British Lion 1957
Only Two Can Play British Lion 1961
(*That Uncertain Feeling*)
Take a Girl Like You Columbia 1971

ASIMOV, Isaac
Born in Russia 1920. Naturalized American 1928.
In addition to the novels and short stories listed below, Asimov has published upwards of eighty other works. It is impossible even to list them within this work, though few would be of interest to the collector of literature. However, the October 1966 issue of the *Magazine of Fantasy and Science Fiction* (NY) carried a full bibliography, should such information be required.

1. *Pebble in the Sky* (novel) Doubleday 1950; 1st Eng. Sidgwick & Jackson 1968
2. *I, Robot* (stories) Gnome Press 1950; 1st Eng. Grayson 1952
3. *The Stars, Like Dust* (novel) Doubleday 1951
4. *Foundation* (novel) Gnome Press 1951; 1st Eng. Weidenfeld 1953
5. *Foundation and Empire* (novel) Gnome Press 1952
6. *The Currents of Space* (novel) Doubleday 1952; 1st Eng. Boardman 1955
7. *Second Foundation* (novel) Gnome Press 1953
8. *The Caves of Steel* (novel) Doubleday 1954; 1st Eng. Boardman 1954
9. *The End of Eternity* (novel) Doubleday 1955
10. *The Martian Way and Other Stories* Doubleday 1955; 1st Eng. Dobson 1964
11. *The Naked Sun* (novel) Doubleday 1957; 1st Eng. Joseph 1958
12. *Earth Is Room Enough* (stories) Doubleday 1957
13. *Nine Tomorrows: Tales of the Near Future* Doubleday 1959; 1st Eng. Dobson 1963
14. *The Rest of the Robots* (stories plus 8 and 11) Doubleday 1964; 1st Eng. Dobson 1967
15. *Fantastic Voyage* (novel) Houghton Mifflin 1966; 1st Eng. Dobson 1966
16. *Through a Glass, Clearly* (stories) New English Library 1967
17. *A Whiff of Death* (novel) Walker 1968; 1st Eng. Gollancz 1968
18. *Asimov's Mysteries* (stories) Doubleday 1968; 1st Eng. Rapp & Whiting 1968
19. *Nightfall and Other Stories* Doubleday 1969; 1st Eng. Rapp & Whiting 1969
20. *The Gods themselves* (novel) Doubleday 1972; 1st Eng. Gollancz 1972
21. *The Early Asimov* (stories) Doubleday 1972
22. *The Best of Isaac Asimov* (stories) Sidgwick & Jackson 1973; 1st Amer. Doubleday 1974
23. *Tales of the Black Widowers* (stories) Doubleday 1974; 1st Eng. Gollancz 1975
24. *Buy Jupiter and Other Stories* Doubleday 1975; 1st Eng. Gollancz 1976
25. *Authorised Murder* (novel) Doubleday 1976; 1st Eng. Gollancz 1976
26. *The Bicentennial Man and Other Stories* Doubleday 1976; 1st Eng. Gollancz 1977
27. *More Tales of the Black Widowers* (stories) Doubleday 1976; 1st Eng. Gollancz 1977

Asimov has also published six juveniles under the pseudonym of Paul French:
David Starr: Space Ranger Doubleday 1952
Lucky Starr and the Pirates of the Asteroids Doubleday 1954

Lucky Starr and the Oceans of Venus Doubleday 1954
Lucky Starr and the Big Sun of Mercury Doubleday 1956
Lucky Starr and the Moons of Jupiter Doubleday 1957
Lucky Starr and the Rings of Saturn Doubleday 1958

These were published in England—under Asimov's real name—by NEL in 1972–73. His first novel and *The Caves of Steel*—which some say is his best—might reach Grade C, though largely his work falls into Grade A–B.

AUDEN, W. H.

Born in York, England, 1907. Died 1973. Was at Oxford 1925–28, and then joined the Loyalists in the Spanish Civil War. Emigrated to U.S.A. 1938, and was naturalized in 1946. Auden's great talent was recognized very early on, but he is now generally agreed to be one of the greatest poets of the century—some collectors being of the opinion that his reputation will outlast that of Eliot. A very prolific and diverse output—at once attractive and maddening to the collector, for Auden was an inveterate reviser of his work, often forbidding a poem to be reprinted at all—one of the reasons why *Spain* is so desirable.

It has been necessary to limit the list that follows to books and pamphlets written by Auden and published by commercial English and American publishers, and those he edited and translated that seem to be most pertinent to his *œuvre*. However, an excellent bibliography of Auden exists: *W. H. Auden: A Bibliography 1924–1969* (University Press of Virginia, 2nd ed. 1972). This contains everything—including contributions to periodicals—within 420 pages. The 1st edition of this work, incidentally, is desirable in that Auden wrote the intro., though as it was published in 1964, it is not of such practical use as the current edition.

1. *Poems* S.H.S. 1928

Spender hand-printed this little volume in Frognal, Hampstead, in an edition of less than thirty. No collector has any hope of finding one, unless one of the known owners decides to sell, but the price could easily be £2,000 or more. It is one of the legendary 1sts of the century. Three facsimiles of the book have been published, however, and one of these might be an acceptable substitute:
University Microfilms Xerox 1960
University of Cincinnati Library 1964 (limited to 500 copies)
Ilkley Literature Festival 1973
The Cincinnati facsimile is cloth-bound, with an introduction by Spender, but the Ilkley copy is faithful to the orange wrpps, reproduces the erratum slip for the first time, and has a separate foreword by B. C. Bloomfield, Auden's bibliographer.

2. *Poems* Faber 1930
   This wrappered volume, his first with Faber, is scarce, and could reach Grade I–J.
3. *The Orators: An English Study* Faber 1932
   Black boards. Scarce. Grade F, but Grade I–J if in the cream and blue d/w.
4. *The Dance of Death* Faber 1933
   Green printed boards with d/w of identical design. Grade F.
5. *Poems* Random House NY 1934
   Dark orange boards, cream d/w. Contains *The Orators* and *The Dance of Death*. Grade E.
6. *The Dog Beneath the Skin* (play) Faber 1935; 1st Amer. Random House 1935 (with C. Isherwood)
   Red cloth, yellow d/w. Grade E.
7. *The Ascent of F6* (play) Faber 1936; 1st Amer. Random House 1937 (with C. Isherwood)
   Blue cloth, cream d/w Grade D.
8. *Look, Stranger!* (verse) Faber 1936
   Grey boards, yellow d/w. The title was invented by Faber and called by Auden 'bloody'. He chose the title of the American edition—see 9. Grade D.
9. *On This Island* (verse) Random House 1937
   Same as 8. Brown cloth, cream d/w. Grade D.
10. *Spain* (poem) Faber 1937

Eight-page pamphlet in red wrpps. Scarce and unreprinted since 1942. Grade E.

11. *Letters from Iceland* Faber 1937; 1st Amer. Random House 1937 (with Louis MacNeice) Lime boards with photographic d/w. Grade D.

12. *Selected Poems* Faber 1938 Faber Library series, with usual green cloth. Grade C.

13. *On the Frontier* (play) Faber 1938; 1st Amer. Random House 1939 (with C. Isherwood) Red cloth, cream d/w. Grade D.

14. *Education Today and Tomorrow* (essay) Hogarth Press 1939 (with T. C. Worsley) Day to Day Pamphlets No. 40. Reddish wrpps. Scarce—Grade E. Auden does not 'remember the pamphlet, or how it came to be written'.

15. *Journey to a War* (prose) Faber 1939; 1st Amer. Random House 1939 (with C. Isherwood) Black boards, cream d/w. Scarce. Grade E–F. Reissued in Faber Paper Covered Editions 1973 with new intros by Auden and Isherwood.

16. *Another Time* (verse) Random House 1940; 1st Eng. Faber 1940 Reddish boards, cream d/w. Faber ed.: red boards, red d/w. Both Grade D.

17. *Some Poems* Faber 1940 Pink paper boards, pale blue d/w. Grade C.

18. *The Double Man* (verse) Random House 1941 Brown cloth, cream d/w. Scarce. Grade E–F.

19. *New Year Letter* (verse) Faber 1941 Same as 18. Grey cloth, orange d/w. Grade D.

20. *For the Time Being* (verse) Random House 1944; 1st Eng. Faber 1945 White and mauve boards, grey d/w. Faber ed.: orange cloth, cream d/w. Amer.: Grade D. Eng.: Grade C.

21. *The Collected Poetry* Random House 1945 Bluish cloth, pink d/w. Grade C–D.

22. *The Age of Anxiety* (verse) Random House 1947; 1st Eng. Faber 1948 Bluish cloth, cream d/w. Faber ed.: green cloth, blue d/w. Grade C.

23. *Collected Shorter Poems 1930–1944* Faber 1950 Bright blue cloth, yellow d/w. Grade C.

24. *The Enchafed Flood* (verse) Random House 1950; 1st Eng. Faber 1951 Dark green boards, grey d/w. Faber ed.: blue cloth, white d/w. Grade D.

25. *Nones* (verse) Random House 1951; 1st Eng. Faber 1952 Dark blue and grey boards, grey d/w. Faber ed.: blue cloth, orange d/w. Grade C.

26. *Mountains* Faber 1954 Ariel Poem, in pink envelope. Grade B.

27. *The Shield of Achilles* (verse) Random House 1955; 1st Eng. Faber 1955 Orange and black boards, cream d/w. Faber ed.: wine cloth, yellow d/w. Grade C.

28. *The Magic Flute* (libretto trans.) Random House 1956; 1st Eng. Faber 1957 (with C. Kallman) Black, pink and grey boards, white d/w. Faber ed.: grey cloth, green d/w. Grade C.

29. *Making, Knowing and Judging* (lecture) OUP 1956 18-page pamphlet in grey wrpps. Scarce. Grade C.

30. *W. H. Auden: A Selection by the Author* Penguin 1958 Penguin paperback, originally published at 3/6d. Grade A.

31. *Selected Poetry of W. H. Auden* Modern Library 1959 American edition of 30. Blue cloth, white d/w. Grade A.

32. *Homage to Clio* (verse) Random House 1960; 1st Eng. Faber 1960 Black and orange cloth, cream d/w. Faber ed.: wine cloth, green d/w. Grade C.

33. *The Dyer's Hand* Random House 1962; 1st Eng. Faber 1963 First book of essays. Green cloth, grey d/w. Faber ed.: green cloth, light green d/w. Grade C.

34. *Selected Essays* Faber 1964 Shiny perfect binding. Grade A.

35. *About the House* (verse) Random House 1965; 1st Eng. Faber 1966 Black and grey boards, white d/w. Faber ed.: blue cloth, green and purple d/w. Grade C.

36. *Collected Shorter Poems 1927–1957* Faber 1966; 1st Amer. Random House 1967

Blue cloth, black and yellow d/w. RH ed.: orange and green boards with black and yellow d/w. Grade C.

37. *Selected Poems* Faber 1968
Shiny tan and blue perfect binding. Grade B.

38. *Collected Longer Poems* Faber 1968; 1st Amer. Random House 1969
Blue cloth, grey and orange d/w. RH ed.: orange and green boards with yellow and orange d/w. Grade B–C.

39. *Secondary Worlds* Faber 1969; 1st Amer. Random House 1969 T. S. Eliot Memorial Lectures
Red cloth, white d/w. RH ed.: grey and orange boards, violet and yellow d/w. Faber ed.: Grade B–C. RH ed.: Grade B.

40. *City Without Walls* (verse) Faber 1969; 1st Amer. Random House 1970
Black cloth, cream d/w. Grade B.

41. *A Certain World* Viking Press 1970; 1st Eng. Faber 1971
A Commonplace book. Fine Faber typography on English d/w. Grade B.

42. *Academic Graffiti* (clerihews) Faber 1971; 1st Amer. Random House 1972
Red cloth, white d/w. Auden's 'Old Possum'. Grade A–B.

43. *Epistle to a Godson* (verse) Faber 1972; 1st Amer. Random House 1972
Brown and cream boards, beige and blue d/w. Grade B.

44. *Forewords and Afterwords* Viking Press 1973; 1st Eng. Faber 1973
Second volume of essays—see 33. Grade B.

45. *Auden/Moore: Poems and Lithographs* British Museum 1974
Catalogue of a fine exhibition. Wrpps. Grade A.

46. *Thank You, Fog* (verse) Faber 1974; 1st Amer. Random House 1974
Posthumous publication. Fine Faber typography on d/w, and photo of Auden on rear. Grade B.

Auden was also the editor of many works. A selection appears below.

47. *The Poet's Tongue* (2 vols) Bell 1935 (with John Garrett)

Scarce. Grade D.

48. *The Oxford Book of Light Verse* OUP 1938

49. *Poets of the English Language* (5 vols) Viking Press 1950; 1st Eng. Eyre & Spottiswoode 1952
VP ed. Grade E.

50. *An Elizabethan Song Book* Doubleday 1955; 1st Eng. Faber 1957

51. *The Faber Book of Modern American Verse* Faber 1956

52. *Selected Writings of Sydney Smith* Farrar 1956; 1st Eng. Faber 1957

53. *Van Gogh: A Self-Portrait* New York Graphic Society 1961; 1st Eng. Thames & Hudson 1961

54. *The Viking Book of Aphorisms* Viking Press 1962
The Faber Book of Aphorisms Faber 1965

55. *A Choice of de la Mare's Verse* Faber 1963

56. *Selected Poems, by Louis MacNeice* Faber 1964

57. *Nineteenth Century British Minor Poets* Delacorte 1966; 1st Eng. Faber 1967

58. *G. K. Chesterton: A Selection from His Non-Fiction Prose* Faber 1970

59. *A Choice of Dryden's Verse* Faber 1973

60. *George Herbert* Penguin 1973

The above should all be Grades A–B, except where stated.
The *Collected Poems* was published in 1976 by Faber, and by Random House in America.

BAINBRIDGE, Beryl
Born in Liverpool 1934.

1. *A Weekend with Claude* (novel) Hutchinson 1967

2. *Another Part of the Wood* (novel) Hutchinson 1968

3. *Harriet Said . . .* (novel) Duckworth 1972; 1st Amer. Braziller 1972

4. *The Dressmaker* (novel) Duckworth 1973

5. *The Secret Glass* (same as 4) Braziller 1974

6. *The Bottle Factory Outing* (novel) Duckworth 1974; 1st Amer. Braziller 1974

7. *Sweet William* (novel) Duckworth 1975; 1st Amer. Braziller 1975

8. *A Quiet Life* (novel) Duckworth 1976

A very recent interest with collectors, Beryl

Bainbridge has very quickly acquired quite a reputation. No. 1 might be Grade B, but the rest are Grade A.

BALLARD, J. G.
Born in Shanghai, China, 1930. British.

1. *The Wind from Nowhere* (novel) Berkley NY 1962
2. *The Voices of Time and Other Stories* Berkley 1962
3. *Billenium and Other Stories* Berkley 1962
4. *The Drowned World* (novel) Berkley 1962; 1st Eng. Gollancz 1963
5. *The Four-Dimensional Nightmare* (stories) Gollancz 1963
6. *Passport to Eternity and Other Stories* Berkley 1963
7. *The Terminal Beach* (stories) Gollancz 1964
8. *The Drought* (novel) Cape 1965
9. *The Crystal World* (novel) Cape 1966; 1st Amer. Farrar Straus 1966
10. *The Disaster Area* (stories) Cape 1967
11. *The Day of Forever* (stories) Panther 1968
12. *The Overloaded Man* (stories) Panther 1968
13. *The Atrocity Exhibition* (novel) Cape 1970
14. *Vermilion Sands* (stories) Berkley 1971; 1st Eng. Cape 1973
15. *Crash!* (novel) Cape 1973; 1st Amer. Farrar Straus 1973
16. *Concrete Island* (novel) Cape 1974; 1st Amer. Farrar Straus 1974
17. *High Rise* (novel) Cape 1975
18. *Low-Flying Aircraft* (stories) Cape 1976
19. *The Best of J. G. Ballard* Sidgwick & Jackson 1977

An author gaining in popularity with collectors, like many SF writers. The early Berkley publications might be Grade C–D. though the rest are Grades A–B. It is likely that *Crash!* might become his highlight.

BANKS, Lynne Reid
Born in London 1929.
Author of about a dozen works, but notable for the following:

1. *The L-Shaped Room* (novel) Chatto & Windus 1960; 1st Amer. Simon & Schuster 1962
2. *The Backward Shadow* (novel) Chatto & Windus 1970; 1st Amer. Simon & Schuster 1970
3. *Two Is Lonely* (novel) Chatto & Windus 1974; 1st Amer. Simon & Schuster 1974

These three form a trilogy. No. 1 is Grade B–C, a milestone, and a desirable work. Nos 2 and 3 are Grade A.

Film:
The L-Shaped Room British Lion 1962

BARKER, George
Born in Essex 1913.

1. *Thirty Preliminary Poems* Parton Press 1933
2. *Alanna Autumnal* (novel) Wishart 1933
3. *Poems* Faber 1935
4. *Janus* (2 novelettes) Faber 1935
5. *Calamiterror* (verse) Faber 1937
6. *Elegy on Spain* (verse) Parton Press 1939
7. *Lament and Triumph* (verse) Faber 1940
8. *Selected Poems* Macmillan NY 1941
9. *Sacred and Secular Elegies* (verse) New Directions NY 1943
10. *Eros in Dogma* (verse) Faber 1944
11. *Love Poems* Dial Press NY 1947
12. *The True Confession of George Barker* (verse) Fore 1950; 1st Amer. NAL 1964
13. *News of the World* (verse) Faber 1950
14. *The Dead Seagull* (novel) Lehmann 1950; 1st Amer. Farrar Straus 1951
15. *A Vision of Beasts and Gods* (verse) Faber 1954
16. *Collected Poems 1930–1955* Faber 1957; 1st Amer. Criterion 1958
17. *Two Plays* Faber 1958
(cont. *The Seraphim* and *In the Shade of the Old Apple Tree*)
18. *The View from a Blind I* (verse) Faber 1962
19. *Collected Poems 1930–1965* October House NY 1965
20. *Dreams of a Summer Night* (verse) Faber 1966
21. *The Golden Chains* (verse) Faber 1968
22. *At Thurgarton Church* (verse) Trigram Press 1969
Limited to 100 copies, signed by the author.
23. *Runes and Rhymes and Tunes and Chimes*

(juvenile) Faber 1969
24. *To Aylsham Fair* (juvenile) Faber 1970
25. *The Alphabetical Zoo* (juvenile) Faber 1970
26. *Essays* MacGibbon & Kee 1970
27. *Poems of Places and People* (verse) Faber 1971
28. *III Hallucination Poems* Helikon Press NY 1972
29. *In Memory of David Archer* (verse) Faber 1973
30. *Dialogues, etc.* (verse) Faber 1976

Nos 1 and 2 are very scarce and are Grade G. Nos 3, 4 and 5 are hardly less so, and would be Grade E. Nos 6–9 are Grade C–D, and all the remainder are Grade A–B, with the exception of 22, which would be Grade C.

BARNES, Djuna
Born in New York 1892.

1. *The Book of Repulsive Women* (stories) Bruno Chapbooks NY 1915
2. *A Book* (stories, verse and plays) Boni & Liveright NY 1923
3. *Ryder* (novel) Liveright NY 1928
4. *Nightwood* (novel) Faber 1936; 1st Amer. Harcourt Brace 1937
5. *The Antiphon* (play) Faber 1958; 1st Amer. Farrar Straus 1958
6. *Spillway* (stories) Faber 1962 (shortened form of 2)
7. *Selected Works* Farrar Straus 1962
8. *Vagaries Malicieux: Two Stories* Frank Hallman NY 1975

All these works are scarce. No. 1 would be Grade Q, and No. 2 very little less. *Ryder* would be Grade K, and *Nightwood*—her highlight—Grade G. The remaining three would be Grade C.

BARSTOW, Stan
Born in Yorkshire 1928.

1. *A Kind of Loving* (novel) Joseph 1960; 1st Amer. Doubleday 1961
2. *The Desperadoes* (stories) Joseph 1961
3. *Ask Me Tomorrow* (novel) Joseph 1962
4. *Joby* (novel) Joseph 1964
5. *The Watchers on the Shore* (novel) Joseph 1966;

1st Amer. Doubleday 1967
Sequel to No. 1.
6. *A Raging Calm* (novel) Joseph 1968
7. *The Hidden Part* (same as 6) Coward McCann NY 1969
8. *A Season with Eros* (stories) Joseph 1971
9. *The Right True End* (novel) Joseph 1976
Completes the trilogy of 1 and 5.

Film:
A Kind of Loving Anglo-Amalgamated 1962 (play script) Blackie 1970

Barstow's first novel is one of the important pieces of fiction of the time, and is usually underpriced as a 1st. Grade B, but will rise. His remaining work should not be too difficult to find, and is Grade A–B.

BECKETT, Samuel
Born near Dublin 1906. Educated at Trinity College, Dublin. He worked with Joyce in Paris during the twenties and thirties. Beckett decided to stay in Paris in 1938, and since then has written nearly all his work in French, and then translated it himself into English. In the list that follows, I have recorded the first editions in the English language, but as the French-language edition precedes many of these, the following bibliography should be consulted for the fullest information:
Raymond Federman and John Fletcher *Samuel Beckett, His Works And His Critics: An Essay in Bibliography* (University of California Press, Berkeley 1970).

1. *Our Exagmination Round His Factification for Incamination of Work in Progress* Shakespeare & Co., Paris 1929; 1st Eng. Faber 1936; 1st Amer. New Directions 1939 (cont. Dante . . . Bruno . . . Vico . . . Joyce. By S.B.)
All very scarce. Shakespeare copy: Grade P. Faber: Grade H.
2. *Whoroscope* (verse) Hours Press, Paris 1930
Beckett's first separately published work. Limited to 300 copies, 100 signed. Wrpps. Very scarce. Signed: Grade R. Unsigned: Grade Q.

3. *Proust* Chatto & Windus 1931; 1st Amer.
   Grove Press 1957
   Very scarce. Grade L.
4. *More Pricks than Kicks* (texts) Chatto &
   Windus 1934; 1st Amer. Grove Press 1970
   Very scarce. Grade L.
5. *Echo's Bones* (verse) Europa Press, Paris 1935
   Very scarce. Grade N.
6. *Murphy* (novel) Routledge 1938; 1st Amer.
   Grove Press 1957
   Scarce. Grade K.
7. *Molloy* (novel) Olympia Press, Paris 1955; 1st
   Amer. Grove Press 1955; 1st Eng. Calder
   1959 (French-language ed. 1951)
   Paris ed.: Grade I. Amer. ed.: Grade G. Eng.
   ed.: Grade B.
8. *Waiting for Godot* (play) Grove Press 1954; 1st
   Eng. Faber 1956 (French-language ed. 1952)
   Amer. ed.: Grade E. Eng. ed.: Grade D.
9. *Malone Dies* (novel) Grove Press 1956; 1st
   Eng. Calder 1958 (French-language ed. 1951)
   Amer. ed.: Grade D. Eng. ed.: Grade C.
10. *All That Fall* (play) Grove Press 1957; 1st
    Eng. Faber 1957
    Grade C.
11. *Endgame* (play) Grove Press 1958; 1st Eng.
    Faber 1958 (French-language ed. 1957)
    Grade C.
12. *The Unnamable* Grove Press 1958; 1st Eng.
    Calder 1959 (French-language ed. 1953)
    Grade C.
13. *From an Abandoned Work* Faber 1958
    Wrpps. Grade C.
14. *Krapp's Last Tape* and *Embers* (plays) Faber
    1959; 1st Amer. Grove Press 1960
    Wrpps. Faber ed.: Grade D. Amer. ed.:
    Grade B–C.
15. *Watt* (novel) Grove Press 1959; 1st Eng.
    Calder 1963 (written in English: Olympia
    Press 1953)
    Olympia ed. (true 1st): Grade F. Amer. ed.:
    Grade C. Eng. ed.: B.
16. *Poems in English* Calder 1961; 1st Amer.
    Grove Press 1963
    Grade C.
17. *Happy Days* (play) Grove Press 1961; 1st
    Eng. Faber 1962
    Grade C.
18. *Play* and *Two Short Pieces for Radio* Faber 1964
    (incl. *Words & Music* and *Cascando*)
    Grade C.
19. *How It Is* (novel) Grove Press 1964; 1st Eng.
    Calder 1964 (French-language ed. 1961)
    Grade C.
20. *Imagination Dead Imagine* (text) Calder &
    Boyars 1965 (French-language ed. 1965)
    Grade B.
21. *Proust* and *Three Dialogues with Georges Duthuit*
    Calder 1965
    Grade B.
22. *Come and Go: Dramaticule* Calder & Boyars
    1967
    Grade B.
23. *Eh Joe* and *Other Writings* (play) Faber 1967
    (incl. *Act Without Words* II and *Film*)
    Grade B.
24. *No's Knife: Selected Shorter Prose 1945–1966*
    Calder 1967 (incl. *Stories and Texts for
    Nothing, From an Abandoned Work, Imagination
    Dead Imagine, Enough* and *Ping*)
    Grade B.
25. *Film* (screenplay) Grove Press 1969; 1st Eng.
    Faber 1972
    Amer. ed.: Grade B Faber ed. Grade A.
26. *Breath* and *Other Shorts* Faber 1971 (incl. *Come
    and Go, Act Without Words* I and II, *From an
    Abandoned Work*)
    Grade B.
27. *Lessness* (story) Calder & Boyars 1971
    (French-language ed. 1969)
    Grade A.
28. *First Love* (story) Calder & Boyars 1973; 1st
    Amer. Grove Press 1974 (French-language
    ed. 1970)
    Grade A.
29. *The Lost Ones* (story) Calder & Boyars 1972
    (French-language ed. 1971) Grade A.
30. *Not I* (play) Faber 1973
    Grade A–B.
31. *The North* Enitharmon Press 1973
    Limited to 137 numbered and signed copies.
    Grade L.
32. *Mercier and Camier* (novel) Calder & Boyars
    1974; 1st Amer. Grove Press 1975 (French-
    language ed. 1970)
    Grade A.

33. *Footfalls* (play) Faber 1976
34. *That Time* (play) Faber 1976
35. *For to End Yet Again, and Other Fizzles* Calder 1977
    Published as *Fizzles* by Grove Press in 1977.
36. *Collected Poems in English and French* Calder 1977
37. *Four Novellas* Calder 1977
38. *Ends and Odds* (plays) Grove Press 1977; 1st Eng. Faber 1977 (incl. Nos 30, 33, 34)
    Nos 33 and 34 are Grade A, Nos 35–38 Grade B.

Beckett translated the following:
Anthology of Mexican Poetry Indiana University, Bloomington 1958; 1st Eng. Thames & Hudson 1959 (ed. by Octavio Paz)
Robert Pinget *The Old Tune* in:
Robert Pinget *Three Plays* Hill & Wang NY 1966/Robert Pinget *Plays* Calder & Boyars 1966
Guillaume Apollinaire *Zone* Calder & Boyars/Dolmen Press 1972

Samuel Beckett: An Exhibition (Turret Books 1971) is also a useful book to the collector.

Film:
Film Evergreen Theatre Inc. 1965

BEERBOHM, Max
Born in London 1872. Died 1956.
Beerbohm is collected as much for his caricatures as for his writings, and prices for these are rising fast. However, Beerbohm published too much to list here, but the following work gives the fullest information available: A. E. Gallatin and L. M. Oliver *A Bibliography of the Works of Max Beerbohm* (Soho Bibliographies, Hart-Davis 1952) There follows Beerbohm's first published book, and also his probable highlight.

1. *The Works of Max Beerbohm* Lane 1896; 1st Amer. Scribner 1896
2. *Zuleika Dobson* Heinemann 1911; 1st Amer. Lane 1911
   No. 1 is very scarce, and would be Grade P. No. 2, Grade F.

BEHAN, Brendan
Born in Dublin 1923. Died 1964.

1. *The Quare Fellow* (play) Methuen 1956
2. *The Hostage* (play) Methuen 1958
   (These two plays pub. in America in one vol. by Grove Press 1964)
3. *Borstal Boy* Knopf 1957; 1st Eng. Hutchinson 1958
4. *Brendan Behan's Island* (non-fiction) Hutchinson 1962; 1st Amer. Geis 1962
5. *Hold Your Hour and Have Another* Hutchinson 1963; 1st Amer. Little, Brown 1964
6. *Brendan Behan's New York* Hutchinson 1964; 1st Amer. Geis 1964
7. *The Scarperer* (novel) Doubleday 1964; 1st Eng. Hutchinson 1966
8. *Confessions of an Irish Rebel* Hutchinson 1965; 1st Amer. Geis 1966
9. *Borstal Boy* (play) Random House NY 1971
10. *Richard's Cork Leg* (play) Methuen 1973; 1st Amer. Grove Press 1974

Film:
The Quare Fellow British Lion 1962

Although very popular in the sixties—the reputation of a somewhat bawdy life was a popular thing, then—Behan has been rather neglected since, which is a shame, for his books retain their vitality. This is particularly true of *The Quare Fellow* and *Borstal Boy*, either or both being regarded as his highlight. Nos 1 and 2 are scarce, and Grade C. No. 3 is not very easy to find, but has always been underpriced at Grade B. The rest are all Grade B, but a rise soon is not unlikely.

BELLOW, Saul
Born in Canada 1915. American.

1. *Dangling Man* (novel) Vanguard Press 1944; 1st Eng. Lehmann 1946
2. *The Victim* (novel) Vanguard Press 1945; 1st Eng. Lehmann 1948
3. *The Adventures of Augie March* (novel) Viking Press 1953; 1st Eng. Weidenfeld 1954
4. *Seize the Day, with Three Short Stories and a One Act Play* Viking Press 1956; 1st Eng. Weidenfeld 1957

5. *Henderson the Rain King* (novel) Viking Press 1959; 1st Eng. Weidenfeld 1959
6. *Herzog* (novel) Viking Press 1964; 1st Eng. Weidenfeld 1965
7. *The Last Analysis* (play) Viking Press 1965; 1st Eng. Weidenfeld 1966
8. *Mosby's Memoirs and Other Stories* Viking Press 1968; 1st Eng. Weidenfeld 1969
9. *Mr Sammler's Planet* (novel) Viking Press 1970; 1st Eng. Weidenfeld 1970
10. *Humboldt's Gift* (novel) Viking Press 1975; 1st Eng. Alison Press/Secker & Warburg 1975
11. *To Jerusalem and Back* (non-fiction) Viking Press 1976; 1st Eng. Secker & Warburg 1976

Bellow's reputation has been growing for some time, and it seems as if his 1sts have been quietly bought and put away by the discerning few, for they rarely come onto the market, except for the most recent few. His winning of the Nobel Prize in 1976 will only accelerate this trend, and, I suppose, raise the prices.
No. 1 is very scarce, and there is a record of the American edition being sold for $100. The English edition would be Grade D–E. No. 2 is Grade E–F (American) and C (English). Nos 3, 4 and 5 are Grade C (American) and B (English). The rest are Grade B, though the American *Herzog* might go to Grade C.

BENCHLEY, Peter

Jaws (novel) Doubleday 1974; 1st Eng. Deutsch 1974
Benchley, the grandson of Robert, wrote one novel before *Jaws*, and has published *The Deep* since, but *Jaws* is notable if only for being one of the biggest-selling novels of all time, and the film is at time of writing the biggest box-office success in history.
Not literary criticism, this, but evidence that for best-seller collectors, at least, this is a must. A good novel, I am told, to get stuck into. Grade B.

Film:
Jaws Universal 1975

BENNETT, Alan
Born in Yorkshire 1934.

1. *Beyond the Fringe* (play) Souvenir Press 1962; 1st Amer. Random House 1963
2. *Forty Years On* (play) Faber 1969
3. *Getting On* (play) Faber 1972
4. *Habeas Corpus* (play) Faber 1973

His first play became famous overnight, and established many new comic talents of the sixties. All the succeeding plays have gained an admirable reputation, and are in Grade A. No. 1, Grade B.

BENTLEY, E. C.
Born 1875. Died 1956. He is notable for two major achievements: the writing of, some say, the most perfect detective story (see below), and the invention of the clerihew (his middle name)—e.g.
The digestion of Milton
Was unequal to Stilton.
He was only feeling so-so
When he wrote Il Penseroso.

1. *Trent's Last Case* (novel) Nelson 1913
He wrote other books, including two Trent sequels.
One other volume bound to be of interest:
2. *Clerihews Complete* Werner Laurie 1951
No. 1: Grade D. No. 2: Grade B–C.

Film:
Trent's Last Case 20th Century Fox 1929; British Lion 1950

BERRYMAN, John
Born in Oklahoma 1914. Died 1972.

1. *Five American Poets* New Directions NY 1940 (with others)
2. *Poems* New Directions 1942
3. *The Dispossessed* (verse) Sloane NY 1948
4. *Stephen Crane* (criticism) Sloane 1950; 1st Eng. Methuen 1951
5. *Homage to Mistress Bradstreet* (verse) Farrar Straus NY 1956; 1st Eng. Faber 1959
(The Amer. ed. is just the title poem, whereas the Faber ed. includes a selection from 3 and 6.)

6. *His Thoughts Made Pockets & The Plane Buckt* Frederick NY 1958
7. *77 Dream Songs* (verse) Farrar Straus 1964; 1st Eng. Faber 1964
8. *Berryman's Sonnets* (verse) Farrar Straus & Giroux 1967; 1st Eng. Faber 1968
9. *Short Poems* Farrar Straus & Giroux 1967 (The same as the Eng. ed. of 5, without the title poem, but with one new poem)
10. *His Toy, His Dream, His Rest* (verse) Farrar Straus & Giroux 1968; 1st Eng. Faber 1969
11. *Love and Fame* (verse) Farrar Straus & Giroux 1970; 1st Eng. Faber 1971
12. *Delusions, etc.* (verse) Farrar Straus & Giroux 1972; 1st Eng. Faber 1972
13. *Selected Poems 1938–1968* Faber 1972
14. *Recovery* (novel) Farrar Straus & Giroux 1973; 1st Eng. Faber 1973
15. *The Freedom of the Poet* (essays) Farrar Straus & Giroux 1977; 1st Eng. Faber 1977

A leading American poet who died, some say, at the height of his powers. Very much collected, and appearing less and less in lists and shops. Nos 1 and 2 are scarce, though 2 would probably be the more desirable: Grade I. Nos 3 and 4 would be Grade E—even for the English ed. No. 5 is Berryman's highlight, and would be Grade G, but Grade C for the Faber ed. No. 6 is scarce and Grade D, but the remainder should all be within Grade C, and Grade B for the English editions.

BETJEMAN, John

Born in Highgate, London, 1906. Educated at Marlborough and Magdalen College, Oxford. The most English of poets, and certainly our best known—this largely due to his architectural sallies on television. The vision of Betjeman immortalizing Ruislip Underground remains ever wondrous. One person said to me; 'You mean he writes poems *as well?!*' I once asked a collector what he thought of Betjeman. He replied that he liked him, but he didn't like himself liking him. Betjeman seems to take some people like that. A fine poet, though, and many have realized how worthwhile he is to collect—from every point of view, some of John Murray's productions being really superb. Most of his later work seems very good value, but the early work really is worth the trouble and expense of going after. Betjeman was knighted in 1969, and became Poet Laureate in 1972.

1. *Mount Zion* (verse) James Press 1931
   As with all major writers' first works, very scarce, and expensive. Grade P.
2. *Ghastly Good Taste* (architecture) Chapman & Hall 1933
   Worth buying for the title alone, this really is a fine item. Small format with pink boards and the famous 'gatefold' at the rear. Ensure that this is present. Grade I.
3. *Devon* (architecture) Architectural Press 1936
   A rare book. Grade E.
4. *Continual Dew: A Little Book of Bourgeois Verse* Murray 1937
   The first of a lifelong partnership with John Murray. A charming production, the black boards featuring mock brass hinges and rustic lettering. The title is illustrated on the t/p by a dripping tap, and the book has India paper inserts, decorated by Osbert Lancaster. A fine item, and quite scarce. Grade E–F.
5. *An Oxford University Chest* J. Miles 1938
   A larger-format book; though recently reissued in facsimile, the 1st remains scarce. Grade G.
6. *Antiquarian Prejudice* (essay) Hogarth Press 1939
   Scarce, and made doubly so by Hogarth collectors. Grade C.
7. *Old Light for New Chancels* (verse) Murray 1940
   First of the paperback-size Murray books, with paper label on blue boards. Grade D.
8. *Vintage London* (architecture) Collins 1942
   Pleasing large, slim volume with tipped-in colour plates. Grade C.
9. *English Cities and Small Towns* (architecture) Collins 1943
   In the Britain in Pictures series, and one of the two or three sought by collectors (other

than collectors of the whole series, who invariably collect King Penguins as well). Pleasant production. Grade B.

10. *John Piper* (art) Penguin 1944
Wrappered booklet in series. Grade B.

11. *New Bats in Old Belfries* (verse) Murray 1945
Small, slim volume. Red boards with paper label on front. White d/w with red printed design. Grade D.

12. *Slick, but Not Streamlined: Poems and Short Pieces* Doubleday NY 1947
Only 1,750 copies printed, and edited by W. H. Auden—hence the scarcity. Black cloth, with our dripping tap again (see 4). Grade F–G.

13. *Murray's Buckinghamshire Architectural Guide* Murray 1948 (with John Piper—see 10)
Grade B.

14. *Selected Poems* Murray 1948
Ed. by John Sparrow. Red boards, white paper label. Grade B.

15. *Murray's Berkshire Architectural Guide* Murray 1949
As 13.

16. *Murray's Shropshire Architectural Guide* Murray 1951
As 13.

17. *First and Last Loves* (essays) Murray 1952
Illustrated and d/w by John Piper (see 10). White boards, decorated in pale blue. Grade C.

18. *A Few Late Chrysanthemums* (verse) Murray 1954
Blue cloth, yellow paper label on front, yellow d/w. Grade B.

19. *Poems in the Porch* SPCK 1954
Wrappered pamphlet, illus. by John Piper. Take care with this one, as the verso will always read 'First published in 1954 by SPCK', whereas t/p itself may bear a different date. They must agree. Grade B.

20. *The English Town in the Last Hundred Years* CUP 1956
Architectural work. Grade C.

21. *Collins Guide to English Parish Churches* Collins 1958; 1st Amer. Obolensky 1959
Grade B.

22. *Collected Poems* Murray 1958
Edited by Earl of Birkenhead. White boards, brown d/w. Grade C.

23. *Summoned by Bells* (verse autobiog.) Murray 1960; 1st Amer. Houghton Mifflin, Boston 1960
Green diamond-paned boards, beige d/w. Grade B.

24. *A Ring of Bells* Murray 1963; 1st Amer. Houghton Mifflin 1963
Edited by Irene Slade, being excerpts of 23, intended for children. d/w by Ardizzone. Grade B.

25. *English Churches* (architecture) Studio Vista 1964 (with Basil Clarke)
Grade B.

26. *Cornwall* Faber 1965
Only Faber Betjeman. Grade B.

27. *High and Low* (verse) Murray 1966; 1st Amer. Houghton Mifflin 1967
Yellow cloth, pink d/w. Grade B.

28. *London's Historic Railway Stations* Murray 1972
Pictorial. Photographic d/w. Grade B.

29. *A Pictorial History of English Architecture* Murray 1972; 1st Amer. Macmillan 1972
Fine book, but thousands upon thousands printed for a certain Book Club, so it is not at all difficult. Grade A–B.

30. *A Nip in the Air* (verse) Murray 1974
Yellow cloth, green d/w. Grade A–B.

Latterly, Betjeman has gone in for the signed, limited edition in a fairly big way, Murray usually doing such an edition simultaneously with the 1st, though never announcing it. For instance, *A Nip in the Air* was also published in a limited edition of 175 copies on handmade paper, signed by the author, and bound in yellow buckram. These appreciate in value very quickly, not least of the reasons being the very low limitation, though the published price is generally quite steep. Blond reissued *Ghastly Good Taste* in a revised edition in 1970. The pink-boarded trade edition was everywhere, and still is, but 200 were quarter-bound in leather, cloth-slipcased, numbered and signed by the author. The trade edition would fetch about £1, but the special would be Grade F.

Betjeman has edited many works, too numerous to list, though all are architectural or photographic except *English Love Poems* (Faber 1957; Grade B) and *Altar and Pew: Church of England Verses* (Hulton 1959; Grade A–B).

BOLT, Robert
Born in Lancashire 1924.

1. *Flowering Cherry* (play) Heinemann 1958; 1st Amer. French NY n.d.
2. *The Tiger and the Horse* (play) Heinemann 1961; 1st Amer. French NY n.d.
3. *A Man for All Seasons* (play) Heinemann 1961; 1st Amer. Random House 1962
4. *Gentle Jack* (play) French 1964; 1st Amer. Random House 1965
5. *The Thwarting of Baron Bolligrew* (play) Heinemann 1966; 1st Amer. Theatre Arts 1967
6. *Doctor Zhivago: The Screenplay* Harvill Press 1966; 1st Amer. Random House 1966
7. *Three Plays* Heinemann 1967 (cont. *Flowering Cherry, A Man for All Seasons, Tiger and the Horse*)
8. *Vivat! Vivat Regina!* (play) Heinemann 1971; 1st Amer. Random House 1972

Films:
Lawrence of Arabia (not published) British Lion 1962
Doctor Zhivago MGM 1965
A Man for all Seasons Columbia 1966
Bolt has written two other films, though neither has been published.

A Man for All Seasons is obviously Bolt's highlight, and is difficult to find as a 1st. However, it might be overlooked, as it is small format with printed boards, looking rather like a school edition. Grade B. No. 1 might also be Grade B, but all others Grade A.

BOND, Edward
Born in London 1934.

1. *Saved* (play) Methuen 1966; 1st Amer. Hill & Wang 1966
2. *Narrow Road to the Deep North* (play) Methuen 1968; 1st Amer. Hill & Wang 1968
3. *Early Morning* (play) Calder & Boyars 1968; 1st Amer. Hill & Wang 1969
4. *The Pope's Wedding and Other Plays* Methuen 1971 (incl. *Mr Dog, The King with Golden Eyes, Sharpville Sequence* and *Black Mass*)
5. *Lear* (play) Methuen 1972; 1st Amer. Hill & Wang 1972
6. *The Sea* (play) Eyre Methuen 1973; 1st Amer. Hill & Wang 1973
7. *Bingo* (play) Eyre Methuen 1974
8. *The Fool* and *We Came to the River* (libretto) Eyre Methuen 1976
9. *A-A-America* and *Stone* (plays) Eyre Methuen 1977

Saved, the obvious highlight here, would be Grade B–C, but all other titles would be Grade A.
Bond also wrote the screenplay for the film *Blow Up,* but this was not published.

BOWEN, Elizabeth
Born in Dublin 1899. Died 1973.

1. *Encounters: Stories* Sidgwick & Jackson 1923; 1st Amer. Boni & Liveright 1926
2. *Ann Lee's and Other Stories* Sidgwick & Jackson 1926; 1st Amer. Boni & Liveright 1926
3. *The Hotel* (novel) Constable 1927 1st Amer. Dial Press 1928
4. *The Last September* (novel) Constable 1929; 1st Amer. Dial Press 1929
5. *Joining Charles and Other Stories* Constable 1929; 1st Amer. Dial Press 1929
6. *Friends and Relations* (novel) Constable 1931; 1st Amer. Dial Press 1931
7. *To the North* (novel) Gollancz 1932 1st Amer. Knopf 1933
8. *The Cat Jumps and Other Stories* Gollancz 1934
9. *The House in Paris* (novel) Gollancz 1935; 1st Amer. Knopf 1936
10. *The Death of the Heart* (novel) Gollancz 1938; 1st Amer. Knopf 1939
11. *Look at All Those Roses* (stories) Gollancz 1941; 1st Amer. Knopf 1941
12. *Bowen's Court* (non-fiction) Longman 1942;

1st Amer. Knopf 1942
13. *English Novelists* (non-fiction) Collins 1942;
    1st Amer. Hastings House 1942
14. *Seven Winters* (non-fiction) Cuala Press,
    Dublin 1942; 1st Eng. Longman 1943; 1st
    Amer. Knopf 1943
15. *The Demon Lover and Other Stories* Cape 1945
16. *Ivy Gripped the Steps and Other Stories* Knopf
    1946 (same as 15)
17. *Selected Stories* Fridberg, Dublin 1946
18. *Anthony Trollope: A New Judgement* OUP
    1946; 1st Amer. OUP 1946
19. *Why Do I Write?: An Exchange of Views
    Between Elizabeth Bowen, Graham Greene, and
    V. S. Pritchett* Marshall 1948
20. *The Heat of the Day* (novel) Cape 1949; 1st
    Amer. Knopf 1949
21. *Collected Impressions* Longman 1950; 1st
    Amer. Knopf 1950
22. *The Shelbourne* (non-fiction) Harrap 1951
23. *The Shelbourne Hotel* (same as 22) Knopf 1951
24. *A World of Love* (novel) Cape 1955; 1st
    Amer. Knopf 1955
25. *Stories* Knopf 1959
26. *A Time in Rome* (non-fiction) Longman 1960;
    1st Amer. Knopf 1960
27. *Afterthought: Pieces About Writing* Longman
    1962; 1st Amer. Knopf 1962
28. *The Little Girls* (novel) Cape 1964; 1st Amer.
    Knopf 1964
29. *A Day in the Dark and Other Stories* Cape 1965
30. *The Good Tiger* (juvenile) Knopf 1965; 1st
    Eng. Cape 1970
31. *Eva Trout* (novel) Knopf 1968; 1st Eng. Cape
    1969

Elizabeth Bowen also edited the following
two important works:
The Faber Book of Modern Stories Faber 1937
Stories (by Katherine Mansfield) Knopf 1956
34 Short Stories (same as above) Collins 1957

The early works are scarce, Nos 1 and 2
being Grade F, and 3, 4, 5 and 6 being Grade
D–E. The thirties Gollancz editions would be
Grade B–C, but all the others are quite easy
to come by and should not rise much above
Grade B—with the exception of 14 (the Cuala
Press edition) which was limited to 450

copies, and could be Grade G. The very
recent works, such as 28 in particular, are
very easy, and Grade A.

BRADBURY, Malcolm
Born in Yorkshire 1932.

1. *Eating People Is Wrong* (novel) Secker &
   Warburg 1959; 1st Amer. Knopf 1960
2. *How to Have Class in a Classless Society* Parrish
   1960
3. *All Dressed Up and Nowhere to Go* Parrish
   1962
4. *Evelyn Waugh* (Writers & Critics Series)
   Oliver & Boyd 1964
5. *Stepping Westward* (novel) Secker & Warburg
   1965; 1st Amer. Houghton Mifflin 1966
6. *What Is a Novel?* Arnold 1969
7. *The Social Context of Modern English Literature*
   Blackwell 1971; 1st Amer. Schocken 1971
8. *Possibilities: Essays on the State of the Novel*
   OUP 1973
9. *The History Man* (novel) Secker & Warburg
   1975; 1st Amer. Houghton Mifflin 1976
10. *Who Do You Think You Are* (stories) Secker
    & Warburg 1976

The History Man was hailed by critics as the
Lucky Jim of the seventies. Whether it proves
so from the collector's point of view remains
to be seen, but it is a fine novel, and bought
now would be Grade A. None of the above
should be above Grade B–C.

BRADBURY, Ray
Born in Illinois 1920. American.

1. *Dark Carnival* (stories) Arkham House 1947;
   1st Eng. Hamish Hamilton 1948
2. *The Meadow* (play) Dodd Mead NY 1948 (in
   Best One-Act Plays of 1947–48)
3. *The Martian Chronicles* (stories) Doubleday
   NY 1950
4. *The Illustrated Man* (stories) Doubleday 1951;
   1st Eng. Hart-Davis 1952
5. *The Golden Apples of the Sun* (stories)
   Doubleday 1953; 1st Eng. Hart-Davis 1953
6. *Fahrenheit 451* (novel) Ballantine NY 1953;
   1st Eng. Hart-Davis 1954

7. *Switch on the Night* (juvenile) Pantheon NY 1955; 1st Eng. Hart-Davis 1955
8. *The October Country* (stories) Ballantine 1955; 1st Eng. Hart-Davis 1956
9. *Dandelion Wine* (stories) Doubleday 1957; 1st Eng. Hart-Davis 1957
10. *A Medicine for Melancholy* (stories) Doubleday 1959
11. *The Day It Rained Forever* (same as 10) Hart-Davis 1959
12. *R Is for Rocket* (juvenile) Doubleday 1962; 1st Eng. Hart-Davis 1968
13. *Something Wicked This Way Comes* (novel) Simon & Schuster 1962; 1st Eng. Hart-Davis 1963
14. *The Anthem Sprinters and Other Antics* (play) Dial Press 1963
15. *The Machineries of Joy: Short Stories* Simon & Schuster 1964; 1st Eng. Hart-Davis 1964
16. *The Vintage Bradbury* (stories) Random House NY 1965
17. *The Autumn People* (stories) Ballantine 1965
18. *Tomorrow Midnight* (stories) Ballantine 1966
19. *The Day It Rained Forever* (play) French NY 1966
20. *The Pedestrian* (play) French NY 1966
21. *S Is for Space* (juvenile) Doubleday 1966; 1st Eng. Hart-Davis 1968
22. *I Sing the Body Electric!* (stories) Knopf 1969; 1st Eng. Hart-Davis 1970
23. *The Wonderful Ice-Cream Suit and Other Plays* Bantam 1972; 1st Eng. Hart-Davis 1973 (incl. *The Veldt* and *To the Chicago Abyss*)
24. *The Halloween Tree* (novel) Knopf 1972; 1st Eng. Hart-Davis MacGibbon 1973
25. *When Elephants Last in the Dooryard Bloomed: Celebrations for Almost any Day of the Year* (verse) Knopf 1972; 1st Eng. Hart-Davis MacGibbon 1975
26. *The Small Assassin* (stories) NEL NY 1973
27. *Mars and the Mind of Man* (non-fiction) Harper NY 1973
28. *Long After Midnight* (stories) Hart-Davis MacGibbon 1977

Currently very popular with collectors. Nos 1–5 are very scarce, and although a defective copy of No. 1 was catalogued at £12 in London in 1975, a good copy now would reach Grade E–F. Nos 2–5, Grade D. No. 6 is Bradbury's highlight, and would be Grade E–F. The rest should be Grade B–C.

Films:
The Beast from 20,000 Fathoms Warner Bros 1953 (*The Foghorn*—story)
Fahrenheit 451 United Artists 1966
The Illustrated Man Warner Bros 1968

BRAINE, John
Born in Yorkshire 1922.

1. *Room at the Top* (novel) Eyre & Spottiswoode 1957; 1st Amer. Houghton Mifflin 1957
2. *The Vodi* (novel) Eyre & Spottiswoode 1959
3. *From the Hand of the Hunter* (same as 2) Houghton Mifflin 1960
4. *Life at the Top* (novel) Eyre & Spottiswoode 1962; 1st Amer. Houghton Mifflin 1962 Sequel to No. 1.
5. *The Jealous God* (novel) Eyre & Spottiswoode 1965; 1st Amer. Houghton Mifflin 1965
6. *The Crying Game* (novel) Eyre & Spottiswoode 1968; 1st Amer. Houghton Mifflin 1968
7. *Stay with Me till Morning* (novel) Eyre & Spottiswoode 1970
8. *The View from Tower Hill* (same as 7) Coward McCann NY 1971
9. *The Queen of a Distant Country* (novel) Methuen 1972; 1st Amer. Coward McCann 1973
10. *Writing a Novel* (non-fiction) Eyre Methuen 1974; 1st Amer. Coward McCann 1974
11. *The Pious Agent* (novel) Eyre Methuen 1975; 1st Amer. Coward McCann 1975
12. *Waiting for Sheila* (novel) Eyre Methuen 1976
13. *Finger of Fire* (novel) Eyre Methuen 1977 Sequel to No. 11.

Films:
Room at the Top British Lion 1958
Life at the Top British Lion 1965

Braine is another Angry Young Man who is no longer quite so angry, and has publicly renounced his former Leftwingmanship. Joe Lampton, though, is one of the enduring characters of fiction, and *Room at the Top* one of the most important novels of the post-war period. It is quite scarce and would be Grade D. No. 4 is desirable to complete the duet, but as it seems to have been remaindered at some quite late stage, it ought to be possible to find a fine copy well within Grade A. All the others would be Grade A, with the possible exception of No. 2.

BRAITHWAITE, E. R.
Born in British Guiana 1922.
Although he has written several books, Braithwaite is notable for one novel, subsequently filmed by Columbia in 1966:

To Sir, with Love Bodley Head 1959
A popular book with collectors of modern fiction. Grade B.

BRAMAH, Ernest
English. Born 1868; died 1942. Real name Ernest Bramah Smith.
It would take a volume specializing in detective fiction to list and grade all of Bramah's works, but the first to start the line of Kai Lung novels was:

The Wallet of Kai Lung Grant Richards 1900
This would now be Grade E, but other Kai Lung 1sts should be found for less, though rarely less than Grade B. During the twenties Grant Richards issued some numbered, signed editions—including a reissue of *The Wallet of Kai Lung*—and these would also be Grade E.

BRAUTIGAN, Richard
Born in Washington 1933. American.

1. *The Return of the Rivers* (verse) Inferno Press, San Francisco 1957
2. *The Galilee Hitch-Hiker* (verse) White Rabbit Press, San Francisco 1958
3. *The Octopus Frontier* (verse) Carp Press, San Francisco 1960
4. *In Watermelon Sugar* (novel) Four Seasons Foundation, San Francisco 1964; 1st Eng. Cape 1970
5. *A Confederate General from Big Sur* (novel) Grove Press NY 1965; 1st Eng. Cape 1971
6. *Trout Fishing in America* (novel) Four Seasons Foundation 1967; 1st Eng. Cape 1970
7. *The Pill Versus the Springhill Mine Disaster (Poems 1957–1968)* Four Seasons Foundation 1968; 1st Eng. Cape 1971
8. *Rommel Drives On Deep into Egypt* (verse) Dell NY 1970
9. *The Abortion: An Historical Romance* Simon & Schuster 1971; 1st Eng. Cape 1973
10. *Revenge of the Lawn: Stories 1962–1970* Simon & Schuster 1971; 1st Eng. Cape 1972
11. *The Hawkline Monster: A Gothic Western* Simon & Schuster 1974; 1st Eng. Cape 1975
12. *Willard and His Bowling Trophy: A Perverse Mystery* Simon & Schuster 1975; 1st Eng. Cape 1976
13. *Sombrero Fallout* (novel) Simon & Schuster 1976; 1st Eng. Cape 1977

Though far more popular in America than in England, the early verse would be Grade E. The rest of Brautigan's work would be Grade B–C, though probably Grade A in England. The most recent few may be found at publication price and, very often, at less.

BRENAN, Gerald
Born in Malta 1894.

1. *Jack Robinson* (novel) Chatto & Windus 1933 (pseud. George Beaton)
2. *Doctor Partridge's Almanack for 1935* (novel) Chatto & Windus 1934 (pseud. George Beaton)
3. *The Spanish Labyrinth* (non-fiction) CUP 1943
4. *Spanish Scene* (non-fiction) Current Affairs pamphlet 1946
5. *The Face of Spain* (non-fiction) Turnstile Press 1950; 1st Amer. Pellegrini & Cudahy 1951
6. *The Literature of the Spanish People* CUP 1951; 1st Amer. CUP 1951
7. *South from Granada* (non-fiction) Hamilton 1957; 1st Amer. Farrar, Straus & Giroux 1957
8. *A Holiday by the Sea* (novel) Hamilton 1961; 1st Amer. Farrar, Straus & Giroux 1961
9. *A Life of One's Own* (autobiog.) Hamilton 1962; 1st Amer. Farrar, Straus & Giroux 1962

10. *The Lighthouse Always Says Yes* (novel) Hamilton 1966
11. *Personal Record 1920–1972* (autobiog.) Cape 1974; 1st Amer. Knopf 1975

The publication of No. 11 rekindled a lot of interest in Brenan, in England and in America, and served as an introduction to many people. His early work has always been difficult to come by, the two pseudonymous novels being Grade F, although—as with all pseudonymous work—there is a chance of picking them up for a fraction of that. The Spanish books of the forties and fifties are Grade B–C, and the recent novels Grade A–B. No. 11 is Grade B. Cape reissued No. 9 in 1975 in matching format.

BROOKE, Rupert
Born at Rugby 1887. Died 1915.

1. *The Pyramids* Rugby Press 1904
2. *The Bastille* Rugby Press 1905
3. *Prize Compositions* Rugby Press 1905
4. *Poems 1911* Sidgwick & Jackson 1911
5. *1914 and Other Poems* Sidgwick & Jackson 1914
   (An American edition seems to have been printed by Doubleday in 1915 for copyright reasons only, and never published)
6. *1914: Five Sonnets* Sidgwick & Jackson 1915
7. *The Collected Poems of Rupert Brooke* Lane NY 1915; 1st Eng. Sidgwick & Jackson 1918
8. *Lithuania* (drama) Chicago Little Theatre 1915; 1st Eng. Sidgwick & Jackson 1935
9. *Letters from America* Scribner 1916 1st Eng. Sidgwick & Jackson 1916
10. *John Webster* (drama) Lane 1916; 1st Eng. Sidgwick & Jackson 1916
11. *Selected Poems* Sidgwick & Jackson 1917
12. *The Complete Poems of Rupert Brooke* Sidgwick & Jackson 1932
13. *Twenty Poems* Sidgwick & Jackson 1935
14. *The Poetical Works of Rupert Brooke* Faber 1946
15. *Democracy and the Arts* Hart-Davis 1946
16. *The Prose of Rupert Brooke* Sidgwick & Jackson 1956
17. *The Letters of Rupert Brooke* Faber 1968

For fullest information on Brooke, see the following:
Christopher Hassall *Rupert Brooke: A Biography* (Faber 1964)
Geoffrey Keynes *Rupert Brooke: A Bibliography* (Soho Bibliographies, Hart-Davis 1959)
Nos 1, 2 and 3 were printed for private distribution only, and are consequently of legendary rarity. None has come up for some time, but each could be expected to reach £500 or more. The early Sidgwick titles would be Grade F, No. 5 being the highlight. No. 8 is very rare in the Chicago edition, and is Grade I. The dramas and prose writings generally, however, seem to be of much less interest than the poems, and a 1st of No. 10, for instance, would not exceed Grade C. The abundance of *Collecteds, Completes* and *Works* is confusing, but No. 12 is usually regarded as the standard edition, and would be C.

BUNTING, Basil
Born in Northumberland 1900.

1. *Redimiculum Matellarum* (verse) Grafica Moderna, Milan 1930
2. *Poems 1950* Cleaners Press, Texas 1950
3. *First Book of Odes* Fulcrum Press 1965
4. *Loquitur* (verse) Fulcrum Press 1965
5. *Ode II/2* (verse) Fulcrum Press 1965
6. *Briggflatts* (verse) Fulcrum Press 1966
7. *Two Poems* Unicorn Press, California 1967
8. *What the Chairman Told Tom* Pym Randall Press, Massachusetts 1967
9. *Collected Poems* Fulcrum Press 1968

A very peculiar publishing history, as will be seen from the above. All private press, and all limited. Although Bunting was virtually unknown until the sixties, his reputation is now high, many pointing to *Briggflatts* as his best work.
All are scarce, particularly No. 1. If this came up, it could easily reach Grade K, and *Poems*

1950 could be Grade E–F. All the Fulcrums are in the C–D class, as are Nos 7 and 8.

BURGESS, Anthony
Born in Manchester 1917.

1. *Time for a Tiger* (novel) Heinemann 1956
2. *English Literature: A Survey for Students* Longman 1958 (pseud. John Burgess Wilson)
3. *The Enemy in the Blanket* (novel) Heinemann 1958
4. *Beds in the East* (novel) Heinemann 1959 This, together with Nos 1 and 3, forms the Malayan trilogy.
5. *The Right to an Answer* (novel) Heinemann 1960; 1st Amer. Norton 1961
6. *The Doctor Is Sick* (novel) Heinemann 1960; 1st Amer. Norton 1966
7. *The Worm and the Ring* (novel) Heinemann 1961
8. *Devil of a State* (novel) Heinemann 1961; 1st Amer. Norton 1962
9. *One Hand Clapping* (novel) Davies 1961; 1st Amer. Knopf 1971 (pseud. Joseph Kell)
10. *A Clockwork Orange* (novel) Heinemann 1962; 1st Amer. Norton 1963
11. *The Wanting Seed* (novel) Heinemann 1962; 1st Amer. Norton 1963
12. *Honey for the Bears* (novel) Heinemann 1963; 1st Amer. Norton 1964
13. *Inside Mr Enderby* (novel) Heinemann 1963 (pseud. Joseph Kell)
14. *The Novel Today* (non-fiction) Longman 1963
15. *Nothing Like the Sun: A Story of Shakespeare's Love-Life* Heinemann 1964; 1st Amer. Norton 1964
16. *The Eve of Saint Venus* (novel) Sidgwick & Jackson 1964; 1st Amer. Norton 1967
17. *Languages Made Plain* (non-fiction) English Universities Press 1964; 1st Amer. Crowell 1965
18. *The Long Day Wanes* Norton 1965 (incl. 1, 3 and 4)
19. *A Vision of Battlements* (novel) Sidgwick & Jackson 1965; 1st Amer. Norton 1966
20. *Here Comes Everybody: An Introduction to James Joyce for the Ordinary Reader* Faber 1965
21. *Re Joyce* Norton 1965 (same as 20)
22. *Tremor of Intent* (novel) Heinemann 1966; 1st Amer. Norton 1966
23. *The Novel Now* (non-fiction) Faber 1967; 1st Amer. Norton 1967
24. *Enderby Outside* (novel) Heinemann 1968
25. *Enderby* Norton 1968 (incl. 13 and 24)
26. *Urgent Copy: Literary Studies* Cape 1968; 1st Amer. Norton 1969
27. *Shakespeare* (non-fiction) Cape 1970; 1st Amer. Knopf 1971
28. *MF* (novel) Cape 1971; 1st Amer. Knopf 1971
29. *Joysprick: An Introduction to the Language of James Joyce* Deutsch 1972
30. *Napoleon Symphony* (novel) Cape 1974; 1st Amer. Knopf 1974
31. *The Clockwork Testament: or, Enderby's End* (novel) Hart-Davis MacGibbon 1974; 1st Amer. Knopf 1975
32. *Moses: A Narrative* (prose) Dempsey & Squires 1976
33. *A Long Trip to Teatime* (juvenile) Dempsey & Squires 1976
34. *Beard's Roman Women* (novel) Knopf 1977; 1st Eng. Hutchinson 1977
35. *Abba Abba* (novel) Faber 1977

Burgess has also edited and translated a number of works. For complete details, see: Paul W. Boytinck *Anthony Burgess: An Enumerative Bibliography* (Norwood Editions, USA 1973)
The Malayan trilogy, as Nos 1, 3 and 4 are known, would be Grade G, or Grade C, individually. *A Clockwork Orange* has become his highlight, and is a rare book: Grade D. All others should be Grade B. It is interesting to note that No. 19, though not published until 1965, was the first novel Burgess wrote—seven years before *Time for a Tiger* was published.

Film:
A Clockwork Orange Warner Bros 1971

BURROUGHS, Edgar Rice
Born 1875, died 1950. Rice Burroughs shares the distinction with Conan Doyle and Frank Richards of having created one of the most

famous fictional characters—though some would add Ian Fleming to the select list. The first of the line is detailed below, but in addition to the Tarzan series, Rice Burroughs wrote many other novels, such as *The Gods of Mars* (Methuen 1920) and the *Jungle Woman* books.

Tarzan of the Apes McClurg, Chicago 1914
This book is very, very scarce and expensive. Grade P.
After this came many—too many even to list: *The Beasts of Tarzan, The Return of Tarzan, The Son of Tarzan, Jungle Tales of Tarzan* and so on. Countless films were made *based* on the character.
In America and in England there has been a recent revival of interest, and whereas it was possible to find English 1sts for a pound or two in the sixties, this is now no longer the case. They are all going up, but depending on how early they are, Grades B to G are reasonable.

BURROUGHS, William S.
Born in Missouri 1914. American.

1. *Junk* (novel) Ace NY 1953 (pseud. William Lee)
Junkie Ace 1964; 1st Eng. NEL 1966
2. *The Naked Lunch* (novel) Olympia Press, Paris 1959; 1st Amer. Grove Press 1962; 1st Eng. Calder 1964 (in Amer. and Eng. eds, no *The* in title)
3. *The Exterminator* (verse) Auerhahn Press, San Francisco 1960 (with Brion Gysin)
4. *Minutes to Go: Poems* Two Cities, Paris 1960; 1st Amer. Beach Books, San Francisco 1968 (with others)
5. *The Soft Machine* (novel) Olympia Press, Paris 1961; 1st Amer. Grove Press 1966; 1st Eng. Calder 1968
6. *The Ticket That Exploded* (novel) Olympia Press, Paris 1962; 1st Amer. Grove Press 1967; 1st Eng. Calder 1968
7. *Dead Fingers Talk* (novel) Olympia Press, Paris 1963; 1st Eng. Calder 1964
8. *The Yage Letters* City Lights, San Francisco 1963 (with Allen Ginsberg)

9. *Nova Express* (novel) Grove Press 1964; 1st Eng. Cape 1966
10. *Time* (verse) C Press NY 1965
11. *Valentine Day's Reading* American Theatre for Poets NY 1965
12. *APO-33: A Metabolic Regulator* Beach Books, San Francisco 1966
13. *So Who Owns Death TV* Beach Books 1967 (with Claude Pelieu and Carl Weissner)
14. *The Job: Interviews with William Burroughs* Grove Press 1970; 1st Eng. Cape 1970 (French-language ed.: Belfond, Paris 1969)
15. *The Third Mind* (non-fiction) Grove Press 1970
16. *The Last Words of Dutch Schultz* (filmscript) Cape 1970
17. *The Wild Boys: A Book of the Dead* (novel) Grove Press 1971; 1st Eng. Calder & Boyars 1972
18. *Exterminator* (novel) Viking Press 1974; 1st Eng. Calder & Boyars 1974
19. *White Subway* Aloes Books 1974
20. *The Last Words of Dutch Schultz* (novel) Viking Press 1975
21. *Port of Saints* Covent Garden Press 1975

Nos 1 and 2 would be Grade F in the true 1st editions, as might be No. 5. The American Press books are difficult, and might be Grade C. The rest are reasonable, or should be—1st English editions not commanding very high prices—Grade B. The exception to this is 21, which was limited to 100 signed (pub. £17.50) and 100 unsigned (pub. £7.50). These prices will by now have risen.

CAMUS, Albert
Born in Algeria 1913. Died 1960. French.
All the true 1st editions are, of course, French. There follow the 1st English editions, which were published in England by Hamish Hamilton, and in the United States by Knopf.

1. *The Outsider* (novel) Hamilton 1946
Though first published as *L'Etranger* in France in 1942, this English edition is of great interest to collectors, as it is translated

by Stuart Gilbert, introduced by Cyril Connolly, and has a d/w by Edward Bawden. It is also, of course, the first appearance of Camus in English. Very undervalued, however. It is at the moment Grade B, but must soon be worth much more.
The Knopf edition is entitled *The Stranger*.

2. *Caligula* and *Cross Purpose* (plays) 1947
3. *The Plague* (novel) 1948 (French ed. *La Peste* 1947)
4. *The Rebel* (essays) 1953; 1st Amer. 1954 (French ed. *L'Homme révolté* 1952)
5. *The Myth of Sisyphus* (essays) 1955 (French ed. *Le Mythe de Sisyphe* 1942)
6. *The Fall* (monologue) 1957 (French ed. *La Chute* 1956)
7. *Exile and the Kingdom* (stories) 1958 (French ed. *L'Exil et la royaume* 1957)
8. *The Possessed* (play) 1960 (French ed. *Les Possédés* 1959)
9. *A Happy Death* (novel) 1972 (French ed. *La Mort heureuse* 1971)

As with No. 1, all the English-language editions of Camus seem to be underpriced, most being found in Grade A, though all are at most Grade B.

Film:
The Outsider Paramount 1968

CAPOTE, Truman
Born in New Orleans 1924.

1. *Other Voices, Other Rooms* (novel) Random House NY 1948; 1st Eng. Heinemann 1948
2. *A Tree of Night and Other Stories* Random House 1949
3. *Local Color* (non-fiction) Random House 1950
4. *The Grass Harp* (novel) Random House 1951; 1st Eng. Heinemann 1952
5. *The Grass Harp* (play) Random House 1952
6. *The Muses Are Heard: An Account* Random House 1956
7. *Breakfast at Tiffany's* (stories) Random House 1958; 1st Eng. Heinemann 1959
8. *Observations* Simon & Schuster 1959; 1st Eng. Weidenfeld & Nicolson 1959 (with Richard Avedon)

9. *Selected Writings* Modern Library NY 1963; 1st Eng. Hamilton 1963
10. *A Christmas Memory* (story) Random House 1966
11. *In Cold Blood: A True Account of a Multiple Murder and Its Consequences* Random House 1966; 1st Eng. Hamilton 1966
12. *House of Flowers* (play) Random House 1968
13. *The Thanksgiving Visitor* (play) Random House 1968; 1st Eng. Hamilton 1969
14. *The Dogs Bark: Public People and Private Places* Random House 1973; 1st Eng. Weidenfeld & Nicolson 1974

Films:
Breakfast at Tiffany's Paramount 1961
In Cold Blood Columbia 1968

Nos 1 and 2 are scarce in the true—American—1sts (Grade D), but No. 1 is surprisingly common in the English edition, rarely rising above Grade B, and usually well within Grade A. The highlights, due, no doubt, to the films, are 7 and 11. The American 1st of No. 7 is quite scarce, and might reach Grade C, English Grade B. *In Cold Blood* is not very difficult to find, and is Grade B, English editions being common and Grade A.

CHANDLER, Raymond
Born in Chicago 1888. Died 1959.

1. *The Big Sleep* (novel) Knopf 1939; 1st Eng. Hamilton 1939
2. *Farewell, My Lovely* (novel) Knopf 1940; 1st Eng. Hamilton 1940
3. *The High Window* (novel) Knopf 1942; 1st Eng. Hamilton 1943
4. *The Lady in the Lake* (novel) Knopf 1943; 1st Eng. Hamilton 1944
5. *Five Murderers* (stories) Avon NY 1944 (This, along with 6 and 7, was published in wrappers)
6. *Five Sinister Characters* (stories) Avon 1945
7. *The Finger Man* (stories) Avon 1946
8. *The Little Sister* (novel) Knopf 1949; 1st Eng. Hamilton 1949

9. *Trouble Is My Business* (stories) Penguin 1950
1st Amer. Houghton Mifflin 1951
10. *The Simple Art of Murder* (miscellany)
Houghton Mifflin 1950; 1st Eng. Hamilton
1950
11. *The Long Goodbye* (novel) Hamilton 1953; 1st
Amer. Houghton Mifflin 1953
12. *Playback* (novel) Houghton Mifflin 1958; 1st
Eng. Hamilton 1958
13. *Raymond Chandler Speaking* (non-fiction)
Houghton Mifflin 1962; 1st Eng. Hamilton
1962
14. *Killer in the Rain* (stories) Houghton Mifflin
1964; 1st Eng. Hamilton 1964
15. *The Smell of Fear* (stories) Hamilton 1965
16. *The Blue Dahlia* (screenplay) S. Illinois
University Press 1976; 1st Eng. Elm Tree 1976

Very much collected, very difficult to find—
especially the American editions—and
becoming very expensive. A 1st of *The Big
Sleep* was catalogued in 1975 at £110! Nos
2–8 are Grade H–J, though those of the
fifties should be Grade C. Highlight is
obviously No. 1, but Nos 2 and 11 are also
very noteworthy.

Films:
The Big Sleep Warner Bros 1946
The Falcon Takes Over (*Farewell, My Lovely*)
RKO 1942
Murder, My Sweet (*Farewell, My Lovely*)
RKO 1944
Lady in the Lake MGM 1946
The Brasher Doubloon (*The High Window*) 20th
Century Fox 1947
Marlowe (*The Little Sister*) MGM 1969
The Long Goodbye United Artists 1973
Farewell, My Lovely Kastner/ITC 1976

CHARTERIS, Leslie
Pseudonym of Leslie Charles Bowyer Yin.
Born in Singapore 1907.

Charteris' first book *Meet the Tiger* was
published by Ward Lock in 1928, but the first
to feature Simon Templar in the title was:

Enter the Saint Hodder & Stoughton 1930
Both these are scarce, and would be Grade

D–E. Saint titles following soon afterwards
would be Grade B, and the more recent
books and Omnibuses, Grade A.
Unfortunately, there are too many to list.

Films:
The Saint in New York RKO 1938
The Saint's Vacation (*Getaway*) RKO 1941
The Saint Meets the Tiger (*Meet the Tiger*)
Republic 1943

CHESTERTON, G. K.
Born in London 1874. Died 1936.
Chesterton is another of those very prolific
authors whose works it is impossible to list
here in their entirety. There follows,
therefore, a list of his best-known works, and
those which are probably the most desirable
as 1st editions. Fuller information might very
well be required, however—particularly for
his very many non-fiction works—and for
this I refer you to:
John Sullivan *G. K. Chesterton: A Bibliography*
(University of London Press 1958)

1. *The Napoleon of Notting Hill* Bodley Head 1904
2. *The Man Who Was Thursday* Arrowsmith 1908
3. *The Innocence of Father Brown* Cassell 1911
4. *Manalive* Nelson 1912
5. *The Flying Inn* Methuen 1914
6. *The Wisdom of Father Brown* Cassell 1914
7. *The Man Who Knew Too Much* Cassell 1922
8. *The Incredulity of Father Brown* Cassell 1926
9. *The Collected Poems of G. K. Chesterton* Palmer
1927
10. *The Secret of Father Brown* Cassell 1927
11. *The Scandal of Father Brown* Cassell 1935
12. *Autobiography* Hutchinson 1936

Films:
Father Brown, Detective Paramount 1935 (*The
Wisdom of Father Brown*)
Father Brown Columbia 1954 (based on the
Father Brown stories)

It is the Father Brown stories that are of most
interest today, which is consistent with the
current enthusiasm for detective fiction. No.
3 might reach Grade D, though the others

would be Grade B–C. It is difficult to find them in fine state, and almost impossible in d/w. Nos 1 and 2 are Grade D, and 4 Grade B. No. 9 is usually Grade B, but so fine a book is it that this seems low. The *Autobiography* is also Grade B.

CHRISTIE, Agatha
Born in Devon 1890. Died 1976.

1. *The Mysterious Affair at Styles* (novel) Lane NY 1920; 1st Eng. Lane 1921
2. *The Secret Adversary* (novel) Lane 1922; 1st Amer. Dodd Mead 1922
3. *Murder on the Links* (novel) Lane 1923; 1st Amer. Dodd Mead 1923
4. *The Man in the Brown Suit* (novel) Lane 1924; 1st Amer. Dodd Mead 1924
5. *Poirot Investigates* (stories) Lane 1924; 1st Amer. Dodd Mead 1925
6. *The Secret of Chimneys* (novel) Lane 1925; 1st Amer. Dodd Mead 1925
7. *The Road of Dreams* (verse) Bles 1925
8. *The Murder of Roger Ackroyd* (novel) Collins 1926; 1st Amer. Dodd Mead 1926
9. *The Big Four* (novel) Collins 1927; 1st Amer. Dodd Mead 1927
10. *The Mystery of the Blue Train* (novel) Collins 1928; 1st Amer. Dodd Mead 1928
11. *The Seven Dials Mystery* (novel) Collins 1929; 1st Amer. Dodd Mead 1929
12. *Partners in Crime* (stories) Collins 1929; 1st Amer. Dodd Mead 1929
13. *The Underdog* (story) Reader's Library 1929 (with *Blackman's Wood* by E. Phillips Oppenheim)
14. *The Murder at the Vicarage* (novel) Collins 1930; 1st Amer. Dodd Mead 1930
15. *The Mysterious Mr Quin* (stories) Collins 1930; 1st Amer. Dodd Mead 1930
16. *Giant's Bread* (novel) Collins 1930; 1st Amer. Doubleday 1930 (as Mary Westmacott)
17. *The Sittaford Mystery* (novel) Collins 1931
18. *The Murder at Hazelmoor* Dodd Mead 1931 (same as 17)
19. *Peril at End House* (novel) Collins 1932; 1st Amer. Dodd Mead 1932
20. *The Thirteen Problems* (stories) Collins 1932

21. *The Tuesday Club Murders* Dodd Mead 1933 (same as 20)
22. *Lord Edgware Dies* (novel) Collins 1933
23. *Thirteen at Dinner* Dodd Mead 1933 (same as 22)
24. *The Hound of Death and Other Stories* Odhams 1933
25. *Parker Pyne Investigates* (stories) Collins 1934
26. *Mr Parker Pyne, Detective* Dodd Mead 1934 (same as 25)
27. *The Listerdale Mystery and Other Stories* Collins 1934
28. *Black Coffee* (play) Ashley 1934
29. *Why Didn't They Ask Evans?* (novel) Collins 1934
30. *Murder on the Orient Express* (novel) Collins 1934
31. *Murder on the Calais Coach* Dodd Mead 1934 (same as 30)
32. *Murder in Three Acts* (novel) Dodd Mead 1934
33. *Unfinished Portrait* (novel) Collins 1934; 1st Amer. Doubleday 1934 (as Mary Westmacott)
34. *Boomerang Clue* Dodd Mead 1935 (same as 29)
35. *Three Act Tragedy* Collins 1935 (same as 32)
36. *Death in the Clouds* (novel) Collins 1935
37. *Death in the Air* Dodd Mead 1935 (same as 36)
38. *The A.B.C. Murders: A New Poirot Mystery* Collins 1936; 1st Amer. Dodd Mead 1936
39. *Cards on the Table* (novel) Collins 1936; 1st Amer. Dodd Mead 1936
40. *Murder in Mesopotamia* (novel) Collins 1936; 1st Amer. Dodd Mead 1936
41. *Murder in the Mews and Other Stories* Collins 1937
42. *Dead Man's Mirror and Other Stories* Dodd Mead 1937 (same as 41)
43. *Death on the Nile* (novel) Collins 1937; 1st Amer. Dodd Mead 1938
44. *Dumb Witness* (novel) Collins 1937
45. *Poirot Loses a Client* Dodd Mead 1937 (same as 44)
46. *Appointment With Death: A Poirot Mystery* Collins 1938; 1st Amer. Dodd Mead 1938
47. *The Regatta Mystery and Other Stories* Dodd Mead 1939
48. *Hercule Poirot's Christmas* (novel) Collins 1939
49. *Murder for Christmas: A Poirot Story* Dodd

Mead 1939 (same as 48)

50. *Murder Is Easy* (novel) Collins 1939
51. *Easy to Kill* Dodd Mead 1939 (same as 50)
52. *Ten Little Niggers* (novel) Collins 1939
53. *And Then There Were None* Dodd Mead 1940 (same as 52)
54. *One, Two, Buckle My Shoe* (novel) Collins 1940
55. *Sad Cypress* (novel) Collins 1940; 1st Amer. Dodd Mead 1940
56. *The Patriotic Murders* Dodd Mead 1941 (same as 54)
57. *Evil Under the Sun* (novel) Collins 1941; 1st Amer. Dodd Mead 1941
58. *N or M?* (novel) Collins 1941; 1st Amer. Dodd Mead 1941
59. *The Body in the Library* (novel) Collins 1942; 1st Amer. Dodd Mead 1942
60. *The Moving Finger* (novel) Dodd Mead 1942; 1st Eng. Collins 1943
61. *Five Little Pigs* (novel) Collins 1942
62. *Murder in Retrospect* Dodd Mead 1942 (same as 61)
63. *Death Comes as the End* (novel) Dodd Mead 1942; 1st Eng. Collins 1945
64. *Towards Zero* (novel) Collins 1944; 1st Amer. Dodd Mead 1944
65. *Absent in the Spring* (novel) Collins 1944; 1st Amer. Farrar & Rinehart NY 1944 (as Mary Westmacott)
66. *Ten Little Niggers* (play) French 1944
67. *Sparkling Cyanide* (novel) Collins 1945
68. *Remembered Death* Dodd Mead 1945 (same as 67)
69. *Appointment with Death* (play) French 1945
70. *The Hollow* (novel) Collins 1946; 1st Amer. Dodd Mead 1946
71. *Come Tell Me How You Live* (travel) Collins 1946; 1st Amer. Dodd Mead 1946
72. *Ten Little Indians* (play) French NY 1946 (same as 66)
73. *Murder on the Nile* (play) French 1946; 1st Amer. French NY 1946
74. *The Labours of Hercules: Short Stories* Collins 1947
75. *Labors of Hercules* Dodd Mead 1947 (same as 74)
76. *Taken at the Flood* (novel) Collins 1948

77. *There Is a Tide . . .* Dodd Mead 1948 (same as 76)
78. *The Rose and the Yew Tree* (novel) Heinemann 1948; 1st Amer. Rinehart 1948 (as Mary Westmacott)
79. *Witness for the Prosecution* (stories) Dodd Mead 1948
80. *Crooked House* (novel) Collins 1949; 1st Amer. Dodd Mead 1949
81. *A Murder Is Announced* (novel) Collins 1950; 1st Amer. Dodd Mead 1950
82. *Three Blind Mice and Other Stories* Dodd Mead 1950
83. *Under Dog and Other Stories* Dodd Mead 1951
84. *They Came to Baghdad* (novel) Collins 1951; 1st Amer. Dodd Mead 1951
85. *The Hollow* (play) French 1952; 1st Amer. French NY 1952
86. *They Do It with Mirrors* (novel) Collins 1952
87. *Murder with Mirrors* Dodd Mead 1952 (same as 86)
88. *Mrs McGinty's Dead* (novel) Collins 1952; 1st Amer. Dodd Mead 1952
89. *A Daughter's a Daughter* (novel) Heinemann 1952 (as Mary Westmacott)
90. *After the Funeral* (novel) Collins 1953
91. *Funerals Are Fatal* Dodd Mead 1953 (same as 90)
92. *A Pocket Full of Rye* (novel) Collins 1953; 1st Amer. Dodd Mead 1954
93. *Witness for the Prosecution* (play) French 1954; 1st Amer. French NY 1954
94. *Destination Unknown* (novel) Collins 1954
95. *So Many Steps to Death* Dodd Mead 1955 (same as 94)
96. *Hickory, Dickory, Dock* (novel) Collins 1955
97. *Hickory, Dickory, Death* Dodd Mead 1955 (same as 96)
98. *The Mousetrap* (play) French 1956; 1st Amer. French NY 1956
99. *Dead Man's Folly* (novel) Collins 1956; 1st Amer. Dodd Mead 1956
100. *The Burden* (novel) Heinemann 1956 (as Mary Westmacott)
101. *The Spider's Web* (play) French 1957; 1st Amer. French NY 1957
102. *Towards Zero* (play) French 1957; 1st Amer. Dramatists Play Service 1957

103. *4.50 from Paddington* (novel) Collins 1957
104. *What Mrs McGillicuddy Saw!* Dodd Mead 1957 (same as 103)
105. *Verdict* (play) French 1958
106. *The Unexpected Guest* (play) French 1958
107. *Ordeal by Innocence* (novel) Collins 1958; 1st Amer. Dodd Mead 1958
108. *Cat Among the Pigeons* (novel) Collins 1959; 1st Amer. Dodd Mead 1959
109. *The Adventure of the Christmas Pudding* (stories) Collins 1960
110. *Go Back for Murder* (play) French 1960 (adaptation of 61)
111. *Double Sin and Other Stories* Dodd Mead 1961
112. *13 for Luck* (stories) Dodd Mead 1961; 1st Eng. Collins 1966
113. *The Pale Horse* (novel) Collins 1961; 1st Amer. Dodd Mead 1962
114. *The Mirror Crack'd from Side to Side* (novel) Collins 1962
115. *The Mirror Crack'd* Dodd Mead 1963 (same as 114)
116. *Rule of Three* (plays) French 1963 (cont. *Afternoon at the Seaside*, *The Patient* and *The Rats*)
117. *The Clocks* (novel) Collins 1963; 1st Amer. Dodd Mead 1964
118. *A Caribbean Mystery* (novel) Collins 1964; 1st Amer. Dodd Mead 1965
119. *Star over Bethlehem and Other Stories* Collins 1965; 1st Amer. Dodd Mead 1965 (as A. C. Mallowan)
120. *Surprise! Surprise!* (stories) Dodd Mead 1965
121. *13 Clues for Miss Marple* (stories) Dodd Mead 1965
122. *At Bertram's Hotel* (novel) Collins 1965; 1st Amer. Dodd Mead 1965
123. *Third Girl* (novel) Collins 1966; 1st Amer. Dodd Mead 1967
124. *Endless Night* (novel) Collins 1967; 1st Amer. Dodd Mead 1968
125. *By the Pricking of My Thumbs* (novel) Collins 1968; 1st Amer. Dodd Mead 1968
126. *Passenger to Frankfurt* (novel) Collins 1970; 1st Amer. Dodd Mead 1970
127. *Nemesis* (novel) Collins 1971; 1st Amer. Dodd Mead 1971
128. *The Golden Ball and Other Stories* Dodd Mead 1971
129. *Elephants Can Remember* (novel) Collins 1972; 1st Amer. Dodd Mead 1972
130. *Postern of Fate* (novel) Collins 1973; 1st Amer. Dodd Mead 1973
131. *Akhnaton* (play) Collins 1973; 1st Amer. Dodd Mead 1973
132. *Poems* Collins 1973; 1st Amer. Dodd Mead 1973
133. *Hercule Poirot's Early Cases* (stories) Collins 1974; 1st Amer. Dodd Mead 1974
134. *Murder on Board: Three Complete Mystery Novels* Dodd Mead 1974 (cont. *The Mystery of the Blue Train*, *Death in the Air*, *What Mrs McGillicuddy Saw!*)
135. *Curtain: Hercule Poirot's Last Case* Collins 1975; 1st Amer. Dodd Mead 1975
136. *Sleeping Murder* (novel) Collins 1976; 1st Amer. Dodd Mead 1976

Films:
Ten Little Niggers 20th Century Fox 1945
Witness for the Prosecution United Artists 1957
The Spider's Web United Artists 1960
Murder She Said (4.50 from Paddington) MGM 1961
Murder Most Foul (Mrs McGinty's Dead) MGM 1963
Murder at the Gallop (After the Funeral) MGM 1963
Murder Ahoy (based on Miss Marple) MGM 1964
Ten Little Indians (Ten Little Niggers) Associated British 1965
The Alphabet Murders (The A.B.C. Murders) MGM 1966
Endless Night British Lion 1971
Murder on the Orient Express EMI 1974

Most fertile ground for a collector here. Admittedly, a complete collection would require considerable space, but when did such considerations stand in a collector's way?
Generally speaking, the earlier the Christie, the more difficult, and the more expensive. Since the film *Murder on the Orient Express*, there has been a great resurgence of interest—if the interest ever flagged—and a

new interest from collectors. The poetry of Miss Christie's publishing *Curtain*—the final Poirot—and then expiring herself as interest grew yet stronger, has had the result of early titles almost vanishing from the market, and quite common sixties titles doubling in price. It is difficult to see whether this trend will continue, but it is certain that she will be remembered as one of the greatest exponents of the genre, and her accepted 'greats' will always remain desirable. As I say, though—acquiring them may be murder.

Obviously, the most scarce is No. 1. Either edition would be well into Grade K. Nos 2–7 would be E, and No. 8 Grade G, as it is generally recognized as her greatest effort. All the others of the twenties and thirties would be Grade D. *Murder on the Orient Express* and *Ten Little Niggers* (despite the now reprehensible title, since altered to *Ten Little Indians*) might rise above this, as they are highlights. Forties Christies are Grade B–C, and those of the fifties, Grade B. An exception to this is *The Mousetrap*, published in wrappers and rare: Grade C–D. The recent books are still easy, and all those of the sixties and seventies are Grade A. An exception might prove to be *Curtain,* which was reprinted twice, very rapidly.

Do not despair of finding No. 1—it has been known. Many collectors have to settle for *An Agatha Christie Omnibus* (Lane 1931) which contains it, but even this is not common, and might be Grade B–C.

CLARKE, Arthur C.

Born in Somerset 1917.

Arthur C. Clarke has published nearly thirty non-fiction works, in addition to his better-known novels and short stories. Space, as it were, does not allow me to list these, but below are the novels and stories in full.

1. *Prelude to Space* (novel) New World NY 1951; 1st Eng. Sidgwick & Jackson 1953
2. *The Sands of Mars* (novel) Sidgwick & Jackson 1951; 1st Amer. Gnome Press 1952
3. *Islands in the Sky* (novel) Winston, Philadelphia 1952; 1st Eng. Sidgwick & Jackson 1952
4. *Against the Fall of Night* (novel) Gnome Press 1953
5. *Childhood's End* (novel) Ballantine 1953; 1st Eng. Sidgwick & Jackson 1954
6. *Expedition to Earth* (stories) Ballantine 1953; 1st Eng. Sidgwick & Jackson 1954
7. *Earthlight* (novel) Ballantine 1955; 1st Eng. Muller 1955
8. *The City and the Stars* (novel) Harcourt Brace 1956; 1st Eng. Muller 1956
9. *Reach for Tomorrow* (stories) Ballantine 1956; 1st Eng. Gollancz 1962
10. *Tales from the White Hart* (stories) Ballantine 1957; 1st Eng. Sidgwick & Jackson 1972
11. *The Deep Range* (novel) Harcourt Brace 1957; 1st Eng. Muller 1957
12. *The Other Side of the Sky* (stories) Harcourt Brace 1958; 1st Eng. Gollancz 1961
13. *Across the Sea of Stars* Harcourt Brace 1959 (incl. 5, 7 and stories)
14. *A Fall of Moondust* (novel) Harcourt Brace 1961; 1st Eng. Gollancz 1961
15. *From the Oceans, From the Stars* Harcourt Brace 1962 (incl. 11, 8 and stories)
16. *Tales of Ten Worlds* (stories) Harcourt Brace 1962; 1st Eng. Gollancz 1963
17. *Dolphin Island* (novel) Holt Rinehart 1963; 1st Eng. Gollancz 1963
18. *Glide Path* (novel) Harcourt Brace 1963; 1st Eng. Sidgwick & Jackson 1969
19. *Prelude to Mars* Harcourt Brace 1965 (incl. 1, 2 and stories)
20. *An Arthur C. Clarke Omnibus* Sidgwick & Jackson 1965 (incl. 1, 5 and 6)
21. *The Nine Billion Names of God* (stories) Harcourt Brace 1967
22. *2001: A Space Odyssey* (novel) NAL 1968; 1st Eng. Hutchinson 1968
23. *An Arthur C. Clarke Second Omnibus* Sidgwick & Jackson 1968 (incl. 2, 7 and 14)
24. *The Lion of Comarre* (novel) Harcourt Brace 1968; 1st Eng. Gollancz 1970
25. *A Meeting with Medusa* (stories) Harcourt Brace 1972
26. *The Wind from the Sun* (stories) Harcourt Brace 1972; 1st Eng. Gollancz 1972

27. *Of Time and Stars* (stories) Gollancz 1972
28. *The Lost Worlds of 2001* (miscellany) NAL 1972; 1st Eng. Sidgwick & Jackson 1972
29. *The Best of Arthur C. Clarke (1937–1971)* Sidgwick & Jackson 1973
30. *Rendezvous with Rama* (novel) Harcourt Brace 1973; 1st Eng. Gollancz 1973
31. *Imperial Earth* (novel) Gollancz 1975; 1st Amer. Harcourt Brace 1976

Film:
2001: A Space Odyssey MGM 1968
Although there is ever-growing interest in Arthur C. Clarke from collectors, prices have stayed quite low. The highlight of his work has become *2001*, and in fact the novel was based on the film, instead of the other way round. This is now Grade C. The screenplay itself was written by Clarke with Stanley Kubrick, but was not published. All the others, though, are Grade B–C, with the exception of No. 1, which would be Grade C.

CONNOLLY, Cyril

Cyril Connolly was born in Coventry in 1903. He was at Eton with George Orwell, Anthony Powell, Henry Green and John Lehmann, among others, and was at Balliol under Maurice Bowra, who called him the cleverest boy of his generation.

It is often said that Connolly never quite lived up to his gifts, and that he himself knew it. Although this may be so, to look back on his work now is to see a very impressive performance indeed, for surely the founding and editing of *Horizon* is testimony enough. *Horizon*, certainly the best of the 'little magazines', came into being in 1939 and closed in 1950. Virtually every writer of importance appeared in its pages, and such works as Evelyn Waugh's *The Loved One* and Augustus John's *Autobiography* appeared first, in their entirety, in the magazine. *Horizon* has been collected for many years now, and a complete set of 121 issues would fetch £150–£200 in a fine state. One can still find odd numbers quite cheaply, and it is possible to build up a set, although it might

be wise to begin with a sizeable run. Connolly's own publications are very varied and interesting, as will be seen below, and are avidly collected, prices having risen sharply over the past few years. This Connolly took as a great tribute, as he was a collector of Modern Firsts himself.

Cyril Connolly was made CBE in 1972, and died in 1974.

1. *The Rock Pool* (novel) Obelisk Press, Paris 1936; 1st Amer. Scribner 1936; 1st Eng. Hamilton 1947
This was his only novel, and is of course very scarce in the Paris and American editions. Obelisk: Grade L. Scribner: Grade E. The English edition, 11 years later, is not very difficult, but in d/w it might be Grade C.
2. *Enemies of Promise* Routledge 1938; 1st Amer. Little Brown, Boston 1939
Scarce. Eng. ed.: Grade G. Amer. ed.: Grade E.
3. *The Unquiet Grave* Horizon 1944
This, under the pseudonym Palinurus, is Connolly's masterpiece. This edition was limited to 1,000 copies, and is scarce. Grade H. A revised edition was published the following year (1945) by Hamish Hamilton, and by Harper in New York. The Hamilton edition has John Piper d/w, but is not too difficult. Grade B.
4. *The Condemned Playground* (essays) Routledge 1945; 1st Amer. Macmillan 1946
Quite difficult, particularly in d/w. Grade C–D.
5. *The Missing Diplomats* Queen Anne Press 1952
Wrappers, yellow d/w. This slight volume, about Burgess and Maclean, is quite scarce, and would be Grade C.
6. *Ideas and Places* Weidenfeld & Nicolson 1953; 1st Amer. Harper 1953
Although fairly recent, a scarce item in its grey d/w. Grade C.
7. *Les Pavillons* Macmillan NY 1962; 1st Eng. Hamilton 1962 (with Jerome Zerbe)
A large-format illustrated book with photographic d/w. Very difficult to find, although some say it was once in a National Book Sale. Grade D.

8. *Bond Strikes Camp*
   This spoof of James Bond first appeared in the *London Magazine* for April 1963, the words 'Cyril Connolly' featuring strongly on its green wrappers. One might pick this up for pennies, but in a list, it would be Grade B. It is reprinted in 9.
9. *Previous Convictions* Hamilton 1963; 1st Amer. Harper 1964
   A collection of pieces, mostly from *The Sunday Times*. Orange and grey d/w, not dissimilar in style to that of 6. Grade B.
10. *The Modern Movement: 100 Key Books from England, France and America 1880–1950* Deutsch/Hamilton 1965; 1st Amer. Atheneum 1966
    White d/w. This little book is of interest to book collectors, and is most useful as a small bibliography. Grade B. In 1971 there was an exhibition based on this book at the University of Texas at Austin. The blue-wrappered catalogue is, apart from being a desirable and scarce Connolly item, a mine of bookish information, and reproduces much manuscript material.
11. *The Evening Colonnade* Bruce & Watson 1973; 1st Amer. Harcourt Brace 1975
    Connolly held a signing session in London on publication of this book, so it might be possible to find an autographed copy. Otherwise, in its amazing collage d/w, Grade B.
12. *A Romantic Friendship: The Letters of Cyril Connolly to Noel Blakiston* Constable 1975
    Posthumously published. Grade B.

Connolly edited the following:
Horizon Stories Faber 1943; 1st Amer. Vanguard Press 1946
Great English Short Novels Dial Press NY 1953
The Golden Horizon Weidenfeld & Nicolson 1953; 1st Amer. University Books 1956
Connolly translated the following:
Vercors *Put Out the Light* Macmillan 1944
This translation of *Le Silence de la mer* was published in America by Macmillan in the same year under the more reasonable title *Silence of the Sea*.

Contributions include essays in Leonard Russell *Press Gang!* and *Parody Party* (Hutchinson 1936 and 1937), and an introduction to the first English edition of Albert Camus *The Outsider* (Hamilton 1946).

CORVO, Baron
Real name: Frederick Rolfe. Born in London 1860. Died 1913.
Below I list some highlights of Corvo's work, but for complete bibliographical details, see:
Cecil Woolf *A Bibliography of Baron Corvo, Frederick Rolfe* (Soho Bibliographies, Hart-Davis 1972)

Biography:
A. J. A. Symons *The Quest for Corvo* (Cassell 1934; 1st Amer. Michigan State University 1955)

1. *Stories Toto Told Me* Lane 1898
   This wrappered volume is Corvo's first book, and scarce. Grade N.
2. *Hadrian the Seventh* Chatto & Windus 1904; 1st Amer. Knopf 1925
   Probably Corvo's best-known work. He designed the patterned boards. Grade L.
3. *Don Tarquinio* Chatto & Windus 1905
   Corvo designed the covers. Scarce. Grade L.
4. *The Desire and Pursuit of the Whole* Cassell 1934; 1st Amer. New Directions 1953
   Although published 21 years after his death, this book has become one of his best-known works. Grade F.
   The 1st Amer., though much later, is also interesting for the facts that the Foreword is by W. H. Auden, and the d/w is by Andy Warhol.

CROMPTON, Richmal
Full name Richmal Crompton Lamburn. Born in Lancashire 1890. Died 1969.
As it is only the famous William series that seems to interest collectors, I have not listed her other works. One might mention that the first few Williams were written for adults,

and it was later that she began to write them specifically for children.

Virtually all these books are now out of print, and it is very difficult to come across 1sts, particularly in fine condition. No. 1 might well be Grade D–E, though the others should be within Grade B, the more recent being Grade A. The prices could well go up sharply soon, now that the texts are no longer available. All, except *, were published by Newnes.

1. *Just William* 1922
2. *More William* 1922
3. *William Again* 1923
4. *William the Fourth* 1924
5. *Still William* 1925
6. *William the Conqueror* 1926
7. *William in Trouble* 1927
8. *William the Outlaw* 1927
9. *William the Good* 1928
10. *William* 1929
11. *William the Bad* 1930
12. *William's Happy Days* 1930
13. *William's Crowded Hours* 1931
14. *William the Pirate* 1932
15. *William the Rebel* 1933
16. *William the Gangster* 1934
17. *William the Detective* 1935
18. *Sweet William* 1936
19. *William the Showman* 1937
20. *William the Dictator* 1938
21. *William and A.R.P.* 1939 (title later changed to *William's Bad Resolution*)
22. *William and the Evacuees* 1940 (later title *William the Film Star*)
23. *William Does His Bit* 1941
24. *William Carries On* 1942
25. *William and the Brains Trust* 1945
26. *Just William's Luck* 1948
27. *William the Bold* 1950
28. *William and the Tramp* 1952
29. *William and the Moon Rocket* 1954
30. *William and the Space Animal* 1956
31. *William's Television Show* 1958
32. *William the Explorer* 1960
33. *William's Treasure Trove* 1962
34. *William and the Witch* 1964

35. *William and the Ancient Briton** 1965
36. *William and the Monster** 1965
37. *William the Globetrotter** 1965
38. *William the Cannibal** 1965
39. *William and the Pop Singers* 1965
40. *William and the Masked Ranger* 1966
41. *William the Superman* 1968
42. *William the Lawless* 1970

The four marked * above were published by Mayfair.

Film:
Just William Associated British 1940

cummings, e. e.
Born in Massachusetts 1894. Died 1962. cummings published quite a few strictly limited editions and signed pamphlets which I have not been able to list within this book, though details of these may be found in: George J. Firmage *E. E. Cummings: A Bibliography* (Wesleyan University Press 1960)

1. *The Enormous Room* (novel) Boni & Liveright 1922; 1st Eng. Cape 1928
   The 1st Eng. has an Intro. by Robert Graves
2. *Tulips and Chimneys* (verse) Seltzer 1923
3. *XLI Poems* Dial Press 1925
4. *Is 5* (verse) Boni & Liveright 1926
5. *Him* (prose) Boni & Liveright 1927
6. *Vi Va* (verse) Liveright Inc 1931
7. *Tom* (ballet) Arrow Editions NY 1935 (limited to 1500 copies)
8. *One Over Twenty* (verse) Contemporary Poetry & Prose Editions, London 1936
9. *Collected Poems* Harcourt Brace 1938
10. *One Times One* (verse) Holt NY 1944; 1st Eng. Horizon 1947
11. *Santa Claus* (prose) Holt 1946
12. *XAIPE* (verse) OUP NY 1950
13. *i: Six Nonlectures* Harvard University Press 1953
14. *Poems 1923–1954* Harcourt Brace 1954
15. *95 Poems* Harcourt Brace 1958 (300 copies limited and signed, 5000 ordinary)
16. *100 Selected Poems* Grove Press 1959

17. *Selected Poems* Faber 1960
18. *73 Poems* Faber 1964
19. *Collected Poems* (2 vols) MacGibbon & Kee 1968
20. *Selected Letters* Harcourt Brace 1969; 1st Eng. Deutsch 1972
21. *Complete Poems* Harcourt Brace 1972

cummings is very difficult to collect in England, as will be seen from the above, but even in America he is scarce and expensive. No. 1 would be Grade Q, and Grade D–E in the English ed. Nos 2–8 would be Grade G, though those of the forties and fifties should be Grade D–E. The recent English eds are Grade B.

DAHL, Roald

Dahl was born in South Wales in 1916. He has become probably the finest living writer of short stories, and one of the best children's writers—certainly one of the most popular with children. He publishes rarely, but each book is very special. Although many reference works still do not list him, and he is hardly a 'household name', it is my opinion that his reputation will continue to grow, as will the prices and rarity of his books in 1st Edition, already by no means common. He is married to the actress Patricia Neal, and although they live in England, all his books are first published in the U.S.A.

1. *The Gremlins* (juvenile) Random House 1943; 1st Eng. Collins 1944
   This book is virtually unknown, but probably Grade C.
2. *Over to You* (stories) Reynal & Hitchcock 1945; 1st Eng. Hamilton 1947
   This first example of his masterly stories is very scarce, and has been out-of-print for a long time. Grade C.
3. *Sometime Never* (novel) Scribner 1948; 1st Eng. Collins 1949
   His only novel. Scarce. Grade C.
4. *Someone Like You* (stories) Knopf 1953; 1st Eng. Secker & Warburg 1954

Rare, and Grade B, but Michael Joseph reissued the book in 1961, with two extra stories, and this may be found more easily.

5. *Kiss, Kiss* (stories) Knopf 1960; 1st Eng. Joseph 1960
   This must be Dahl's highlight. The great success of this book prompted Joseph to reissue 4 the following year (see above) with a similar d/w—red and blue shapes on a background of net curtain. Grade B–C.
6. *James and the Giant Peach* (juvenile) Knopf 1961; 1st Eng. Allen & Unwin 1967
   Published in the usual way in America in boards and d/w. Allen & Unwin published it in laminated boards, rather like the *Beano Book*. These shiny boards have not stood the test of time, and it will be hard to find good copies. Knopf ed. Grade B. English ed. Grade A.
7. *Charlie and the Chocolate Factory* (juvenile) Knopf 1964; 1st Eng. Allen & Unwin 1967
   His best-known children's book. Knopf ed.: Grade B–C. Eng. ed.: Grade A.
8. *The Magic Finger* (juvenile) Harper 1966; 1st Eng. Allen & Unwin 1968
   Less well known. Grade A–B.
9. *Twenty-Nine Kisses* Joseph 1969
   As the title suggests, a collection of past stories. Grade A.
10. *Selected Stories* Random House 1970
    No new material. Grade A.
11. *Fantastic Mr Fox* (juvenile) Knopf 1970; 1st Eng. Allen & Unwin 1970
    Recent, though little known. Grade A–B.
12. *Charlie and the Great Glass Elevator* (juvenile) Knopf 1972; 1st Eng. Allen & Unwin 1973
    Successful, because of the word 'Charlie', though less successful in England, because of the word 'Elevator'. Grade A–B.
13. *Switch Bitch* (stories) Knopf 1974; 1st Eng. Joseph 1974
    Only his third collection of stories, this time on the theme of sex. Grade A–B.
14. *Danny: The Champion of the World* (juvenile) Knopf 1975; 1st Eng. Cape 1975
    Grade A–B.

Films:
Willie Wonka and the Chocolate Factory

Paramount 1971 (*Charlie and the Chocolate Factory*)
Dahl wrote the screenplay for the above, as well as the screenplays for Ian Fleming's *You Only Live Twice* (United Artists 1965) and *Chitty-Chitty-Bang-Bang* (United Artists 1968). None has been published.

DAVIES, W. H.

Born in Monmouthshire 1871. Died 1940.
Davies wrote about fifty books, mostly verse, and it is impossible to list them, though a certain amount of bibliographical information may be found in *The New Cambridge Bibliography of English Literature* vol. 4. The highlight, however, appears below.

The Autobiography of a Super-Tramp Fifield 1908; 1st Amer. Knopf 1917
Bernard Shaw wrote the Preface for this work, which helped a great deal to get it noticed and read. It has now become a classic, and is quite scarce. Grade E.

DAY-LEWIS, C.

Born in Ireland 1904. Poet Laureate 1968. Died 1972.
Day-Lewis published about fifty books under his own name, occasionally omitting the hyphen, as well as the detective novels under the pseudonym Nicholas Blake. A checklist may be found in *The New Cambridge Bibliography of English Literature* vol. 4. For fuller details, an excellent bibliography is G. Handley-Taylor and Timothy d'Arch Smith *C. Day-Lewis: The Poet Laureate* (St James Press 1968).
Apart from his translations of Virgil, Day-Lewis is probably best remembered for
The Poetic Image Cape 1947; 1st Amer. Oxford 1947
This is Grade B–C.
Of late, the Blake novels have come to the fore, and these are listed below:

1. *A Question of Proof* Collins 1935; 1st Amer. Harper 1935
2. *Thou Shell of Death* Collins 1936; 1st Amer. Harper 1936
   The American edition omits *Thou* from the title.
3. *There's Trouble Brewing* Collins 1937; 1st Amer. Harper 1937
4. *The Beast Must Die* Collins 1938; 1st Amer. Harper 1938
5. *The Smiler with the Knife* Collins 1939; 1st Amer. Harper 1939
6. *Malice in Wonderland* Collins 1940
   This was published in America in the same year by Harper as *Summer Camp Mystery*.
7. *The Case of the Abominable Snowman* Collins 1941
   The title of the American edition, published in the same year by Harper, was *Corpse in the Snowman*.
8. *Minute for Murder* Collins 1947; 1st Amer. Harper 1948
9. *Head of a Traveller* Collins 1949; 1st Amer. Harper 1949
10. *The Dreadful Hollow* Collins 1953; 1st Amer. Harper 1953
11. *The Whisper in the Gloom* Collins 1954; 1st Amer. Harper 1954
12. *A Tangled Web* Collins 1956; 1st Amer. Harper 1956
13. *End of Chapter* Collins 1957; 1st Amer. Harper 1957
14. *A Penknife in my Heart* Collins 1958; 1st Amer. Harper 1958
15. *The Widow's Cruise* Collins 1959; 1st Amer. Harper 1959
16. *The Worm of Death* Collins 1961; 1st Amer. Harper 1961
17. *The Deadly Joker* Collins 1963; 1st Amer. Harper 1963
18. *The Sad Variety* Collins 1964; 1st Amer. Harper 1964
19. *The Morning after Death* Collins 1966; 1st Amer. Harper 1966
20. *The Nicholas Blake Omnibus* Collins 1966 (incl. Nos 4, 12 and 14)
21. *The Private Wound* Collins 1968; 1st Amer. Harper 1968

The early titles are scarce, with No. 1 at Grade E–F, Nos 2, 3 and 4 at Grade D, and the remainder Grade B, except the most recent few, which are Grade A.

Film:
Que la Bête meure (Killer/This Man Must Die) La Boétie/Rizzoli 1969 (*The Beast Must Die*)

DEIGHTON, Len

Deighton was born in London in 1929. His spy novels reach ever-growing audiences, and although lately he has experimented with many types of novel, the public was delighted when he returned to the 'Ipcress' style. Nowadays, he and his publishers seem to go to great lengths to ensure that the word 'Spy' is somewhere in the title. Educated at the Royal College of Art, Deighton is known to have a very high regard for the designs of the d/ws of his first three books—by Raymond Hawkey—and indeed they did have an enormous influence at the time.

1. *The Ipcress File* (novel) Hodder & Stoughton 1962; 1st Amer. Simon & Schuster 1963
Secret File No. 1. Very distinctive black and white photographic d/w, and orange boards. It is scarce, and Grade C.
2. *Horse Under Water* (novel) Cape 1964; 1st Amer. Putnam 1968
Secret File No. 2. First book with Cape, who have since published all his novels. The appearance is very similar to 1, though. Quite difficult. Grade B.
3. *Funeral in Berlin* (novel) Cape 1964; 1st Amer. Putnam 1965
Secret File No. 3. Continuing the theme and design of 1 and 2, this forms a trilogy, in a sense. Grade B.
4. *Action Cook Book: Len Deighton's Guide to Eating* Cape 1965
Printed boards, text printed in comic-strip style. Another original design, and an attractive book. Because original owners used it, however, it is difficult to find a nice copy. Grade A–B.
5. *Où Est le Garlic; or, Len Deighton's French Cook Book* Penguin 1965
First published as a paperback, this was as successful as his three Secret Files. Although they were everywhere in 1965, I suspect that a clean copy of this Penguin would be hard to find. Still Grade A, however.
6. *Cookstrip Cook Book* Geis NY 1966
This is the American edition of No. 4. Grade A.
7. *Billion Dollar Brain* (novel) Cape 1966; 1st Amer. Putnam 1966
Another superb Hawkey d/w, though now appearing fearfully sixties, in its silver and black shininess. The d/w announced (on the front!) that the book was to be filmed 'by the producers of James Bond', and that *The New York Times* described it as 'even better than *The Spy Who Came In from the Cold*' (see le Carré). The endpapers continue a fine tradition with a very official 'Automath Statement'. (No. 1's endpapers were plain, but on No. 2's was printed a crossword by Cape, and Gothic German in negative for No. 3.) This title is only Grade A, though. Maybe B.
8. *An Expensive Place to Die* (novel) Cape 1967; 1st Amer. Putnam 1967
The d/w is still by Hawkey, but in colour for the first time, perhaps losing some of its style. The endpapers here are a trendy black and white Art Nouveau, but the very special feature is a very effectively produced TOP SECRET buff wallet, with letters and documents within—reminiscent of Wheatley's Dossiers (see Wheatley). Needless to say, a copy *must* have this wallet. Grade A–B.
9. *London Dossier* (non-fiction) Penguin 1967
Deighton edited this volume. It is an interesting book, and now quite scarce. Grade A.
10. *Only When I Larf* (novel) Joseph 1968
This comic novel was also published (simultaneously) by Sphere in paperback, and this can be found quite easily. The Joseph edition, however is quite difficult. Both share the teeth on the cover design, but the hardback must be worth tracking down, if only for the photograph of Deighton at the rear. Not published in America, perhaps

because of the Cockney phoneticism of the title. Grade B.

11. *Len Deighton's Continental Dossier* (non-fiction) Joseph 1968
    A follow-up to 9, but very little known. Grade B.

12. *Bomber* (novel) Cape 1970; 1st Amer. Harper 1970
    Deighton's longest book, and a change of style. Grade A–B.

13. *Declarations of War* (stories) Cape 1971
    His only book of stories. Grade A–B.

14. *Close-Up* (novel) Cape 1972; 1st Amer. Atheneum 1972
    Unusual subject-matter for Deighton. Grade A.

15. *Spy Story* (novel) Cape 1974; 1st Amer. Harcourt Brace 1974
    The triumphant return, with the title leaving nothing to doubt. Grade B.

16. *Yesterday's Spy* (novel) Cape 1975; 1st Amer. Harcourt Brace 1975
    A repeat of 15's success story in the bestseller charts, and a welcome change from black and red dust-wrappers. Grade A–B.

17. *Eleven Declarations of War* (stories) Harcourt Brace 1975
    The same as 13. Grade A.

18. *Twinkle, Twinkle, Little Spy* (novel) Cape 1976; 1st Amer. Harcourt Brace 1976
    Not to be confused (if you can help it) with le Carré's *Tinker, Tailor,* etc. Grade B.

Films:
The Ipcress File Rank 1964
Funeral in Berlin Paramount 1966
Billion Dollar Brain United Artists 1967
Only When I Larf Paramount 1969
Spy Story Gala 1976
Deighton wrote the screenplay for *Only When I Larf,* as well as that for *Oh! What a Lovely War.* Neither was published.
He also wrote the introduction to Arthur Conan Doyle *The Valley of Fear* (reissue of the Sherlock Holmes stories; Murray/Cape 1974).

de la MARE, Walter
Born in Kent 1873. Died 1956.
de la Mare published over a hundred works, including many for children—some of these illustrated by some of the most collected artists of the day, such as Whistler and Ardizzone, to name two. It is impossible to list all the works, though a complete checklist may be found in *The New Cambridge Bibliography of English Literature* vol. 4. Some bibliographical information is also supplied in *The Complete Poems of Walter de la Mare* (Faber 1969). Below are a few highlights.

1. *Songs of Childhood* Longmans, Green 1902 (pseud. Walter Ramal. Author's first book)
2. *The Listeners* Constable 1912
3. *Peacock Pie* Constable 1913
4. *Memoirs of a Midget* Collins 1921

No. 1 is very scarce, and would be Grade K. The others are Grade D.

DELANEY, Shelagh
Born in Lancashire 1939.
Shelagh Delaney has published several works, but it is her first that is important, and of interest to collectors of recent drama.

A Taste of Honey (play) Methuen 1959; 1st Amer. Grove Press 1959
This is now scarce, and is Grade B–C.

Film:
A Taste of Honey British Lion 1961
She wrote the screenplay, with Tony Richardson. She also wrote the screenplay for the film *Charlie Bubbles,* but neither was published.

DONLEAVY, J. P.
Born in New York 1926. Became Irish citizen in 1967.

1. *The Ginger Man* (novel) Olympia Press, Paris 1955; 1st Eng. Spearman 1956; 1st Amer. McDowell Obolensky 1958; 1st complete ed. Corgi 1963; 1st complete Amer. ed. Lawrence-Delacorte Press 1965

This is Donleavy's highlight. Paris ed.:
Grade F–G. London ed.: Grade D. Amer.
ed.: Grade B. The others are Grade A.

2. *Fairy Tales of New York* (play) Penguin 1961;
   1st Amer. Random House 1961
3. *The Ginger Man* (play) Random House 1961
4. *What They Did in Dublin with the Ginger Man*
   McGibbon & Kee 1962 (same as 3)
5. *A Singular Man* (novel) Little Brown, Boston
   1963; 1st Eng. Bodley Head 1964
6. *Meet My Maker the Mad Molecule* (stories)
   Little Brown 1964; 1st Eng. Bodley Head
   1965
7. *A Singular Man* (play) Bodley Head 1965
8. *The Saddest Summer of Samuel S* (novel)
   Lawrence-Delacorte 1966; 1st Eng. Eyre &
   Spottiswoode 1967
9. *The Beastly Beatitudes of Balthazar B* (novel)
   Lawrence-Delacorte 1968; 1st Eng. Eyre &
   Spottiswoode 1969
10. *The Onion Eaters* (novel) Lawrence-Delacorte
    1971; 1st Eng. Eyre & Spottiswoode 1971
11. *The Plays of J. P. Donleavy* Lawrence-
    Delacorte 1972; 1st Eng. Penguin 1974 (incl.
    3, 2, 7 and the play of 8)
12. *A Fairy Tale of New York* (novel) Lawrence-
    Delacorte 1973; 1st Eng. Eyre Methuen
    1973
13. *The Unexpurgated Code: A Complete Manual of
    Survival and Manners* Lawrence-Delacorte
    1975; 1st Eng. Wildwood House 1975

Apart from No. 1, none of these is
particularly hard to find, and all should be
within Grade B.

DOUGLAS, Keith

Born in Tunbridge Wells 1920. Died 1944.
Because of Douglas's tragically short life,
nothing was published during his lifetime.
His war journals, entitled *Alamein to Zem-
Zem,* were published in 1946. These
contained a few poems, which were reprinted
in:

1. *Collected Poems* Editions Poetry London 1951
   This is scarce, and Grade F.
   Almost half the poems in the above were

reprinted in:
2. *Selected Poems* Faber 1964; 1st Amer.
   Chilmark Press 1964
   This is edited and has an Introduction by Ted
   Hughes, and is also sought after by Hughes
   collectors. Grade C.

Biography:
Desmond Graham *Keith Douglas 1920–1944*
(OUP 1974)

DOYLE, Arthur Conan

Born in Edinburgh 1859. Knighted 1902.
Died 1930.
Conan Doyle wrote many books on many
subjects, but whether he liked it or not, it
was Sherlock Holmes who captured the
public's imagination, and continues to do so.
This is also true of collectors: over the past
ten years the prices of Holmes books have
truly rocketed, and look as if they will
continue to do so. This is hardly surprising,
for apart from the magnificence of the tales,
Conan Doyle created in Holmes one of the
most famous fictional characters ever—along
with Tarzan, Billy Bunter and (some would
say) James Bond. Collectors tend to be drawn
to 'greats' and landmarks, which perhaps
explains some of it.
A complete checklist of Conan Doyle may be
found in *The New Cambridge Bibliography of
English Literature* vol. 3, and some valuable
information in:
John Dickson Carr *The Life of Sir Arthur
Conan Doyle* (Murray 1949)
Below are all the Sherlock Holmes books.

1. *A Study in Scarlet* 28th Beeton's Christmas
   Annual 1887; 1st book form Ward Lock 1887
   The wrappered annual which ushered
   Holmes into the world is fantastically scarce,
   and could easily fetch £2,000. The book is
   also very scarce, and would be Grade Q.
2. *The Sign of Four* Lippincott's Magazine 1890;
   1st book form Blackett 1890
   Very, very scarce. At least Grade P.
3. *The Adventures of Sherlock Holmes* Strand
   Magazine 1891–92; 1st book form Newnes 1892

The Strand Magazine, which began in 1891, issued bound volumes of six months' issues, and Newnes (who owned the *Strand*) published the *Adventures* in a similar format— pale blue bevelled boards, with gold blocking. It is strange that there is so much difference between the prices of the bound magazines and the 1st book forms. The *Strands* might fetch Grade B prices per volume, whereas the *Adventures* separate would be Grade N and over. This is true also of many of the following titles, but it is apparent now that bound *Strands* are not as common as they used to be, and a marked rise in price seems inevitable.

4. *The Memoirs of Sherlock Holmes* Strand Magazine 1892–93; 1st Book form Newnes 1894
   Same situation as in 3. Identical format, but in dark blue cloth.
5. *The Hound of the Baskervilles* Strand magazine 1901–02; 1st book form Newnes 1902
   The *Strands* would be Grade A–B per volume. Newnes ed., with its attractively decorated red cover, Grade L.
6. *The Return of Sherlock Holmes* Strand Magazine 1903–04; 1st book form Newnes 1905
   The *Strands* are Grade A–B per volume, but the Newnes 1st is one of the most difficult to find. Blue cloth. Grade P.
7. *The Valley of Fear* Strand Magazine 1914–15; 1st book form Smith, Elder 1915
   Strands Grade A–B per volume. 1st book in red cloth. Grade K.
8. *His Last Bow* Murray 1917
   These stories were scattered throughout *The Strand Magazine* over the period 1893–1917. The 1st is Grade G.
9. *The Case-Book of Sherlock Holmes* Murray 1927
   These too were scattered in the *Strand* over many years. Grade G.

There have been a vast number of books on Holmes, each specializing in putting forward theories more fantastic than the last, and indicating flaws in their predecessors' deductions, hopefully in the manner of the great man himself. Two works that strike me as essential are:
William S. Baring-Gould (ed.) *The Annotated Sherlock Holmes* (2 vols, Murray 1968)
Michael and Mollie Hardwick *The Sherlock Holmes Companion* (Murray 1962).

Films:
Sherlock Holmes films are too numerous to list here, but those based on Conan Doyle's stories include:
The Return of Sherlock Holmes Paramount 1929
The Sign of Four Wide World 1932
The Hound of the Baskervilles First Division 1932; 20th Century Fox 1939; United Artists 1959
A Study in Scarlet Wide World 1933
Sherlock Holmes and the Voice of Terror Universal 1942 (*His Last Bow*)
Adventure of the Five Pips Universal 1945 (*The Five Orange Pips*)
The Man with the Twisted Lip Gaumont 1951

DRABBLE, Margaret
Born in Yorkshire 1939.

1. *A Summer Bird-Cage* (novel) Weidenfeld & Nicolson 1963; 1st Amer. Morrow 1964
2. *The Garrick Year* (novel) Weidenfeld & Nicolson 1964; 1st Amer. Morrow 1965
3. *The Millstone* (novel) Weidenfeld & Nicolson 1965; 1st Amer. Morrow 1966
4. *Wordsworth* (non-fiction) Evans 1966
5. *Jerusalem the Golden* (novel) Weidenfeld & Nicolson 1967; 1st Amer. Morrow 1967
6. *The Waterfall* (novel) Weidenfeld & Nicolson 1969; 1st Amer. Knopf 1969
7. *The Needle's Eye* (novel) Weidenfeld & Nicolson 1972; 1st Amer. Knopf 1972
8. *Arnold Bennett: A Biography* Weidenfeld & Nicolson 1974; 1st Amer. Knopf 1974
9. *The Realms of Gold* (novel) Weidenfeld & Nicolson 1975; 1st Amer. Knopf 1975
10. *The Genius of Thomas Hardy* (ed.) Weidenfeld & Nicolson 1976; 1st Amer. Knopf 1976
11. *The Ice Age* (novel) Weidenfeld & Nicolson 1977; 1st Amer. Knopf 1977

Film:
A Touch of Love British Lion 1969

(The screenplay is written by Drabble, and adapted from *The Millstone*)

The first two novels are surprisingly difficult to find, though they would probably not be much above Grade B. All of the others would probably be in this range also.

du MAURIER, Daphne

Born in London 1907.
Although Daphne du Maurier has published upwards of thirty books, it tends only to be the highlights that interest collectors, and these appear below.

1. *The Loving Spirit* (novel) Heinemann 1931; 1st Amer. Doubleday 1931
   Her first book. Grade C–D.
2. *Jamaica Inn* (novel) Gollancz 1936; 1st Amer. Doubleday 1936
   Quite scarce. Grade C.
3. *Rebecca* (novel) Gollancz 1938; 1st Amer. Doubleday 1938
   Grade B.
4. *Frenchman's Creek* (novel) Gollancz 1941; 1st Amer. Doubleday 1942
5. *The Breaking Point* (stories) Gollancz 1959; 1st Amer. Doubleday 1959 (incl. *The Birds*)
   Grade B, as is No. 4.

Films:
There have been nine films made from Daphne du Maurier's books, four of which are listed above.
Jamaica Inn Paramount 1939
Rebecca United Artists 1940
Frenchman's Creek Paramount 1944
The Birds Rank 1963

DUNN, Nell

Born in London 1936. Notable for two books:

1. *Up the Junction* (stories) MacGibbon & Kee 1963; 1st Amer. Lippincott 1966
2. *Poor Cow* (novel) MacGibbon & Kee 1967; 1st Amer. Doubleday 1967
   No. 1: Grade B. No. 2: Grade A.

Films:
Poor Cow Warner Bros 1967
Up the Junction Paramount 1968

DURRELL, Lawrence

British, though born in India in 1912. He had many non-literary jobs before, with Henry Miller and Alfred Perles, editing *The Booster* in Paris just before the Second World War. He is much travelled, and was the Cyprus correspondent for *The Economist* in the early fifties. His early work received attention only from a select band, but the *Alexandria Quartet* is probably responsible for furthering his fame as a writer. *Spirit of Place* and his private correspondence with Henry Miller (see below) will fill in a good deal of biographical information. G. S. Fraser *Lawrence Durrell: A Study* (Faber 1968) is also essential reading, and contains a bibliography by Alan G. Thomas. Durrell now lives in France and Greece.

1. *Quaint Fragment* (poems) Cecil Press 1931
   Durrell says that this was never published; but Thomas (see above) says that several have passed through the salerooms, though it is extremely scarce. Very difficult to grade such an item, as it would seem to be on a par with Auden's *Poems* (1928). £1000 would be likely, though.
2. *Ten Poems* Caduceus Press 1932
   Very limited, and very rare—the remaining stock having been destroyed in the Blitz. Again, difficult to grade, though the price would be in hundreds of pounds.
3. *Bromo Bombastes* Caduceus Press 1933
   This parody of Shaw's *Black Girl* is far more scarce than the original, and was limited to 100 copies. Could be Grade Q.
4. *Transition* (poems) Caduceus Press 1934
   The same situation as No. 2.
5. *Pied Piper of Lovers* (novel) Cassell 1935
   The first commercially published work, with d/w by Nancy Myers, Durrell's first wife. Very scarce. Grade P.
6. *Panic Spring* (novel) Faber 1937; 1st Amer. Covici-Friede 1937

Although Durrell's first book with Faber, it was published under the pseudonym Charles Norden at their request, because No. 5 had sold so badly. This item is very scarce, and Grade N.

It was also the first Durrell book to be published in America.

7. *The Black Book* (novel) Obelisk Press, Paris 1938; 1st Amer. Dutton 1960; 1st Eng. Faber 1973
The Paris edition is Grade P, and the Amer. ed. would Grade D. For the publication of the work in England, Durrell held a signing session in Longon, and so autographed copies might turn up soon. Ordinary copies are still Grade B.

8. *A Private Country* (verse) Faber 1943
Grey boards, grey d/w with red lettering. First poetry published by Faber, and scarce. Grade F.

9. *Prospero's Cell* (non-fiction) Faber 1945; 1st Amer. Dutton 1960
Although quite an early work, it seems to come up fairly often, but it is still Grade D–E.

10. *Cities, Plains and People* (verse) Faber 1946
Quite scarce. Grade E.

11. *Cefalû* (novel) Editions Poetry London 1947
Scarce. It was apparently issued in both brown and green cloth, but either is particularly difficult in the d/w. Grade E.

12. *On Seeming to Presume* (verse) Faber 1948
Red boards, with cream d/w printed in black and red. Grade C.

13. *Sappho* (play) Faber 1950; 1st Amer. Dutton 1958
Grey boards with purple d/w. Grade C.

14. *Key to Modern Poetry* (lectures) Nevill 1952
This is particularly scarce, though quite recent. Grade E.

15. *A Key to Modern British Poetry* Oklahoma Press 1952 (same as 14). Grade C.

16. *Reflections on a Marine Venus* (travel) Faber 1953; 1st Amer. Dutton 1960
Quite scarce. Grade D.

17. Emmanuel Royidis *Pope Joan* Verschoyle 1954; 1st Amer. Dutton 1961
Translated from the Greek by L.D. Quite

scarce, particularly in the d/w. Grade C.

18. *The Tree of Idleness* (verse) Faber 1955
Quite difficult, and Grade C, although there is an abundance of second impressions around!

19. *Selected Poems* Faber 1956; 1st Amer. Grove Press 1956
Grade B.

20. *Bitter Lemons* (travel) Faber 1957; 1st Amer. Dutton 1958
His best-known travel work, this book on Cyprus has become quite a classic. Grade C— the d/w can be hard to find. Be careful of the Book Society editions, of which there are plenty around, as they are not the true 1st, although printed by Faber.

21. *Esprit de Corps* (stories) Faber 1957; 1st Amer. Dutton 1958
The first of the Antrobus trilogy. Grade B.

22. *Justine* (novel) Faber 1957; 1st Amer. Dutton 1957
The 1st edition has always been very difficult, and many are the Alexandria Quartets lacking the first volume! It is Grade E, despite the fact that Durrell says there were about '250 errors which were put right in the 2nd'. An important work—see *Balthazar, Mountolive* and *Clea* below.

23. *White Eagles over Serbia* (novel) Faber 1957; 1st Amer. Criterion 1957
Durrell thought it a detective story, Faber thought it a juvenile, and as such was it published. Quite scarce. Grade D.

24. *The Dark Labyrinth* Ace NY 1958
The same as No. 11. Faber published it under this title in 1961.

25. *Balthazar* (novel) Faber 1958; 1st Amer. Dutton 1958
The second of the Quartet. Grade C.

26. *Mountolive* (novel) Faber 1958; 1st Amer. Dutton 1959
The third of the Quartet. Grade C.

27. *Stiff Upper Lip* (stories) Faber 1958; 1st Amer. Dutton 1959
The second of the Antrobus trilogy (see 21). Nicolas Bentley drew the pictures. Grade B.

28. *Art and Outrage* Putnam 1959; 1st Amer. Dutton 1960

A correspondence about Henry Miller between Alfred Perles and Lawrence Durrell. Quite difficult. Grade B–C.

29. *Clea* (novel) Faber 1960; 1st Amer. Dutton 1960
The completion of the Quartet. The four look dynamic together, with their bold, graphic d/ws—yellow, grey, green and off-white, respectively, with red and black designs and lettering. *Clea* is Grade B–C.

30. *Collected Poems* Faber 1960; 1st Amer. Dutton 1960
Grade B–C.

31. *The Alexandria Quartet* Faber 1962; 1st Amer. Dutton 1962
This one-volume edition was issued in an ordinary trade edition (Grade C), and one limited to 500 copies, signed by L.D. This is Grade K.

32. *Lawrence Durrell and Henry Miller: A Private Correspondence* Dutton 1963; 1st Eng. Faber 1963
Grade B–C.

33. *Beccafico Le Becfigue* (verse) La Licorne, France 1963
Limited to 150 copies, signed. Grade G.

34. *An Irish Faustus* (play) Faber 1963; 1st Amer. Dutton 1964
Grade B.

35. *La Descente du Styx* (verse) La Murène, France 1964
Limited to 250 copies, signed. Grade G–H.

36. *Selected Poems 1935–1963* Faber 1964
Paper-covered edition. Grade A.

37. *Acte* (play) Faber 1965; 1st Amer. Dutton 1965
Grade B.

38. *Sauve Qui Peut* (stories) Faber 1966; 1st Amer. Dutton 1967
The final Antrobus (see 21 and 27). Nicolas Bentley drew the pictures. Remaindered in the seventies, and therefore abundant. Grade A.

39. *The Ikons* (poems) Faber 1966; 1st Amer. Dutton 1967
Grade B.

40. *Tunc* (novel) Faber 1968; 1st Amer. Dutton 1968
The first of the *Revolt of Aphrodite* duet. Grade B.

41. *Spirit of Place* (travel) Faber 1969; 1st Amer. Dutton 1969
Essays edited by Alan G. Thomas. Grade B.

42. *Nunquam* (novel) Faber 1970; 1st Amer. Dutton 1970
The completion of the duet (see 40). Grade B.

43. *The Red Limbo Lingo* (poetry notebook) Faber 1971
An unusual venture for Faber. Limited edition, 100 of which signed. Red cloth in slipcase. Grade D unsigned; Grade E signed.

44. *On the Suchness of the Old Boy* (verse) Turret 1972
Illustrated by Sappho Durrell. Limited. Grade E.

45. *Vega and Other Poems* Faber 1973
Very quickly replaced by a paperback edition, and may already prove quite hard to find. Grade B.

46. *The Big Supposer* Abelard-Schuman 1973; 1st Amer. Grove Press 1974
A dialogue with Marc Alyn. First published in French as *Le Grand Suppositoire* by Editions Pierre Belfond (Paris 1972). Grade A–B.

47. *The Revolt of Aphrodite* Faber 1974
Nos 40 and 42 in one volume. Grade A–B.

48. *The Best of Antrobus* Faber 1974
A selection from 21, 27 and 38. Grade A.

49. *Monsieur: or, The Prince of Darkness* (novel) Faber 1974; 1st Amer. Viking Press 1974
The publication of this work saw a signing session with Durrell in London, so check title pages! Grade A–B.

50. *Prospero's Cell* Faber 1975
A reissue of No. 9, with a new Preface. Grade A–B.

51. *Sicilian Carousel* (travel) Faber 1977
Grade B.

Film:
Justine 20th Century Fox 1969

Durrell also edited many works, including, most notably:
A Henry Miller Reader New Directions 1959
The Best of Henry Miller Heinemann 1960
(same as above)

New Poems 1963: A P.E.N. Anthology
Hutchinson 1963
Wordsworth Penguin 1973
The *Miller Reader* would be Grade C, though the other two are Grade A.

DYER, Charles

Born in Shropshire 1928.
Although Dyer has written and had produced fifteen or more plays, only a few of these have been published. Of these few, the following are of particular note:

1. *Rattle of a Simple Man* (play) French 1963
2. *Rattle of a Simple Man* (novel) Elek 1964
3. *Staircase* (play) French 1967

The two French editions were published simultaneously in England and America. Grade A–B. The novel version of *Rattle of a Simple Man* is not common, but should not rise above Grade B.

Films:
Rattle of a Simple Man Warner Bros 1964
Staircase 20th Century Fox 1969

ELIOT, T. S.

Thomas Stearns Eliot was born in St Louis, Missouri, in 1888. He graduated from Harvard, and went on to study at Oxford and at the Sorbonne in Paris. He became a teacher in London, and then a bank clerk, but his literary friends decided that he was wasting his very apparent talents, and helped him to be independent of such drudgery, encouraging him to write. Virginia Woolf, who was very much in the forefront of this, was soon to publish his poems at the Hogarth Press. Eliot was received very quickly, and became revered by almost everyone. He became a director at Faber & Faber, who were to publish most of his work. His reputation has worn extremely well since his death in 1965, his books selling in large quantities each year. From the collector's point of view, the essential book is:

Donald Gallup *T. S. Eliot: A Bibliography* (Faber 1969)
This extremely fine bibliography lists absolutely everything, though I must limit myself to a checklist of his books. He wrote many Introductions and the like, all of which may be found in Gallup.

1. *Prufrock and Other Observations* Egoist Ltd 1917
2. *Ezra Pound: His Metric and Poetry* Knopf NY 1917 (published anonymously)
3. *Poems* Hogarth Press 1919
4. *Ara Vos Prec* (verse) Ovid Press 1920
5. *Poems* Knopf 1920 (same as 4)
6. *The Sacred Wood* (essays) Methuen 1920; 1st Amer. Knopf 1921
7. *The Waste Land* (verse) Boni & Liveright NY 1922; 1st Eng. Hogarth Press 1923
8. *Homage to John Dryden* (verse) Hogarth Press 1924
9. *Poems 1909–1925* Faber & Gwyer 1925; 1st Amer. Harcourt Brace 1932
10. *Journey of the Magi* (poem) Faber & Gwyer 1927; 1st Amer. Rudge 1927
    Faber ed.: 5000 copies printed. Rudge ed.: 27 copies printed.
11. *Shakespeare and the Stoicism of Seneca* (address) OUP 1927
12. *A Song for Simeon* (poem) Faber & Gwyer 1928
13. *For Lancelot Andrewes* (essays) Faber & Gwyer 1928; 1st Amer. Doubleday 1929
14. *Dante* (essay) Faber 1929
15. *Animula* (poem) Faber 1929
16. *Ash-Wednesday* (verse) Faber 1930; 1st Amer. Putnam 1930
    Slightly preceded by limited, signed edition.
17. *Anabasis: A Poem by St J. Perse* Faber 1930; 1st Amer. Harcourt Brace 1938; 1st rev. ed. Harcourt Brace 1949; 1st Eng. rev. ed. Faber 1959
    Translated by T.S.E.
18. *Marina* (poem) Faber 1930
19. *Thoughts After Lambeth* (*Criterion* miscellany) Faber 1931
20. *Triumphal March* (poem) Faber 1931
21. *Charles Whibley: A Memoir* OUP 1931

22. *Selected Essays 1917–1932* Faber 1932; 1st Amer. Harcourt Brace 1932
23. *John Dryden: The Poet, the Dramatist, The Critic* Holliday NY 1932
24. *Sweeney Agonistes* (drama) Faber 1932
25. *The Use of Poetry and the Use of Criticism* Faber 1933; 1st Amer. Harvard 1933
26. *After Strange Gods* (lectures) Faber 1934; 1st Amer. Harcourt Brace 1934
27. *The Rock* (play) Faber 1934; 1st Amer. Harcourt Brace 1934
28. *Elizabethan Essays* Faber 1934
29. *Murder in the Cathedral* (play) Goulden 1935; 1st complete ed. Faber 1935; 1st Amer. Harcourt Brace 1935
30. *Essays Ancient and Modern* Faber 1936; 1st Amer. Harcourt Brace 1936
31. *Collected Poems 1909–1935* Faber 1936; 1st Amer. Harcourt Brace 1936
    Cont. first appearance of *Burnt Norton*.
32. *The Family Reunion* (play) Faber 1939; 1st Amer. Harcourt Brace 1939
33. *Old Possum's Book of Practical Cats* Faber 1939; 1st Amer. Harcourt Brace 1939; 1st Illus. ed. Faber 1940
    1939 ed.: d/w by T.S.E. 1940 ed.: Nicolas Bentley drew the pictures.
34. *The Idea of a Christian Society* (lectures) Faber 1939; 1st Amer. Harcourt Brace 1940
35. *The Waste Land and Other Poems* Faber 1940; 1st Amer. Harcourt Brace 1955
36. *East Coker* (poem) Faber 1940
    Published previously in *The New English Weekly* Easter no. of the same year.
37. *Burnt Norton* (poem) Faber 1941
    1st separate ed. See 31.
38. *Points of View* (essays) Faber 1941
    Contains no new material.
39. *The Dry Salvages* (poem) Faber 1941
40. *The Classics and the Man of Letters* (address) OUP 1942
41. *The Music of Poetry* (lecture) Jackson, Glasgow 1942
42. *Little Gidding* (poem) Faber 1942
    This, with 36, 37 and 39, completes the Four Quartets.
43. *Four Quartets* Harcourt Brace 1943; 1st Eng. Faber 1944
44. *What Is a Classic?* (address) Faber 1945
45. *On Poetry* (address) Concord, Massachusetts 1947
    750 copies printed, and distributed gratis.
46. *Milton* (lecture) Cumberlege, London 1947
    500 copies printed.
47. *A Sermon* CUP 1948
    300 copies printed, and distributed gratis.
48. *Selected Poems* Penguin 1948; 1st Amer. Harcourt Brace 1967
49. *Notes Towards the Definition of Culture* Faber 1948; 1st Amer. Harcourt Brace 1949
50. *From Poe to Valéry* (lecture) Harcourt Brace 1948
    1500 copies printed for distribution to friends of publisher.
51. *The Undergraduate Poems* Harvard Advocate, Massachusetts 1949
    Unauthorized publication. 1000 copies printed.
52. *The Aims of Poetic Drama* Poets' Theatre Guild 1949
53. *The Cocktail Party* (play) Faber 1950; 1st Amer. Harcourt Brace 1950
54. *Poetry and Drama* (lecture) Cambridge, Massachusetts 1951; 1st Eng. Faber 1951
55. *The Value and Use of Cathedrals in England Today* Chichester 1952
56. *An Address to Members of the London Library* London 1952
    500 copies printed.
57. *The Complete Poems and Plays (1909–1950)* Harcourt Brace 1952
58. *Selected Prose* Penguin 1953
59. *American Literature and the American Language* Washington University 1953
    500 copies printed.
60. *The Three Voices of Poetry* (lecture) NBL 1953; 1st Amer. CUP 1954
61. *The Confidential Clerk* (play) Faber 1954; 1st Amer. Harcourt Brace 1954
62. *Religious Drama: Mediaeval and Modern* House of Books NY 1954
    326 copies printed. 300 numbered, 26 lettered and signed.
63. *The Cultivation of Christmas Trees* (poem) Faber 1954; 1st Amer. Farrar, Straus & Cudahy 1956

Illus. David Jones.
64. *The Literature of Politics* (address) Conservative Centre 1955
65. *The Frontiers of Criticism* (lecture) Minnesota 1956
   10,050 copies printed, and distributed gratis.
66. *On Poetry and Poets* (essays) Faber 1957; 1st Amer. Farrar, Straus & Cudahy 1957
67. *The Elder Statesman* (play) Faber 1959; 1st Amer. Farrar, Straus & Cudahy 1959
68. *Geoffrey Faber 1889–1961* (memoir) Faber 1961
   Limited to 100 copies, distributed gratis.
69. *Collected Plays* Faber 1962
70. *George Herbert* (essay) NBL 1962
71. *Collected Poems 1909–1962* Faber 1963; 1st Amer. Harcourt Brace 1963
72. *Knowledge and Experience in the Philosophy of F. H. Bradley* Faber 1964; 1st Amer. Farrar Straus 1964
73. *To Criticize the Critic* (essays) Faber 1965; 1st Amer. Farrar, Straus & Giroux 1965
74. *Poems Written in Early Youth* Faber 1967; 1st Amer. Farrar, Straus & Giroux 1967
   Preceded only by a privately printed edition in 1950, which was limited to 12 copies.
75. *The Complete Poems and Plays* Faber 1968
76. *The Waste Land: A Facsimile and Transcript* Faber 1971; 1st Amer. Harcourt Brace 1971

Eliot edited and introduced a vast number of books, a few of the more important being:
Ezra Pound: Selected Poems Faber & Gwyer 1928
A Choice of Kipling's Verse Faber 1941; 1st Amer. Scribner 1943
Introducing James Joyce Faber 1942
Literary Essays of Ezra Pound Faber 1954; 1st Amer. New Directions 1954

Film:
Murder in the Cathedral Film Traders 1951
T. S. Eliot and George Hoellering *The Film of Murder in the Cathedral* was published by Faber in 1952, and by Harcourt Brace in America in the same year.

Although the more recent items are not difficult to find, and are quite reasonably priced, to collect Eliot seriously is an expensive business. The early work is very rare, and this is reflected in the price.

I have some booksellers' catalogues for 1950, in which Eliot is very much in evidence, although the prices quoted are more than enough to make any Modern Firsts collector drool and dream of what might have been. The Ariel Poem *Animula*, for instance, was published in an ordinary edition (3000 copies) and a signed edition (400 copies). In 1950, one of the 400 signed copies commanded 17/6d ($=87\frac{1}{2}$p, for those who cannot remember). Today, it would be Grade I. Even one of the ordinary edition would be Grade C. The same catalogue quotes *Anabasis* at 25s (today's value Grade G), *For Lancelot Andrewes* at 7/6d (today's value Grade F)— and most amazingly of all: *Ezra Pound: His Metric and Poetry,* Eliot's second book, at £8.10s (today's value: Grade Q). It is sweet agony to read such catalogues, and quite irresistible.

With regard to today's values, it must be noted that very many of Eliot's works were issued in an ordinary edition, and a signed, limited edition simultaneously (for details of these you must refer to Gallup), and that his signature on any copy of any book enormously increases its value, particularly so with a close association. An outstanding instance of this occurred in 1975, when in one well-known London bookseller's list appeared a 1st of *Journey of the Magi* at £5, which was cheap, and in that of another a similar copy but with an autograph dedication from Eliot to his wife: this was priced at £400. It is up to the collector's instinct and wallet when this sort of situation occurs, as I have said in the essay at the front of this book.

Prufrock would now fetch about £400, and Nos 2 and 3 would be Grade Q. No. 4 was limited to 264 copies, some signed, some not for sale, and all numbered. It is scarce, and depending on the copy would be Grade P–Q. No. 6: Grade F. No. 7: Grade K. No. 8: Grade F. No. 9: Grade E. No. 10: Grade C, but the legendary American edition could go to Grade P. No. 11: Grade E. No. 12: Grade C. Nos 13 and 14: Grade F (the latter has a cover by Rex Whistler). Nos 15 and 16: Grade C. No. 17: Grade G. Nos 18, 19 and 20: Grade C. Nos 21–27: Grade D. No. 28: Grade C. The Goulden edition of No. 29 (750 copies) might reach Grade H, Faber ed. Grade D. Nos 30 and 31: Grade D. No. 32: Grade C. No. 33: Grade E. Nos 34, 35 and 40: Grade C. Nos 36, 37, 39 and 42 (the Four Quartets) together would be Grade I. No. 38: Grade B. No. 41: Grade E. Nos 43, 44 and 48: Grade B. Nos 45, 46, 47, 50, 52, 55, 56, 59 and 60 (all limited addresses and lectures) are Grade D–E. No. 49: Grade C. No. 51: Grade I. No. 53: Grade C. No. 54: Grade B. No. 57: Grade C. Nos 58, 61 and 63: Grade B. No. 62: Grade H, or Grade P for one of the 26 signed. Nos 64, 65, 66, 67, 69 and 76: Grade C. No. 68: Grade I. Nos 70, 71, 72, 73, 74 and 75: Grade B.

Of the works edited and introduced by Eliot quoted, *Ezra Pound: Selected Poems* is the most scarce, being Grade G. *Kipling's Verse* and Pound's *Literary Essays* are Grade C, and the *Joyce* is Grade B.

The Film of Murder in the Cathedral was remaindered during the early seventies, and could be bought for 80 pence. It is now Grade B, and rising.

FAULKNER, William

Born in New Albany, Mississippi, 1867. Died 1962.

1. *The Marble Faun* (verse) privately printed 1924
2. *Soldier's Pay* (novel) Liveright 1926; 1st Eng. Chatto & Windus 1930
3. *Mosquitoes* (novel) privately printed 1927
   A revised ed. was published by Garden City in 1937, and in England by Chatto & Windus in 1964.
4. *Sartoris* (novel) Harcourt Brace 1929; 1st Eng. Chatto & Windus 1933
5. *The Sound and the Fury* (novel) H. Smith 1929; 1st Eng. Chatto & Windus 1931

6. *As I Lay Dying* (novel) H. Smith 1930; 1st Eng. Chatto & Windus 1935
7. *Sanctuary* (novel) H. Smith 1930; 1st Eng. Chatto & Windus 1931
8. *These 13* (stories) H. Smith 1930; 1st Eng. Chatto & Windus 1933
9. *Light in August* (novel) Random House 1932; 1st Eng. Chatto & Windus 1933
10. *A Green Bough* (verse) H. Smith 1933
11. *Doctor Martino and Other Stories* H. Smith 1934; 1st Eng. Chatto & Windus 1934
12. *Pylon* (novel) H. Smith 1935; 1st Eng. Chatto & Windus 1936
13. *Absalom, Absalom!* (novel) Random House 1936; 1st Eng. Chatto & Windus 1937
14. *The Unvanquished* (novel) Random House 1938; 1st Eng. Chatto & Windus 1938
15. *The Wild Palms* (stories) Random House 1939; 1st Eng. Chatto & Windus 1939
16. *The Hamlet* (novel) Random House 1940; 1st Eng. Chatto & Windus 1940
17. *Go Down, Moses* (novel) Random House 1942; 1st Eng. Chatto & Windus 1942
18. *Intruder in the Dust* (novel) Random House 1948; 1st Eng. Chatto & Windus 1949
19. *Knight's Gambit* (stories) Random House 1949; 1st Eng. Chatto & Windus 1951
20. *Collected Stories* Random House 1950; 1st Eng. Chatto & Windus 1951
21. *Requiem for a Nun* (novel) Random House 1951; 1st Eng. Chatto & Windus 1953
22. *A Fable* (novel) Random House 1954; 1st Eng. Chatto & Windus 1954
23. *Faulkner's Country* (stories) Chatto & Windus 1955
24. *The Town* (novel) Random House 1957; 1st Eng. Chatto & Windus 1958
25. *New Orleans Sketches* Rutgers University Press 1958; 1st Eng. Sidgwick & Jackson 1959
26. *The Collected Stories* (3 vols) Chatto & Windus 1958
27. *The Mansion* (novel) Random House 1959; 1st Eng. Chatto & Windus 1960
   With Nos 16 and 24, this forms a trilogy.
28. *The Reivers* (novel) Random House 1962; 1st Eng. Chatto & Windus 1962
29. *Selected Short Stories* Random House 1962
30. *Early Prose and Poetry* Little Brown 1962; 1st

Eng. Cape 1962

31. *Essays, Speeches, and Public Letters* Random House 1966; 1st Eng. Chatto & Windus 1966

There is great interest in Faulkner at the moment, and prices—particularly for the American editions—are riding high. Nos 1, 2, 5 and 7 (the latter two being highlights) would be Grade O and over, for the American editions, though substantially less for the English. The English ed. of No. 2 had a Preface by Richard Hughes, and would be Grade G. The prices thereafter tend to descend with the decades, most of those of the thirties being Grade G, and those of the forties Grade D–E—although No. 18, his best-selling detective novel, may go higher. Nos 20, 21, 22 and 26 are Grade C, and Nos 23, 24, 25, 27, 28, 29, 30 and 31 are Grade B.

Films:
The Story of Temple Drake (Sanctuary) Paramount 1933
Intruder in the Dust MGM 1949
The Long, Hot Summer (The Hamlet) 20th Century Fox 1957
The Tarnished Angels (Pylon) United Artists 1957
The Sound and the Fury 20th Century Fox 1959
Sanctuary (based on *Requiem for a Nun* and *Sanctuary*) 20th Century Fox 1960
The Reivers Warner Bros 1969

FEIFFER, Jules
Born in New York 1929.
Feiffer is above all a cartoonist, but he has published one novel:

1. *Harry, the Rat with Women* McGraw-Hill NY 1963; 1st Eng. Collins 1963
He has also published about ten plays, the highlight being:

2. *Little Murders* Random House NY 1968; 1st Eng. Faber 1970

Of most interest, however, are probably the cartoons:

3. *Sick, Sick, Sick* McGraw-Hill 1958; 1st Eng.

Collins 1959
4. *Passionella and Other Stories* McGraw-Hill 1959; 1st Eng. Collins 1960
5. *The Explainers* McGraw-Hill 1960; 1st Eng. Collins 1961
6. *Boy, Girl, Boy, Girl* Random House 1961; 1st Eng. Collins 1962
7. *Hold Me!* Random House 1963
8. *Feiffer's Album* Random House 1963
9. *The Unexpurgated Memoirs of Bernard Mergendeiler* Random House 1965; 1st Eng. Collins 1966
10. *The Penguin Feiffer* Penguin 1966

Film:
Little Murders 20th Century Fox 1971 (Feiffer wrote the screenplay)
Non of the above is outstandingly difficult, and all would be within Grade B. No. 10 is Grade A.

FERLINGHETTI, Lawrence
Born in Yonkers, New York, 1919.

1. *Pictures of the Gone World* (verse) City Lights San Francisco 1955
2. *A Coney Island of the Mind* (verse) New Directions NY 1958
3. *Tentative Description of a Dinner Given to Promote the Impeachment of President Eisenhower* (verse) Golden Mountain, San Francisco 1958
4. *Her* (novel) New Directions 1960; 1st Eng. MacGibbon & Kee 1966
5. *One Thousand Fearful Words for Fidel Castro* (verse) City Lights 1961
6. *Berlin* (verse) Golden Mountain 1961
7. *Starting From San Francisco: Poems* New Directions 1961
8. *Penguin Modern Poets* 5 Penguin 1963 (with Allen Ginsberg and Gregory Corso)
9. *Unfair Arguments with Existence* (plays) New Directions 1963 (incl. *The Soldiers of No Country, Three Thousand Red Ants, The Alligation, The Victims of Amnesia, Motherlode, The Customs Collector in Baggy Pants, The Nose of Sisyphus*)
10. *Routines* (plays) New Directions 1964
11. *Where Is Vietnam?* (verse) City Lights 1965

12. *To Fuck Is to Love Again; Kyrie Eleison Kerista* (verse) Fuck You Press NY 1965
13. *An Eye on the World: Selected Poems* MacGibbon & Kee 1967
14. *After the Cry of the Birds* (verse) Haslewood, San Francisco 1967
15. *Moscow in the Wilderness, Segovia in the Snow* (verse) Beach, San Francisco 1967
16. *The Secret meaning of Things* (verse) New Directions 1969
17. *Tyrannus Nix?* (verse) New Directions 1969
18. *The Mexican Night* (travel) New Directions 1970
19. *Back Roads to Far Places* (verse) New Directions 1971
20. *Open Eye, Open Heart* (verse) New Directions 1973

Ferlinghetti has also edited several works, and has translated Jacques Prévert *Selections from Paroles* (City Lights 1958; 1st Eng. Penguin 1963).

It will be seen from the above that only four of Ferlinghetti's publications were ever available in England: a Penguin selection, a Penguin translation, his only novel, and a further selection. All of these would be Grade A, as would be the most recent New Directions publications. Nos 1–2 Grade D, Nos 3–7 Grade C, and the remainder Grade B.

FIRBANK, Ronald
Arthur Annesley Ronald Firbank. Born in London 1886. Died 1926.
Details of the works may be found in:
M. J. Benkowitz *A Bibliography of Ronald Firbank* (Soho Bibliographies, Hart-Davis 1963)
Brigid Brophy *Prancing Novelist: A Defence of Fiction in the Form of a Critical Biography in Praise of Ronald Firbank* (Cape 1972; 1st Amer. Barnes & Noble 1973)

1. *Odette d'Antrevernes* and *A Study in Temperament* (stories) Elkin Mathews 1905
2. *Vainglory* (novel) Grant Richards 1915 (Frontis. by Felicien Rops)
3. *Odette* Grant Richards 1916 (same as in No. 1)
4. *Inclinations* Grant Richards 1916
5. *Caprice* Grant Richards 1917 (Frontis. by Augustus John)
6. *Valmouth: A Romantic Novel* Grant Richards 1919 (Frontis. by Augustus John)
7. *The Princess Zoubaroff: A Comedy* Grant Richards 1920
8. *Santal* (story) Grant Richards 1921
9. *The Flower Beneath the Foot* (biog.) Grant Richards 1923 (Portraits by Augustus John and Wyndham Lewis)
10. *Prancing Nigger* (novel) Brentano's NY 1924
11. *Sorrow in Sunlight* Brentano's UK 1925 (same as 10)
12. *Concerning the Eccentricities of Cardinal Pirelli* (novel) Grant Richards 1926 (Portrait by Augustus John)
13. *The Artificial Princess* (novel) Duckworth 1934

Two of the several collected editions are:
The Collected Works of Ronald Firbank Duckworth 1929 (6 vols; Intro. by Arthur Waley, with an essay by Osbert Sitwell)
Five Novels (6, 10, 9, 13 and 12) Duckworth 1949 (Intro. by Osbert Sitwell, portrait by Augustus John) No. 1 is the most scarce of a very scarce author, and is Grade M (only 500 were printed, in wrappers). Nos. 2, 3, 4, 5, 6, 7 and 8 are Grade H. No. 10, Grade H–I. Nos 9, 11, 12 and 13 are Grade E–F.

FITZGERALD, F. Scott
Born in Minnesota 1896. Died 1940.
Collected editions and anthologies have been omitted.

1. *This Side of Paradise* (novel) Scribner 1920; 1st Eng. Grey Walls Press 1948
2. *Flappers and Philosophers* (stories) Scribner 1920; 1st Eng. Collins 1922
3. *The Beautiful and Damned* (novel) Scribner 1922; 1st Eng. Collins 1922
4. *Tales of the Jazz Age* (stories) Scribner 1922; 1st Eng. Collins 1923
5. *The Great Gatsby* (novel) Scribner 1925; 1st Eng. Chatto & Windus 1925

6. *All the Sad Young Men* (stories) Scribner 1926
7. *John Jackson's Arcady* (stories) Baker NY 1928
8. *Tender Is the Night* (novel) Scribner 1934; 1st Eng. Chatto & Windus 1934
9. *Taps at Reveille* (stories) Scribner 1935
10. *The Last Tycoon* (unfinished novel) Scribner 1941; 1st Eng. Grey Walls Press 1949
11. *The Crack-Up* (letters and essays) New Directions 1945; 1st Eng. Grey Walls Press 1947
12. *Afternoon of an Author* (stories) Scribner 1957; 1st Eng. Bodley Head 1958

Recently, there has been enormous interest in Fitzgerald, and his 1sts—never common—have now become extremely hard to find, and extremely expensive. *The Great Gatsby* is his highlight, and the Scribner 1st would reach over Grade P. Even the English 1st would be Grade K. No. 1 would be Grade P–Q, and Nos 2, 3 and 4 Grade K–L. Nos 6, 7, 8 and 9 would be Grade K (possibly more for No. 8), and No. 10 would be Grade E–F. No. 11 is Grade E, and No. 12 Grade C.

Films:
The Great Gatsby Paramount 1949; Paramount 1974
The Last Time I Saw Paris MGM 1954 (*Babylon Revisited*: story)
Tender Is the Night 20th Century Fox 1962
The Last Tycoon Paramount 1976

Bibliography:
Charles E. Shane *Scott Fitzgerald* (University of Minnesota American Authors Pamphlet)

FITZGIBBON, Constantine
Born 1919, FitzGibbon has written several books, but is noted for the following:

1. *When the Kissing Had to Stop* (novel) Cassell 1960; 1st Amer. Norton 1960
   An important and controversial novel of the period. Quite scarce. Grade B–C.
2. *The Life of Dylan Thomas* (biog.) Dent 1965; 1st Amer. Atlantic, Little 1965
   The definitive biography. Grade B–C.

FLEMING, Ian
Born 1909. Was at Eton, in the shadow of his brilliant brother Peter, Sandhurst (ingloriously), and then into the Diplomatic Service. He also worked for Reuter, *The Times, The Sunday Times*, and Naval Intelligence. His very earliest writings appeared in *Horizon* (see Connolly), to be followed by an essay in a rather dull manual of journalism. After this came *Casino Royale*, which he arranged to have published with William Plomer, then director of Cape, the publishers of Peter's travel books. Thus was born James Bond, one of the lasting characters of popular fiction. Each Bond after that increased the reputation, and seemed to sell more than the last; although Bond was slow to catch on in America, the Bond industry of the sixties soon propelled the digits 007 into the language. The films smashed all records, and fitted well with the Swinging London image of the time. They failed to do justice to the books, however, for although the first one or two were reasonably close to the original, those succeeding became less and less recognizable, transforming Bond into a plastic man who killed someone horribly, cracked a ghastly quip, and then seduced some nubile Russian lady—veritably the 'cardboard booby' that Fleming had himself privately christened him. As Corgi Toys put out a model of the 007 Aston Martin (in the books it was a vintage 3-litre Bentley), as Zippo sold thousands of lighters with J.B.007 etched into them, and as salaried travellers and 'Bondbirds' vanished beneath an ocean of vodka-martinis (shaken, not, of course, stirred), it became difficult to recall that initially it was all about novels. It is these novels we now discuss.

The early ones are difficult to acquire, as will be seen below, though some titles are quite common. Prices have been rising steadily, and will probably continue to do so—particularly so with *Casino Royale*. Fleming died in 1964, when forty million copies of his books had been sold; that was well over a decade ago, and their popularity shows no sign of decline.

1. *Casino Royale* (Bond novel) Cape 1953; 1st Amer. Macmillan 1954
   Black boards, as are all the Bond books, with red heart motif. Grey (gunmetal?) d/w, repeating heart motif, devised by I.F. This is the very first appearance of Bond, and it is very, very scarce. 4,750 copies were printed of the 1st edition, many of these going to public libraries. It could easily be sold for Grade K, and will never become a common book—nor can I see the price ever coming down. It is particularly difficult in d/w.

2. *Live and Let Die* (Bond novel) Cape 1954; 1st Amer. Macmillan 1955
   Medallion motif on boards. Scarlet d/w with yellow lettering, devised by I.F. Very difficult. Grade D–E.

3. *Moonraker* (Bond novel) Cape 1955; 1st Amer. Macmillan 1955
   Silver titling on boards, yellow and orange flame design on d/w, with black lettering, devised by I.F. Very difficult. Grade C–D.

4. *Diamonds Are Forever* (Bond novel) Cape 1956; 1st Amer. Macmillan 1956
   Blind-stamped diamond-pane motif on boards. Black, tan, pink and white d/w lettered in black and white. Grade C.

5. *From Russia, with Love* (Bond novel) Cape 1957; 1st Amer. Macmillan 1957
   Gun and rose motif on boards, repeated on the superb Chopping d/w, depicting a sawn-off Smith and Wesson and a red rose against a pale wood ground. The famous stencil lettering appears to be inked onto the wood, but beneath the rose stem. This is the first of Richard Chopping's *trompe l'œil* d/ws, which continued, with the exception of No. 7, to the end of the Bond saga. Grade C.

6. *The Diamond Smugglers* (non-fiction) Cape 1957; 1st Amer. Macmillan 1958
   Black boards, red, black and grey d/w. Quite scarce. Grade C.

7. *Dr No* (Bond novel) Cape 1958; 1st Amer. Macmillan 1958
   Brown and black d/w with a girl's silhouette, repeated on boards. One feels Cape might

have compared this d/w with that of No. 5, and recalled Chopping quickly! Grade C.

8. *Goldfinger* (Bond novel) Cape 1959; 1st Amer. Macmillan 1959
   Skull motif with gold coins on boards, repeated on Chopping d/w. Grade C.

9. *For Your Eyes Only* (Bond stories) Cape 1960; 1st Amer. Viking Press 1960
   Matisse-like eye motif on boards. Chopping d/w. Grade B–C.

10. *Thunderball* (Bond novel) Cape 1961; 1st Amer. Viking Press 1961
    Blind-stamped skeletal hand motif, repeated on Chopping d/w. Grade B.

11. *The Spy Who Loved Me* (Bond novel) Cape 1962; 1st Amer. Viking Press 1962
    Silver dagger motif on boards, repeated on Chopping d/w. t/p reads: by Ian Fleming with Vivienne Michel. This is not a genuine collaboration: Fleming wrote this novel as Vivienne Michel in the first person. Hence, the 'Spy' in the title is none other than 007. Grade B.

12. *On Her Majesty's Secret Service* (Bond novel) Cape 1963; 1st Amer. NAL 1963
    White gunsmoke motif on boards. Chopping d/w. Grade A–B.

12a. *On Her Majesty's Secret Service* (ltd ed.) Cape 1963
    Same motif on black boards, as in 12, but with white vellum spine. Coloured frontis. portrait of I.F. by Amherst Villiers. t/p printed in red and black. Verso of t/p reads: 'This special edition is limited to 250 numbered copies only for sale, each signed by the author. Copy number . . .', followed by I.F.'s signature. As is apparent from the limitation, this book is very, very scarce, and a copy would be in Grade K.

13. Hugh Edwards *All Night at Mr Stanyhurst's* Cape 1963
    This thriller of the thirties was reissued by Cape at Fleming's request, and there is a 14-page Intro. by him. Black boards, green and orange d/w. Scarce. Grade B–C.

14. *Thrilling Cities* (non-fiction) Cape 1963; 1st Amer. NAL 1964
    Grey mottled boards with white cloth spine.

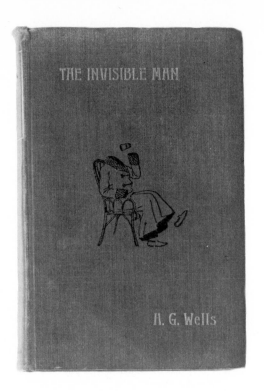

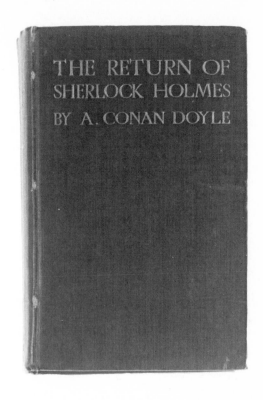

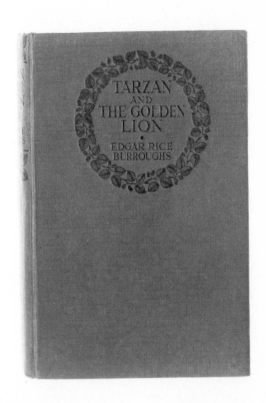

The Invisible Man (1897), a Sherlock Holmes (1905), *The Four Just Men* (1905), and a Tarzan (1924).

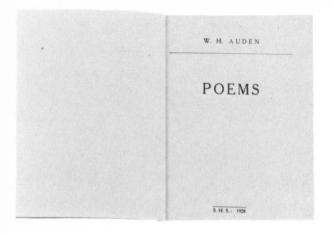

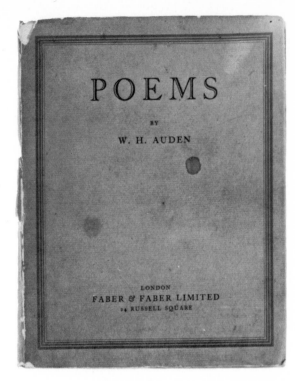

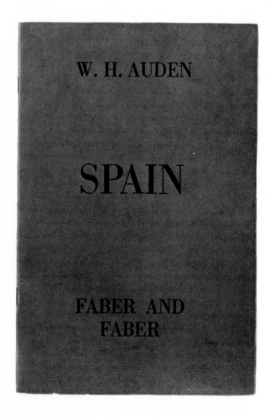

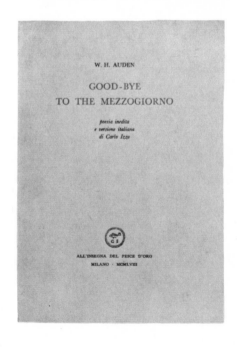

Four wrappered volumes by Auden. The small *Poems* (1928) is the Ilkley facsimile, the *Poems* (1930) next to it being his first commercially published book. Also shown: *Spain* (1937), and a poem with parallel text in English and Italian, published in Milan (1958) and limited to 1,000 copies.

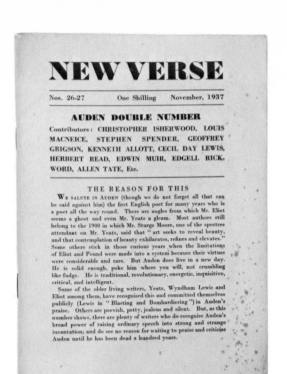

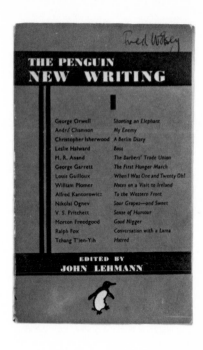

The Auden double number of Grigson's *New Verse* (1937), No. 1 of Lehmann's *Penguin New Writing*
(1936), and No. 1 of his *London Magazine* (1954).
The *Agenda* is the second David Jones special issue (1973/4).

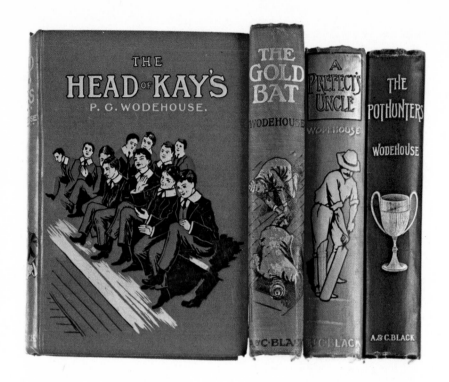

Some early Wodehouse (1902–10) in decorated bindings.

Golden period Wodehouse (1929–36). The design of *If I Were You* is by Heath Robinson.

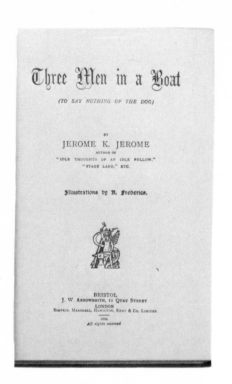

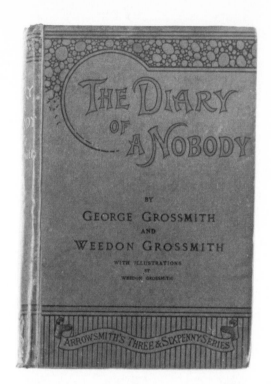

The title page and case design, respectively, of two deathless *fin-de-siècle* funnies.
Huxley's highlight (1932), Amis's first novel (1953), and the only Chandler to be
first published in England (1953).

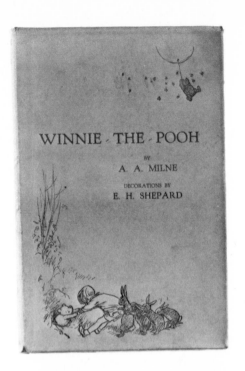

Four for children, all very different: *Winnie the Pooh* (1926), the first Billy Bunter (1947),
Smith of Wootton Major (1967), and *Charlie and the Chocolate Factory* (1964).

Four by Virginia Woolf, all with Vanessa Bell artwork. *The Years* is 1937,
the other three from the fifties.

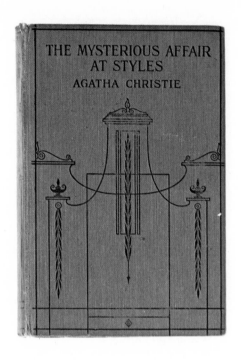

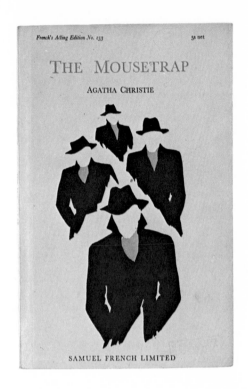

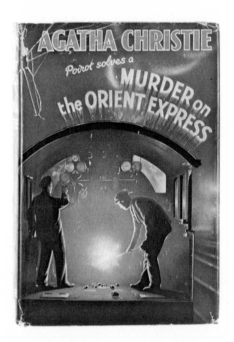

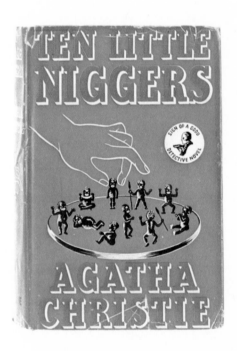

Agatha Christie's first book (1921), her most famous play (1956), and two highlights (1934, 1939).

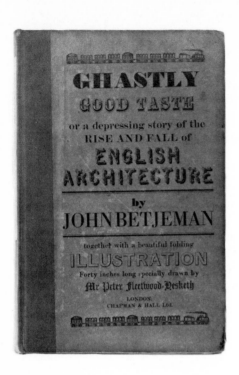

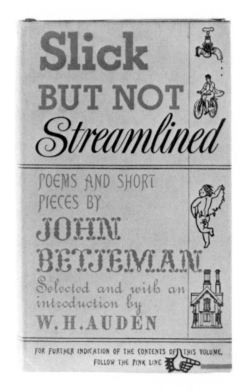

A representative selection of Betjeman (1933–47), with artwork in sympathy.

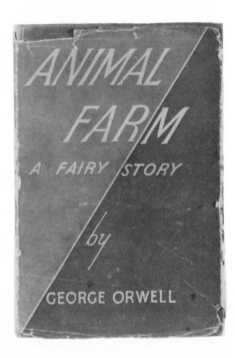
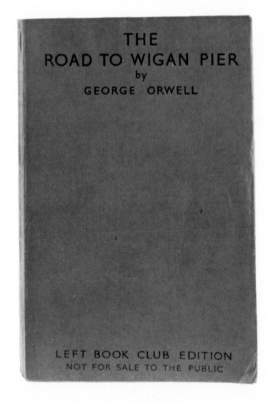

Waugh's first novel (1928), with his own d/w design, together with the war trilogy (1952–61).
The Orwells (1945 and 1937) are highlights.

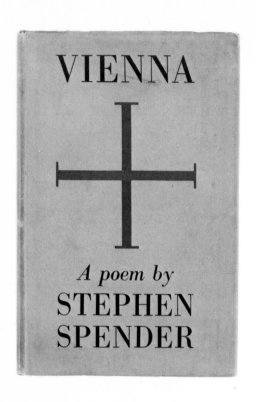

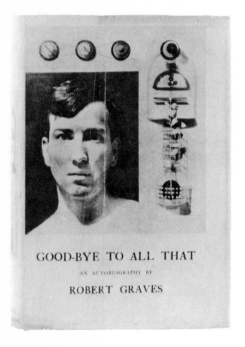

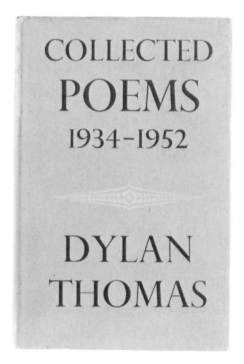

Representative works by four outstanding poets. *Vienna* is 1934, the *Cantos* 1954;
the Graves is 1929, and the Dylan Thomas 1957.

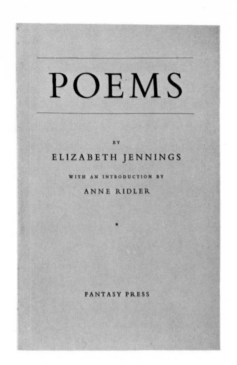

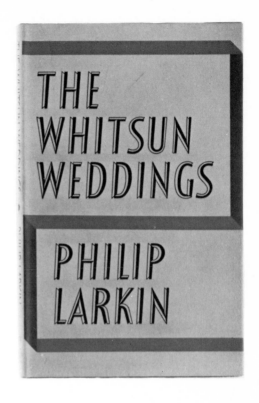

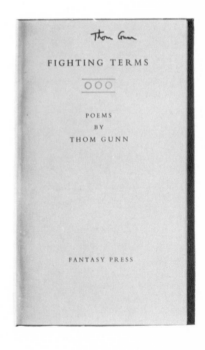

Elizabeth Jennings' first book (1953), highlights by Larkin (1964) and Plath (1965),
and the signed title-page of Gunn's *Fighting Terms* (1954).

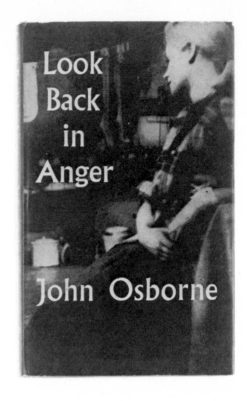

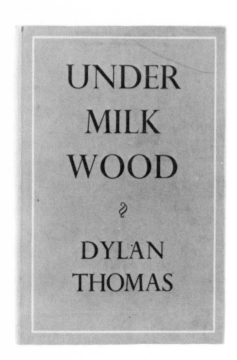

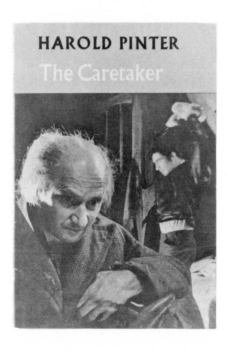

Four landmarks in the history of drama (1954–60): Beckett, Osborne, Dylan Thomas, and Pinter.

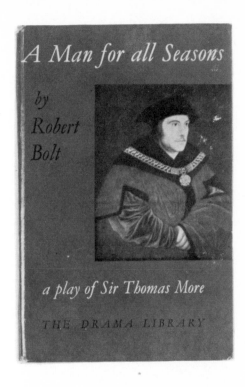

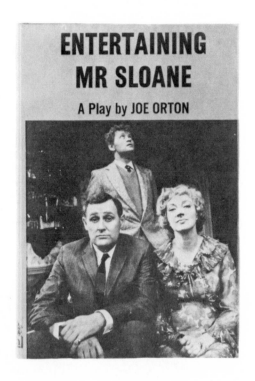

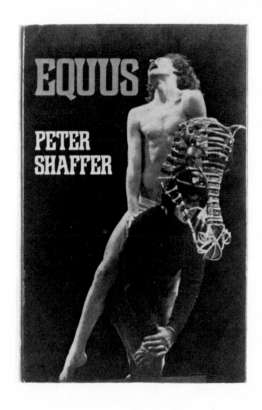

Four important plays, all quite recent (1959–73).

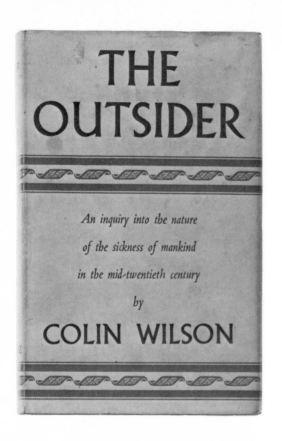

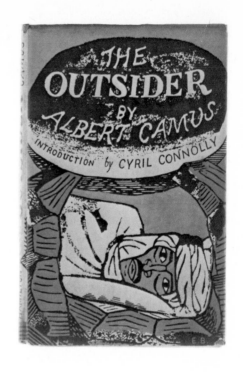

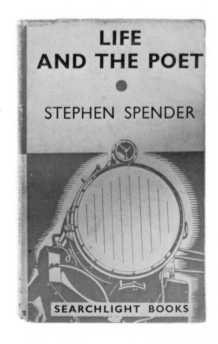

The two *Outsiders* (the Colin Wilson is 1956, the Camus 1946), the first British unexpurgated *Lady Chatterley* (1960), and the Spender title in Orwell's Searchlight Books (1942).

Daliesque d/w by Paul Davis in monochrome with shocking-pink spine and lettering. Quite scarce. Grade C.

15. *You Only Live Twice* (Bond novel) Cape 1964; 1st Amer. NAL 1964
Chinese characters motif on boards. Chopping d/w. Grade A–B.

16. *Chitty-Chitty-Bang-Bang* (juveniles) Cape 1964–65; 1st Amer. Random House 1964
There are three of these books, all admirably illustrated by John Burningham. The pictorial boards are also by Burningham, the identical designs being reproduced on the laminated d/ws. The first has 'Adventure Number 1' within a red disc on the cover (1964), the second (1964) bears a turquoise disc reading 'Adventure Number 2', and the third (1965) has 'Adventure Number 3' on a lilac disc. They are very difficult, particularly in fine condition—as is the case with all children's books. The three would be Grade C–D, though probably Grade A individually.

17. *The Man with the Golden Gun* (Bond novel) Cape 1965; 1st Amer. NAL 1965
The only Bond to lack a motif on the boards. The blurbs, which used to be very newsy, have grown simpler now. This one reads: The New James Bond. Enough said. Chopping d/w. Grade A.

18. *Ian Fleming Introduces Jamaica* (non-fiction) Deutsch 1965; 1st Amer. Hawthorne 1965
Rust cloth, laminated photographic d/w. Despite the two-inch-high lettering of 'Ian Fleming' on the d/w, it contains only an 11-page Intro. by him. Nonetheless, a handsome book, with many fine coloured photographs. The second impression was remaindered, but the 1st remains elusive. Grade B–C.

19. *Octopussy* and *The Living Daylights* (Bond stories) Cape 1966; 1st Amer. NAL 1966
Intended to be a sequel (i.e. a book of short stories) to No. 9, but sadly, Fleming died having completed only these two. Chopping d/w. Grade A.

The essential book about Fleming is the very fine biography:
John Pearson *The Life of Ian Fleming* Cape 1966; 1st Amer. McGraw Hill 1966
Pearson has also written the amusing, and very convincing:
James Bond: The Authorized Biography Sidgwick & Jackson 1973; 1st Amer. Morrow 1973
Several books have been written about Bond, though the best is:
Kingsley Amis *The James Bond Dossier* Cape 1965; 1st Amer. NAL 1965
Amis (q.v.) has also written the Bond novel *Colonel Sun.*
In addition to the above, Fleming himself wrote an Intro. to Herbert O. Yardley *The Education of a Poker Player* (1959), and there is an interview with him in Roy Newquist (ed.) *Counterpoint* (Allen & Unwin 1965).

Films:
Dr No United Artists 1962
From Russia, with Love United Artists 1963
Goldfinger United Artists 1963
Thunderball United Artists 1964
You Only Live Twice United Artists 1966
Casino Royale Columbia 1966
Chitty-Chitty-Bang-Bang United Artists 1968
On Her Majesty's Secret Service United Artists 1969
Diamonds Are Forever United Artists 1971
Live and Let Die United Artists 1974
The Man with the Golden Gun United Artists 1974

FORESTER, C. S.
Born in Cairo 1899. Educated in Britain. Died 1966.
The Hornblower series would appear to be the highlight, as far as the collector is concerned, with two notable exceptions:

1. *A Pawn Among Kings* (novel) Methuen 1924
This is his first book. Scarce. Grade E–F.

2. *The African Queen* (novel) Little Brown, Boston 1935; 1st Eng. Heinemann 1935
Not a title always associated with Forester, but a highlight of his work. Grade C.

Herewith follows the Hornblower series, in entirety, but omitting collections, anthologies, Omnibus volumes and extracts—of which there seem to have been an amazing number.

3. *Beat to Quarters* Little Brown 1937
4. *The Happy Return* Joseph 1937 (same as 3)
5. *A Ship of the Line* Little Brown 1938; 1st Eng. Joseph 1938
6. *Flying Colours* Little Brown 1938; 1st Eng. Joseph 1938
7. *To the Indies* Little Brown 1940
8. *The Earthly Paradise* Joseph 1940 (same as 7)
9. *Commodore Hornblower* Little Brown 1945
10. *The Commodore* Joseph 1945 (same as 9)
11. *Lord Hornblower* Little Brown 1946; 1st Eng. Joseph 1946
12. *Mr Midshipman Hornblower* Little Brown 1950; 1st Eng. Joseph 1950
13. *Lieutenant Hornblower* Grosset NY 1952; 1st Eng. Joseph 1952
14. *Hornblower and the Atropos* Little Brown 1953; 1st Eng. Joseph 1953
15. *Admiral Hornblower in the West Indies* Little Brown 1958
16. *Hornblower in the West Indies* Joseph 1958 (same as 15)
17. *Hornblower and the Hotspur* Little Brown 1962; 1st Eng. Joseph 1962

Nos 3 and 4 might reach Grade C, though all the others would be Grade B, with the exception of the last three, which are Grade A.

Films:
The African Queen Romulus 1951
Captain Hornblower R.N. Warner Bros 1951

FORSTER, E. M.
Born in England 1879. Died 1970.
The details of the works may be found in: B. J. Kirkpatrick *A Bibliography of E. M. Forster* (Soho Bibliographies, Hart-Davis 1968)
A complete checklist appears below.

1. *Where Angels Fear to Tread* (novel) Blackwood 1905; 1st Amer. Knopf 1920
2. *The Longest Journey* (novel) Blackwood 1907; 1st Amer. Knopf 1922
3. *A Room with a View* (novel) Arnold 1908; 1st Amer. Putnam 1911
4. *Howard's End* (novel) Arnold 1910; 1st Amer. Putnam 1910
5. *The Celestial Omnibus* (stories) Sidgwick & Jackson 1911; 1st Amer. Knopf 1923
6. *The Story of the Siren* Hogarth Press 1920
7. *Egypt* (non-fiction) Labour Research Dept. 1920
8. *Alexandria* (history) Whitehead Morris 1922; 1st Amer. Doubleday 1961
9. *Pharos and Pharillon* (essays) Hogarth Press 1923; 1st Amer. Knopf 1923
10. *A Passage to India* (novel) Arnold 1924; 1st Amer. Harcourt Brace 1924
11. *Anonymity* (essay) Hogarth Press 1925
12. *Aspects of the novel* (prose) Arnold 1927; 1st Amer. Harcourt Brace 1927
13. *The Eternal Moment* (stories) Sidgwick & Jackson 1928; 1st Amer. Harcourt Brace 1928
14. *A Letter to Madan Blanchard* (essay) Hogarth Press 1931; 1st Amer. Harcourt Brace 1932
15. *Goldsworthy Lowes Dickinson* Arnold 1934; 1st Amer. Harcourt Brace 1934
16. *Abinger Harvest* (essays) Arnold 1936; 1st Amer. Harcourt Brace 1936
17. *What I Believe* (essay) Hogarth Press 1939
18. *Reading as Usual* (lecture) Tottenham Public Libraries 1939
19. *England's Pleasant Land* (prose) Hogarth Press 1940
20. *Nordic Twilight* (essay) Macmillan 1940
21. *Virginia Woolf* (lecture) CUP 1942; 1st Amer. Harcourt Brace 1942
22. *The Development of English Prose* (lecture) Jackson, Glasgow 1945
23. *The Collected Tales* Knopf 1947
24. *Collected Short Stories* Sidgwick & Jackson 1948 (same as 23)
25. *Two Cheers for Democracy* (essays) Arnold 1951; 1st Amer. Harcourt Brace 1951
26. *Billy Budd* Boosey & Hawkes 1951 (libretto for Britten's opera)
27. *The Hill of Devi* Arnold 1953; 1st Amer. Harcourt Brace 1953
28. *Marianne Thornton* (biography) Arnold 1956; 1st Amer. Harcourt Brace 1956
29. *Maurice* (novel) Arnold 1971; 1st Amer. Norton 1971

30. *The Life to Come* (stories) Arnold 1972; 1st Amer. Norton 1973

Some of Forster is very scarce and expensive, and some surprisingly cheap. No. 1 is Grade P, and Nos 2, 3 and 4 are all Grade K–L. No. 5: Grade I. No. 6 is very scarce—only 500 copies printed—and an early Hogarth Press item: Grade L. Nos 7 and 9 are Grade G, and Nos 8 and 10 are Grade K—much of the stock of No. 8 having been destroyed; No. 10 (*A Passage to India*) is, of course, together with *Howard's End* (No. 4), Forster's highlight. No. 11 is Grade D, and Nos 12, 16, 17, 18, 19 and 20 are Grade C. No. 13 is Grade E, and Nos 14, 15, 21, 24, 25, 27, 28, 29 and 30 are all Grade B. Nos 22, 23 and 26 are Grade C.

FORSYTH, Frederick
Born in England 1939.

1. *The Biafra Story* (non-fiction) Penguin 1969
2. *The Day of the Jackal* (novel) Hutchinson 1971; 1st Amer. Viking Press 1971
3. *The Odessa File* (novel) Hutchinson 1972; 1st Amer. Viking Press 1972
4. *The Dogs of War* (novel) Hutchinson 1974; 1st Amer. Viking Press 1974
5. *The Shepherd* (story) Hutchinson 1975; 1st Amer. Viking Press 1976

Forsyth is a very recent success, and No. 1 was very untypical of his work to come. It was a Penguin Special, though it would now be Grade A–B. No. 2 will be desirable to the collector of contemporary fiction, but it is quite difficult as it was reprinted before publication, so huge was the advance publicity. Grade C. The others are all Grade A, and should be very easy to find.

Films:
The Day of the Jackal Universal 1972
The Odessa File Columbia 1974

FOWLES, John
Born in Essex in 1926, Fowles has published comparatively few books, but his place in literature seems secure. He founded his reputation with his first novel, and no book since has disappointed, although they have been very diverse. *The Aristos* has not received a great deal of attention—and, indeed, it is a difficult work to classify—but all his other books are very eagerly sought and read. From the collector's point of view, however, *The Aristos* is probably the most hard to come by—I myself know of two otherwise complete Fowles collections, the owners always scowling if I even mention the title.

1. *The Collector* (novel) Cape 1963; 1st Amer. Little Brown 1963
   Very distinctive in its 'Chopping-style' d/w by Tom Adams, which was used for both the English and American editions. It is interesting to note that the advance proof of the Cape edition was issued in the d/w, though in place of the quotation on the rear, there is an announcement of the sale of film rights, and that it has been 'sold to Little Brown . . . for a very big advance'. This on the proof of a yet-unpublished first novel! It is scarce, and getting more scarce each year. I have heard of a copy changing hands privately for £50, but Grade E would be nearer the mark.
2. *The Aristos* Little Brown 1964; 1st Eng. Cape 1965
   Although the American edition precedes, either is desirable, and as I have said above, very difficult. Grade E. It is worth noting that the Pan paperback edition (1968) is not a straight reprint, but 'specially revised for Pan by the author', and has a new Preface. This Preface begins: 'This book was first published against the advice of almost everyone who read it. I was told it would do my "image" no good.'
3. *The Magus* (novel) Cape 1966; 1st Amer. Little Brown 1966
   Another very fine d/w by Tom Adams for Fowles' longest book. Although it used to be quite common, it is becoming less so. Grade

C, but rising. A revised and supplemented edition was published by Cape in 1977.

In the seventies Fowles signed quite a large number of second impressions for the New Fiction Society.

4. *The French Lieutenant's Woman* (novel) Cape 1969; 1st Amer. Little Brown 1969
   Superb d/w of gold engraved letters on a claret stippled ground. Although quite recent, quite elusive. Grade B, rising to Grade C.
5. S. Baring-Gould *Mehalah* Chatto & Windus 1969
   Fowles wrote the Introduction to this Landmark Library reissue. Grade B.
6. *Poems* Ecco Press NY 1973
   Unfortunately not published in England. Grade D.
7. *The Hound of the Baskervilles* Murray/Cape 1974
   Fowles wrote the Introduction to this volume of the Collected Edition of Sherlock Holmes.
8. Perrault *Cinderella* Cape 1974; 1st Amer. Little Brown 1975
   A large-format, thin shiny book, published at the very low price of £1.25. As soon as it is reprinted, or goes out of print, the 1st will rise to Grade B. Fowles translated the original of 1697, and Sheilah Beckett illustrated it.
9. *The Ebony Tower* (novellas) Cape 1974; 1st Amer. Little Brown 1974
   Handsome green d/w, the typography reminiscent of No. 4. This was reprinted very quickly, and the 1st is now Grade B.
10. *Shipwreck* Cape 1974; 1st Amer. Little Brown 1975
    A slim, landscape volume of photographs of shipwrecks, with text by Fowles. Grade A.

An interview with John Fowles was included in Roy Newquist (ed.) *Counterpoint* (Allen & Unwin 1965), and one book has been written about him:
William J. Palmer *The Fiction of John Fowles* (University of Missouri Press Columbia, 1974)

Films:
The Collector British Lion 1964
The Magus 20th Century Fox 1969

FRANCIS, Dick
Born in Pembrokeshire 1920.

1. *The Sport of Queens: The Autobiography of Dick Francis* Joseph 1957; 1st Amer. Harper 1969
2. *Dead Cert* (novel) Joseph 1962; 1st Amer. Holt Rinehart 1962
3. *Nerve* (novel) Joseph 1964; 1st Amer. Harper 1964
4. *For Kicks* (novel) Joseph 1965; 1st Amer. Harper 1965
5. *Odds Against* (novel) Joseph 1965; 1st Amer. Harper 1966
6. *Flying Finish* (novel) Joseph 1966; 1st Amer. Harper 1967
7. *Blood Sport* (novel) Joseph 1967; 1st Amer. Harper 1968
8. *Forfeit* (novel) Joseph 1968; 1st Amer. Harper 1969
9. *Enquiry* (novel) Joseph 1969; 1st Amer. Harper 1969
10. *Rat Race* (novel) Joseph 1970; 1st Amer. Harper 1971
11. *Bonecrack* (novel) Joseph 1971; 1st Amer. Harper 1972
12. *Smokescreen* (novel) Joseph 1972; 1st Amer. Harper 1972
13. *Slay-Ride* (novel) Joseph 1973; 1st Amer. Harper 1974
14. *Knock-Down* (novel) Joseph 1974; 1st Amer. Harper 1975
15. *Across the Board* Harper 1975 (incl. 6, 7 and 9)
16. *High Stakes* (novel) Joseph 1975; 1st Amer. Harper 1976
17. *In the Frame* (novel) Joseph 1976

Film:
Dead Cert United Artists 1974

At the moment, all Francis's books are within Grade A, though this situation might not last too much longer.

FRAYN, Michael
Born in London 1933.

1. *The Day of the Dog* (articles) Collins 1962; 1st Amer. Doubleday 1963
2. *The Book of Fub* (articles) Collins 1963
3. *Never Put Off to Gomorrah* Pantheon NY 1964 (same as 2)
4. *On the Outskirts* (articles) Collins 1964
5. *The Tin Men* (novel) Collins 1965; 1st Amer. Little Brown, Boston 1966
6. *The Russian Interpreter* (novel) Collins 1966; 1st Amer. Viking Press 1966
7. *Towards the End of Morning* (novel) Collins 1967
8. *Against Entropy* Viking Press 1967 (same as 7)
9. *At Bay in Gear Street* (articles) Fontana 1967
10. *A Very Private Life* (novel) Collins 1968; 1st Amer. Viking Press 1968
11. *The Two of Us* (play) Fontana 1970
12. *Sweet Dreams* (novel) Collins 1974; 1st Amer. Viking Press 1974
13. *Constructions* (philosophy) Wildwood House 1974
14. *Alphabetical Order, Donkey's Years* and *Clouds* (plays) Eyre Methuen 1977

No. 5, his first novel, might reach Grade B, though all the others are Grade A. Frayn is much talked of as one of our greatest humorists, however, and so this situation may not last.

FROST, Robert
Born in San Francisco 1874. Died 1963.
Frost published very many single poems, and other limited and privately printed editions. These unfortunately have had to be omitted.

1. *A Boy's Will* (verse) Holt NY 1913
2. *North of Boston* (verse) Holt NY 1914
3. *Mountain Interval* (verse) Holt NY 1916
4. *New Hampshire* (verse) Holt NY 1923
5. *Selected Poems* Heinemann 1923
6. *West-Running Brook* (verse) Holt NY 1928
7. *Collected Poems* Holt NY 1930; 1st Eng. Longman 1930
8. *The Lone Striker* (verse) Holt NY 1933
9. *A Further Range* (verse) Holt NY 1936; 1st Eng. Cape 1937
10. *From Snow to Snow* (verse) Holt NY 1936
11. *A Witness Tree* (verse) Holt NY 1942; 1st Eng. Cape 1943
12. *A Masque of Reason* (verse) Holt NY 1945; 1st Eng. Cape 1948
13. *Steeple Bush* (verse) Holt NY 1947
14. *A Masque of Mercy* (verse) Holt NY 1947
15. *In the Clearing* (verse) Holt NY 1962; 1st Eng. Holt 1962
16. *The Poetry of Robert Frost* Holt NY 1969; 1st Eng. Cape 1971

In addition to No. 5, a further *Selected Poems* was published in England by Cape in 1936, with several introductory essays, including one by W. H. Auden.
Very many of the above were issued simultaneously with a limited, signed edition, but the prices here refer to the ordinary trade editions.
No 1 is very scarce, and would be Grade J–K. No. 2, Grade G. Nos 3, 4 and 6 are Grade E, and the remainder are Grade D, with the exceptions of Nos 15 and 16, which are Grade B, and No. 7, which is Grade C. The English editions of Nos 7, 9, 11 and 12 are Grade B–C, and of Nos 15 and 16, Grade B. Incidentally, the Cape edition of No. 12 contains the texts of 13 and 14 also.

Bibliography:
W. B. Sherbrick Caymer *Robert Frost: A Bibliography* (Jones Library Inc. USA 1937)

GARDNER, Erle Stanley
Born in Massachusetts 1889. Died 1970.
Best known as the inventor of the character Perry Mason, who featured in a vast number of books, each chronicling the exploits of this super attorney. The first of these was:

The Case of the Velvet Claws Morrow 1933; 1st Eng. Harrap 1933
This would be Grade E. Other early Morrow titles, in the dynamic black and red d/ws, would be Grade B, though the more recent ones may be found very cheaply.

Film:
The Case of the Velvet Claws International 1936
In addition to this, five other Perry Mason novels have been filmed, as well as the very successful television series.

GIBBONS, Stella
Born in London 1902.
Although she has published over thirty books, she is remembered for her first novel, a classic.

Cold Comfort Farm Longman 1932; 1st Amer. Longman 1933
It is scarce, and very desirable. Grade F.

GINSBERG, Allen
Born in New Jersey 1926.

1. *Howl and Other Poems* City Lights, San Francisco 1956
2. *Empty Mirror: Early Poems* Totem Press-Corinth NY 1961
3. *Kaddish and Other Poems* City Lights 1961
4. *Reality Sandwiches* (verse) City Lights 1963
5. *Penguin Modern Poets* 5 Penguin 1963 (with Lawrence Ferlinghetti and Gregory Corso)
6. *The Yage Letters* City Lights 1963 (with William S. Burroughs)
7. *The Change* (verse) Writers Forum, London 1963
8. *Kral Majales* (verse) Oyez, Berkeley 1965
9. *Wichita Vortex Sutra* (verse) Peace News, London 1966
10. *Housemans* (verse) Coyote Books, San Francisco 1966
11. *T.V. Baby Poems* Cape Goliard 1967; 1st Amer. Grossman 1968
12. *Wales—A Visitation, July 29 1967* Cape Goliard 1968
13. *Scrap Leaves, Tasty Scribbles* (verse) Poets Press NY 1968
14. *The Heart Is a Clock* (verse) Gallery Upstairs NY 1968
15. *Message II* (verse) Gallery Upstairs 1968; 1st Eng. Ad Infinitum 1968
16. *Planet News 1961–1967* (verse) City Lights 1968
17. *Airplane Dreams* (verse) House of Anansi, Toronto 1968; 1st Amer. City Lights 1969
18. *Ankor-Wat* (verse) Fulcrum Press, London 1969
19. *Notes After an Evening with William Carlos Williams* (verse) Charters NY 1970
20. *Iron Horse* (verse) Coach House Press, Toronto 1972
21. *The Fall of America* (verse) City Lights 1972
22. *Kaddish* (play) City Lights 1973

Bibliography:
George Dowden *A Bibliography of the Works of Allen Ginsberg* (City Lights, San Francisco 1970)

Penguin Modern Poets 5 was responsible for introducing the three famous Beat Poets to England, though as can be seen from the above list, very little else was published in this country. No. 11, the Cape Goliard, was a limited edition of 100 copies, signed, and is now Grade I., but generally speaking, the popularity of the Beats—including Ginsberg—has declined in England, and the prices seem to have declined in sympathy. It is true to say that Ginsberg hardly ever appears on a list in England any more, and although this may be attributed to rarity, one prominent London bookseller recently had the same two items in two successive catalogues—this would not have occurred in the sixties.
Nonetheless, No. 1 remains a valuable book, at Grade K and up, though *Kaddish* is probably his most popular work, and Grade G upwards. So many of the successive volumes are from small presses, limited or special in some other way, that it is very difficult even to attempt to give valuations, though I believe it to be true to say that all have retained at least their cover price (which may not be said of all recent poetry) and much has increased substantially. I feel we will have to wait for the mooted sixties revival for real interest to be stimulated again in Ginsberg, though I am told that this is already on the way, and an upturn is discernible.

GOLDING, William

Golding was born in Cornwall in 1911. Although he published some poems in his twenties, he was 43 when his explosive first novel was published. Its effect was immediate, and its impact was lasting. *Lord of the Flies* stands firmly as one of the few post-war classics. He publishes rarely, and although his last work—*The Scorpion God*—was not received as enthusiastically as the preceding novels, the standard of his work has remained extremely high.

1. *Poems* Macmillan 1934; 1st Amer. Macmillan 1935
   Very, very scarce. Grade K would seem reasonable today, though it is one of these books that is worth what a collector is willing to pay!
2. *Lord of the Flies* (novel) Faber 1954; 1st Amer. Coward McCann 1955
   Not only Golding's highlight, but one of the key novels of recent years. It is a small volume, with a d/w bearing fine artwork and the magnificent Faber Albertus type, as do most of his works. It is very scarce. E. M. Forster singled it out for special attention on publication, and the second and third impressions came swiftly. By now, the editions are beyond count, and it has long been a 'set book' in schools. Very satisfying, then, to have the 1st, but it would be Grade H and rising fast—any price, though, is a good price, as a collection of modern fiction would never be complete without it.
3. *The Inheritors* (novel) Faber 1955; 1st Amer. Harcourt Brace 1962
   Similar in format to 2. Quite scarce. Grade C–D.
4. *Pincher Martin* (novel) Faber 1956
   Grade C.
5. *The Two Deaths of Christopher Martin* Harcourt Brace 1957 (same as No. 4)
6. *The Brass Butterfly* (play) Faber 1958; 1st Amer. NAL 1962
   Grade C.
7. *Free Fall* (novel) Faber 1959; 1st Amer. Harcourt Brace 1960
   Grade C.
8. *The Spire* (novel) Faber 1964; 1st Amer. Harcourt Brace 1965. Grade B–C.
9. *The Hot Gates* (occasional pieces) Faber 1965; 1st Amer. Harcourt Brace 1965
   Grade C.
10. *The Pyramid* (novel) Faber 1967; 1st Amer. Harcourt Brace 1967
11. *The Scorpion God* (stories) Faber 1971
    One of the stories—*Envoy Extraordinary*—was first published in *Sometime, Never—Three Tales of Imagination* (Eyre & Spottiswoode 1956; Ballantine NY 1956). Grade B—as is No. 10.

Film:
Lord of the Flies British Lion 1963

There have been many books on the writings of Golding, and the following are recommended:
Bernard S. Oldsey and Stanley Weintraub *The Art of William Golding* Harcourt Brace 1965
Mark Kinkead-Weekes and Ian Gregor *William Golding: A Critical Study* Faber 1967
Leighton Hodson *Golding* Oliver & Boyd 1969

GRAHAME, Kenneth

Born in Edinburgh 1859. Died 1932. Grahame published few works, the three most notable being:

1. *The Golden Age* (juvenile) Lane 1895; 1st Amer. Stone & Kimball 1895
2. *Dream Days* (juvenile) Lane 1898; 1st Amer. Lane 1898
3. *The Wind in the Willows* (juvenile) Methuen 1908; 1st Amer. Scribner 1908

Nos 1 and 2 would be Grade D, and No. 3 Grade F. *The Wind in the Willows* is the real highlight here, but as all the great illustrators have at one stage rendered their interpretations, these later editions often exceed the prices of the 1sts. For example, Lane published an edition of No. 1 in 1900 illustrated by Maxfield Parrish—very much in vogue at the moment. This would probably be Grade F now.

Films (cartoons):

The Reluctant Dragon (story) Disney 1941
The Adventures of Ichabod and Mr Toad Disney 1949 (based in part on *The Wind in the Willows*)

GRASS, Günter
Born in Danzig 1927
The author's first book, and his most important, is:

The Tin Drum (novel) Random House 1963; 1st Eng. Secker & Warburg 1963
This was, of course, originally published in Germany as *Die Blechtrommel* in 1959. The English editions, however, are by no means common, and in the d/w would be Grade C.

GRAVES, Robert
Born in London 1895.
Graves' output is prodigious. The collector would, at least, have vast scope. He is indeed a very worthwhile poet to collect, and the works in 1st edition would be an impressive sight. It is impossible to list them in this book—there are over fifty books of verse, and about seventy other works—but the following bibliography will be of assistance: Fred H. Higginson *A Bibliography of the Works of Robert Graves* (Vane 1966)
There follows a necessarily brief selection of the highlights.

1. *Lars Porsena; or, The Future of Swearing and Improper Language* Kegan Paul 1927; 1st Amer. Dutton 1927
   Grade C.
2. *Lawrence and the Arabs* (biog.) Cape 1927
   Grade B–C. Published in America as *Lawrence and the Arabian Adventure* by Doubleday in 1928.
3. *Good-bye to All That: An Autobiography* Cape 1929; 1st Amer. Cape & Smith 1930
   This is Graves' best-known work, though there is an important issue point which greatly affects the value. In the first issue, there is a long poem by Siegfried Sassoon, beginning on page 341. This is replaced in the second issue by asterisks. The title pages are

identical. 1st issue: Grade K. 2nd issue: Grade C. Both, however, are very scarce in the d/w, which is a black-and-white montage of artwork and photographs.

4. *I, Claudius* (novel) Barker 1934; 1st Amer. Smith & Haas 1934
   Quite difficult. Grade E.
5. *Claudius the God* (novel) Barker 1934; 1st Amer. Smith & Haas 1935
   Sequel to No. 4. Grade C.

Although the prose works are the best known, the poetry is very desirable—particularly the very early books. Many are called simply *Poems,* followed by the relevant dates. The first was *Over the Brazier* (Poetry Bookshop 1916); the seemingly definitive *Collected Poems 1975* was published by Cassell.

GRAY, Simon
Born in Hampshire 1936.
The author of a dozen books, mostly plays, but notable for:

Butley (play) Methuen 1971; 1st Amer. Viking Press 1972
Grade A, at the moment.

GREEN, Henry
Pseudonym of Henry Vincent Yorke. Born 1905. Died 1973.

1. *Blindness* (novel) Dutton 1926; 1st Eng. Dent 1926
2. *Living* (novel) Dutton 1929; 1st Eng. Dent 1929
3. *Party Going* (novel) Hogarth Press 1939; Longman, Toronto 1939
4. *Pack My Bag* (autobiog.) Hogarth Press 1940; Macmillan, Toronto 1940
5. *Caught* (novel) Hogarth Press 1943; Macmillan, Toronto 1943
6. *Loving* (novel) Hogarth Press 1945; Macmillan, Toronto 1945
7. *Back* (novel) Hogarth Press 1946; Oxford, Toronto 1946
8. *Concluding* (novel) Hogarth Press 1948; 1st

Amer. Viking Press 1950

9. *Nothing* (novel) Hogarth Press 1950; 1st Amer. Viking Press 1950

10. *Doting* (novel) Hogarth Press 1952; 1st Amer. Viking Press 1952

The first four are difficult, though even the others are vanishing fast from the market. Nos. 1 and 2 are Grade E–F, Nos 3 and 4 Grade D. The remainder are Grade C, though the most recent may be found within Grade B.

d/ws are important, as they are by artists of renown, such as Vanessa Bell, John Piper and Lynton Lamb.

Since Green's death, his reputation has been gaining, and I feel that soon all his 1sts will be very scarce, the values rising accordingly.

GREENE, Graham

Born in Hertfordshire in 1904, Greene is often talked of today as (one of) our greatest living novelist(s). He is certainly one of the most collected. A book collector himself, Greene seems to delight in producing esoteric pamphlets quietly, when no-one is looking. Collectors usually find out about these a year later, when they are long out-of-print. He has been known to publish books first in some quite incredible language in a strictly limited edition, and later in England. It is then that collectors read 'First published in Great Britain . . .', and proceed to go mad again. Neither does Greene sign very much, as is reflected in the following prices from two booksellers' catalogues in 1975: *Heart of the Matter*. VG in d/w. £4, and a similar copy with inscription: £48. The various signed editions he has produced—e.g. *May We Borrow Your Husband?*—come considerably cheaper than this, but are not so popular, and justly so.

There follows a complete list of Greene's books, but for the very severely bitten, there is:

J. D. Vann *Graham Greene* (bibliography) (Kent State University Press, Ohio 1970)

1. *Babbling April: Poems* Blackwell, Oxford 1925
Of legendary scarcity, despite the fact that it appears at sales not irregularly. It is now over Grade P, though.

2. *The Man Within* (novel) Heinemann 1929; 1st Amer. Doubleday 1929
Very scarce, particularly in d/w. Grade O.

3. *The Name of Action* (novel) Heinemann 1930; 1st Amer. Doubleday 1931
Same situation as No. 2. Grade O.

4. *Rumour at Nightfall* (novel) Heinemann 1931; 1st Amer. Doubleday 1932
Again, very scarce. Grade L.

5. *Stamboul Train* (novel) Heinemann 1932
Classed by Greene as 'An entertainment', this was published in America as *Orient Express* by Doubleday in 1933, anticipating Agatha Christie's *Murder . . .* by just one year. This is the easiest of the early Greenes, though difficult in d/w. An unwrapped copy should not be above Grade D.

6. *It's a Battlefield* (novel) Heinemann 1934; 1st Amer. Doubleday 1934
Again, scarce in d/w, but otherwise Grade F.

7. *England Made Me* (novel) Heinemann 1935; 1st Amer. Doubleday 1935
Scarce. Grade I.

8. *The Basement Room* (stories) Cresset Press 1935
Very scarce. Grade I.

9. *A Gun for Sale* (novel) Heinemann 1936
An entertainment. Published in America as *This Gun for Hire* by Doubleday in 1936. Grade H.

10. *Journey Without Maps* (travel) Heinemann 1936; 1st Amer. Doubleday 1936
Quite scarce. Grade F.

11. *Brighton Rock* (novel) Heinemann 1938
Greene's highlight. Not only scarce in d/w, this, but legendary. I know several ardent Greene collectors who despair of ever seeing it, let alone acquiring it. Grade H, but if one came up in d/w, the price could double. In America only it was classed as 'An entertainment' and published in the same year by a new publisher, the Viking Press.

12. *The Confidential Agent* (novel) Heinemann 1939; 1st Amer. Viking Press 1939

Scarce. Grade E.

13. *Twenty-Four Stories* Cresset Press 1939 (with James Laver and Sylvia Townsend Warner) An unusual item, but not above Grade D.

14. *The Lawless Roads* (travel) Longman 1939 Published in America as *Another Mexico* by the Viking Press in the same year. Grade F.

15. *The Power and the Glory* (novel) Heinemann 1940
Another Greene highlight. Published in America as *The Labyrinthine Ways*, for some reason, by the Viking Press in the same year. Grade G.

16. *British Dramatists* (non-fiction) Collins 1942 One of the Britain in Pictures series. Grade B. Not published separately in America, but included in *The Romance of English Literature* (Hastings House 1944)

17. *The Ministry of Fear* (novel) Heinemann 1943; 1st Amer. Viking Press 1943
Not too difficult. Grade D.

18. *The Little Train* (juvenile) Eyre & Spottiswoode 1946; 1st Amer. Lothrop 1958 Published anonymously while Greene was a director at E & S. Scarce. Grade F.

19. *Nineteen Stories* Heinemann 1947; 1st Amer. Viking Press 1949
Grade B–C. Heinemann published a supplemented edition as *Twenty-One Stories* in 1954.

20. *The Heart of the Matter* (novel) Heinemann 1948; 1st Amer. Viking Press 1948
One of the easy Greenes. Grade B, but beware the Book Society edition—these are very common, and are worth no more than £1.

21. *Why Do I Write?: An Exchange of Views Between Elizabeth Bowen, Graham Greene, and V. S. Pritchett* Marshall 1948
Quite scarce. Grade B–C.

22. *The Little Fire Engine* (juvenile) Parrish 1950 Scarce, and Grade E. It was published in America by Lothrop in 1952 as *The Little* Red *Fire Engine*, so as to make no mistake.

23. *The Third Man* (novel) Viking Press 1950 An entertainment. Quite scarce. Grade C.

24. *The Third Man* and *The Fallen Idol* (novels) Heinemann 1950

Quite difficult. Grade B–C.

25. *The End of the Affair* (novel) Heinemann 1951; 1st Amer. Viking Press 1951
Quite easy. Grade B.

26. *The Lost Childhood* (essays) Eyre & Spottiswoode 1951; 1st Amer. Viking Press 1952
Grade B–C.

27. *The Little Horse Bus* (juvenile) Parrish 1952; 1st Amer. Lothrop 1954
Scarce. Grade D.

28. *The Little Steam Roller* (juvenile) Parrish 1953; 1st Amer. Lothrop 1955
Scarce. Grade D.

29. *The Living Room* (play) Heinemann 1953; 1st Amer. Viking Press 1954
His first play, and not common. Grade C.

30. *Loser Takes All* (novel) Heinemann 1955; 1st Amer. Viking Press 1957
Grade A–B.

31. *The Quiet American* (novel) Heinemann 1955; 1st Amer. Viking Press 1956
Grade B.

32. *The Potting Shed* (play) Viking Press 1957; 1st Eng. Heinemann 1958
Grade B.

33. *Our Man in Havana* (novel) Heinemann 1958; 1st Amer. Viking Press 1958
An entertainment. Grade B.

34. *The Complaisant Lover* (play) Heinemann 1959; 1st Amer. Viking Press 1961
Grade B.

35. *In Search of a Character: Two African Journals* Bodley Head 1961; 1st Amer. Viking Press 1961
Grade B. One of the journals, *Convoy to West Africa,* was first published in Geoffrey Grigson (ed.) *The Mint* (Routledge 1946)

36. *A Burnt-Out Case* (novel) Heinemann 1961; 1st Amer. Viking Press 1961
Grade B.

37. *A Sense of Reality* (stories) Bodley Head 1963; 1st Amer. Viking Press 1963
Grade A–B.

38. *Carving a Statue* (play) Bodley Head 1964
Grade B.

39. *The Comedians* (novel) Bodley Head 1966; 1st Amer. Viking Press 1966

Grade A–B.

40. *May We Borrow Your Husband?* (stories) Bodley Head 1967; 1st Amer. Viking Press 1967
    Grade A.
41. *The Third Man: A Film* (non-fiction) Lorrimer 1969 (with Carol Reed)
    Grade B.
42. *Collected Essays* Bodley Head 1969; 1st Amer. Viking Press 1969
    Grade B.
43. *Travels with My Aunt* (novel) Bodley Head 1969; 1st Amer. Viking Press 1970. Grade A.
44. *A Sort of Life* (autobiog.) Bodley Head 1971; 1st Amer. Simon & Schuster 1971
    Grade B.
45. *The Pleasure Dome: The Collected Film Criticism 1935–40* Secker & Warburg 1972; 1st Amer. Simon & Schuster 1972
    Grade B.
46. *The Collected Stories* Bodley Head/Heinemann 1972; 1st Amer. Viking Press 1973
    Grade B.
47. *The Honorary Consul* (novel) Bodley Head 1973; 1st Amer. Viking Press 1973
48. *The Portable Graham Greene* Viking Press 1973
49. *Lord Rochester's Monkey* (biog.) Bodley Head 1974; 1st Amer. Viking Press 1974
    The above three items are all Grade B.
50. *Shades of Greene* (stories) Bodley Head/Heinemann 1975
51. *The Return of A. J. Raffles* (play) Bodley Head 1975
    The above two items are Grade A.

Greene has edited the following:
The Old School: Essays by Divers Hands Cape 1934; 1st Amer. Smith 1934
Greene also has an essay in this. Scarce. Grade F.
The Spy's Bedside Book Hart-Davis 1957 (with Hugh Greene)
An Impossible Woman: The Memories of Dottoressa Moor of Capri Bodley Head 1975; 1st Amer. Viking Press 1976

Films:
Orient Express (*Stamboul Train*) 20th Century Fox 1934

This Gun for Sale (*A Gun for Sale*) Paramount 1942
Ministry of Fear Paramount 1944
Confidential Agent Warner Bros 1945
The Man Within 20th Century Fox 1947
The Fugitive (*The Power and the Glory*) RKO 1947
The Fallen Idol 20th Century Fox 1948
Brighton Rock Associated British 1948
The Third Man General 1950
The Heart of the Matter British Lion 1953
The End of the Affair Columbia 1954
Loser Takes All British Lion 1956
Short Cut to Hell (*A Gun for Sale*) Paramount 1957
Across the Bridge (story) Rank 1957
The Quiet American United Artists 1957
Our Man in Havana Columbia 1959
The Power and the Glory Paramount 1962
The Comedians MGM 1967
England Made Me Hemdale 1972
Travels with My Aunt MGM 1972

Greene wrote the screenplays for *Brighton Rock, The Fallen Idol, The Third Man, Our Man in Havana* and *The Comedians*, though they have not been published.

GREENWOOD, Walter
Born in Lancashire 1903. Died 1974.
Although the author of several books, he is remembered for the following modern classic:

Love on the Dole Cape 1933; 1st Amer. Doubleday 1934
It is scarce, and Grade D–E.

Film:
Love on the Dole United Artists 1941

GRIGSON, Geoffrey
Born in Cornwall 1905.
Although known as a poet, Grigson has in fact published only a dozen books of verse, against his fifty prose works. These are chiefly on art or natural history, many having become standard works, and sought after in

their own right—such as his *Samuel Palmer* (Kegan Paul 1947). *Britain Observed* (Phaidon 1975), a book of English landscape art, looks to be already on its way to become a classic of the future. He has also edited over three dozen works, mostly poetry anthologies; as his *œuvre* totals more or less a hundred books, I must content myself with a checklist of his own verse.

1. *Several Observations: Thirty Five Poems* Cresset Press 1939
2. *Under the Cliff and Other Poems* Routledge 1943
3. *The Isles of Scilly and Other Poems* Routledge 1946
4. *The Collected Poems 1924–1962* Phoenix House 1963
5. *A Skull in Salop and Other Poems* Macmillan 1967; 1st Amer. Dufour 1967
6. *Ingestion of Ice-Cream and Other Poems* Macmillan 1969
7. *Discoveries of Bones and Stones* Macmillan 1971
8. *Sad Grave of an Imperial Mongoose* Macmillan 1973
9. *Angles and Circles* Gollancz 1974

No. 1 is Grade C, Nos 2, 3 and 4 Grade B, and Nos 5–9 Grade A.
It is of note that Grigson was the founder of the little magazine *New Verse*, which ran from 1933 until 1939. Most of the major poets of the day appeared within its covers, and odd copies may be found for as little as £1. There were special issues, however—such as the Auden double number—which would be Grade B–C.

GROSSMITH, George and Weedon

George (1847–1912) and Weedon (1854–1919) Grossmith are not strictly within our brief, as their classic work was published in the last century, but one feels that any great comic work which has been loved and re-read for so long, deserves an entry:

The Diary of a Nobody Arrowsmith 1892
Originally a series of contributions to *Punch*, and then enlarged and developed for this book. Illustrated by Weedon, and published

in Arrowsmith's Three-and-sixpenny series (!), this fine work is now Grade E–F, and getting more and more scarce each year.

GUNN, Thom

Born in Kent in 1929, Gunn made his mark very rapidly, publishing his first volume of verse at the age of 24. With Ted Hughes, he was recognized as being one of the outstanding new poets. Although he has published a lot of private press material, as will be seen below, the standard slim volumes have appeared rarely, and have always been well received.

1. *Poetry from Cambridge 1951–52* Fortune Press 1952
Bound in cloth, with d/w, this volume is edited by Gunn, and contains four poems by him, these being his first published. There are other poets represented in the book. Scarce. Grade G.
2. *Fighting Terms* (verse) Fantasy Press 1954; 1st Amer. Hawks Well Press 1958
This is his first book proper, and it is very scarce. It was catalogued at Grade K in 1974, and could easily have reached Grade L or M by now. The American edition, four years later, was revised, and is the first appearance of Gunn in the U.S.A. It is Grade E, and the revised edition published by Faber in 1962 is Grade B.
3. *The Sense of Movement* (verse) Faber 1957; 1st Amer. University of Chicago 1959
Gunn's first book with Faber, bound in wine cloth and sporting a fine Faber d/w—pale green with an orange circle, and black upper- and lower-case lettering. Quite scarce. Grade E.
4. *My Sad Captains* (verse) Faber 1961; 1st Amer. University of Chicago 1961
Wine cloth, pale blue d/w with red and grey design and Albertus typeface. Quite scarce. Grade D.
5. *Selected Poems* Faber 1962 (with Ted Hughes)
This paper-covered edition did much to bring these two poets a far wider audience. It has been reprinted countless times, and a 1st

in nice condition could be difficult, but nonetheless should not exceed Grade A.

6. *A Geography* (verse) Stone Wall Press, Iowa 1966
Printed only in America, and scarce. Grade

7. *Positives* (verse) Faber 1966; 1st Amer. University of Chicago 1967
This large-format volume is illustrated with photographs by Ander Gunn, Thom's brother. This went into paperback quite quickly, and the 1st is difficult. Grade C.

8. *Touch* (verse) Faber 1967; 1st Amer. University of Chicago 1968
Black cloth, and the d/w in brown, cream and black is really one of Faber's greatest efforts. Grade B–C.

9. *The Garden of the Gods* (verse) Pym Randall, Mass. 1968
Limited to 200 copies signed by the author. Grade D–E.

10. *The Explorers: Poems* Gilbertson, Devon 1969

11. *The Fair in the Woods* (verse) Sycamore Press, Oxford 1969
The above two private press items were limited. Grade D.

12. *Poems 1950–1966: A Selection* Faber 1969
Paper-covered edition. Grade A.

13. *Sunlight* (verse) Albondocani Press NY 1969
Limited and signed edition. Grade E.

14. *Moly* (verse) Faber 1971
Another fine Faber production in yellow cloth, and d/w similar in design to that of No. 8, but this time in yellow, white and black. Grade B.

15. *Poem After Chaucer* Albondocani Press 1971
Limited edition of 300 copies, though it was issued as a greeting from author and publisher, and none was sold. Grade C.

16. *The Spell* (poem) Steane, Kettering 1973
This is a poem on a poster, with a design by Nina Carroll. Grade B.

17. *Moly* and *My Sad Captains* (verse) Farrar Straus NY 1973
First publication in U.S.A. of No. 14, together with a reprint of No. 4. Grade A.

18. *Mandrakes* (verse) Rainbow Press 1973
Limited to 150 numbered and signed copies, illustrated by Leonard Baskin (see Ted

Hughes: *Crow*, No. 25), bound in quarter vellum by Sangorski & Sutcliffe, and in a fleece-lined (!) slip-case. What they call a 'collector's item'. Grade K.

19. *Songbook* (verse) Albondocani Press 1973
Limited to 226 copies—200 numbered and signed, 26 lettered and signed. Illustrated by Bill S. Marbled wrpps. Grade C–E.

20. *To the Air* (verse) Godine Press, Boston 1974
Blue and white patterned boards, issued without d/w. Cover has *trompe l'œuil* paper labels. Grade B.

21. *Jack Straw's Castle* (verse) Faber 1976; 1st Amer. Farrar Straus & Giroux 1976
This was preceded by an American edition (Hallman 1975), limited to 400 copies, 100 signed, bearing the same title, but containing only the title poem.

Gunn has edited the following:
Five American Poets Faber 1963 (with Ted Hughes)
Selected Poems of Fulke Greville Faber 1968; 1st Amer. University of Chicago 1968
Ben Jonson Penguin 1974

Five American Poets and *Fulke Greville* are Grade B, and *Ben Jonson* Grade A.

HALL, Radclyffe
Born in Bournemouth 1886. Died 1943. Among her works is one book which caused a furore in its time, although this seems unbelievable today. The courts declared the book obscene, and ordered it to be destroyed—an act which might or might not have saved England's morals from destruction, but which has made the bibliophile's task harder. 1sts are not common, and when one does find one, it always seems to have been well read.

The Well of Loneliness (novel) Cape 1928; 1st Amer. Covici 1928
The American edition might well be a lot easier, as the book was cleared of charges in the States. Grade B for an average copy, but Grade C if in the scarce d/w.

HAMMETT, Dashiell
Born in America 1894. Died 1961.
Author of several detective stories, and recently very popular with collectors, though always hard to find. His highlight appears below.

The Maltese Falcon (novel) Knopf 1930; 1st Eng. Cassell 1931
Both editions are scarce, but the Knopf ed. would be Grade I upwards, for a nice copy, and the Cassell ed. would be Grade D–E.

Films:
The Maltese Falcon Warner Bros 1931; Warner Bros 1941
It was also filmed as *Satan Met a Lady* by First National in 1937.
Several other Hammett stories have been filmed, notably *The Glass Key* and *The Thin Man*.

HARDY, Thomas
Born in Dorset 1840. Died 1928.
Although many disagree upon whether Hardy should be classed as a 'Modern' or not, it seems impossible to omit such a writer, although it was just his poetry that appeared in the twentieth century, all the novels having been published earlier. The popularity of these novels at the moment is enormous, and interest in the verse has been revived (if it needed revival) by the publication of *The Complete Poems* (Macmillan 1976).
Such novels as *Tess of the d'Urbervilles* are extremely rare, and very expensive, but the following ought to be in any collection of fiction, and—unlike *Tess*—it is not a three-decker, and not too difficult to come by.

1. *Jude the Obscure* Osgood, McIlvaine1896; 1st Amer. Harper 1896
This volume is uniform with the Wessex Novels edition of the works. It is getting more scarce each year, but it might be found within Grade E.
2. *The Early Life of Thomas Hardy* Macmillan 1928; 1st Amer. Macmillan 1928
3. *The Later Years of Thomas Hardy* Macmillan 1930; 1st Amer. Macmillan 1930
The above two volumes 'by Florence Emily Hardy' were written by Hardy himself, and are essential reading. The two volumes together would be Grade F.
The essential book for the collector, however, is:
Richard Little Purdy *Thomas Hardy: A Bibliographical Study* (OUP 1968)
Dozens and dozens of books have been published about Hardy, but two of the very best are:
F. B. Pinion *A Hardy Companion* Macmillan 1968
Robert Gittings *Young Thomas Hardy* Heinemann 1975

Film:
Far from the Madding Crowd Warner Bros 1966

HARTLEY, L. P.
Leslie Poles Hartley. Born in Cambridgeshire 1895. Died 1972. A bibliography is contained in Peter Bien *L. P. Hartley* (Chatto & Windus 1963)

1. *Night Fears and Other Stories* Putnam 1924
2. *Simonetta Perkins* (novel) Putnam 1925; 1st Amer. Putnam 1925
3. *The Killing Bottle* (stories) Putnam 1932
4. *The Shrimp and the Anemone* (novel) Putnam 1944
5. *The West Window* Doubleday NY 1945 (same as 4)
6. *The Sixth Heaven* (novel) Putnam 1946; 1st Amer. Doubleday 1947
7. *Eustace and Hilda* (novel) Putnam 1947
Nos 4, 6 and 7 form a trilogy.
8. *The Travelling Grave* (stories) Arkham House 1948; 1st Eng. Barrie & Jenkins 1951
9. *The Boat* (novel) Putnam 1950; 1st Amer. Doubleday 1950
10. *My Fellow Devils* (novel) Barrie & Jenkins 1951
11. *The Go-Between* (novel) Hamilton 1953; 1st Amer. Knopf 1954
12. *A White Wand and Other Stories* Hamilton 1954

13. *A Perfect Woman* (novel) Hamilton 1955; 1st Amer. Knopf 1956
14. *The Hireling* (novel) Hamilton 1957; 1st Amer. Rinehart 1958
15. *Facial Justice* (novel) Hamilton 1960; 1st Amer. Doubleday 1961
16. *Two for the River* (stories) Hamilton 1961
17. *The Brickfield* (novel) Hamilton 1964
18. *The Betrayal* (novel) Hamilton 1966
19. *Poor Clare* (novel) Hamilton 1968
20. *The Collected Stories* Hamilton 1968; 1st Amer. Horizon Press 1969
21. *The Love-Adept* (novel) Hamilton 1969
22. *My Sister's Keeper* (novel) Hamilton 1970
23. *The Harness Room* (novel) Hamilton 1971
24. *Mrs Carteret Receives* (stories) Hamilton 1971
25. *The Will and the Way* (novel) Hamilton 1973

Since Hartley died, a revival seems to have taken place, collectors showing more interest in gathering the works than previously. The trilogy has always been a popular work, the three volumes in 1sts fetching Grade G, and *The Go-Between* has been of considerable interest since the film. This is now Grade B–C. His first two books are very scarce, and Grade I. Nos 3 and 8 are Grade B–C, Nos 9–20 (with the exception of 11) are Grade B, and the most recent works are Grade A.

Films:
The Go-Between MGM/EMI 1971
The Hireling Columbia/Warner Bros 1973

HEANEY, Seamus
Born in County Derry, Northern Ireland, 1939.

1. *Eleven Poems* Festival, Belfast 1965
2. *Death of a Naturalist* (verse) Faber 1966; 1st Amer. OUP 1966
3. *A Lough Neagh Sequence* Phoenix Pamphlet Poets Press 1969
4. *Door into the Dark* (verse) Faber 1969; 1st Amer. OUP 1969
5. *Night Drive: Poems* Gilbertson, Crediton 1970
6. *Boy Driving His Father to Confession* Sceptre Press 1970

7. *Wintering Out* (verse) Faber 1972; 1st Amer. OUP 1973
8. *North* (verse) Faber 1975; 1st Amer. OUP 1976

Heaney has edited *New Poems 1970–1971* (with Alan Brownjohn and Jon Stallworthy; Hutchinson 1971) and *Soundings 72* (Blackstaff Press, Belfast 1972). Both these are Grade A. No. 1 is very scarce and Grade C–D. All the others are Grade B, with the exception of No. 5. This is limited to 100 copies, signed (Grade B–C), 25 of which contain a poem in the author's hand (Grade D). No. 6 was limited to 150 numbered copies, 50 signed. No. 7, it is interesting to note, appeared first in wrpps, and later in boards and d/w. The 1st is always of smaller format, with limp covers.

HEATH-STUBBS, John
Born in London 1918.

1. *Wounded Thammuz* (verse) Routledge 1942
2. *Beauty and the Beast* (verse) Routledge 1943
3. *The Divided Ways* (verse) Routledge 1947
4. *The Charity of the Stars* (verse) Sloane NY 1949
5. *The Swarming of the Bees* (verse) Eyre & Spottiswoode 1950
6. *The Darkling Plain* (criticism) Eyre & Spottiswoode 1950
7. *A Charm Against the Toothache* (verse) Methuen 1954
8. *Charles Williams* (criticism) Longman 1955
9. *The Triumph of the Muse and Other Poems* OUP 1958
10. *The Blue-Fly in His Head: Poems* OUP 1962
11. *Selected Poems* OUP 1965
12. *Satires and Epigrams* (verse) Turret 1968
13. *The Verse Satire* (criticism) OUP 1969
14. *The Ode* (criticism) OUP 1969
15. *The Pastoral* (criticism) OUP 1969
16. *Artorius* (verse) Burning Deck, USA 1970; 1st Eng. Enitharmon Press 1973
17. *Indifferent Weather* (verse) McKelvie 1975

Heath-Stubbs' plays (*Helen in Egypt, The Talking Ass* and *The Harrowing of Hell*) were published in *Helen in Egypt and Other Plays* (OUP 1958).

Heath-Stubbs has edited the following:

18. *Selected Poems of Shelley* Falcon Press 1947
19. *Selected Poems of Tennyson* Falcon Press 1947
20. *Selected Poems of Swift* Falcon Press 1947
21. *The Forsaken Garden* (anthology) Lehmann 1950 (with David Wright)
22. *Images of Tomorrow* (anthology) SCM Press 1953
23. *The Faber Book of Twentieth-Century Verse* Faber 1953 (with David Wright)
24. *Selected Poems of Alexander Pope* Heinemann 1964; 1st Amer. Barnes & Noble 1966
25. *Homage to George Barker on His 60th Birthday* O'Keeffe 1973 (with Martin Green)

Heath-Stubbs has translated the following:

26. *Poems from Giacomo Leopardi* Lehmann 1946
27. *Aphrodite's Garland* Crescendo Press 1952
28. *Thirty Poems of Hafiz of Shiraz* Murray 1955
29. Giacomo Leopardi *Selected Poetry and Prose* OUP 1966; 1st Amer. NAL 1967 (with Iris Origo)

Nos 1–4: Grade C–D. Nos 5–11: Grade B. No. 12: Grade C. All the remainder, including edited volumes and translations, Grade B.

HELLER, Joseph
Born in Brooklyn, NY, 1923.

1. *Catch-22* (novel) Simon & Schuster 1961; 1st Eng. Cape 1962
2. *We Bombed in New Haven* (play) Knopf 1968; 1st Eng. Cape 1969
3. *Catch-22* (play) French NY 1971
4. *Clevinger's Trial* (play) French NY 1973
5. *Something Happened* (novel) Knopf 1974; 1st Eng. Cape 1974

Catch-22 is of course one of the most famous post-war novels, the title having entered the language. It is scarce, and Grade G. The Cape edition is Grade B–C. The plays are Grade A, and No. 5 Grade B.

Film:
Catch-22 Paramount 1969

HEMINGWAY, Ernest
Born in Illinois 1899. Died 1961.

Below is a checklist of Hemingway's major works, excluding private press material and special editions. A short bibliography was published in New York in 1951 by Lee Samuels, and S. Sanderson *Hemingway* (Writers and Critics series, Oliver & Boyd 1961), also gives some information.

1. *Three Stories and Ten Poems* Paris 1923
2. *In Our Time* (stories) Boni & Liveright 1924; 1st Eng. Cape 1924
3. *The Torrents of Spring* (novel) Scribner 1926
4. *The Sun Also Rises* (novel) Scribner 1926
5. *Fiesta* Cape 1927 (same as 4)
6. *Men Without Women* (stories) Scribner 1927; 1st Eng. Cape 1927
7. *A Farewell to Arms* (novel) Scribner 1929; 1st Eng. Cape 1929
8. *Death in the Afternoon* (non-fiction) Scribner 1932; 1st Eng. Cape 1932
9. *Winner Take Nothing* (stories) Scribner 1933; 1st Eng. Cape 1934
10. *Green Hills of Africa* (non-fiction) Scribner 1935; 1st Eng. Cape 1936
11. *To Have and Have Not* (novel) Scribner 1937; 1st Eng. Cape 1937
12. *The Fifth Column and the first Forty-Nine Stories* (play and stories) Scribner 1938; 1st Eng. Cape 1941
13. *For Whom the Bell Tolls* (novel) Scribner 1940; 1st Eng. Cape 1941
14. *Across the River and into the Trees* (novel) Scribner 1950; 1st Eng. Cape 1950
15. *The Old Man and the Sea* (novel) Scribner 1952; 1st Eng. Cape 1952
16. *A Moveable Feast* (non-fiction) Scribner 1964; 1st Eng. Cape 1964
17. *Islands in the Stream* (novel) Scribner 1970; 1st Eng. Collins 1970

In 1947 Cape published *The Essential Hemingway*, which contains extracts from his works.

There is a great difference between the prices for the American and the English editions. On the whole, the prices of the Cape editions are cheaper than might be expected, sometimes as little as one-third of the Scribner value. Autograph inscriptions also make a big difference with Hemingway, as may be seen from the following two items, quoted from the same catalogue of a London bookseller in 1975:

A Farewell to Arms 1st U.S. Fine, d/w. Inscribed. £225
A Farewell to Arms 1st G.B. V.G., d/w. £10
No. 1 is extremely scarce, and would be Grade R or over. Nos 2 and 3 are Grade I. No. 4 is Grade G, and No. 5 Grade D. Nos 6, 7, 9, 10 and 11 are Grade G–H in the American editions, though only Grade B–C in the English. No. 8 is Grade D. Nos 12 and 13 are Grade E in the American, and Grade B–C in the English editions. Nos 14, 15 and 16 are Grade C, American, and Grade B, English. No. 17 is A.

Films:
A Farewell to Arms Paramount 1932; 20th Century Fox 1957
For Whom the Bell Tolls Paramount 1943
To Have and Have Not Warner Bros 1944
  (as *The Breaking Point*) Warner Bros 1950
  (as *The Gun Runners*) United Artists 1958
The Killers (story) Universal 1946; Rank 1964
The Macomber Affair (story) Universal 1947
Under My Skin 20th Century Fox 1950 (*My Old Man*—story)
The Snows of Kilimanjaro (story) 20th Century Fox 1952
The Sun Also Rises 20th Century Fox 1957
The Old Man and the Sea Warner Bros 1958
Hemingway's Adventures of a Young Man 20th Century Fox 1962

HESSE, Hermann
Born in Germany 1877. Died 1962. Notable for quite a few novels, all first published in Germany, but in particular:

Steppenwolf Secker 1929; 1st Amer. Holt, Rinehart 1929

This was published in Germany as *Der Steppenwolf* in 1927.
The Secker edition would now be Grade D, largely because of the great popularity of Hesse at the moment.

HIGHSMITH, Patricia
Born in Fort Worth, Texas, 1921.

1. *Strangers on a Train* (novel) Harper 1950; 1st Eng. Cresset Press 1951
2. *The Price of Salt* (novel) Coward McCann NY 1952 (pseud. Claire Morgan)
3. *The Blunderer* (novel) Coward McCann 1954; 1st Eng. Cresset Press 1956
4. *The Talented Mr Ripley* (novel) Coward McCann 1955; 1st Eng. Cresset Press 1957
5. *Deep Water* (novel) Harper 1957; 1st Eng. Heinemann 1958
6. *A Game for the Living* (novel) Harper 1958; 1st Eng. Heinemann 1959
7. *Miranda the Panda Is on the Verandah* (juvenile) Coward McCann 1958 (with Doris Sanders)
8. *This Sweet Sickness* (novel) Harper 1960; 1st Eng. Heinemann 1961
9. *The Cry of the Owl* (novel) Harper 1962; 1st Eng. Heinemann 1963
10. *The Two Faces of January* (novel) Doubleday 1964; 1st Eng. Heinemann 1964
11. *The Glass Cell* (novel) Doubleday 1964; 1st Eng. Heinemann 1965
12. *The Story-Teller* (novel) Doubleday 1965
13. *A Suspension of Mercy* Heinemann 1965 (same as 12)
14. *Plotting and Writing Suspense Fiction* Writer, Boston 1966
15. *Those Who Walk Away* (novel) Doubleday 1967; 1st Eng. Heinemann 1967
16. *The Tremor of Forgery* (novel) Doubleday 1969; 1st Eng. Heinemann 1969
17. *Ripley Under Ground* (novel) Doubleday 1970; 1st Eng. Heinemann 1971
18. *The Snail-Watchers* (stories) Doubleday 1970
19. *Eleven* (stories) Heinemann 1970 (same as 18)
20. *A Dog's Ransom* (novel) Knopf 1972; 1st Eng. Heinemann 1972
21. *Ripley's Game* (novel) Knopf 1974; 1st Eng. Heinemann 1974

22. *The Animal Lover's Book of Beastly Murder* (stories) Heinemann 1975
23. *Edith's Diary* (novel) Heinemann 1977

The Queen of psychological crime is popular with collectors quite suddenly, prices having been rising slightly over the past two years. A fairly sharp upward surge in the near future would not be unexpected. At the moment, No. 1—her highlight—is Grade C, and all the others are Grade B, with the exception of the most recent few, which are A.

Films:
Strangers on a Train Warner Bros 1951
Purple Noon Hillcrest 1961 (*The Talented Mr Ripley*)

HILL, Susan
Born in Yorkshire 1942.

1. *The Enclosure* (novel) Hutchinson 1961
2. *Do Me a Favour* (novel) Hutchinson 1963
3. *Gentlemen and Ladies* (novel) Hamilton 1968; 1st Amer. Walker 1969
4. *A Change for the Better* (novel) Hamilton 1969
5. *I'm the King of the Castle* (novel) Hamilton 1970; 1st Amer. Saturday Review Press 1970
6. *Strange Meeting* (novel) Hamilton 1971; 1st Amer. Saturday Review Press 1972
7. *The Albatross and Other Stories* Hamilton 1971
8. *The Bird of Night* (novel) Hamilton 1972; 1st Amer. Saturday Review Press 1972
9. *The Custodian* (story) Covent Garden Press 1972
10. *A Bit of Singing and Dancing* (stories) Hamilton 1973
11. *In the Springtime of the Year* (novel) Hamilton 1974; 1st Amer. Saturday Review Press 1974
12. *The Land of Lost Content* (novel) Hamilton 1977

Nos 1 and 2 are Grade B, and the remainder Grade A.

HILTON, James
Born in Lancashire 1900. Died 1954.

Author of several books, eight of which have been filmed, but it is for the following that he is known:

Goodbye, Mr Chips (novel) Hodder & Stoughton 1934; 1st Amer. Little Brown 1934
This novel was first published as a supplement to the magazine *British Weekly*, the Hodder edition being 1st book form. A sequel *To You, Mr Chips* was published in 1938, also by Hodder (Musson in Toronto). Despite both books being very well produced, printed and illustrated, prices have remained low—Grade B for a fine *Goodbye, Mr Chips* in d/w, and Grade A for the sequel.

Films:
Goodbye, Mr Chips MGM 1939; MGM 1969

HOUSEHOLD, Geoffrey
Born in Bristol 1900.

1. *The Terror of Villadonga* (juvenile) Hutchinson 1936
2. *The Spanish Cave* Little Brown, USA 1936 (same as No. 1, revised)
3. *The Third Hour* (novel) Chatto & Windus 1937 1st Amer. Little Brown 1938
4. *The Salvation of Pisco Gabar* (stories) Chatto & Windus 1938; 1st Amer. Little Brown 1940
5. *Rogue Male* (novel) Chatto & Windus 1939; 1st Amer. Little Brown 1939
6. *Arabesque* (novel) Chatto & Windus 1948; 1st Amer. Little Brown 1948
7. *The High Place* (novel) Joseph 1950; 1st Amer. Little Brown 1950
8. *A Rough Shoot* (novel) Joseph 1951; 1st Amer. Little Brown 1951
9. *A Time to Kill* (novel) Little Brown 1951; 1st Eng. Joseph 1952
10. *Tales of Adventurers* (stories) Joseph 1952; 1st Amer. Little Brown 1952
11. *Fellow Passenger* (novel) Joseph 1955; 1st Amer. Little Brown 1955
12. *The Exploits of Xenophon* (juvenile) Random House NY 1955
Published in England as *Xenophon's Adventure* by The Bodley Head in 1961.

13. *The Brides of Solomon* (stories) Joseph 1958; 1st Amer. Little Brown 1958
14. *Watcher in the Shadows* (novel) Joseph 1960; 1st Amer. Little Brown 1960
15. *Thing to Love* (novel) Joseph 1963; 1st Amer. Little Brown 1963
16. *Olura* (novel) Joseph 1965; 1st Amer. Little Brown 1965
17. *Sabres on the Sand* (stories) Joseph 1966; 1st Amer. Little Brown 1966
18. *Prisoner of the Indies* (juvenile) Bodley Head 1967; 1st Amer. Little Brown 1967
19. *The Courtesy of Death* (novel) Joseph 1967; 1st Amer. Little Brown 1967
20. *Dance of the Dwarfs* (novel) Joseph 1968; 1st Amer. Little Brown 1968
21. *Doom's Caravan* (novel) Joseph 1971; 1st Amer. Little Brown 1971
22. *The Three Sentinels* (novel) Joseph 1972; 1st Amer. Little Brown 1972
23. *The Lives and Times of Bernardo Brown* (novel) Joseph 1973; 1st Amer. Little Brown 1974
24. *Red Anger* (novel) Joseph 1975; 1st Amer. Little Brown 1976
25. *Escape Into Daylight* (juvenile) Bodley Head 1976
26. *Hostage: London* (novel) Joseph 1977; 1st Amer. Little Brown 1977

A degree of the bibliographical fact may be found in his autobiography *Against the Wind* (Joseph 1958; Little Brown 1958).
One very rarely sees Household 1sts— particularly the very early ones. *Rogue Male* is his highlight, and is Grade G–H. Those preceding it would be Grade D. All the others are Grade B, though possibly Nos 6–9 would be higher.

Films:
Manhunt (*Rogue Male*) 20th Century Fox 1941
Brandy for the Parson (story) MGM 1952
Rough Shoot United Artists 1953

HOWARD, Elizabeth Jane
Born in London 1923.

1. *The Beautiful Visit* (novel) Cape 1950; 1st Amer. Random House 1950

2. *We Are for the Dark: Six Ghost Stories* Cape 1951 (with Robert Aickman)
3. *The Long View* (novel) Cape 1956; 1st Amer. Reynal 1956
4. *The Sea Change* (novel) Cape 1959; 1st Amer. Harper 1960
5. *After Julius* (novel) Cape 1965; 1st Amer. Viking Press 1965
6. *Something in Disguise* (novel) Cape 1969; 1st Amer. Viking Press 1970
7. *Odd Girl Out* (novel) Cape 1972; 1st Amer. Viking Press 1972
8. *Mr Wrong* (stories) Cape 1975; 1st Amer. Viking Press 1975

All of these are Grade A, at the moment.

HUGHES, Richard
Born in Surrey 1900. Died 1976.
Hughes published a fair amount of private press material which does not appear here. A list may be found in *The New Cambridge Bibliography of English Literature* vol. 4, and the Golden Cockerel Press items may be found in their own checklist of publications.

1. *The Sister's Tragedy* (play) Blackwell 1922
2. *The Sister's Tragedy and Other Plays* Heinemann 1924 (incl. *The Man Born to be Hanged, A Comedy of Good and Evil* and *Danger*)
   Published in the same year in America by Knopf as *A Rabbit and a Leg: Collected Plays*.
3. *Confessio Juvenis: Collected Poems* Chatto & Windus 1925
4. *A Moment of Time* (stories) Chatto & Windus 1926
5. *A High Wind in Jamaica* (novel) Chatto & Windus 1929
6. *The Innocent Voyage* Harper NY 1929 (same as 5)
7. *Richard Hughes: An Omnibus* (stories, plays and poems) Harper 1931
8. *The Spider's Palace* (juvenile stories) Chatto & Windus 1931; 1st Amer. Harper 1932
9. *In Hazard* (novel) Chatto & Windus 1938; 1st Amer. Harper 1938
10. *Don't Blame Me and Other Stories* (juvenile)

Chatto & Windus 1940; 1st Amer. Harper 1940

11. *The Fox in the Attic* (novel) Chatto & Windus 1961; 1st Amer. Harper 1961
12. *Gertrude's Child* (juvenile) Harlin Quist NY 1966; 1st Eng. Allen 1967
13. *The Wooden Shepherdess* (novel) Chatto & Windus 1973; 1st Amer. Harper 1973
14. *The Wonder-Dog: The Collected Stories* (juvenile) Chatto & Windus 1977

A High Wind in Jamaica is his highlight. It should be pointed out that book publication was preceded by the appearance in *Life and Letters* magazine, and that Chatto published a limited, signed edition simultaneously with the trade edition. This has patterned boards, red spine, is limited to 150 copies, plus seven complimentary, and is Grade I, against the trade edition's Grade B, for it is not a rare book. Nos 1, 2, 3 and 4 are Grade D. No. 9 is Grade C, and the remainder Grade B. Nos 11 and 13 are the first two parts of *The Human Predicament*, alas never to be complete. Interest has increased since Hughes' death, and prices seem likely to rise.

Film:
A High Wind in Jamaica 20th Century Fox 1964

HUGHES, Ted
Born in Yorkshire 1930. One of our foremost living poets, and avidly collected. His early books have been steadily rising in price and decreasing in availability for some years now, the prices reflecting both the quality of the work and its scarcity. Of recent years, however, a vast amount of privately printed, limited, signed, and extraordinarily bound editions have descended upon the market. These editions make it difficult and expensive for the collector to keep up—and, indeed, I have had quite a hard time even cataloguing them. I can only hope that they are all here, so quickly and silently are they published. I know of several Hughes collectors who have opted out of this compulsory purchase of each new ephemeral and expensive item—

and, indeed, this is understandable, for if one possesses Hughes' signature on half-a-dozen limited items, the lure of a seventh might seem irresistible. Nonetheless, any collector worth the name would be prepared to pay quite a lot of money for the true 1sts—such as a *Hawk in the Rain* or *Lupercal*—if one can find them.

1. *The Hawk in the Rain* (verse) Faber 1957; 1st Amer. Harper 1957
2. *Lupercal* (verse) Faber 1960; 1st Amer. Harper 1960
3. *Meet My Folks!* (juvenile) Faber 1961; 1st Amer. Bobbs Merrill 1973
4. *Selected Poems* Faber 1962 (with Thom Gunn)
5. *The Earth-Owl and Other Moon-People* (juvenile) Faber 1963; 1st Amer. Atheneum 1964
6. *How the Whale Became* (juvenile) Faber 1963; 1st Amer. Atheneum 1964
7. *Nessie the Mannerless Monster* (juvenile) Faber 1964; 1st Amer. Chilmark Press 1964
8. *The Burning of the Brothel* (verse) Turret 1966
9. *Recklings* (verse) Turret 1966
10. *Scapegoats and Rabies* (poem) Poet & Printer 1967
11. *Animal Poems* Gilbertson, Crediton 1967
12. *Wodwo* (miscellany) Faber 1967; 1st Amer. Harper 1967
13. *Poetry in the Making* (anthology) Faber 1967
14. *Five Autumn Songs for Children's Voices* Gilbertson 1968
15. *The Iron Man* (juvenile) Faber 1968 Published in America in the same year by Harper as *The Iron Giant*
16. *Seneca's Oedipus* (play trans. and adapt.) Faber 1969; 1st Amer. Doubleday 1972
17. *The Demon of Adachigahara* (musical) OUP 1969 (with Gordon Crosse)
18. *I Said Goodbye to Earth* (poem) Turret 1969
19. *The Martyrdom of Bishop Farrar* (poem) Gilbertson 1969
20. *Poetry Is* Doubleday NY 1970 (same as 13)
21. *The Coming of the Kings and Other Plays* Faber 1970 (incl. *The Tiger's Bones, Beauty and the Beast* and *Sean, the Fool, The Devil and the Cats*)

22. *Crow* (verse) Faber 1970; 1st Amer. Harper 1971
23. *A few Crows* (verse) Rougemont Press 1970
24. *Four Crow Poems* Lloyd 1970
25. *A Crow Hymn* Sceptre Press 1970
26. *Shakespeare's Poems* Lexham Press 1971
27. *Crow Wakes: Poems* Poet & Printer 1971
28. *Poems* Rainbow Press 1971 (with Alan Sillitoe and Ruth Fainlight)
29. *Eat Crow* (verse) Rainbow Press 1971
30. *Crow* (revised ed. of 22) Faber 1972
31. *Selected Poems 1957–1967* Faber 1972; 1st Amer. Harper 1974
32. *In the Little Girl's Angel Gaze* (poem) Steam Press 1972
33. *Prometheus on His Crag* Rainbow Press 1973
34. *The Tiger's Bones* (augmented ed. of 21) Viking Press NY 1973
35. *Crow* (illus. ed. of 30) Faber 1973
36. *The Story of Vasco* (libretto) OUP 1974
37. *Spring, Summer, Autumn, Winter* (verse) Rainbow Press 1974
38. *The Interrogator* (poem) Ilkley Festival 1975
39. *Season Songs* (juvenile verse) Viking Press 1975; 1st Eng. Faber 1976
40. *Earth Moon* (verse) Rainbow Press 1976 200 copies, illustrated, numbered and signed by author. Published at £18 and £22, depending on binding.
41. *Moon-Whales and Other Moon Poems* (juvenile) Viking Press 1976 Illus. Leonard Baskin.
42. *Gaudete* (verse) Faber 1977; 1st Amer. Viking Press 1977

Hughes had three stories in *Introduction* (Faber 1960).
Hughes edited the following:
New Poems 1962 Hutchinson 1962 (with Patricia Beer and Vernon Scannell)
Five American Poets Faber 1963 (with Thom Gunn)
Here Today (anthology) Hutchinson 1963
Keith Douglas *Selected Poems* Faber 1964; 1st Amer. Chilmark Press 1964
A Choice of Emily Dickinson's Verse Faber 1968
A Choice of Shakespeare's Verse Faber 1971

Published in America in the same year by Doubleday as *With Fairest Flowers While Summer Lasts*.
Sylvia Plath *Crossing the Water* Faber 1971; 1st Amer. Harper 1971

Keith Sagar *The Art of Ted Hughes* (Cambridge 1975) is highly recommended. It contains a bibliography, including all magazine and periodical contributions, reviews, etc.

No. 1 is very scarce, and the prized representation of Hughes' work: Grade F–G. Nos 2 and 3 are not much less rare, though 2 would be Grade D–E, and 3 Grade D. No. 4 is a paper-covered edition, and Grade A. Nos 5, 6 and 7 are all quite scarce, and Grade C. The two Turret Press titles—8 and 9—are the first of many private press books. In this case, No. 8 was limited to 150 signed copies, and is Grade F, and No. 9 was limited to 300, 75 signed. This would be Grade C, unsigned, and Grade E–F signed. The Turret Press also issued in 1967 a series of six poster poems (from *Wodwo*), each limited to 40 copies and signed: these would be Grade C–D. No. 10 was limited to 400 copies, and is Grade C, whereas No. 11—the first of Gilbertson's publications—was limited to only 100 copies, each signed. This is Grade F. *Wodwo* is Grade C, although it precedes the Turret poster poems mentioned above. No. 13 was published by Faber Educational Books in laminated boards, without d/w, and sold non-net. It is, for this reason, scarce, and Grade C; No. 20 (the American edition) might be easier to find, although three years later. It was issued in a usual edition, with a Leonard Baskin d/w. No. 14 was limited to 500 copies, 188 signed: this is Grade B unsigned, Grade D signed. No. 15 is quite scarce, and Grade C. No. 16 was issued in hardcover and paper simultaneously, the hardcover being the more difficult: Grade B. No. 17 is Grade B, and No. 18 (a poster poem, limited to 75 signed copies) is Grade C–D. No. 19 is also Grade C–D, though this was limited to 100 signed copies. No. 21 is Grade B, and No. 22—the

original *Crow,* and one of Hughes'
highlights—is Grade B–C. No. 23 begins
the dizzying array of variations
on the *Crow* theme. It was limited to
75 signed copies, and is Grade G; 150
numbered copies were also done, now Grade
D. No. 24 is a silkscreen print in a limited
edition of only 20; Grade G. No. 25 was
limited to 100 copies, 26 signed: Grade D
(unsigned), Grade F (signed). No. 26 was
limited to 150 copies, but only 75 for sale,
and these signed: Grade D–E. No. 27 was
limited to 200 copies, and is Grade D. No.
No. 28 was limited to 300 leather-bound
copies, signed by all three authors. Grade F.
No. 29 was limited to 150 leather-bound
signed copies, with a drawing by Leonard
Baskin: Grade H. No. 30 is Grade A, as is
No. 31. No. 32 is a broadsheet designed by
Ralph Steadman, and limited to 50 signed
copies: Grade F. No. 33 has a frontis. by
Leonard Baskin, and is limited to 160 copies,
signed by author and artist, and morocco-
bound: Grade F–G. No. 34 is Grade A. No.
35 has twelve drawings by Leonard Baskin,
and is limited to 400 copies, signed by author
and artist: Grade H. No. 36 is Grade B. No.
37 is limited to 140 signed copies, and is
Grade I, mainly due to publication price of
£32. No. 38 is Grade B, and Nos 39 and 41
are Grade A.
All the volumes Hughes edited are Grade B,
except the Keith Douglas and Sylvia Plath's
Crossing the Water, which are Grades C and
B–C respectively.

HUME, Fergus
Born in England 1859. Died 1932.
Hume wrote over a hundred books in his
lifetime, though he never recaptured the
phenomenal success of:

The Mystery of a Hansom Cab 1886
This was first published in Australia, by
Kemp & Boyce of Melbourne, in 1886. The
first English edition was published in the
following year by The Hansom Cab
Publishing Company. Both editions were
issued in pictorial wrappers, and are very
scarce—particularly in fine state. The English
edition would be Grade P, and the true 1st—
of which very few copies are known to
exist—might be three times that.

HUXLEY, Aldous
Born in Surrey 1894. Died 1963.
Huxley published over sixty books. Full
details of all of these—including periodical
contributions, etc.—may be found in:
C. J. Eschelbach and J. L. Shober *Aldous
Huxley: A Bibliography 1916–59* (Berkeley 1961)
This is continued in:
T. D. Clareson and C. S. Andrews *Huxley: A
Bibliography 1960–4* (*Extrapolation* 6; 1964)
The most famous work by Huxley, and
certainly his highlight as far as collectors are
concerned, is

Brave New World (novel) Chatto & Windus
1932; 1st Amer. Garden City 1932
This great futuristic novel (which preceded
Orwell's *1984* by seventeen years) is not as
scarce as one might suppose, but it is
particularly difficult in the d/w. In this case,
the presence of a clean, sound d/w could raise
the value from Grade C to Grade F.

The essential and definitive biography:
Sybille Bedford *Aldous Huxley* Vol. 1:
1894–1939 Chatto/Collins 1973; Vol. 2:
1939–63 Chatto/Collins 1974

ISHERWOOD, Christopher
Born in Cheshire 1904.

1. *All the Conspirators* (novel) Cape 1928; 1st
   Amer. New Directions 1958
2. *The Memorial* (novel) Hogarth Press 1932; 1st
   Amer. New Directions 1946
3. *Mr Norris Changes Trains* (novel) Hogarth
   Press 1935
4. *The Last of Mr Norris* Morrow NY 1935
   (same as 3)
5. *The Dog Beneath the Skin* (play) Faber 1935;
   1st Amer. Random House 1935 (with W. H.
   Auden)
6. *The Ascent of F6* (play) Faber 1936; 1st Amer.

Random House 1937 (with W. H. Auden)
7. *Sally Bowles* (novel) Hogarth Press 1937
8. *On The Frontier* (play) Faber 1938; 1st Amer. Random House 1939 (with W. H. Auden)
9. *Lions and Shadows* (prose) Hogarth Press 1938; 1st Amer. New Directions 1948
10. *Goodbye to Berlin* (novel) Hogarth Press 1939; 1st Amer. Random House 1939
11. *Journey to a War* (non-fiction) Faber 1939; 1st Amer. Random House 1939 (with W. H. Auden)
12. *Prater Violet* (novel) Random House 1945; 1st Eng. Methuen 1946
13. *The Berlin Stories* New Directions 1946 (cont. 3, 7 and 10)
14. *The Condor and the Cows* (travel) Random House 1949; 1st Eng. Methuen 1949
15. *The World in the Evening* (novel) Random House 1954; 1st Eng. Methuen 1954
16. *Down There on a Visit* (novel) Simon & Schuster 1962; 1st Eng. Methuen 1962
17. *A Single Man* (novel) Simon & Schuster 1964; 1st Eng. Methuen 1964
18. *Ramakrishna and His Disciples* (non-fiction) Simon & Schuster 1965; 1st Eng. Methuen 1965
19. *Exhumations* (miscellany) Simon & Schuster 1966; 1st Eng. Methuen 1966
20. *A Meeting by the River* (novel) Simon & Schuster 1967; 1st Eng. Methuen 1967
21. *Kathleen and Frank* (biog.) Simon & Schuster 1971; 1st Eng. Methuen 1971
22. *Frankenstein: The True Story* (screenplay) Avon NY 1973
23. *The Berlin of Sally Bowles* Hogarth Press 1975 (same as 13)
24. *Christopher and His Kind* (autobiog.) Simon & Schuster 1977; 1st Eng. Methuen 1977

Isherwood's interest in Vedanta is shown by the two books he wrote—*An Approach to Vedanta* and *Essentials of Vedanta* (both Vedanta Press USA, 1963 and 1969), as well as the two books he edited:
Vedanta and the Western World Rodd 1946; 1st Eng. Allen & Unwin 1948
Vedanta for Modern Man Harper 1951; 1st Eng. Allen & Unwin 1952

No. 1 is very scarce, and Grade I–J. Nos 2 and 3 are also rare, and nice copies in the d/w would be Grade G, although No. 3— probably Isherwood's most famous book— is particularly rare in the d/w, as well as being a highlight, and therefore might rise higher. Nos 5 and 6 are mainly hunted down by Auden collectors, and are Grade D–E. No. 7—*Sally Bowles*—has become very much more popular since the film *Cabaret*, and is a highlight: scarce, and Grade I. No. 8 is also primarily an Auden item, and Grade D, as is No. 11, though this is rarer and Grade E–F. Nos 9 and 10 are Grade F, and No. 12 is Grade B–C.

At this point, the prices descend quite sharply, as all the more recent works are quite common. No. 13 is Grade C, and the rest are Grade B, with the possible exception of *Down There on a Visit*, hailed by many as his best novel. This is Grade B–C at the moment.

Films:
I Am a Camera Monogram 1955 (based on the *Berlin Stories*)
Cabaret Cinerama 1972 (based on *I Am a Camera*)
Frankenstein: The True Story Universal 1973

JARRELL, Randall
Born in Tennessee 1914. Died 1965.
An American poet, whose highlights nonetheless seem to be a volume of criticism and a novel.

1. *Poetry and the Age* (criticism) Knopf 1953; 1st Eng. Faber 1955
2. *Pictures from an Institution* (novel) Knopf 1954; 1st Eng. Faber 1954

The *Complete Poems* were first published by Farrar Straus NY in 1969.
Nos 1 and 2 are Grade C, and Grade B in the Faber editions.

JELLICOE, Ann
Born in Yorkshire 1927.

She has published a dozen or more works, but is notable for the following:

1. *The Sport of My Mad Mother* (play) Faber 1958
This was published in *The Observer Plays* along with other plays, including N. F. Simpson's *A Resounding Tinkle*. The Preface is by Kenneth Tynan. Grade B.
2. *The Knack* (play) Encore 1962; 1st Amer. French 1962
Quite scarce. Grade B.

Two Plays: The Knack and The Sport of My Mad Mother was published in America by Dell in 1964.

Film:
The Knack United Artists 1965

JENNINGS, Elizabeth
Born in Lincolnshire 1926.

1. *Poems* Fantasy Press 1953
2. *A Way of Looking: Poems* Deutsch 1955; 1st Amer. Rinehart 1956
3. *A Sense of the World: Poems* Deutsch 1958; 1st Amer. Rinehart 1959
4. *Let's Have Some Poetry* (prose) Museum Press 1960
5. *Song for a Birth or a Death* (verse) Deutsch 1961; 1st Amer. Dufour 1962
6. *Every Changing Shape* (prose) Deutsch 1961
7. *Recoveries: Poems* Deutsch 1964; 1st Amer. Dufour 1964
8. *Frost* (criticism) Oliver & Boyd 1964; 1st Amer. Barnes & Noble 1965
9. *Christianity and Poetry* (prose) Burnes & Oates 1965
This was published in America in the same year by Hawthorn Books as *Christian Poetry*.
10. *The Mind Has Mountains* (verse) Macmillan 1966; 1st Amer. St Martin's Press 1966
11. *The Secret Brother* (children's verse) Macmillan 1966; 1st Amer. St Martin's Press 1966
12. *Collected Poems 1967* Macmillan 1967; 1st Amer. Dufour 1967
13. *The Animals' Arrival* (verse) Macmillan 1969; 1st Amer. Dufour 1969
14. *Lucidities* (verse) Macmillan 1970
15. *Relationships* (verse) Macmillan 1972
16. *Growing-Points* (verse) Carcanet Press 1975
17. *Seven Men of Vision: An Appreciation* (non-fiction) Vision Press 1976
18. *New Poems* Carcanet Press 1977

Elizabeth Jennings has edited the following:
New Poems 1956 Joseph 1956 (with Dannie Abse and Stephen Spender)
The Batsford Book of Children's Verse Batsford 1958
An Anthology of Modern Verse 1940–1960 Methuen 1961
A Choice of Christina Rossetti's Verse Faber 1970

She translated *The Sonnets of Michaelangelo* (Folio Society 1961). A revised edition was published by Allison & Busby in 1969, and in America by Doubleday in 1970.
The early books by Elizabeth Jennings are scarce. Particularly so is the first: this Fantasy Press publication is a slim, wrappered booklet, and would now reach Grade D. Nos 2–7 are Grade B, as are Nos 9–13 and 17. No. 8 and the most recent volumes are Grade A.

JEROME, Jerome K.
Born in Staffordshire 1859. Died 1927
The fact that only Jerome's two or three most popular works are still in print would seem to indicate that there is little interest in him any more, but this could not be farther from the truth. The scarce Jerome items—and there are quite a few—are avidly hunted, and prices are going up. A complete Jerome collection is a rare thing, one of the reasons being that no-one admits to knowing exactly how many books he published. *The Cambridge Bibliography of English Literature*, no less, follows an incomplete list of his prose with a statement to the effect that Jerome wrote a lot of plays, some of which were published. A short bibliography has been published (Robert G. Logan *Jerome K. Jerome: A Concise Bibliography* Walsall Libraries 1971), and it is certainly the best checklist of Jerome to have appeared, listing periodical contributions etc., but even Logan, in his

Introduction, says: 'Various factors have conspired to make this bibliography less comprehensive and possibly less accurate than I would have wished . . .'.

The following list is the nearest *I* can come.

1. *On the Stage—And Off* (pieces) Field & Tuer 1885
   This tiny book (about four inches by three) was soon followed by an illustrated edition (Leadenhall Press, illus. by Kenneth M. Skeaping)
2. *Barbara* (play) Lacy 1886
3. *The Idle Thoughts of an Idle Fellow* (essays) Field & Tuer 1886
   The earliest editions make no mention of 'edition' on cover.
4. *Sunset* (play) Fitzgerald NY n.d.
5. *Fennel* (play) French n.d.
6. *Woodbarrow Farm* (play) French n.d.
7. *Stage-Land* (satire) Chatto & Windus 1889
8. *Three Men in a Boat* (novel) Arrowsmith 1889
   The obvious highlight, but a tricky 1st to spot. Essentially, though all early editions are dated 1889, the very earliest do not have '11 Quay Street' as the publisher's address at the foot of t/p, but simply 'Quay Street'.
9. *Told After Supper* (essays) Leadenhall Press 1891
10. *The Diary of a Pilgrimage* (novel) Arrowsmith 1891
    Earliest editions also contain six essays, and make no mention of edition on cover.
11. *Novel Notes* (articles) Leadenhall Press 1893
12. *John Ingerfield* (stories) McClure 1894
13. *My First Book* (essays, with other writers) Chatto & Windus 1894
    Blue cloth. The 1897 red-bound edition is often mistaken for the 1st.
14. *The Prude's Progress* (play) French 1895
15. *Sketches in Lavender, Blue and Green* (stories) Longman 1897
16. *The Second Thoughts of an Idle Fellow* Hurst & Blackett 1898
17. *Three Men on the Bummel* (novel) Arrowsmith 1900
18. *The Observations of Henry* (stories) Arrowsmith 1901
19. *Miss Hobbs* (play) French 1902
20. *Paul Kelver* (novel) Hutchinson 1902
21. *Tea-Table Talk* (essays) Hutchinson 1903
22. *Tommy and Co.* (novel) Hutchinson 1904
23. *American Wives and Others* (essays) Stokes 1904
    A miscellany published only in U.S.A.
24. *Idle Ideas in 1905* (essays) Hurst & Blackett 1905
25. *The Passing of the Third Floor Back* (essays, stories) Hurst & Blackett 1907
26. *The Angel and the Author* (essays) Hurst & Blackett 1908
27. *They and I* (novel) Hutchinson 1909
28. *Fanny and the Servant Problem* (play) Lacy 1909
29. *The Passing of the Third Floor Back* (play) Hurst & Blackett 1910
30. *The Master of Mrs Chilvers* (play) T. Fisher Unwin 1911
31. *Robina in Search of a Husband* (play) Lacy 1914
32. *Malvina of Brittany* (stories) Cassell 1916
33. *All Roads Lead to Calvary* (novel) Hutchinson 1919
34. *Anthony John* (novel) Cassell 1923
35. *A Miscellany of Sense and Nonsense* Arrowsmith 1923
36. *The Celebrity* (play) Hodder & Stoughton 1926
37. *The Soul of Nicholas Synders* (play) Hodder & Stoughton 1927
38. *My Life and Times* (autobiog.) Hodder & Stoughton 1926

Contributions by Jerome are included in: *Humours of Cycling* (ed. James Bowden) Chatto & Windus 1905

Jerome also edited two magazines, *The Idler* and *Today*. *The Idler* was founded in 1892 by Robert Barr, who offered Jerome the joint editorship. They edited it until 1898, although the magazine ran until 1911. *The Idler* was issued in bound volumes, which are now Grade B each.

Today was a weekly founded by Jerome himself in 1893. He edited it until 1898 and the magazine ran until 1905, when it merged with *London Opinion*. Bound volumes of *Today* were also published, but these are much more scarce than *The Idler*, and Grade C.

The list above is of English 1st editions, though it should be noted that in America No. 17 was published as *Three Men on Wheels,* No. 32 as *The Street of the Blank Wall,* No. 28 as *Lady Bantock* and No. 36 as *Cook.*

All of Jerome's books are scarce, though some very much more than others. Although the plays are particularly difficult, however, these do not command a very high price, I suppose because of their popularity in relation to his better-known humorous works. Nos 4, 5, 6, 10, 11, 14, 16, 19, 21, 24, 26, 27, 28, 29, 30, 31, 32, 33, 34, 35, 36 and 37 are Grade B. Nos 2, 3, 7, 9, 12, 13, 15, 17, 18, 20, 22, 23, 25 and 38 are Grade C. No. 1 was paper-covered and is very scarce. Grade E.

No. 8, the highlight, is not particularly rare in 1st edition, but in 1st state or issue. Any Arrowsmith edition dated 1889 is Grade B, but if the 1st issue (see No. 8 for basic explanation) Grade D–E.

In addition to the above-mentioned bibliography, the following might be of interest:

Ruth Marie Faurot *Jerome K. Jerome* Twayne NY 1974

Films:
The Passing of the Third Floor Back Gaumont British 1936
Three Men in a Boat British Lion 1956

JOHNS, W. E.
Born in Hertford 1893. Died 1968.
A very large number of stories concerning the famous character Biggles were published, most of the earlier ones having been published by Oxford. Johns' first book, however, was:

1. *The Camels Are Coming* (novel) J. Hamilton 1932
   and the first Biggles followed two years later:
2. *Biggles of the Camel Squadron* (novel) J. Hamilton 1934

Either of these would be Grade B–C, though other Biggles titles would probably be Grade A.

JONES, David
Born 1895. Died 1974.

1. *In Parenthesis* Faber 1937; 1st Amer. Chilmark 1961
   Although the Amer. ed. is 24 years after the English, it contains an Intro. by T. S. Eliot, reprinted in the first English paperback edition (Faber 1963).
2. *The Anathemata* Faber 1952; 1st Amer. Chilmark 1963
3. *Epoch and Artist* Faber 1959; 1st Amer. Chilmark 1964
4. *The Tribune's Visitation* Fulcrum Press 1969
5. *The Sleeping Lord* Faber 1974
6. *The Kensington Mass* Agenda Editions 1975
7. *Letters to Vernon Watkins* University of Wales Press 1976

d/ws are extremely important with David Jones, as those of Nos 2, 3, 4 and 5 bear his exquisite typography. No. 1 is Grade G–H, No. 2 Grade E, No. 3 Grade D, No. 4 Grade C, and Nos 5 and 6 Grade A–B.

There have been two *Agenda* special numbers devoted to David Jones (Vol. 5 Nos 1–3 1967, and Vol. 11 No. 4–Vol. 12 No. 1 1973/74), and one slight book on his art (Penguin Modern Painters 1949); it is one of the most scarce of the series, and Grade B. One book of literary criticism has appeared: David Blamires *David Jones, Artist and Writer* (Manchester University Press 1971). (See also Raine, K., No. 25.)

In 1975, The Tablet published Peter Levi *In Memory of David Jones.* The d/w and frontis. of Peter Levi *Fresh Water, Sea Water* (Black Raven Press 1966) reproduces Jones' superb design for Levi's ordination certificate.

JOYCE, James
Born in Ireland 1882. Died 1941.
For a major writer, Joyce published comparatively few titles, but they were done in many editions, particularly *Ulysses,* most of which are 1sts in one way or another. For example, a work first published in English in Paris would be the 1st edition, but the very

same text published later for the first time in England would also constitute a desirable collector's item. In short, collecting Joyce—though very worthwhile—can be a confusing and expensive pursuit, and the following work is not merely recommended—it is absolutely essential:
John J. Slocum and Herbert Cahoon *A Bibliography of James Joyce* (Yale University Press, USA 1953)
Below are 1st and some other notable editions of Joyce's major work.

1. *Chamber Music* (poems) Elkin Mathews 1907; 1st Amer. Cornhill Co. 1918
   This edition was unauthorized. The authorized edition was published in the same year by Huebsch.
2. *Dubliners* (stories) Grant Richards 1914; 1st Amer. Huebsch 1916
3. *A Portrait of the Artist as a Young Man* Huebsch 1916; 1st Eng. Egoist Ltd 1917
   The 1st English was American sheets. In the following year The Egoist Ltd published a 2nd edition, printed in England.
4. *Exiles* (play) Grant Richards 1918; 1st Amer. Huebsch 1918
   This play was reissued in 1951 by the Viking Press 'with hitherto unpublished notes by the author'. This was published in England by Cape in 1952.
5. *Ulysses* (novel) Shakespeare Press, Paris 1922
   Limited to 1000 copies, 100 signed. Published in France.
6. *Ulysses* Egoist Press 1922
   This was the 1st English edition, though printed in France. Limited to 2000 numbered copies.
7. *Ulysses* Shakespeare Press, Paris 1929
   This was the 1st American edition, though unauthorized. The 1st authorized American edition was published in 1934 by Random House, though set up from the Shakespeare edition. The first printing of the Random House ed., due to copyright, was only 100 copies, and the second printing 10,300.
8. *Ulysses* Bodley Head 1936
   This was the 1st English edition actually printed in England.
9. *Pomes Penyeach* Shakespeare & Co, Paris 1927
   The 1st American edition was published by Sylvia Beach in 1931. The 1st English edition—but printed in France—was by the Obelisk Press in 1932, and the 1st English edition printed in England was by Faber in 1933.
10. *Anna Livia Plurabelle* (fragment) Crosby Gaige NY 1928; 1st Eng. Faber 1930
    The American ed. was limited to 850 signed copies, but the Faber ed. was in the Criterion Miscellany series, and unlimited.
11. *Tales Told of Shem and Shaun* Black Sun Press, Paris 1929
    Limited to 650 copies, 100 signed.
12. *Two Tales of Shem and Shaun* Faber 1932
    Extract from No. 11. 1st English.
13. *Haveth Childers Everywhere* (fragment) Fountain Press 1930
    Printed in France, but published in America. Limited to 685 copies, 100 signed. The 1st English edition was published by Faber in the following year, in an unlimited edition.
14. *Collected Poems* Black Sun Press NY 1936
    Limited to 800 copies, 50 signed. A trade edition followed in 1937 from the Viking Press.
15. *Finnegans Wake* Faber 1939; 1st Amer. Viking Press 1939
16. *Stephen Hero* (draft) Cape 1944; 1st Amer. New Directions 1944
17. *The Essential James Joyce* (extracts) Cape 1948
18. *The Letters* Vol. I Faber 1957
19. *The Critical Writings* Faber 1959
20. *The Cat and the Devil* (juvenile) Faber 1965
21. *The Letters* Vol. II Faber 1966
22. *The Letters* Vol. III Faber 1966
23. *Giacomo Joyce* Viking Press 1968 1st Eng. Faber 1968

There have been a vast number of books on Joyce, but below appears a selection of the best:
T. S. Eliot *Introducting James Joyce* Faber 1942
Harry Levin *James Joyce: A Critical Introduction* Faber 1944
Richard Ellmann *James Joyce* OUP 1959

Anthony Burgess *Here Comes Everybody* Faber 1965
John Gross *Joyce* Fontana 1971
A good deal of information is also given in Stanislaus Joyce *My Brother's Keeper*. This was edited by Richard Ellmann, and has a Preface by T. S. Eliot (Faber 1958).

Firstly, it must be said that anything signed by Joyce is worth a great deal of money. Those limited editions, therefore, bearing his signature always cost hundreds of pounds. I shall try to be more explicit further on, but prices are rising so rapidly, and booksellers disagree quite strongly on values, this making a price guide particularly difficult. No. 1 would be Grade Q, Nos 2 and 3, Grade P and over. No. 4 is not so scarce as other early items, and Grade G. As regards *Ulysses,* No. 5, the actual 1st, would be around £300, though probably twice that, at least, if one of the signed copies. No. 6 is Grade P. No. 7 is Grade I–J, but the Random House ed. is Grade F. No. 8 was the first to bear the Eric Gill 'bow' design, and 1000 copies were printed, 100 of which were signed; one of these would now be about £500–£600, and one of the 900 Grade P. No. 9 is Grade K–L, and the Faber ed. Grade E. The American limited ed. of No. 10 would be Grade Q and over, but Grade C for the Faber ed. Of No. 11, one of the signed copies would be about £200, and unsigned Grade N; No. 12 (the Faber ed.) is Grade C. No. 13 would also be around £200 for the signed ed., but Grade K unsigned. The Faber ed. is Grade C. No. 14 is in the same situation. No. 15 is Grade L, and Grade J for the American ed. Nos 16, 19 and 23 are Grade C, Nos 17 and 20 are Grade B, and the three volumes of letters are Grade E–F. A selection from these three volumes, with one or two new ones, was published by Faber in 1976 at £12·50. Of the books on Joyce, the Gross is well within Grade A, the Eliot, Levin and Burgess are Grade B, and the Ellmann Grade C.

Films:
Ulysses British Lion 1966

Passages from Finnegans Wake Expanding Cinema 1965

KÄSTNER, Erich
Born in Germany 1899. Died 1974.
Author of several books, but remembered for one great highlight:

Emil and the Detectives (juvenile) Cape 1930; 1st Amer. Doubleday 1930
This was first published in Germany in 1929 as *Emil und die Detektive*. The 1st English edition is scarce, and Grade C–D.

Film:
Emil and the Detectives United Artists 1931; Disney 1965

KAZANTZAKIS, Nikos
Born in Greece 1885. Died 1957.
Author of several books, though notable for the following:

Zorba the Greek (novel) Lehmann 1952; 1st Amer. Simon & Schuster 1953
The novel was originally published in Greek in 1946. The Lehmann edition spells his name Kazantzaki. It is scarce. Grade D.

Film:
Zorba the Greek 20th Century Fox 1964

KEROUAC, Jack
Born in Massachusetts 1922. Died 1969.
Notable particularly for the following three books:

1. *On the Road* Viking Press 1957; 1st Eng. Deutsch 1958
2. *The Dharma Bums* Viking Press 1958; 1st Eng. Deutsch 1959
3. *Big Sur* Farrar Straus 1962; 1st Eng. Deutsch 1963

No. 1 is Grade C–D, No. 2 Grade B–C, and No. 3 Grade B.

KESEY, Ken
Born in Colorado 1935.
Although he has published many stories in

various journals, Kesey has written only two novels, one of which has recently made his name very much better known by being turned into a highly successful, Oscar-scooping film.

1. *One Flew over the Cuckoo's Nest* (novel) Viking Press 1962; 1st Eng. Methuen 1963
2. *Sometimes a Great Notion* (novel) Viking Press 1964; 1st Eng. Methuen 1966

The American 1st of *Cuckoo* would be Grade D, English Grade B, and No. 2 is Grade B.

Film:
One Flew over the Cuckoo's Nest United Artists 1975

KOESTLER, Arthur
British. Born in Hungary 1905.

1. *Spanish Testament* (autobiog.) Gollancz 1937 This is the orange-wrapped Left Book Club edition. An abridged edition was published in America by Macmillan in 1942 as *Dialogue with Death*.
2. *The Gladiators* (novel) Cape 1939; 1st Amer. Macmillan 1939
3. *Darkness at Noon* (novel) Cape 1940; 1st Amer. Macmillan 1941
4. *Scum of the Earth* (autobiog.) Cape 1941; 1st Amer. Macmillan 1941
5. *Arrival and Departure* (novel) Cape 1943; 1st Amer. Macmillan 1943
6. *The Yogi and the Commissar* (essays) Cape 1945; 1st Amer. Macmillan 1945
7. *Thieves in the Night* (novel) Macmillan 1946; 1st Amer. Macmillan 1946
8. *Insight and Outlook* (essay) Macmillan 1949; 1st Amer. Macmillan 1949
9. *Promise and Fulfilment* (non-fiction) Macmillan 1949; 1st Amer. Macmillan 1949
10. *The Age of Longing* (novel) Collins 1951; 1st Amer. Macmillan 1951
11. *Arrow in the Blue* (autobiog.) Collins/Hamilton 1952; 1st Amer. Macmillan 1952
12. *The Invisible Writing* (autobiog.) Collins/Hamilton 1954; 1st Amer. Macmillan 1954
13. *The Trail of the Dinosaur* (essays) Collins 1955; 1st Amer. Macmillan 1955
14. *Reflections on Hanging* (essay) Gollancz 1957; 1st Amer. Macmillan 1957
15. *The Sleepwalkers* (non-fiction) Hutchinson 1959; 1st Amer. Macmillan 1959
16. *The Lotus and the Robot* (essays) Hutchinson 1960; 1st Amer. Macmillan 1961
17. *Hanged by the Neck* (essay) Penguin 1961
18. *The Act of Creation* (non-fiction) Hutchinson 1964; 1st Amer. Macmillan 1964
19. *The Ghost in the Machine* (non-fiction) Hutchinson 1967; 1st Amer. Macmillan 1968
20. *Drinkers of Infinity: Essays 1955–1967* Hutchinson 1968; 1st Amer. Macmillan 1969
21. *The Case of the Midwife Toad* (non-fiction) Hutchinson 1971; 1st Amer. Random House 1972
22. *The Call-Girls* (novel) Hutchinson 1972; 1st Amer. Random House 1973
23. *The Roots of Coincidence* (non-fiction) Hutchinson 1972; 1st Amer. Random House 1972
24. *The Lion and the Ostrich* (essay) OUP 1973
25. *The Challenge of Chance* (non-fiction) Hutchinson 1973; 1st Amer. Random House 1975 (with Alister Hardy and Robert Harvie)
26. *The Heel of Achilles: Essays 1968–1973* Hutchinson 1974; 1st Amer. Random House 1975
27. *The Thirteenth Tribe* (non-fiction) Hutchinson 1976; 1st Amer. Random House 1976

Darkness at Noon is the highlight, and quite scarce: Grade C. Virtually all the others are Grade B, and sometimes less.

LANCASTER, Osbert
Born in England 1908.
Lancaster has illustrated very many books, and has designed d/ws and paperback covers for even more. This list is limited to books he has written—all of which, incidentally, are illustrated and have d/ws by him. The small volumes of 'Pocket Cartoons' have been appearing since 1940, but these have not been listed. It might be noted that recently Murray have taken to issuing very limited editions—

specially bound, and signed—simultaneously with the trade edition.

1. *Our Sovereigns: From Alfred to Edward VIII* Murray 1936
2. *Progress at Pelvis Bay* Murray 1936
3. *Pillar to Post* Murray 1938; 1st Amer. Scribner 1939
4. *Homes Sweet Homes* Murray 1939; 1st Amer. Transatlantic 1939
5. *Classical Landscape with Figures* Murray 1947; 1st Amer. Houghton 1949
6. *The Saracen's Head* Murray 1948; 1st Amer. Houghton 1949
7. *Draynflete Revealed* Murray 1949
8. *There'll Always be a Draynflete* Houghton 1950 (same as 7)
9. *Facades and Faces* Murray 1950; 1st Amer. Musson 1950
10. *All Done from Memory* Murray 1953; 1st Amer. Houghton 1953
11. *Here, of All Places* Houghton 1958; 1st Eng. Murray 1959 (incl. 3 and 4)
12. *A Cartoon History of Architecture* (extracts) Houghton 1964
13. *With an Eye to the Future* Murray 1967; 1st Amer. Houghton 1967
14. *Sailing to Byzantium* Murray 1969; 1st Amer. Gambit 1969
15. *The Littlehampton Bequest* Murray 1973; 1st Amer. Gambit 1974

No. 1 is Grade C, Nos 2–9 are Grade B, and Nos 10–15 are Grade A.

LARKIN, Philip

Born in Warwickshire 1922. Larkin has published very few books of verse, but each has been ecstatically received, and his reputation is extremely fine, some even ranking him as our finest living poet. Many people want his work, therefore, and the collector finds nothing but high prices wherever he looks—*if* he can find the books at all. All are scarce, and even his latest work, published in 1974, is becoming difficult to find.

1. *The North Ship* (verse) Fortune Press 1945

If the verso of the Contents page reads 'First Published 1945', then, confusingly, the book you are handling is *not* the 1st edition—but nonetheless a desirable, finely-printed, Fortune Press item. A revised edition was published by Faber in 1966.
2. *Jill* (novel) Fortune Press 1946
A revised edition was published in 1964 by Faber, and in America by the St Martin's Press.
3. *A Girl in Winter* (novel) Faber 1947; 1st Amer. St Martin's Press 1957
4. *Poems* Fantasy Press 1954
5. *The Less Deceived* (verse) Marvell Press 1955; 1st Amer. St Martin's Press 1960
6. *The Whitsun Weddings* (verse) Faber 1964; 1st Amer. Random House 1964
7. *All What Jazz: A Record Diary 1961–68* Faber 1970; 1st Amer. St Martin's Press 1970
8. *The Oxford Book of Twentieth-Century English Verse* OUP 1973
This very important book was edited by Larkin.
9. *High Windows* (verse) Faber 1974; 1st Amer. Farrar Straus 1974

Larkin also wrote the Preface for *The Arts Council Collection of Modern Literary Manuscripts 1963–1972* (Turret Books 1974), a fascinating and valuable book in itself.
A useful study is David Timms *Philip Larkin* (Oliver & Boyd 1973; Barnes & Noble 1974).
No. 1 is Grade J–K. Nos 2 and 3 are Grade G, and Nos 4 and 5 are Grade F. No. 6—a veritable highlight—is Grade D–E, and the rest are Grade B.

LAWRENCE, D. H.

Born in Nottinghamshire 1885. Died 1930. There is a very good bibliography, essential to all Lawrence collectors:
Warren Roberts *A Bibliography of D. H. Lawrence* (Soho Bibliographies, Hart-Davis 1963)
Below is all his main work, though I have omitted a few privately printed items, special editions, etc. In some cases, however—notably

Lady Chatterley's Lover—there are several relevant editions, and these have been included.

1. *The White Peacock* (novel) Duffield NY 1911; 1st Eng. Heinemann 1911
2. *The Trespasser* (novel) Duckworth 1912; 1st Amer. Kennerley 1912
3. *Love Poems and Others* Duckworth 1913; 1st Amer. Kennerley 1913
4. *Sons and Lovers* (novel) Duckworth 1913; 1st Amer. Kennerley 1913
5. *The Widowing of Mrs Holroyd* (play) Kennerley 1914; 1st Eng. Duckworth 1914
6. *The Prussian Officer* (stories) Duckworth 1914; 1st Amer. Huebsch 1916
7. *The Rainbow* (novel) Methuen 1915; 1st Amer. Huebsch 1916
8. *Twilight in Italy* (travel) Duckworth 1916; 1st Amer. Huebsch 1916
9. *Amores* (verse) Duckworth 1916; 1st Amer. Huebsch 1916
10. *New Poems* Secker 1918; 1st Amer. Huebsch 1920
11. *The Lost Girl* (novel) Secker 1920; 1st Amer. Seltzer 1921
12. *Women in Love* (novel) Secker 1921
    This was the 1st trade edition.
13. *Sea and Sardinia* (travel) Seltzer 1921; 1st Eng. Secker 1923
14. *Aaron's Rod* (novel) Seltzer 1922; 1st Eng. Secker 1922
15. *Fantasia of the Unconscious* (non-fiction) Seltzer 1922; 1st Eng. Secker 1923
16. *England, My England* (essays) Seltzer 1922; 1st Eng. Secker 1924
17. *The Ladybird* (novelettes) Secker 1923 (incl. *The Fox* and *The Captain's Doll*)
18. *The Captain's Doll* Seltzer 1923 (same as 17)
19. *Kangaroo* (novel) Secker 1923; 1st Amer. Seltzer 1923
20. *Birds, Beasts and Flowers* (verse) Seltzer 1923; 1st Eng. Secker 1923
21. *The Boy in the Bush* (novel) Secker 1924; 1st Amer. Seltzer 1924
22. *The Plumed Serpent* (novel) Secker 1926; 1st Amer. Knopf 1926
23. *David* (play) Secker 1926; 1st Amer. Knopf 1926
24. *Mornings in Mexico* (travel) Secker 1927; 1st Amer. Knopf 1927
25. *The Woman Who Rode Away* (stories) Secker 1928; 1st Amer. Knopf 1928
26. *Lady Chatterley's Lover* (novel) privately printed 1928
    Printed and published in Florence.
27. *Lady Chatterley's Lover* Secker 1932; Knopf 1932
    These are the first English and American *expurgated* editions.
28. *Lady Chatterley's Lover* Grove Press 1959; Penguin 1960; Heinemann 1961
    These are the first American and English *unexpurgated* editions, the Penguin following the infamous trial. The Heinemann edition is really a hardback version of the Penguin.
29. *Collected Poems* (2 vols) Secker 1928
30. *Pornography and Obscenity* (essay) Faber 1929
31. *Pansies* (verse) Secker 1929
32. *Nettles* (verse) Faber 1930
33. *The Virgin and the Gypsy* (novel) Secker 1930; 1st Amer. Knopf 1930
    These were preceded by a limited edition published by Orioli, Florence.
34. *The Man Who Died* (novelette) Secker 1931
    This had been published as *The Escaped Cock* in Paris in 1929.
35. *The Letters* (ed. Aldous Huxley) Heinemann 1932
36. *The Lovely Lady* (stories) Secker 1933; 1st Amer. Viking Press 1933
37. *Last Poems* Secker 1933
38. *The Plays* Secker 1933
39. *The Tales* Secker 1934
40. *A Collier's Friday Night* (play) Secker 1934
41. *Pornography and So On* (essay) Faber 1936
42. *Poems* (2 vols) Heinemann 1939
43. *The Complete Poems* (3 vols) Heinemann 1957
44. *The Complete Poems* (2 vols) Heinemann 1964
45. *The Complete Plays* Heinemann 1965

The books and articles on Lawrence number many hundreds, and continue to be published. Two of the most important are: Harry T. Moore *The Intelligent Heart* Heinemann 1955
(revised ed.: *The Priest of Love* Heinemann 1974)

Richard Aldington *Portrait of a Genius, but . . .*
Heinemann 1950

No. 1 would be Grade M, and Nos 2, 3, 4, 6
and 7 are Grade H–I. Nos 5, 8, 9, 10 and 11
are Grade F–G. The Secker ed. of No. 12 is
Grade C, and Nos 13, 14, 15, 16 are Grade
E. Nos 17, 18, 19, 21 and 22 are Grade F.
Nos 20 and 23 are Grade E, as is No. 24. No.
25 is Grade D. As to *Lady Chatterley,* No. 26
is Grade R, No. 27 is Grade G, and No. 28
Grade B.
Nos 29, 31, 33, 34, 37, 40 are Grade D. Nos
30, 32, 35, 36, 38, 39, 42, 43 and 44 are
Grade C. No. 41 is Grade B, as is No. 45.

Films:
The Rocking Horse Winner (story) Two Cities
1949
Lady Chatterley's Lover Columbia 1956
Sons and Lovers 20th Century Fox 1960
The Fox Warner Bros 1968
Women in Love United Artists 1969
The Virgin and the Gypsy London
Screenplays 1971

LAWRENCE, T. E.

Born in Caernarvonshire 1888. Died 1935.
Variously known as J. H. Ross, T. E. Shaw
and T. E. Lawrence, he is very difficult and
expensive to collect seriously, though trade
editions of his major works may be
acquired quite easily, and usually at
surprisingly low prices.
*The New Cambridge Bibliography of English
Literature* vol. 4 lists all of Lawrence's works,
and gives a few bibliographies, but these all
seem to have been limited editions, or
duplicated in small numbers.
Below are the major works.

1. *Revolt in the Desert* Cape 1927; 1st Amer.
   Doran 1927
   The ordinary trade edition is Grade C,
   though there were simultaneous limited
   editions—of 315 and 250 copies, respectively,
   in England and America.
2. *Seven Pillars of Wisdom* Cape 1936; 1st Amer.
   Doubleday 1936

This, it must be noted, is the first *trade*
edition, and Grade C. The 1st edition was
privately printed in Oxford in 1922 in an
edition of 8 copies. It was printed again in
1925, privately, in a revised edition of 100
copies, and once more, in 1926—text
completely revised, with a new prefatory
note—privately printed in England and
America in editions of 202 and 22 copies,
respectively.
3. *The Letters of T. E. Lawrence* Cape 1938; 1st
   Amer. Doubleday 1939
   Edited by David Garnett. Grade C. Garnett
   also edited *The Essential T. E. Lawrence* (Cape
   1951).
4. *The Mint* Cape 1955; 1st Amer. Doubleday 1955
   Once more, this is the first *trade* edition, and
   Grade B. It was first published in New York
   in 1936 in an edition of 50.

There are a vast number of books on
Lawrence, though no definitive biography
has yet emerged. One outstanding title is:
Robert Graves *Lawrence and the Arabs* Cape
1927
Published by Doubleday in America in 1928
as *Lawrence and the Arabian Adventure.*

Film:
Lawrence of Arabia British Lion 1962 (*Seven
Pillars of Wisdom*)

LEACOCK, Stephen

Born in Hampshire 1869. Died 1944. Parents
emigrated to Canada.
Although the author of many serious
works—*Elements of Political Science* (1906), to
give an example—he is remembered for his
humorous works. There are a great number
of these, and collectors have recently shown
fair interest in them. The early titles, such as
the two examples quoted below, might reach
Grade C, but generally speaking, Grade A–B
is the norm.

1. *Literary Lapses* Dodd 1910; 1st Eng. Lane 1910
2. *Moonbeams from the Larger Lunacy* Lane 1915;
   1st Eng. Lane 1915

le CARRÉ, John

Pseudonym of David Cornwell. Born in Dorset in 1931.

1. *Call for the Dead* (novel) Gollancz 1960; 1st Amer. Walker 1962
2. *A Murder of Quality* (novel) Gollancz 1962; 1st Amer. Walker 1963
3. *The Spy Who Came In from the Cold* (novel) Gollancz 1963; 1st Amer. Coward McCann 1963
4. *The Looking-Glass War* (novel) Heinemann 1965; 1st Amer. Coward McCann 1965
5. *A Small Town in Germany* (novel) Heinemann 1968; 1st Amer. Coward McCann 1968
6. *The Naive and Sentimental Lover* (novel) Hodder & Stoughton 1971; 1st Amer. Knopf 1971
7. *Tinker, Tailor, Soldier, Spy* (novel) Hodder & Stoughton 1974; 1st Amer. Knopf 1974

No. 3 is the highlight, and reprinted four or five times *before* publication; hence scarce, and Grade C. Nos 1 and 2, though little known, are hard to come by, and also Grade C. The rest are Grade A, with the possible exception of No. 7, which was reprinted very quickly, and might now be Grade B.

Films:
The Spy Who Came In from the Cold Paramount 1963
The Deadly Affair British Lion 1966 (*Call for the Dead*)
The Looking-Glass War Columbia 1969

LEE, Laurie

Born in Gloucestershire 1914.

1. *The Sun My Monument* (verse) Hogarth Press 1944; 1st Amer. Doubleday 1947
2. *Land at War* (non-fiction) HMSO 1945
3. *We Made a Film in Cyprus* (with Ralph Keene) Longman 1947
4. *The Bloom of Candles* (verse) Lehmann 1947
5. *Peasant's Priest* (play) Goulden, Canterbury 1947
6. *The Voyage of Magellan* (play) Lehmann 1948
7. *My Many-Coated Man* (verse) Deutsch 1955; 1st Amer. Coward McCann 1957
8. *A Rose for Winter* (travel) Hogarth Press 1955; 1st Amer. Morrow 1956
9. *Cider with Rosie* (autobiog.) Hogarth Press 1959
10. *The Edge of Day* Morrow 1960 (same as 9)
11. *Poems* Studio Vista 1960
12. *Man Must Move* (juvenile) Rathbone 1960
13. *The Wonderful World of Transportation* Doubleday 1961 (same as 12)
14. *As I Walked Out One Midsummer Morning* (autobiog.) Deutsch 1969; 1st Amer. Atheneum 1969
15. *I Can't Stay Long* (pieces) Deutsch 1975; 1st Amer. Atheneum 1975

No. 9, and its sequel No. 14, are the highlights here, and Grade C and B respectively. No. 1 is Grade D, Nos 2–7 are Grade C, and the rest Grade B.

LEHMANN, John

Born in Buckinghamshire 1907.
Important mainly for his fine work in publishing and editing. Once partner in the Hogarth Press, he founded John Lehmann Ltd, which published quite a few of the books mentioned in this volume. He then founded *New Writing, Daylight, Penguin New Writing* and *The London Magazine*. Between them, these publications printed the work of just about everybody, many single issues having become collectors' items, although sets are pursued as well. Particularly collected lately is the *Penguin New Writing* (40 vols, 1936–50), a nice run being Grade I.
Also of note is his three-volume autobiography:

1. *The Whispering Gallery* Longman 1955; 1st Amer. Harcourt Brace 1955
2. *I Am My Brother* Longman 1960; 1st Amer. Reynal 1960
3. *The Ample Proposition* Eyre & Spottiswoode 1966

The three together would be Grade C.

LENNON, John

Born in Liverpool 1940.

Although possibly better known for activities other than writing, Lennon's two little books have almost become period pieces, and although still Grade A, are getting harder to find.

1. *In His Own Write* Cape 1964; 1st Amer. Simon & Schuster 1964
2. *A Spaniard in the Works* Cape 1965; 1st Amer. Simon & Schuster 1965

Beatles material is now being collected, and although it might be difficult to know quite where to begin, the two items following seem essential:
Brian Epstein *A Cellarful of Noise* Souvenir Press 1964
Hunter Davies *The Beatles* Heinemann 1968

LESSING, Doris

British. Born in Persia 1919.

1. *The Grass Is Singing* (novel) Joseph 1950; 1st Amer. Crowell 1950
2. *This Was the Old Chief's Country* (stories) Joseph 1951; 1st Amer. Crowell 1952
3. *Martha Quest* (novel) Joseph 1952
4. *Five: Short Novels* Joseph 1953
5. *Retreat to Innocence* (novel) Joseph 1953
6. *A Proper Marriage* (novel) Joseph 1954; 1st Amer. Simon & Schuster 1964
   The American ed. includes No. 3.
7. *Going Home* (non-fiction) Joseph 1957; 1st Amer. Ballantine 1968
8. *The Habit of Loving* (stories) MacGibbon & Kee 1957; 1st Amer. Crowell 1958
9. *A Ripple from the Storm* (novel) Joseph 1958
10. *Fourteen Poems* Scorpion Press 1959
11. *In Pursuit of the English: A Documentary* Joseph 1960
12. *Portrait of the English* Simon & Schuster 1961 (same as 11)
13. *Play with a Tiger* (play) Joseph 1962
14. *The Golden Notebook* (novel) Joseph 1962; 1st Amer. Simon & Schuster 1962
15. *A Man and Two Women: Stories* MacGibbon & Kee 1963; 1st Amer. Simon & Schuster 1963
16. *African Stories* Joseph 1964; 1st Amer. Simon & Schuster 1965
17. *Landlocked* (novel) MacGibbon & Kee 1965; 1st Amer. Simon & Schuster 1966
    The Amer. ed. includes No. 9.
18. *Particularly Cats* (non-fiction) Joseph 1967; 1st Amer. Simon & Schuster 1967
19. *Nine African Stories* Longman 1968
20. *The Four-Gated City* (novel) MacGibbon & Kee 1969; 1st Amer. Knopf 1969
    This completes the *Children of Violence* sequence, the other volumes being Nos 3, 6, 9 and 17.
21. *Briefing for a Descent into Hell* (novel) Cape 1971; 1st Amer. Knopf 1971
22. *The Story of a Non-Marrying Man* (stories) Cape 1972
23. *The Temptation of Jack Orkney* Knopf 1972 (same as 22)
24. *The Summer Before the Dark* (novel) Cape 1973; 1st Amer. Knopf 1973
25. *A Small Personal Voice* (pieces) Knopf 1974
26. *The Memoirs of a Survivor* (novel) Octagon Press 1974; 1st Amer. Knopf 1975

Nos 1–6 are Grade C. Nos 7–17 are Grade B, and Nos 18 on, Grade A.

LEVI, Peter

Born in Middlesex 1931.

1. *Earthly Paradise* (verse) privately printed 1958
2. *The Gravel Ponds: Poems* Deutsch 1960; 1st Amer. Macmillan 1960
3. *Beaumont: 1861–1961* (non-fiction) Deutsch 1961
4. *Orpheus Head* (verse) privately printed 1962
5. *Water, Rock and Sand* (verse) Deutsch 1962; 1st Amer. Dufour 1962
6. *The Shearwaters* (verse) Allison, Oxford 1965
7. *Fresh Water, Sea Water* (verse) Black Raven Press 1966
8. *Pancakes for the Queen of Babylon* (verse) Anvil Press 1968
9. *Ruined Abbeys* (verse) Anvil Press 1968
10. *Life Is a Platform* (verse) Anvil Press 1971

11. *Death Is a Pulpit* (verse) Anvil Press 1971
12. *The Light Garden of the Angel King* (travel) Collins 1972
13. *In Memory of David Jones* (memoir) The Tablet 1975
14. *Collected Poems 1955–1975* Anvil Press 1976

The recent Anvil Press editions were done in limited, signed editions, as well as a regular trade edition.
Nos 1 and 4 are Grade C. Nos 2, 3, 5, 6, 7, 8, 9 are Grade B, and the rest are Grade A, though No. 14 would be Grade B, on account of the retail price.

LEVIN, Bernard
Born in London 1928.
Levin's book has become a minor classic of its kind. It was reprinted before publication, and is quite difficult to find. Grade B.

The Pendulum Years Cape 1970

LEWIS, C. S.
Born in Belfast 1898. Died 1963.
Lewis published a large number of books, many of them theological, and many of very specific literary criticism. A checklist may be found in *The New Cambridge Bibliography of English Literature* vol. 4, but below are his absolute highlights, of which there are quite a few.

1. *The Allegory of Love* (non-fiction) OUP 1936; 1st Amer. OUP 1936
2. *Out of the Silent Planet* (novel) Bodley Head, Lane 1938; 1st Amer. Macmillan 1943
3. *The Screwtape Letters* (religious) Bles 1942; 1st Amer. Saunders 1942
4. *Perelandra* (novel) Bodley Head, Lane 1943; 1st Amer. Macmillan 1944
5. *That Hideous Strength* (novel) Bodley Head, Lane 1945; 1st Amer. Macmillan 1946
   Nos 2, 4 and 5 form his SF trilogy.
6. *The Lion, the Witch, and the Wardrobe* (juvenile) Bles 1950; 1st Amer. Macmillan 1950
7. *Prince Caspian* (juvenile) Bles 1951; 1st Amer. Macmillan 1951)
8. *The Voyage of the Dawn Treader* (juvenile) Bles 1952; 1st Amer. Macmillan 1952
9. *The Silver Chair* (juvenile) Bles 1953; 1st Amer. Macmillan 1953
10. *The Horse and His Boy* (juvenile) Bles 1954; 1st Amer. Macmillan 1954
11. *The Magician's Nephew* (juvenile) Bodley Head 1955; 1st Amer. Macmillan 1955
12. *Surprised by Joy* (autobiog.) Bles 1955; 1st Amer. Harcourt Brace 1956
13. *The Last Battle* (juvenile) Bodley Head 1956; 1st Amer. Macmillan 1956
    Nos 6, 7, 8, 9, 10, 11 and 13 form the *Chronicles of Narnia.*
14. *The Four Loves* (philosophy) Bles 1960; 1st Amer. Harcourt Brace 1960
15. *Studies in Words* (essay) CUP 1960; 1st Amer. Macmillan 1960
16. *Experiment in Criticism* CUP 1961; 1st Amer. Macmillan 1961
17. *A Grief Observed* (essay) Faber 1961; 1st Amer. Seabury 1963 (pseud. N. W. Clerk)

Nos 1 and 3 are Grade C. The SF trilogy (Nos 2, 4 and 5) is scarce and Grade I. The juveniles are much sought after, partly because of the vast interest in this field: No. 6 is Grade C, and Nos 7, 8, 9, 10, 11 and 13 are Grade B. All the others are Grade A–B.

LEWIS, P. Wyndham   189422
Born in U.S.A. of English parents 1884. Died 1957.
Hugh Kenner *Wyndham Lewis* (Makers of Modern Literature, Norfolk, Conn. 1954) gives a bibliography, and a checklist appears in vol. 4 of *The New Cambridge Bibliography of English Literature.*
In 1914, Lewis founded the periodical *BLAST: Review of the Great English Vortex,* though it ran for only two issues, these two now being Grade P. Although remembered just as much for his Vorticist art as for his writing, one novel stands out:

The Apes of God Arthur Press 1930; 1st Amer. MacBride 1932
The Arthur Press edition was limited and signed, and is now Grade L. A 25th

anniversary edition was published in 1955 by Arco Ltd, limited to 1000 numbered and signed copies—published at three guineas, but now Grade G–H.

The *Agenda* special Wyndham Lewis issue (1969–70) is of great interest, and reproduces some of his pictures, as well as much writing by and about Lewis.

LOFTING, Hugh
Born in Maidenhead 1886. Died 1947.
Author of a long line of Dr Dolittle books, which have become children's classics. Most of these are Grade B–C—in the d/w, designed by Lofting himself (as were the illustrations) and hence of importance. The first one, however, would be Grade D–E.

The Story of Dr Dolittle Stokes 1920; 1st Eng. Cape 1922

Film:
Dr Dolittle 20th Century Fox 1966

LONDON, Jack
Born in San Francisco 1876. Died 1916.
Author of many books, but two in particular have become classics.

1. *The Call of the Wild* (novel) Macmillan 1903; 1st Eng. Heinemann 1903
2. *White Fang* (novel) Macmillan 1906; 1st Eng. Methuen 1907

No. 1 is scarce in the American ed. and Grade K. *White Fang* is not so difficult, and Grade D.

Films:
Call of the Wild United Artists 1935; MGM-EMI 1972
White Fang 20th Century Fox 1936; 20th Century Fox 1974

LOOS, Anita
Born in California 1893.
Known in particular for one book, the title of which entered the language, and became a

statement as famous as Dorothy Parker's 'Men seldom make passes at girls who wear glasses'—and equally doubtful:

1. *Gentlemen Prefer Blondes* Boni & Liveright 1925; 1st Eng. Brentano's 1926
   The sequel seems an attempt to redress the balance.
2. *But Gentlemen Marry Brunettes* Boni & Liveright 1928; 1st Eng. Brentano's 1928
   The *Blondes* is scarce, and Grade D, and the *Brunettes* is Grade B. (Preference comes more expensive than marriage.)

Films:
Gentlemen Prefer Blondes 20th Century Fox 1953
Gentlemen Marry Brunettes United Artists 1955

LOVECRAFT, H. P.
Born in Providence 1890. Died 1937.
Lovecraft is an unusual literary figure, for although now verging upon being a cult, collectors (particularly of SF) standing on each other's backs to get at the few 1sts around, this popularity occurred considerably after his death. Amis said in *New Maps Of Hell*: 'Lovecraft's intrinsic importance is small', and although the reference books and bibliographies seem to agree with him—information is extremely hard to come by—it is evident that collectors do not.
Many of Lovecraft's books are being reissued in whole and in part by the paperback companies, and some title changes seem to have taken place, to add to the confusion. It is possible, therefore, that the list below is not as complete as I should have wished.

1. *Shadow over Innsmouth* (novel) Visionary Publications 1936
2. *Notes and Commonplace Book Employed by the Author* Futile Press 1938
3. *The Outsider and Others* (stories) Arkham House 1939
4. *Beyond the Wall of Sleep* (novel) Arkham House 1943
5. *Best Supernatural Stories* World Publishers 1945; 1st Eng. Gollancz 1952

6. *Marginalia* Arkham House 1945
7. *The Lurker at the Threshold* Arkham House 1948; 1st Eng. Museum Press 1948 (with A. W. Derleth)
8. *Something About Cats* (stories) Arkham House 1949
9. *The Haunter of the Dark* (stories) Gollancz 1951
10. *The Case of Charles Dexter Ward* (novel) Gollancz 1952
11. *Dream Quest of Unknown Kadath* Dawn Press 1955
12. *Survivor, and Others* (stories) Arkham House 1957 (with A. W. Derleth)
13. *Cry Horror* (stories) Corgi 1959
14. *The Shuttered Room* (stories) Arkham House 1959
15. *Dreams and Fancies* (stories) Arkham House 1962
16. *Collected Poems* Arkham House 1963
17. *The Dunwich Horror and Other Stories* Arkham House 1963
18. *The Mountains of Madness* (stories) Gollancz 1966
19. *Dagon* (novel) Gollancz 1967
20. *Shadow out of Time* (stories) Gollancz 1968

The early books very rarely come up, but would now fetch quite a lot—certainly Grade E–F for Nos 1–3. Nos 4–8 would be Grade D, Nos 9–14 would be Grade C, with the exception of No. 13, at Grade A. The remainder would be Grade B.
A biography has recently been published:
L. Sprague de Camp *Lovecraft* (NEL 1976).
Also recently published:
Mark Owings *The Revised Lovecraft Bibliography* (Mirage Press 1973)

Films:
The Haunted Palace American International 1963 (*The Case of Charles Dexter Ward*)
Monster of Terror (Die Monster Die) American International 1965 (*Color Out of Space*—story)
Dunwich Horror American International 1969

LOWELL, Robert
Born Boston 1914.

1. *The Land of Unlikeness* (verse) Cummington Press USA 1944
2. *Lord Weary's Castle* (verse) Harcourt Brace NY 1946
3. *Poems 1938–1949* Faber 1950
4. *The Mills of the Kavanaughs* Harcourt Brace NY 1951
5. *Life Studies* (verse) Faber 1959; 1st Amer. Farrar Straus 1959
6. *Imitations* (verse) Farrar Straus 1961; 1st Eng. Faber 1962
7. *Phaedra and Figaro* (plays trans.) Farrar Straus 1961
8. *Phaedra* Faber 1963 (as in 7)
9. *For the Union Dead* (verse) Farrar Straus 1964; 1st Eng. Faber 1965
10. *The Old Glory* (play) Farrar Straus 1964
An expanded version was published by Faber in 1966, and by Farrar Straus in 1968.
11. *Selected Poems* Faber 1965
12. *Near the Ocean* (verse) Farrar Straus 1967; 1st Eng. Faber 1967
13. *The Voyage* (Baudelaire trans.) Farrar Straus 1968; 1st Eng. Faber 1968
14. *Notebook 1967–1968* Farrar Straus 1969
An augumented edition, called simply *Notebook,* was published in 1970 by Faber and Farrar Straus.
15. *Prometheus Bound* (adapt.) Farrar Straus 1969; 1st Eng. Faber 1970
16. *For Lizzie and Harriet* (verse) Faber 1973; 1st Eng. Farrar Straus 1973
17. *History* (verse) Faber 1973; 1st Amer. Farrar Straus 1973
18. *The Dolphin* (verse) Faber 1973; 1st Amer. Farrar Straus 1973
19. *Poems: A Selection* Faber 1974

No. 1 is extremely scarce, a copy having recently been sold in America for $1000! No. 2 is Grade I–J, No. 3 Grade E, No. 4 Grade E–F. Nos 5, 6 and 7 are Grade C, Nos 9, 12, 13 and 14 Grade B, and the remainder Grade A.

McCARTHY, Mary
Born in Washington 1912.
Below is a checklist of her fictional work, and

one autobiographical. The remainder of her non-fiction work tends to the political, but details of all her books may be found in: Sherli Goldman *Mary McCarthy: A Bibliography* (Harcourt Brace 1968)

1. *The Company She Keeps* (novel) Simon & Schuster 1942; 1st Eng. Weidenfeld & Nicolson 1957
2. *The Oasis* (novel) Random House 1949
3. *A Source of Embarrassment* Heinemann 1950 (same as 2)
4. *Cast a Cold Eye* (stories) Harcourt Brace 1950; 1st Eng. Heinemann 1952
5. *The Groves of Academe* (novel) Harcourt Brace 1952; 1st Eng. Heinemann 1953
6. *A Charmed Life* (novel) Harcourt Brace 1955; 1st Eng. Weidenfeld & Nicolson 1956
7. *Memories of a Catholic Girlhood* (autobiog.) Harcourt Brace 1957; 1st Eng. Heinemann 1957
8. *The Group* (novel) Harcourt Brace 1963; 1st Eng. Weidenfeld & Nicolson 1963
9. *Birds of America* (novel) Harcourt Brace 1971; 1st Eng. Weidenfeld & Nicolson 1971

No. 1 is Grade C. Nos 2 and 4 are Grade B, and the rest—including *The Group*, a highlight—are Grade A.

Film:
The Group United Artists 1965

MacDIARMID, Hugh

Pseudonym of Christopher Grieve. Born in Dumfriesshire 1892.
MacDiarmid has published over forty books of verse, about thirty other works, and a dozen more that he has edited. He has also translated a number of works. A checklist appears in *The New Cambridge Bibliography of English Literature* vol. 4, and the bibliography appears below.
W. R. Aitken *A Hugh MacDiarmid Bibliography* (cont. in Duncan Glen (ed.) *Hugh MacDiarmid: A Critical Survey* Scottish Academic Press 1972)
Below appear the two volumes of autobiography, and the complete poems.

1. *Lucky Poet* Methuen 1943
2. *The Company I've Kept* Hutchinson 1966; 1st Amer. University of California 1967
3. *Complete Poems* Martin Brian & O'Keeffe 1974

Lucky Poet is quite scarce, and Grade C. It was reissued recently by Cape. The other volume is Grade B, as are the *Poems*.

MACKENZIE, Compton

Born in West Hartlepool 1883. Died 1972. Author of over a hundred books, a checklist of which may be found in *The New Cambridge Bibliography of English Literature* vol. 4. Mackenzie became established with the novel *Sinister Street* (2 vols, Secker 1913–14), though possibly it is for the comparatively recent novel below that he is best remembered.

Whisky Galore Chatto & Windus 1947 Grade A only. It was published in America by Houghton Mifflin in 1950 as *Tight Little Island*.
His *Autobiography* has gained a considerable reputation; this was published in ten volumes (*Octaves*[*sic*]) by Chatto & Windus 1963–70. The set is Grade E.

Films:
Whisky Galore Ealing 1949
Three other Mackenzie books have been filmed.

MacLEAN, Alistair

Born in Inverness-shire 1923.
MacLean has published over a score of novels, nine of which have been filmed. His first novel, below, sold a quarter of a million copies in six months, its successors selling as well. All are still in print. With his first novel is his highlight. They are Grade A.

1. *H.M.S. Ulysses* Collins 1955; 1st Amer. Doubleday 1956
2. *The Guns of Navarone* Collins 1957; 1st Amer. Doubleday 1957

Films:
The Guns of Navarone Columbia 1959

As mentioned above, eight other films of MacLean novels have been made.

MacNEICE, Louis
Born in Belfast 1907. Died 1963.

1. *Blind Fireworks* (verse) Gollancz 1929
2. *Roundabout Way* (novel) Putnam 1932 (pseud. Louis Malone)
3. *Poems* Faber 1935; 1st Amer. Random House 1937
4. *The Agamemnon of Aeschylus* (trans.) Faber 1936; 1st Amer. Harcourt Brace 1937
5. *Out of the Picture* (play) Faber 1937; 1st Amer. Harcourt Brace 1938
6. *Letters from Iceland* (non-fiction) Faber 1937; 1st Amer. Harcourt Brace 1937 (with W. H. Auden)
7. *I Crossed the Minch* (travel) Longman 1938
8. *Zoo* (non-fiction) Joseph 1938
9. *Modern Poetry: A Personal Essay* OUP 1938
10. *The Earth Compels* (verse) Faber 1938
11. *Autumn Journal* (verse) Faber 1939; 1st Amer. Random House 1939
12. *The Last Ditch* (verse) Cuala Press, Dublin 1940
13. *Selected Poems* Faber 1940
14. *Poems 1925–1940* Random House 1940
15. *Plant and Phantom* (verse) Faber 1941
16. *The Poetry of W. B. Yeats* (criticism) OUP 1941
17. *Meet the U.S. Army* (essay) Board of Education 1943
18. *Springboard: Poems 1941–44* Faber 1944; 1st Amer. Random House 1945
19. *Christopher Columbus* (play) Faber 1944
20. *The Dark Tower* (plays) Faber 1947
21. *Holes in the Sky: Poems 1944–47* Faber 1948; 1st Amer. Random House 1949
22. *Collected poems 1925–48* Faber 1949; 1st Amer. OUP 1949
23. *Goethe's Faust Parts I & II* (trans.) Faber 1951; 1st Amer. OUP 1952
24. *Ten Burnt Offerings* (verse) Faber 1952; 1st Amer. OUP 1953
25. *Autumn Sequel* (verse) Faber 1954
26. *The Other Wing* (Ariel Poem) Faber 1954
27. *The Penny That Rolled Away* (juvenile) Putnam 1954

This was published in England, no doubt for sound economic reasons, as *The Sixpence That Rolled Away* by Faber in 1956.

28. *Visitations* (verse) Faber 1957; 1st Amer. OUP 1958
29. *Eighty-Five Poems* Faber 1959; 1st Amer. OUP 1959
30. *Solstices* (verse) Faber 1961; 1st Amer. OUP 1961
31. *The Burning Perch* (verse) Faber 1963; 1st Amer. OUP 1963
32. *Selected Poems* Faber 1964 (ed. and Intro. by W. H. Auden)
33. *The Mad Islands* and *The Administrator* (plays) Faber 1964
34. *Astrology* (non-fiction) Aldus 1964; 1st Amer. Doubleday 1964
35. *The Strings Are False* (autobiog.) Faber 1965; 1st Amer. OUP 1966
36. *Varieties of Parable* (lecture) CUP 1965
37. *Collected Poems* Faber 1966; 1st Amer. OUP 1967
38. *One for the Grave* (play) Faber 1968
39. *Persons from Porlock and Other Plays* BBC 1969 (Intro. by W. H. Auden)

Nos 1 and 2 are particularly scarce, and Grade G. Nos 3, 4 and 5 are Grade C, whereas No. 6 is Grade D, partly for the Auden interest, as are Nos 7 and 8, neither of which is a common book. Nos 9, 10, and 11 are Grade C, No. 12 is Grade D, and Nos 13 and 14 are Grade A. Nos 16, 17, 22 and 27 are Grade C, Nos 15, 18, 19, 20, 21, 23, 24, 25, 28, 29, 30, 31, 37 and 39 are Grade B, and Nos 26, 32, 33, 34, 35, 36 and 38 are Grade A.
See Christopher Armitage and Neil Clark *A Bibliography of the Works of Louis MacNeice* (Kaye & Ward 1973).

MAILER, Norman
Born in New Jersey 1923.
In addition to the novels, plays and verse below, Mailer has published about twenty other works—as diverse as *Cannibals and Christians* (Dial Press 1966; 1st Eng. Deutsch 1967) and *Marilyn* (Grosset & Dunlap 1973;

1st Eng. Hodder & Stoughton 1973). Details of all of these, however, may be found in: Laura Adams *Norman Mailer: A Comprehensive Bibliography* (Scarecrow Press, New Jersey 1974)

1. *The Naked and the Dead* (novel) Rinehart 1948; 1st Eng. Wingate 1949
2. *Barbary Shore* (novel) Rinehart 1951; 1st Eng. Cape 1952
3. *The Deer Park* (novel) Putnam 1955; 1st Eng. Wingate 1957
4. *Advertisements for Myself* (miscellany) Putnam 1959; 1st Eng. Deutsch 1961
5. *Deaths for the Ladies and Other Disasters* (verse) Putnam 1962; 1st Eng. Deutsch 1962
6. *An American Dream* (novel) Dial Press 1965; 1st Eng. Deutsch 1965
7. *The Deer Park* (play) Dial Press 1967; 1st Eng. Weidenfeld & Nicolson 1970
8. *Why Are We in Vietnam?* (novel) Putnam 1967; 1st Eng. Weidenfeld & Nicolson 1969

Nos 1 and 6 are the highlights, and are Grade C and B respectively, though less for the English editions. Nos 2, 3, 4 and 5 are also Grade B, and Nos 7 and 8 are Grade A.

Films:
The Naked and the Dead Warner Bros 1958
See You in Hell, Darling Warner Bros 1966
(*An American Dream*)

MANSFIELD, Katherine
Pseudonym of Kathleen Mansfield Beauchamp. Born in New Zealand 1888. Died 1923.
She published about a score of books, details of which may be found in R. Mantz *The Critical Bibliography of Katherine Mansfield* (Constable 1931) with an Intro. by J. Middleton Murry, her husband.
Her stories are her most important work, two early books of which appear below, together with the first English and American collected editions.

1. *Bliss and Other Stories* Constable 1920; 1st Amer. Knopf 1921

2. *The Garden Party and Other Stories* Constable 1922; 1st Amer. Knopf 1922
3. *The Short Stories of Katherine Mansfield* Knopf 1937 (Intro. J. M. Murry)
4. *The Collected Stories of Katherine Mansfield* Constable 1945

Nos 1 and 2 are Grade D, No. 3 Grade C, and No. 4 Grade B.

MARCUS, Frank
British. Born in Germany 1928.
Author of over a dozen plays, though notable in particular for one, which is quite hard to find, and Grade B.

The Killing of Sister George Hamilton 1965; 1st Amer. Random House 1966

Film:
The Killing of Sister George Cinerama 1968

MARSH, Ngaio
New Zealander. Born in Christchurch 1899.

1. *A Man Lay Dead* (novel) Bles 1934; 1st Amer. Sheridan 1942
2. *Enter a Murderer* (novel) Bles 1935; 1st Amer. Sheridan 1942
3. *Death in Ecstasy* (novel) Bles 1936; 1st Amer. Sheridan 1941
4. *The Nursing Home Murder* (novel) Bles 1936; 1st Amer. Sheridan 1941 (with H. Jellett)
5. *Vintage Murder* (novel) Bles 1937; 1st Amer. Sheridan 1940
6. *Artists in Crime* (novel) Bles 1938; 1st Amer. Furman 1938
7. *Death in a White Tie* (novel) Bles 1938; 1st Amer. Furman 1938
8. *Overture to Death* (novel) Collins 1939; 1st Amer. Little Brown 1939
9. *Death at the Bar* (novel) Collins 1940; 1st Amer. Little Brown 1940
10. *Death of a Peer* (novel) Little Brown 1940
11. *Surfeit of Lampreys* Collins 1941 (same as 10)
12. *Death and the Dancing Footman* (novel) Collins 1941; 1st Amer. Little Brown 1941

13. *Colour Scheme* (novel) Collins 1943; 1st Amer. Little Brown 1943
14. *Died in the Wool* (novel) Collins 1945; 1st Amer. Little Brown 1945
15. *Final Curtain* (novel) Collins 1947; 1st Amer. Little Brown 1947
16. *Swing Brother Swing* (novel) Collins 1949
17. *Wreath for Riviera* Little Brown 1949 (same as 16)
18. *Opening Night* (novel) Collins 1951
19. *Night at the Vulcan* Little Brown 1951 (same as 18)
20. *Spinsters in Jeopardy* (novel) Little Brown 1953; 1st Eng. Collins 1954
21. *Scales of Justice* (novel) Collins 1955; 1st Amer. Little Brown 1955
22. *Death of a Fool* (novel) Little Brown 1956
23. *Off with His Head* Collins 1957 (same as 22)
24. *Singing in the Shrouds* (novel) Little Brown 1958; 1st Eng. Collins 1959
25. *False Scent* (novel) Little Brown 1959; 1st Eng. Collins 1960
26. *Hand in Glove* (novel) Little Brown 1962; 1st Eng. Collins 1962
27. *Dead Water* (novel) Little Brown 1963; 1st Eng. Collins 1964
28. *Killer Dolphin* (novel) Little Brown 1966
29. *Death at the Dolphin* Collins 1967 (same as 28)
30. *Clutch of Constables* (novel) Collins 1968; 1st Amer. Little Brown 1969
31. *When in Rome* (novel) Collins 1970; 1st Amer. Little Brown 1970
32. *Tied up in Tinsel* (novel) Collins 1972; 1st Amer. Little Brown 1972
33. *Black as He's Painted* (novel) Collins 1974; 1st Amer. Little Brown 1974
34. *Last Ditch* (novel) Collins 1977; 1st Amer. Little Brown 1977

There is more interest in Ngaio Marsh now, as with all detective writers, and No. 1 would fetch Grade F. Nos 2–7 are Grade D–E, Nos 8–19 are Grade C, Nos 20–22 are Grade B, and the rest Grade A.

MASEFIELD, John
Born in Herefordshire 1878. Died 1967. Author of an almost incredible number of books (few short of 150), Masefield has declined sharply in popularity with collectors since the boom years of the thirties, and although a few well-loved works still fetch reasonable prices, and his limited and signed editions continue to hold their value, only one work seems constantly to be in demand, and never fails to make at least £100 in the salerooms—his first book:

Salt Water Ballads (verse) Richards 1902

There is a checklist of works in *The New Cambridge Bibliography of English Literature* vol. 4, but the bibliography to be consulted is G. Handley-Taylor *Masefield O. M.: A Bibliography and Eighty-First Birthday Tribute* (Cranbrook Tower Press 1960).

MAUGHAM, W. Somerset
British. Born in Paris 1874. Died 1965. Maugham published a very large number of books, and, like Masefield (above), was avidly collected during the thirties. Interest was almost non-existent in the sixties—except of course for the few constant favourites— but recently, a slight return to favour is discernible. Fred Bason published a bibliography in 1931 (Unicorn Press), in a limited edition with a Maugham Preface, but the most comprehensive is Raymond Toole Stott *Maughamiana* (Heinemann 1950), supplements appearing in 1956, 1961 and 1964.
Below appears a selection of highlights.

1. *Liza of Lambeth* (novel) T. Fisher Unwin 1897; 1st Amer. Doubleday 1921
In this, Maugham's first book, an interesting point arises. Bason, in his bibliography, quotes his copy of the 1st as having the word 'belly' included in place of the later substitution 'stomach'—the former word being thought overstrong for the novel-reading public of the time. He deduces that thus can a 1st be recognized. Stott, however, says 'the word belly was not included in the first edition of this book', but appears for the first time in the Travellers Library edition of

1930. Controversy notwithstanding, the book is a rare one, and Grade N upwards.

2. *Of Human Bondage* (novel) Heinemann 1915; 1st Amer. Doran 1915
Scarce. Grade J.

3. *Ashenden* (novel) Heinemann 1928; 1st Amer. Doran 1928

4. *Cakes and Ale* (novel) Heinemann 1930; 1st Amer. Doran 1930

The above two are Grade F–G.

Films:
Of Human Bondage RKO 1934; Warner Bros 1946; MGM 1963
Secret Agent (*Ashenden*) Gaumont British 1936
There have been fifteen other films made from Maugham's novels, though not, strangely enough, *Liza of Lambeth* or *Cakes and Ale*.

MILLER, Arthur
Born in New York 1915.
Author of over twenty plays, among other works, those appearing below having become theatre classics. Details may be found in Tetsumaro Hayashi *Arthur Miller: A Checklist of His Published Works* (in *The Serif*, Kent, Ohio 1967).

1. *All My Sons* (play) Reynal & Hitchcock 1947
2. *Death of a Salesman* (play) Viking Press 1949; 1st Eng. Cresset Press 1949
3. *The Crucible* (play) Viking Press 1953; 1st Eng. Cresset Press 1956
4. *A View from the Bridge* and *A Memory of Two Mondays* Viking Press 1955
5. *A View from the Bridge* (revised) Cresset Press 1956
6. *Collected Plays* Viking Press 1957; 1st Eng. Cresset Press 1958 (incl. 1, 2, 3 and 4)
7. *Incident at Vichy* (play) Viking Press 1965; 1st Eng. Secker & Warburg 1966

Nos 1, 2 and 3 are Grade C, though less for the English editions. Nos 4, 5 and 6 are Grade B, and No. 7 Grade A.

Films:
All My Sons Universal 1948

Death of a Salesman Columbia 1951
The Witches of Salem Films de France 1957 (*The Crucible*)
A View from the Bridge Transcontinental 1961
The Misfits (story) United Artists 1961
The screenplay of *The Misfits* was published by Dell in 1961 (1st Eng. Secker & Warburg 1961): Grade A.

MILLER, Henry
Born in New York 1891.
In addition to Miller's fictional work, which appears below, he has published about sixty other books. There has been more than one bibliography, though the most recent is:
T. H. Moore (ed.) *Bibliography of Henry Miller* (Henry Miller Literary Society, Minneapolis 1961)

1. *Tropic of Cancer* (novel) Obelisk Press, Paris 1934; 1st Amer. Grove Press 1961; 1st Eng. Calder 1963
The Obelisk Press ed. of this very famous novel is extremely scarce, and expensive. A copy was sold *to a dealer* in 1973 for £240, though the retail price today would exceed this. A worn copy, of course, would be considerably less. The American ed. is Grade C–D, and the English Grade B.

2. *Black Spring* (novel) Obelisk Press, Paris 1936; 1st Amer. Grove Press 1963; 1st Eng. Calder 1965
Again, a scarce book, and Grade P in the Paris edition, Grade B in the American, and Grade A in the English.

3. *Tropic of Capricorn* (novel) Obelisk Press, Paris 1939; 1st Amer. Grove Press 1961; 1st Eng. Calder 1964
Grade P for the true 1st, Grade C for the American, and Grade B for the English.

4. *Sexus* (novel) Obelisk Press, Paris 1949; 1st Amer. Grove Press 1965; 1st Eng. Weidenfeld 1969
Grade K, B and A, respectively. The Paris ed. is in 2 vols.

5. *Plexus* (novel) Olympia Press, Paris 1953; 1st Eng. Weidenfeld 1963; 1st Amer. Grove Press 1965

The Paris ed. was in 2 vols, and is Grade J. English and American eds are Grade B.

6. *Quiet Days in Clichy* (novel) Olympia Press, Paris 1956; 1st Amer. Grove Press 1965; 1st Eng. Calder 1966
Paris ed.: Grade G. American and English eds.: Grade A–B.

7. *Nexus* (novel) Olympia Press, Paris 1960; 1st Eng. Weidenfeld 1964; 1st Amer. Grove Press 1965
This combines with Nos 4 and 5 to form *The Rosy Crucifixion* trilogy. Grade F, Paris ed., and Grade A–B for the English and American.

8. *Just Wild About Harry* (play) New Directions 1963; 1st Eng. MacGibbon & Kee 1964
Grade B–C in the American ed., and Grade A–B in the English.

Film:
Tropic of Cancer Paramount 1969

MILNE, A. A.
Born in London 1882. Died 1956.
Milne published thirty prose works, and two dozen books of plays. He also wrote some children's books, and it is for these that he is remembered:

1. *When We Were Very Young* (verse) Methuen 1924; 1st Amer. Dutton 1924

2. *Winnie the Pooh* (stories) Methuen 1926; 1st Amer. Dutton 1926

3. *Now We Are Six* (verse) Methuen 1927; 1st Amer. Dutton 1927

4. *The House at Pooh Corner* (stories) Methuen 1928; 1st Amer. Dutton 1928

5. *Toad of Toad Hall* (play) Methuen 1929; 1st Amer. Scribner 1929
This is an adaptation of Kenneth Grahame's *The Wind in the Willows*.

These books, with their attractive format and E. H. Shepard illustrations, have been gaining in price very steadily. Fine copies, in d/ws—difficult, as with all children's books—would be Grade I for Nos 1 and 2—No. 1 being more scarce, but No. 2 being the highlight—and Grade F for Nos 3 and 4. No. 5 is Grade C–D.

Films (cartoons):
Winnie the Pooh and the Honey Tree Disney 1965
Winnie the Pooh and the Blustery Day Disney 1968
Winnie the Pooh and Tigger Too Disney 1974

MITCHELL, Margaret
Born in Atlanta 1900. Died 1949.
Author of only one book, of which she is quoted as saying: 'I know good work and I know good writing, and I didn't think mine good.' The world disagreed with her at the time, and seems to find it difficult to decide now. It is the book people love to hate, but nonetheless, one of the best-selling novels of all time.

Gone with the Wind Macmillan 1936; 1st Eng. Macmillan 1936
It is very uncommon in a 1st, but would probably never rise above Grade C, such is its image.

Film:
Gone with the Wind MGM 1939

MITFORD, Nancy
Born in London 1904. Died 1973.
In addition to the four highlights below, she published four other early fictional works and some historical non-fiction.
All the books below are Grade A.

1. *The Pursuit of Love* (novel) Hamilton 1945; 1st Amer. Random House 1946

2. *Love in a Cold Climate* (novel) Hamilton 1949; 1st Amer. Random House 1949

3. *The Blessing* (novel) Hamilton 1951; 1st Amer. Random House 1951

4. *Don't Tell Alfred* (novel) Hamilton 1960; 1st Amer. Harper 1960

Also notable is the following volume which she edited, responsible for the whole U and non-U 'controversy' of the fifties:
Noblesse Oblige Harper 1956; 1st Eng. Hamilton 1957

Biography:

Harold Acton *Nancy Mitford* (Hamilton 1975; Harper Row 1976)

Film:
Count Your Blessings MGM 1959 (*The Blessing*)

MONSARRAT, Nicholas
Born in Liverpool 1910.
Author of over thirty books, mainly novels, Monsarrat—although a best-seller—has never been a collector's choice. One quite early novel, however, is perhaps exceptional:

The Cruel Sea Cassell 1951; 1st Amer. Knopf 1951
The American edition actually preceded, by about three weeks.
Grade A–B in the d/w, but the Book Society edition—issued simultaneously—is very common, and very cheap.

Films:
The Cruel Sea General Films 1952
Two more films have been made from Monsarrat's books.

MOORE, Marianne
Born in St Louis 1887. Died 1972.
Author of about a dozen books, predominantly verse, as well as a somewhat controversial translation of La Fontaine. The early books are scarce—her first, *Poems, 1921,* especially so—though the later works such as *Like a Bulwark* (1956) and *The Arctic Ox* (1964), are not too difficult, and Grade B. More details are to be found in *A Marianne Moore Reader* (Viking Press 1961). Below appear her two collections:

1. *Collected Poems* Macmillan 1951; 1st Eng. Faber 1951
2. *Complete Poems* Macmillan 1967; 1st Eng. Faber 1968
No. 1 is Grade C, and No. 2 is Grade B.

MORTIMER, Penelope
Born in Rhyl 1918.
Author of under a dozen books, though

notable for the following:

The Pumpkin Eater (novel) Hutchinson 1962; 1st Amer. McGraw-Hill 1963
Grade A–B.

Films:
The Pumpkin Eater British Lion 1963
Although she did not write the screenplay for this film, she did collaborate with her playwright husband John Mortimer to produce the screenplay for *Bunny Lake Is Missing,* though this was not published.

MUIR, Edwin
Born on the Isle of Orkney 1887. Died in 1959.
Author of several volumes of verse and books of criticism, as well as many translations, with Willa Muir, of such authors as Kafka. A checklist of works may be found in *The New Cambridge Bibliography of English Literature*, vol. 4, and details in:
E. W. Mellown *Bibliography of the Writings of Muir* (University of Alabama 1964)
Probably his most enduring work is:

Structure of the Novel (criticism) Hogarth Press 1928; 1st Amer. Harcourt Brace 1929
This is quite a difficult book, and Grade C.

MURDOCH, Iris
Born in Dublin in 1919, Iris Murdoch is one of our most enduring new novelists, lately building on each success—a new novel better than the last now seems to be the rule. Her first novel was received very well, as has been each since. From the collector's point of view, the novels form a very handsome set, many of the d/ws designed by fine artists. Each novel is identical in format, and all the d/ws are artwork, not photography.

1. *Sartre: Romantic Rationalist* (non-fiction) Bowes & Bowes 1953; 1st Amer. Yale University 1953
2. *Under the Net* (novel) Chatto & Windus 1954; 1st Amer. Viking Press 1954
3. *The Flight from the Enchanter* (novel) Chatto &

Windus 1956 1st Amer. Viking Press 1956

4. *The Sandcastle* (novel) Chatto & Windus 1957; 1st Amer. Viking Press 1957
5. *The Bell* (novel) Chatto & Windus 1958; 1st Amer. Viking Press 1958
6. *A Severed Head* (novel) Chatto & Windus 1961; 1st Amer. Viking Press 1961
7. *An Unofficial Rose* (novel) Chatto & Windus 1962; 1st Amer. Viking Press 1962
8. *The Unicorn* (novel) Chatto & Windus 1963; 1st Amer. Viking Press 1963
9. *The Italian Girl* (novel) Chatto & Windus 1964; 1st Amer. Viking Press 1964
10. *A Severed Head* (play) Chatto & Windus 1964 (with J. B. Priestley)
11. *The Red and the Green* (novel) Chatto & Windus 1965; 1st Amer. Viking Press 1965
12. *The Time of the Angels* (novel) Chatto & Windus 1966; 1st Amer. Viking Press 1966
13. *The Sovereignty of Good* (lecture) CUP 1967
14. *The Nice and the Good* (novel) Chatto & Windus 1968; 1st Amer. Viking Press 1968
15. *Bruno's Dream* (novel) Chatto & Windus 1969; 1st Amer. Viking Press 1969
16. *The Italian Girl* (play) French 1969 (with James Saunders)
17. *A Fairly Honourable Defeat* (novel) Chatto & Windus 1970; 1st Amer. Viking Press 1970
18. *The Sovereignty of Good* (essays) Routledge 1971
    Contains No. 13, together with other unpublished essays.
19. *An Accidental Man* (novel) Chatto & Windus 1971; 1st Amer. Viking Press 1972
20. *The Black Prince* (novel) Chatto & Windus 1973; 1st Amer. Viking Press 1973
21. *The Three Arrows* and *The Servants and the Snow: Two Plays* Chatto & Windus 1973; 1st Amer. Viking Press 1974
22. *The Sacred and Profane Love Machine* (novel) Chatto & Windus 1974; 1st Amer. Viking Press 1974
23. *A Word Child* (novel) Chatto & Windus 1975; 1st Amer. Viking Press 1975
24. *Henry and Cato* (novel) Chatto & Windus 1976; 1st Amer. Viking Press 1976
25. *The Fire and the Sun: Why Plato Banished the Artists* (philosophy) OUP 1977

A story entitled *Something Special* appears in *Winter's Tales* 3 (Macmillan 1957).
Her first book *Sartre* is scarce, and Grade D, but just as scarce and even more sought after is her first novel, *Under the Net*. This is Grade E–F in d/w. Nos 3 and 4 are also rare, particularly in d/w; they are both Grade D. The remainder should not be too difficult to acquire, with the exception of No. 13—a flimsy pamphlet, now difficult, and Grade B. Nos 5, 6, 7, 8, 9, 10 and 18 are Grade B, and the rest Grade A, though many are of the opinion that these are undervalued, and this situation might alter in the near future.

Film:
A Severed Head Columbia 1969

NABOKOV, Vladimir

Born in St Petersburg (Leningrad) 1899. Nabokov is a difficult author to collect, not least because most collections must probably be compromises, for many of his works were first published in Russian in different countries, sometimes long before the first English editions, although in most cases the translations into English were by Nabokov himself. In the checklist below, I have taken the chronology of the English editions, though stating whether Russian-language publication preceded. Some works—notably the very early verse—did not appear under their original titles in English, but details of these and of his translations of other works, etc., may be found in:
Andrew Field *Nabokov: A Bibliography* (McGraw-Hill 1974)

1. *Camera Obscura* (novel) Long, London 1937
   A revised edition was published in America by Bobbs Merrill in 1938 as *Laughter in the Dark*, and by Weidenfeld & Nicolson in 1961. First publication, in Russian, was in Paris and Berlin 1933.
2. *Despair* (novel) Long, London 1937
   A revised edition was published in America by Putnam, and in England by Weidenfeld & Nicolson, in 1966. First publication was in Berlin 1936.

3. *The Real Life of Sebastian Knight* (novel) New Directions 1941; 1st Eng. Editions Poetry 1945
4. *Nikolai Gogol* (non-fiction) New Directions 1944; 1st Eng. Editions Poetry 1947
5. *Bend Sinister* (novel) Holt 1947; 1st Eng. Weidenfeld & Nicolson 1960
6. *Nine Stories* New Directions 1947
7. *Conclusive Evidence: A Memoir* Harper 1951
   Published in England by Gollancz in 1952 as *Speak, Memory: A Memoir*. A revised edition *Speak, Memory: An Autobiography Revisited* was published in America by Putnam in 1966, and in England by Weidenfeld & Nicolson in 1967.
8. *Lolita* (novel) Olympia Press, Paris 1955; 1st Amer. Putnam 1958; 1st Eng. Weidenfeld & Nicolson 1959
   The Paris edition is in two volumes.
9. *Pnin* (novel) Doubleday 1957; 1st Eng. Heinemann 1957
10. *Nabokov's Dozen* (stories) Doubleday 1958; 1st Eng. Heinemann 1959
11. *Invitation to a Beheading* (novel) Putnam 1959; 1st Eng. Weidenfeld & Nicolson 1960
    First publication, in Russian, was in Paris 1938.
12. *Poems* Doubleday 1959; 1st Eng. Weidenfeld & Nicolson 1961
13. *Pale Fire* (novel) Putnam 1962; 1st Eng. Weidenfeld & Nicolson 1962
14. *The Gift* (novel) Putnam 1963; 1st Eng. Weidenfeld & Nicolson 1963
    First published, in Russian, in New York 1952.
15. *The Defense* (novel) Putnam 1964
    The Defence 1st Eng. Weidenfeld & Nicolson 1964
    First published, in Russian, in Berlin 1930.
16. *Nabokov's Quartet* (stories) Phaedra 1966; 1st Eng. Weidenfeld & Nicolson 1967
17. *King, Queen, Knave* (novel) McGraw-Hill 1968; 1st Eng. Weidenfeld & Nicolson 1968
18. *Nabokov's Congeries* (anthology) Viking Press 1968
19. *Ada* (novel) McGraw-Hill 1969; 1st Eng. Weidenfeld & Nicolson 1969
20. *Mary* (novel) McGraw-Hill 1970; 1st Eng.

Weidenfeld & Nicolson 1971
This, his first novel, was published in Russian in Berlin 1926.
21. *Glory* (novel) McGraw-Hill 1971; 1st Eng. Weidenfeld & Nicolson 1972
    First publication, in Russian, was in Paris 1932.
22. *Poems and Problems* McGraw-Hill 1971; 1st Eng. Weidenfeld & Nicolson 1972
23. *Transparent Things* (novel) McGraw-Hill 1973; 1st Eng. Weidenfeld & Nicolson 1973
24. *A Russian Beauty and Other Stories* McGraw-Hill 1973; 1st Eng. Weidenfeld & Nicolson 1973
25. *Strong Opinions* (essays) McGraw-Hill 1973; 1st Eng. Weidenfeld & Nicolson 1974
26. *Look at the Harlequins!* (novel) McGraw-Hill 1974; 1st Eng. Weidenfeld & Nicolson 1975
27. *Lolita: A Screenplay* McGraw-Hill 1974
28. *Tyrants Destroyed and Other Stories* McGraw-Hill 1975; 1st Eng. Weidenfeld & Nicolson 1975
29. *Details of a Sunset and Other Stories* McGraw-Hill 1976; 1st Eng. Weidenfeld & Nicolson 1976

Nos 1 and 2 are scarce, and Grade H–I. Nos 3–7 are Grade C. No. 8 is, of course, the highlight, and the Paris edition is Grade K, the American Grade C, and the English Grade B. Nos 9–15 are Grade B, and the remainder Grade A.

Films:
Lolita MGM 1962
Laughter in the Dark United Artists 1969

NAIPAUL, V. S.
British. Born in Trinidad 1932.

1. *The Mystic Masseur* (novel) Deutsch 1957; 1st Amer. Vanguard Press 1959
2. *The Suffrage of Elvira* (novel) Deutsch 1958
3. *Miguel Street* (novel) Deutsch 1959; 1st Amer. Vanguard Press 1960
4. *A House for Mr Biswas* (novel) Deutsch 1961; 1st Amer. McGraw-Hill 1962
5. *The Middle Passage* (non-fiction) Deutsch 1962; 1st Amer. Macmillan 1963

6. *Mr Stone and the Knights Companion* (novel)
   Deutsch 1963; 1st Amer. Macmillan 1964
7. *An Area of Darkness* (travel) Deutsch 1964;
   1st Amer. Macmillan 1965
8. *The Mimic Men* (novel) Deutsch 1967; 1st
   Amer. Macmillan 1967
9. *A Flag on the Island* (stories) Deutsch 1967;
   1st Amer. Macmillan 1968
10. *The Loss of El Dorado* (history) Deutsch 1969;
    1st Amer. Knopf 1970
11. *In a Free State* (novel) Deutsch 1971; 1st
    Amer. Knopf 1971
12. *The Overcrowded Barracoon* (articles) Deutsch
    1972; 1st Amer. Knopf 1972
13. *Guerrillas* (novel) Deutsch 1975; 1st Amer.
    Knopf 1975

No. 1 is Grade B–C, Nos 2–7 are Grade B,
and the rest Grade A.

NASH, Ogden

Born in New York State 1902. Died 1971.
The master of the unique rhyme has
published quite a few volumes, though no
one in particular stands out as a highlight.
Each seems as delightful as the next,
however, and so I print a representative
selection.

1. *Hard Lines* Simon & Schuster 1931; 1st Eng.
   Duckworth 1931
2. *The Primrose Path* Simon & Schuster 1935;
   1st Eng. Bodley Head 1935
3. *The Bad Parent's Garden of Verse* Simon &
   Schuster 1936
4. *The Face is Familiar* Little Brown 1940; 1st
   Eng. Dent 1942
5. *Verses from 1929 on* Little Brown 1961
   This was published in England as *Collected
   Verses* by Dent during the same year.

No. 1 is Grade C, and the rest Grade B.

NAUGHTON, Bill

Born in County Mayo, Ireland, 1910.
Chiefly a playwright, though notable for one
sixties novel:

Alfie MacGibbon & Kee 1966; 1st Amer.
Ballantine 1966
This is Grade A–B.

Films:
Alfie Paramount 1965
Naughton is also responsible for such films as
Spring and Port Wine and *The Family Way*,
though these have not been published.

NICHOLS, Peter

Born in Bristol 1927.
Author of a score of television plays, as well
as his better-known stage successes. His
published highlights appear below.

1. *A Day in the Death of Joe Egg* (play) Faber
   1967
   Published in America in the same year by the
   Grove Press as *Joe Egg*.
2. *The National Health* (play) Faber 1970
3. *Forget-Me-Not-Lane* (play) Faber 1971

All of these are Grade A, at the moment.

Films:
Joe Egg Columbia 1971
The National Health Columbia 1973

O'BRIEN, Edna

Born in County Clare, Ireland, 1932.

1. *The Country Girls* (novel) Hutchinson 1960;
   1st Amer. Knopf 1960
2. *The Lonely Girl* (novel) Cape 1962; 1st Amer.
   Random House 1962
3. *Girls in Their Married Bliss* (novel) Cape 1964;
   1st Amer. Houghton Mifflin 1968
   Nos 1, 2 and 3 form a trilogy.
4. *August Is a Wicked Month* (novel) Cape 1965;
   1st Amer. Simon & Schuster 1965
5. *Casualties of Peace* (novel) Cape 1966; 1st
   Amer. Simon & Schuster 1967
6. *The Love Object* (stories) Cape 1968; 1st Amer.
   Knopf 1969
7. *A Pagan Place* (novel) Weidenfeld & Nicolson
   1970; 1st Amer. Knopf 1970
8. *Zee & Co* (screenplay) Weidenfeld &
   Nicolson 1971

9. *Night* (novel) Weidenfeld & Nicolson 1972; 1st Amer. Knopf 1973
10. *A Pagan Place* (play) Faber 1973
11. *A Scandalous Woman* (stories) Weidenfeld & Nicolson 1974; 1st Amer. Harcourt Brace 1974
12. *Mother Ireland* (autobiog.) Weidenfeld & Nicolson 1976; 1st Amer. Harcourt Brace 1976
13. *Johnnie, I Hardly Knew You* (novel) Weidenfeld & Nicolson 1977

Nos 1 and 2 are quite scarce, and Grade B. The rest are Grade A.

Films:
The Girl with Green Eyes United Artists 1964 (*The Lonely Girl*)
Zee & Co Columbia 1971

O'BRIEN, Flann
Pseudonym for Brian O'Nolan, also known as Myles na Gopaleen. Born in Tyrone, Ireland, 1912. Died 1966.
Author of several books, but notable in particular for the novel below. This Joycean work has been gaining more and more admirers over the years, and has now become a modern classic. It is scarce, and Grade G–H.

At-Swim-Two-Birds Longman 1939; 1st Amer. Pantheon 1951

O'CASEY, Sean
Born in Dublin 1880. Died 1964.
Author of many plays, though his two highlights were first published within the same volume:

Two Plays: Juno and the Paycock; The Shadow of a Gunman Macmillan 1925
This is quite scarce, and Grade D–E.
A checklist of O'Casey's work may be found in *The New Cambridge Bibliography of English Literature* vol. 4, but the only bibliographies, strangely enough, appear in German and Russian.
O'Casey's *Collected Plays* (4 vols) were published by Macmillan (1949–51).

Films:
Juno and the Paycock British International 1930
Two other films have been made from O'Casey's work.

ORTON, Joe
Born in Leicester 1933. Died 1967.
Master of black comedy in his plays, Orton left a small *œuvre* after his premature death. A novel was published posthumously, but his highlights remain the following two plays, the first of which is his first published work.

1. *Entertaining Mr Sloane* (play) Hamilton 1964; 1st Amer. Grove Press 1965
2. *Loot* (play) Methuen 1967; 1st Amer. Grove Press 1968

No. 1 is Grade B, and No. 2 Grade A.

Films:
Entertaining Mr Sloane Warner Bros 1969
Loot British Lion 1971

ORWELL, George
Pseudonym of Eric Blair. Born in Bengal 1903. Died 1950.
The following list omits books edited by, introduced by, and contributed to by Orwell, and also selections. Details, however, may be found in:
Z. G. Zeke and W. White *George Orwell: A Selected Bibliography* (Boston 1962)

1. *Down and Out in Paris and London* (non-fiction) Gollancz 1933; 1st Amer. Harper 1933
2. *Burmese Days* (novel) Harper 1934; 1st Eng. Gollancz 1935
3. *A Clergyman's Daughter* (novel) Gollancz 1935; 1st Amer. Harper 1936
4. *Keep the Aspidistra Flying* (novel) Gollancz 1936; 1st Amer. Harcourt Brace 1956
5. *The Road to Wigan Pier* (non-fiction) Gollancz 1937; 1st Amer. Harcourt Brace 1958
The 1st was published in orange wrpps under The Left Book Club imprint. A hard-covered trade edition followed.

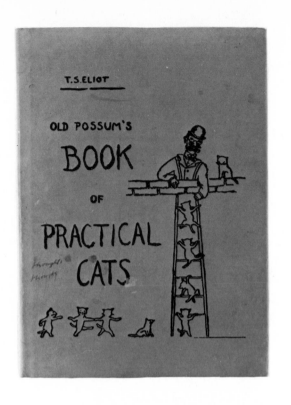

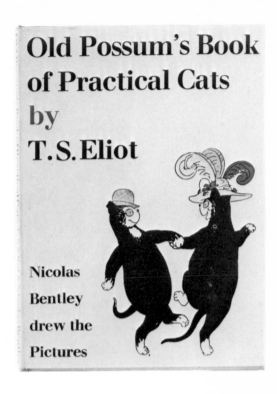

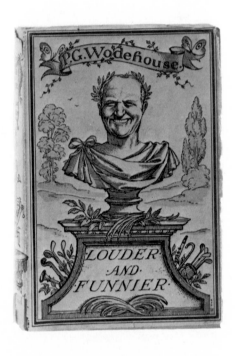

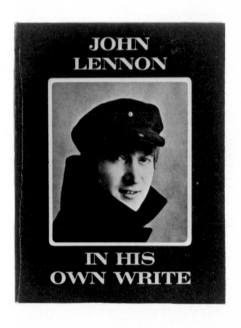

The first (1939) and first illustrated (1940) *Old Possum,* Wodehouse's only book of essays, with a
Rex Whistler d/w (1932), and that Beatle book (1964).

IN PAREN THESIS

Faber and Faber

DAVID JONES

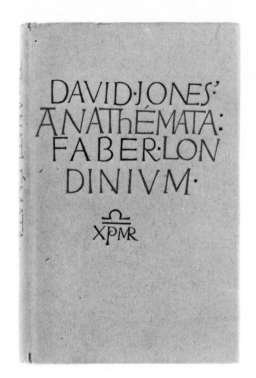

DAVID·JONES'
ANATHÉMATA:
FABER·LON
DINIVM·

XPMR

EPOCH
AND
ARTIST
·
DAVID
JONES
·
FABER
LONDON

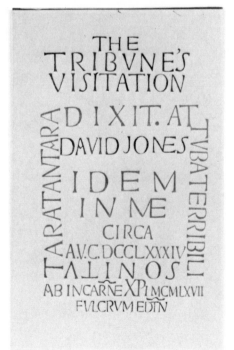

THE
TRIBVNE'S
VISITATION
DIXIT. AT
DAVID JONES
IDEM
IN ME
CIRCA
A.V.C.DCCLXXXIV
TALINOS
AB INCARÑE XPI MCMLXVII
FVLCRVM EDTÑ

TARATANTARA

TVBATERRIBILI

Four by David Jones (1937, 1952, 1959, 1969), three of them with his incomparable artwork.

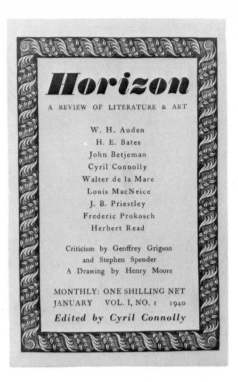

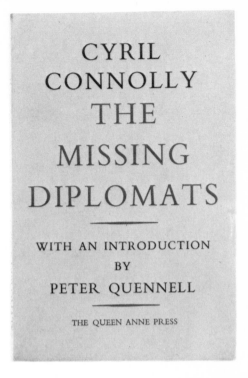

The first issue of *Horizon* (1940), Connolly's book about spies (1952), and the first (limited) Palinurus (1944) next to the first trade edition (1945), with Piper d/w.

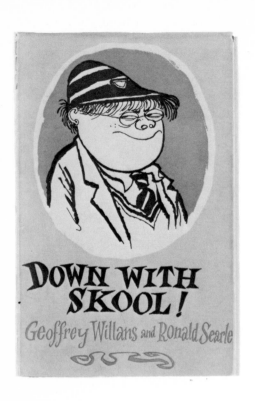

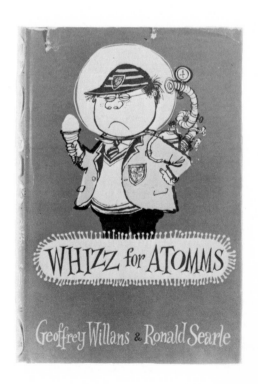

Searle's cover designs for the Molesworth quartet (1953–59).

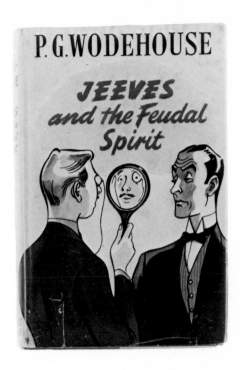

The changing face of Jeeves (1934–71). The last, by Osbert Lancaster, to celebrate
Wodehouse's ninetieth birthday.

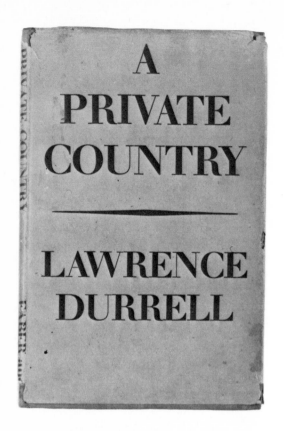

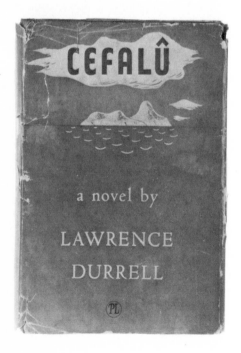
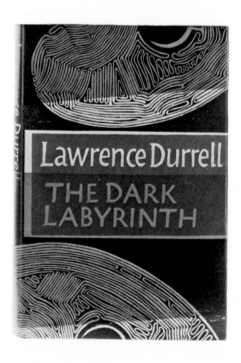

Lawrence Durrell: early verse (1943), the *Alexandria Quartet* (1957–60), and the first edition of *Cefalû* (1947) together with the first Faber edition, called *The Dark Labyrinth* (1961).

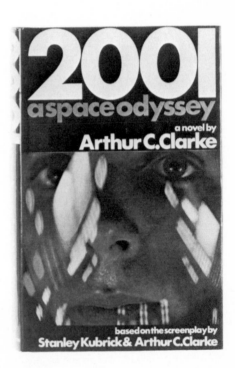

Four works of imagination (1946, 1951, 1954, 1968). The Peake d/w is by Peake.

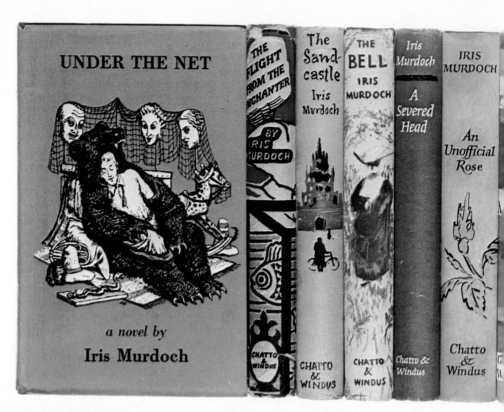

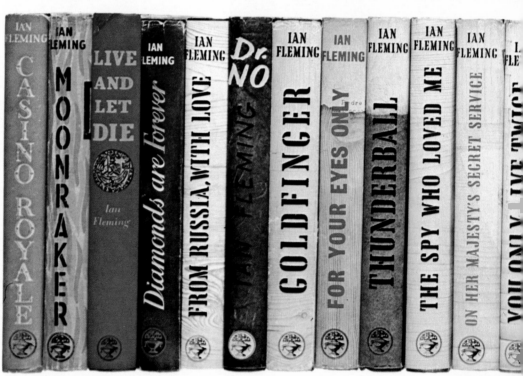

The novels to date (1954–76) of Iris Murdoch, the complete James Bond sequence (1953–66), and
Anthony Powell's *Music of Time* sequence (1951–75).

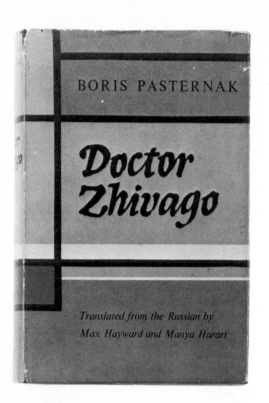

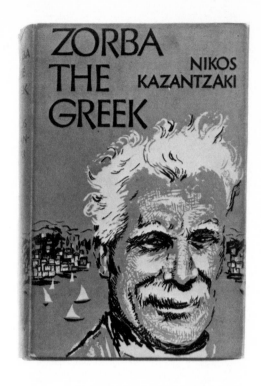

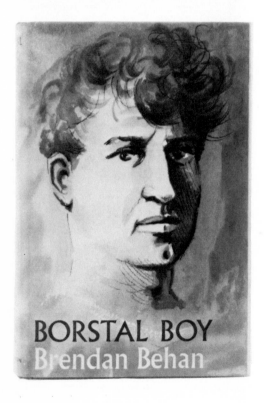

Four prominent novels (1952–63) from Russia, Greece, Ireland and Germany

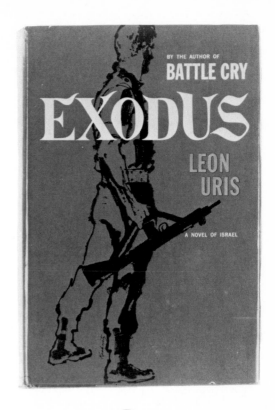

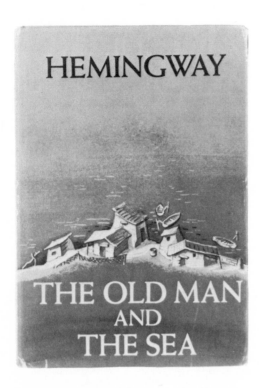

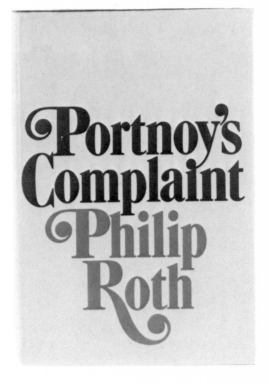

Four outstanding American novels of the fifties and sixties.

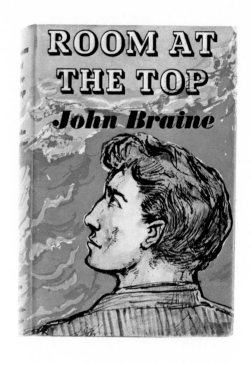

Four influential novels of the fifties: *Saturday Night & Sunday Morning, Room at the Top, A Kind of Loving, Billy Liar.*

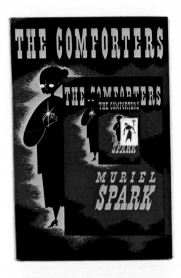
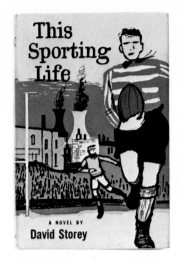

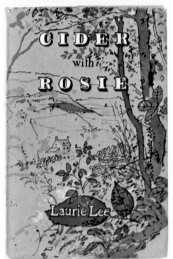
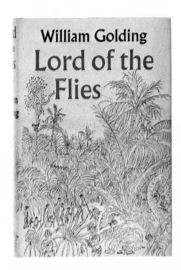
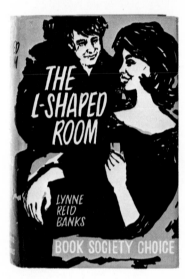

Six prominent novels of the fifties and sixties: *The Comforters, This Sporting Life, The Collector, Cider with Rosie, Lord of the Flies, The L-Shaped Room.*

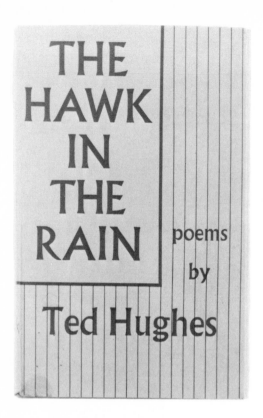

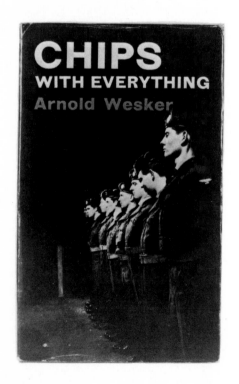

Ted Hughes' first (1957) and second (1960) volumes of verse, Wesker's best-known play (1962), and Stoppard's initial success (1967).

Four plays by Beckett (1959, 1957, 1963, 1964).

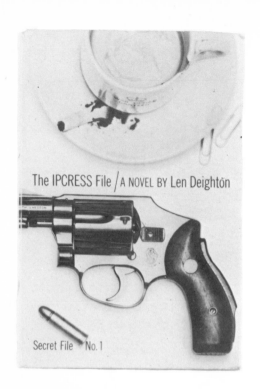

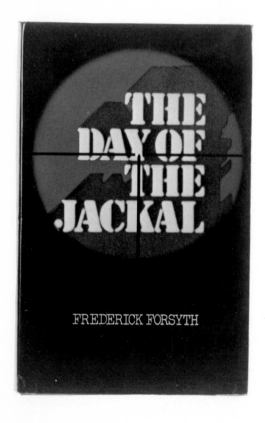

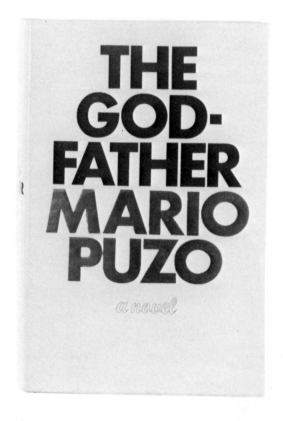

Four famous and filmed thrillers (1962, 1963, 1971, 1969). *The Ipcress File* has the influential Hawkey d/w.

6. *Homage to Catalonia* (non-fiction) Secker & Warburg 1938; 1st Amer. Harcourt Brace 1952
7. *Coming Up for Air* (novel) Gollancz 1939; 1st Amer. Harcourt Brace 1950
8. *Inside the Whale* (essays) Gollancz 1940
9. *The Lion and the Unicorn* (non-fiction) Secker & Warburg 1941
   This was published as Searchlight Books No. 1. Orwell was the editor, with T. R. Fyvel, of ten Searchlight Books, published between 1941 and 1943. Although this was the only one he wrote, he contributed Forewords to two more: T. C. Worsley *The End of the Old School Tie* and J. Cary *The Case for African Freedom.*
10. *Animal Farm* (novel) Secker & Warburg 1945; 1st Amer. Harcourt Brace 1946
11. *James Burnham and the Managerial Revolution* Socialist Book Centre 1946
12. *Critical Essays* Secker & Warburg 1946
13. *Dickens, Dali and Others* Reynal NY 1946 (same as 12)
14. *The English People* (essay) Collins 1947
    This was No. 100 in the Britain in Pictures series.
15. *Nineteen Eighty-Four* (novel) Secker & Warburg 1949; 1st Amer. Harcourt Brace 1949
    The earliest d/w is pink, and not the more common green.
16. *Shooting an Elephant* (essays) Secker & Warburg 1950; 1st Amer. Harcourt Brace 1950
17. *Such, Such Were the Joys* (essays) Harcourt Brace 1953
18. *England, Your England* (essays) Secker & Warburg 1953
    Substantially the same as No. 17.
19. *Selected Essays* Penguin 1957
20. *Selected Writings* Heinemann 1958
21. *Collected Essays* Secker & Warburg 1961 (incl. Nos 12, 16 and 18)
22. *The Collected Essays, Journalism and Letters* (4 vols) Secker & Warburg 1968; 1st Amer. Harcourt Brace 1968

Orwell is extremely popular, and almost all of the early books are very hard to find, and quite expensive; now the good news: *Wigan Pier* was printed in large quantities, and is only Grade C. Not so the rest, however. Nos 1 and 2 could well reach Grade P, and Nos 3 and 4 Grade I–J, or more. Grading is particularly difficult with Orwell, as d/ws are hardly ever present, and therefore the difference in price between a 1st in shabby boards and one in fine d/w can be enormous. Nos 6 and 7 are Grade I, No. 8 Grade C, and No. 9 Grade C also, though more in d/w. Nos 10 and 15, though later works, are highlights, and the prices have been climbing steadily for both. *Animal Farm* is the more scarce, and Grade G–I, depending largely on state of d/w; *1984* has been catalogued within the last year at prices varying between £5 and £45, but generally speaking, a good copy in *pink* d/w could fetch this latter figure, whereas an equally good copy in green d/w would be Grade E–F. Nos 11, 12, 13, 14, 16, 17 and 18 are Grade C. No. 19 is Grade A, Nos 20 and 21 are Grade B, and No. 22 is Grade E.

Films:
Animal Farm Associated British 1954
1984 Associated British 1956

OSBORNE, John
Born in London 1929.

1. *Look Back in Anger* (play) Faber 1957; 1st Amer. Criterion 1957
2. *The Entertainer* (play) Faber 1957; 1st Amer. Criterion 1958
3. *Epitaph for George Dillon* (play) Faber 1958; 1st Amer. Criterion 1958 (with Anthony Creighton)
4. *The World of Paul Slickey* (play) Faber 1959; 1st Amer. Criterion 1961
5. *A Subject of Scandal and Concern* (play) Faber 1961
6. *Luther* (play) Faber 1961; 1st Amer. Dramatic Publishing Co. 1961
7. *Plays for England* Faber 1963; 1st Amer. Criterion 1964 (incl. *The Blood of the Bambergs*

and *Under Plain Cover*)
8. *Tom Jones: A Film Script* Faber 1964; 1st Amer. Grove Press 1964
9. *Inadmissible Evidence* (play) Faber 1965; 1st Amer. Grove Press 1965
10. *A Bond Honoured* (play) Faber 1966
11. *A Patriot for Me* (play) Faber 1966; 1st Amer. Random House 1970
12. *Time Present* and *Hotel in Amsterdam* (plays) Faber 1968
13. *The Right Prospectus* (play) Faber 1970
14. *Very Like a Whale* (play) Faber 1971
15. *West of Suez* (play) Faber 1971
16. *Hedda Gabler* (play: adapt. from Ibsen) Faber 1972
17. *The Gift of Friendship* (play) Faber 1972
18. *A Sense of Detachment* (play) Faber 1973
19. *A Place Calling Itself Rome* (play) Faber 1973
20. *The Picture of Dorian Gray* (play) Faber 1973
21. *The End of Me Old Cigar* (play) Faber 1975
22. *Watch It Come Down* (play) Faber 1975

His earlier works are the most collected, No. 1 being a key work, and Grade D–E. Nos 2, 4 and 6 are Grade C, Nos 3, 5, 7 and 9 are Grade B, and the rest Grade A.

Films:
Look Back in Anger Associated British 1959
The Entertainer British Lion 1960
Inadmissible Evidence Paramount 1968
The film *Tom Jones* (No. 8) was made in 1962 by United Artists.

Two works about Osborne are recommended:
John Russell Taylor *Anger and After* (Methuen 1962)
Simon Trussler *The Plays of John Osborne* (Gollancz 1969)

OWEN, Wilfred
Born in Shropshire 1893. Died 1918.

1. *Poems* Chatto & Windus 1920 (Intro. by Siegfried Sassoon)
2. *The Collected Poems of Wilfred Owen* Chatto & Windus 1963; 1st Amer. New Directions 1964 (Intro. by C. Day Lewis, memoir by Edmund Blunden)
3. *Collected Letters* OUP 1967

No. 1 is exceedingly difficult to find: Grade K upwards. No. 2 is Grade B–C, and No. 3 Grade B.
The prizewinning biography is:
Jon Stallworthy *Wilfred Owen* (OUP/Chatto 1974; US 1975)

PARKINSON, C. Northcote
Born in Durham 1909.
Notable for one book in particular, the title of which has entered the language:

Parkinson's Law Houghton Mifflin 1957; 1st Eng. Murray 1958
Quite uncommon, and Grade B.

PASTERNAK, Boris
Born in Moscow 1890. Died 1960.
Notable in particular for one novel:

Dr Zhivago Collins/Harvill 1958; 1st Amer. Pantheon 1958
Only Grade A–B. First publication was in Italy in 1957.

Film:
Doctor Zhivago MGM 1965

PATTEN, Brian
Born in Liverpool 1946.
Much of Patten's later work has been published by private presses, and these have been omitted. Below appear his books commercially published, all of which are Grade A, at the moment.

1. *Little Johnny's Confession* (verse) Allen & Unwin 1967; 1st Amer. Hill & Wang 1968
2. *Notes to the Hurrying Man* (verse) Allen & Unwin 1969; 1st Amer. Hill & Wang 1969
3. *The Irrelevant Song and Other Poems* Allen & Unwin 1971

Patten has also published two books for children:
The Elephant and the Flower Allen & Unwin 1970

Jumping Mouse Allen & Unwin 1973
He was represented, together with Adrian
Henri and Roger McGough, in *Penguin
Modern Poets* 10: *The Mersey Sound* (1967).

PEAKE, Mervyn

Born in China 1911. Died 1968.
Peake is known just as much for his
illustrations as his writings, but as he
illustrated over twenty books, I must confine
myself to his own works—most of which, of
course, contain his illustrations, and have
d/ws by him.
A bibliography of all his artwork and
exhibitions, however, may be found in:
Maeve Gilmore and Shelagh Johnson *Mervyn
Peake: Writings and Drawings* (Academy 1974).

1. *Captain Slaughterboard Drops Anchor* (juvenile)
   Country Life 1939; 1st Amer. Macmillan
   1967
2. *Shapes and Sounds* (verse) Chatto & Windus
   1941
3. *Rhymes Without Reason* (verse) Eyre &
   Spottiswoode 1944
4. *The Craft of the Lead Pencil* (non-fiction)
   Wingate 1946
5. *Titus Groan* (novel) Eyre & Spottiswoode
   1946; 1st Amer. Reynal & Hitchcock 1946
6. *Letters from a Lost Uncle from Polar Regions*
   (stories) Eyre & Spottiswoode 1948
7. *The Drawings of Mervyn Peake* Grey Walls
   Press 1949
8. *The Glassblowers* (verse) Eyre & Spottiswoode
   1950
9. *Gormenghast* (novel) Eyre & Spottiswoode
   1950; 1st Amer. Weybright & Talley 1967
10. *Mr Pye* (story) Heinemann 1953
11. *Titus Alone* (novel) Eyre & Spottiswoode
    1959; 1st Amer. Weybright & Talley 1967
    This, with Nos 5 and 9, completes the
    trilogy. A revised ed. of *Titus Alone* was
    published by Eyre & Spottiswoode in 1970.
12. *The Rhyme of the Flying Bomb* (verse) Dent
    1962
13. *Selected Poems* Faber 1972
14. *A Book of Nonsense* Owen 1972

Surprisingly, America seems rather
uninterested in this cult figure. In England,
however, enthusiasm is strong, and prices
have risen sharply over the last few years.
Many of the above have been recently
reissued to cope with the demand, but the
1sts remain rare. No. 1 is Grade K or over,
and Nos 2 and 3 are Grade E–F. No. 5 is
the highlight, together with 9 and 11, and
these are Grades G, E and D, respectively—
in the Peake d/ws. Nos 4, 6, 7, 8 and 10 are
Grade D–E, No. 12 is Grade C–D, and Nos
13 and 14 are Grade B.
Two other books of verse were published,
though in limited editions: *Poems and
Drawings* (Keepsake Press 1965; 150 copies),
and *A Reverie of Bone* (Rota 1967; 300 copies).
A biography, containing a bibliography, has
been published:
John Watney *Mervyn Peake* (Joseph 1976).

PERELMAN, S. J.

Born in Brooklyn 1904.
Perelman has written about thirty books—
novels, stories, plays, screenplays,
miscellaneous insanities—all in his own
inimitable style. There are no highlights as
such, though below appears a selection which
deserves to be preserved, if only for the
titles—or, should I say, not least for the titles.

1. *Keep It Crisp* Random House 1946; 1st Eng.
   Heinemann 1947
2. *Acres and Pains* Reynal & Hitchcock 1947;
   1st Eng. Heinemann 1948
3. *Westward Ha! or, Around the World in 80
   Clichés* Simon & Schuster 1947; 1st Eng.
   Reinhardt & Evans 1949
4. *The Swiss Family Perelman* Simon & Schuster
   1950; 1st Eng. Reinhardt & Evans 1951
5. *A Child's Garden of Curses* Heinemann 1951
6. *The Rising Gorge* Simon & Schuster 1961; 1st
   Eng. Heinemann 1962

All the above are Grade B–C (the higher
price for the American eds), and Grade A–B
for No. 6.

Film:
One Touch of Venus Universal 1948
Perelman wrote this screenplay with Ogden
Nash.

PINTER, Harold
Born in London 1930.

1. *The Birthday Party* (play) Encore Publishing
   1959
2. *The Birthday Party and Other Plays* Methuen
   1960 (incl. *The Dumb Waiter* and *The Room*)
3. *The Caretaker* (play) Methuen 1960
4. *A Slight Ache and Other Plays* Methuen
   1961 (incl. *A Night Out, The Dwarfs* and 5
   revue sketches)
5. *The Birthday Party* and *The Room* Grove Press
   NY 1961 (same as No. 2)
6. *The Collection* (play) French 1962
7. *The Caretaker* and *The Room* (plays) Grove
   Press 1962
8. *Three Plays* Grove Press 1962 (incl. *A Slight
   Ache, The Collection, The Dwarfs*)
9. *The Lover* (play) Dramatists Play Service NY
   1965
10. *The Dwarfs* and *Eight Revue Sketches*
    Dramatists Play Service 1965
11. *The Homecoming* (play) Methuen 1965; 1st
    Amer. Grove Press 1966
12. *The Collection* and *The Lover* (plays) Methuen
    1966 (incl. *The Examination*, a prose piece)
13. *Tea Party* (play Grove Press 1966
14. *Tea Party and Other Plays* Methuen 1967 (incl.
    The Basement and *Night School*)
15. *Early Plays* Grove Press 1968 (incl. *A Night
    Out, Night School,* revue sketches)
16. *Poems* Enitharmon Press 1968
    A revised edition was published in 1971, with
    extra poems.
17. *Mac* (memoir) Pendragon Press 1968
18. *Landscape* and *Silence* (plays) Methuen 1969;
    1st Amer. Grove Press 1970 (incl. *Night*)
19. *Five Screenplays* Methuen 1971 (cont. *The
    Caretaker, The Servant, The Pumpkin Eater,
    Accident, The Quiller Memorandum*)
20. *Old Times* (play) Eyre Methuen 1971; 1st
    Amer. Grove Press 1971
21. *Monologue* Covent Garden Press 1973
22. *No Man's Land* (play) Eyre Methuen 1975;
    1st Amer. Grove Press 1975

No. 1 is Grade D. Nos 2, 3 and 4 are Grade
B–C. Nos 5, 7, 8, 9, 10, 11, 12, 13, 14, 15, 18
and 20 are Grade B. No. 6 is Grade A, Nos
16 and 17 Grade B–C. No. 19 is also Grade
B–C, No. 21 is Grade B, and No. 22 is Grade
A.

Films:
The Caretaker British Lion 1963
The Birthday Party Cinerama 1968
In addition to those in No. 19, Pinter also
wrote the screenplay for *The Go-Between*
(MGM/EMI 1971), though this has not been
published.

PLATH, Sylvia
Born in America 1932. Died 1963.

1. *The Colossus and Other Poems* Heinemann
   1960; 1st Amer. Knopf 1962
2. *The Bell Jar* (novel) Heinemann 1963
   This was published under the pseudonym of
   Victoria Lucas. It first appeared under Plath's
   own name in 1966, from Faber.
3. *Ariel* (verse) Faber 1965; 1st Amer. Harper
   Row 1966
4. *Uncollected Poems* Turret Press 1965
   This edition was limited to 150 copies.
5. *Three Women* (play) Turret Press 1968
   This edition was limited to 150 copies.
6. *The Art of Sylvia Plath* (symposium) Faber
   1970; 1st Amer. Indiana University Press
   1970
7. *Crossing the Water* (verse) Faber 1971; 1st
   Amer. Harper Row 1971
8. *Winter Trees* (verse) Faber 1971; 1st Amer.
   Harper Row 1972
9. *The Crystal Gazer* (verse) Rainbow Press 1971
   Limited to 480 copies, 80 specially bound.
10. *Million Dollar Month* (verse) Sceptre Press
    1971
    Limited to 150 copies.
11. *Pursuit* (verse) Rainbow Press 1973
    Limited to 100 copies, Illus. By Leonard
    Baskin, with an original etching.

12. *Letters Home* (letters) Harper Row 1975; 1st Eng. Faber 1976
13. *The Bed Book* (juvenile) Faber 1976; 1st Amer. Harper Row 1976
14. *Johnny Panic and the Bible of Dreams* (prose) Faber 1977

Certainly one of the most popular contemporary poets, and inevitably this is reflected in the prices. Nos 1 and 2 are very scarce, and might fetch anything a dealer cared to ask, though certainly Grade K–L upwards. No. 3 is considered a highlight, and Grade D. The strict limitation on Nos 4 and 5 encourages a high price, No. 4 having been catalogued by a major London dealer in 1974 at £95—though most dealers would regard that as rather high. The same dealer listed No. 5 at £40, which is about right. No. 6, inexplicably, went out of print very quickly, and is now Grade B–C, as are Nos 7, 8, 12 and 14. No. 13 is Grade A, at the moment. No. 9 is Grade F or Grade J, depending on binding, No. 10 Grade C, and no. 11 Grade J.

PLOMER, William
British. Born in South Africa 1903. Died 1973.
Although one thinks of Plomer as a poet, he published far more prose than verse, and indeed it is for some of these prose works that he is best remembered. A selection appears below, though a checklist may be found in *The New Cambridge Bibliography of English Literature* vol. 4, and a bibliography in: John R. Doyle *William Plomer* (Twayne NY 1969)

1. *Turbott Wolfe* (novel) Hogarth Press 1926; 1st Amer. Harcourt Brace 1926
2. *Sado* (novel) Hogarth Press 1931
   This was published in America as *They Never Came Back* by Coward McCann in 1932.
3. *The Case Is Altered* (novel) Hogarth Press 1932; 1st Amer. Farrar & Rinehart 1932
4. *Double Lives* (autobiog.) Cape 1943; 1st Amer. Noonday Press 1956
5. *At Home: Memoirs* Cape 1958; 1st Amer.

Noonday Press 1958
6. *Collected Poems* Cape 1960
7. *The Butterfly Ball and the Grasshopper's Feast* (juvenile) Cape 1973
   Illus. Alan Aldridge.

No. 1 is Plomer's 1st novel, and a desirable Hogarth Press item: Grade D–E. Nos 2 and 3 are Grade B–C, and the remainder Grade A–B.

POUND, Ezra
Born in Idaho 1885. Died in 1972.
There is a first-class bibliography for collectors of Pound, and it is absolutely essential, for he is not an easy man to collect. Many works have been issued in various editions, many limited and private press editions have been published, as well as instalments of the epic *Cantos*—this last leading to several collected editions. Donald Gallup *A Bibliography of Ezra Pound* (Soho Bibliographies, Hart-Davis 1963) Below appears a selection of Pound's works.

1. *A Lume Spento* (verse) Antonini, Venice 1908
   This, Pound's first book, was an edition of only 100 copies. Now extremely rare and near priceless, it was reissued in 1965 by New Directions, USA, and by Faber in England.
2. *Personae* (verse) Mathews 1909
3. *Exultations* (verse) Mathews 1909
4. *The Spirit of Romance* (prose) Dent 1910; 1st Amer. Dutton 1910
5. *Canzoni* (verse) Mathews 1911
6. *Ripostes* (verse) Swift 1912; 1st Amer. Small Maynard 1913
7. *Cathay* (translations) Mathews 1915
8. *Gaudier-Brzeska* (memoir) Bodley Head 1916; 1st Amer. Lane 1916
9. *Poems 1918–21* Boni & Liveright 1921
10. *Selected Poems* Faber & Gwyer 1928
    Includes Introduction by T. S. Eliot.
11. *A Draft of XXX Cantos* Hours Press, Paris 1930; 1st Amer. Farrar & Rinehart 1933; 1st Eng. Faber 1933
    The Paris ed. was limited to 210 copies, 10 signed.

12. *How to Read* (prose) Harmsworth 1931
13. *ABC of Economics* (prose) Faber 1933; 1st Amer. New Directions 1940
14. *ABC of Reading* (prose) Routledge 1934; 1st Amer. Yale 1934
15. *Make It New* (essays) Faber 1934; 1st Amer. Yale 1935
16. *Eleven New Cantos: XXXI–XLI* Farrar & Rinehart 1934
    This was published in 1935 by Faber as *A Draft of Cantos XXXI–XLI.*
17. *Homage to Sextus Propertius* (verse) Faber 1934
18. *Polite Essays* Faber 1937; 1st Amer. New Directions 1940
19. *The Fifth Decad of Cantos* Faber 1937; 1st Amer. Farrar & Rinehart 1937
20. *Guide to Kulchur* (prose) Faber 1938; 1st Amer. New Directions 1938
21. *Cantos LII–LXXI* Faber 1940; 1st Amer. New Directions 1940
22. *The Pisan Cantos* New Directions 1948; 1st Eng. Faber 1949
23. *The Cantos* New Directions 1948
    This was published in 1950 by Faber as *Seventy Cantos.*
24. *The Cantos of Ezra Pound* Faber 1954
    This is as above, but including No. 22. New Collected Editions of the *Cantos* were published by Faber in 1964 and 1976.
25. *Patria Mia* (prose) Seymour 1950; 1st Eng. Owen 1962
26. *The Letters of Ezra Pound* Harcourt Brace 1950; 1st Eng. Faber 1951
27. *The Translations of Ezra Pound* Faber 1953; 1st Amer. New Directions 1953
28. *Literary Essays of Ezra Pound* Faber 1954; 1st Amer. New Directions 1954 (incl. Intro. by T. S. Eliot)
29. *Section Rock-Drill* (cantos) Pesce d'Oro, Milan 1955; 1st Amer. New Directions 1956; 1st Eng. Faber 1957
    The Milan edition consisted of 506 copies.
30. *Thrones* (cantos) Pesce d'Oro, Milan 1959; 1st Amer. New Directions 1959; 1st Eng. Faber 1960
    The Milan edition consisted of 300 copies.
31. *Pound/Joyce* (letters) New Directions 1967; 1st Eng. Faber 1968

32. *Drafts and Fragments of Cantos CX–CXVII* New Directions 1969; 1st Eng. Faber 1970
33. *Selected Prose 1909–65* Faber 1973; 1st Amer. New Directions 1975
34. *Collected Early Poems* Faber 1977
    Published at £12.

Nos 2–6 are very scarce, and prices tend to be huge. A presentation copy of No. 2 was catalogued recently by a London dealer at £475, and this is not excessive—although it is true that Pound's signature adds vastly to the value. No. 31, for instance, is quite an easy book and Grade B–C, though a presentation copy would be at least Grade K or L. Nos 7 and 8 are Grade L–M, No. 9 is Grade I, and No. 10 Grade G. The American or English eds. of No. 11 would be Grade E, though a signed Hours Press edition should top £500. Nos 12–16 are Grade E–G, Nos 17–22 Grade E–F, and Nos 23, 24, 25, 26, 27, 28 and 31 are Grade C. Nos 32 and 33 are Grade B, as are the English and American editions of Nos 29 and 30, though the Milan editions would be Grade E–F.

In addition to the bibliography, two books that are of great value:

Noel Stock *The Life of Ezra Pound* Pantheon 1970; 1st Eng. Routledge 1970

Hugh Kenner *The Pound Era* University of California 1971; 1st Eng. Faber 1972

POWELL, Anthony

Powell was born in London in 1905, and educated at Eton and Balliol. He has been a publisher, a scriptwriter for Warner Bros, and literary editor of *Punch*, as well as reviewing for the *Daily Telegraph, Times Literary Supplement, Observer,* etc. His five pre-war novels, though still in print, are very difficult to find in 1sts, and the price for fine copies is Grade K, up. It is probably for the *Music of Time* sequence that he will be best remembered, however, and these are not so very scarce, and the prices reasonable—a lot lower than they will be in five years' time. *A Question of Upbringing* is the most difficult, and this might be Grade E–G, whereas *A Buyer's Market* and *The Acceptance World* would be Grade D. The rest should be Grade B–C, for all but the most recent, but they are getting hard to find, and this might soon be reflected in a rise. They are pleasing volumes from the collector's point of view—small, and all in uniform red *cloth* with black labels; the fine Broom-Lynne d/ws are worthy of display. For the record, Powell likes his name pronounced with the first syllable rhyming with 'no', as opposed to 'now'.

1. *Afternoon Men* (novel) Duckworth 1931; 1st Amer. Holt 1932
2. *Venusberg* (novel) Duckworth 1932; 1st Amer. Holliday 1952
3. *From a View to a Death* (novel) Duckworth 1933
   This was published as *Mr Zouch: Superman* by the Vanguard Press in 1934, though the Little Brown reissue of 1964 mercifully returns to the original title.
4. *Caledonia: A Fragment* privately printed 1934
5. *Agents and Patients* (novel) Duckworth 1936; 1st Amer. Holliday 1952
6. *What's Become of Waring* (novel) Cassell 1939; 1st Amer. Little Brown 1963
7. *John Aubrey and His Friends* (non-fiction) Heinemann 1948; 1st Amer. Scribner 1949

The following comprise *A Dance to the Music of Time*:

8. *A Question of Upbringing* (novel) Heinemann 1951; 1st Amer. Scribner 1951
9. *A Buyer's Market* (novel) Heinemann 1952; 1st Amer. Scribner 1953
10. *The Acceptance World* (novel) Heinemann 1955; 1st Amer. Farrar Straus 1956
11. *At Lady Molly's* (novel) Heinemann 1957; 1st Amer. Little Brown 1958
12. *Casanova's Chinese Restaurant* (novel) Heinemann 1960; 1st Amer. Little Brown 1960
13. *The Kindly Ones* (novel) Heinemann 1962; 1st Amer. Little Brown 1962
14. *The Valley of Bones* (novel) Heinemann 1964; 1st Amer. Little Brown 1964
15. *The Soldier's Art* (novel) Heinemann 1966; 1st Amer. Little Brown 1966
16. *The Military Philosophers* (novel) Heinemann 1968; 1st Amer. Little Brown 1969
17. *Books Do Furnish a Room* (novel) Heinemann 1971; 1st Amer. Little Brown 1971
18. *Temporary Kings* (novel) Heinemann 1973; 1st Amer. Little Brown 1973
19. *Hearing Secret Harmonies* (novel) Heinemann 1975; 1st Amer. Little Brown 1975

Powell has also published:

20. *The Garden God* and *The Rest I'll Whistle* (plays) Heinemann 1971; 1st Amer. Little Brown 1972
21. *Infants of the Spring* (autobiog.) Heinemann 1976; 1st Amer. Little Brown 1976
    The first volume of *To Keep the Ball Rolling*.

Powell has edited, with an Introduction, the following:

22. *Novels of High Society from the Victorian Age* Pilot 1947
23. *Brief Lives and Other Selected Writings of John Aubrey* Cresset Press 1949; 1st Amer. Scribner 1949
24. *The Complete Ronald Firbank* Duckworth 1961

No. 22 is Grade C, and Nos 20, 21, 23 and 24 Grade B.
The following criticism has been published:

Robert K. Morris *The Novels of Anthony Powell* (University of Pittsburg 1968).

THE POWYS BROTHERS

POWYS, J. C.
Born in Derbyshire 1872. Died 1963.
Author of about fifty books, a checklist of which may be found in *The New Cambridge Bibliography of English Literature* vol. 4, and a more detailed account—though limited to the date of publication—in:
L. E. Siberell *A Bibliography of the First Editions of Powys* (Cincinnati 1934; Intro. by J. C. Powys)
Below appears a selection.

1. *Wolf Solent* (novel) Simon & Schuster 1929; 1st Eng. Cape 1929

The Amer. ed. is in two volumes, the English in one.

2. *The Meaning of Culture* (prose) Norton 1929; 1st Eng. Cape 1930
3. *In Defense of Sensuality* (philosophy) Simon & Schuster 1930; 1st Eng. Gollancz 1930
4. *A Glastonbury Romance* (novel) Simon & Schuster 1932; 1st Eng. Bodley Head 1933
5. *A Philosophy of Solitude* Simon & Schuster 1933; 1st Eng. Cape 1933
6. *Weymouth Sands* (novel) Simon & Schuster 1934
   This was published in England by The Bodley Head in 1935 as *Jobber Skald*.

POWYS, Llewelyn
Born in Dorchester 1884. Died 1939.
Author of about thirty books, a checklist of which appears in *The New Cambridge Bibliography of English Literature* vol. 4, and also in:
Kenneth Hopkins *Llewelyn Powys: A Selection* (1952)
Below is a brief selection:

7. *Apples Be Ripe* (novel) Harcourt Brace 1930; 1st Eng. Longman 1930
8. *Dorset Essays* Bodley Head 1935; 1st Amer. Simon & Schuster 1938
9. *Love and Death* (novel) Bodley Head 1939; 1st Amer. Simon & Schuster 1941

POWYS, T. F.
Born in Dorset 1875. Died 1953.
Author of about three dozen books, a checklist of which may be found in *The New Cambridge Bibliography of English Literature* vol. 4, and more detailed information in:
A. P. Riley *A Bibliography of Powys* (Hastings 1967).
Two of his books appear below.

10. *Mr Weston's Good Wine* (novel) Viking Press 1928; 1st Eng. Chatto & Windus 1928
    The American edition was preceded by a limited ed. (660 copies).
11. *The White Paternoster* (stories) Chatto & Windus 1930; 1st Amer. Viking Press 1931

Two books of note concerning the Powys brothers are:
Louis Marlow *Welsh Ambassadors (Powys Lives and Letters)* (Chapman & Hall 1936)
Kenneth Hopkins *The Powys Brothers* (Phoenix 1967)
The Powys brothers have been collected for a long time, and recent reissues have generated further interest. J. C. Powys remains the favourite with collectors, however, with No. 1 at Grade F, Nos 2, 3, and 4 at Grade D, No. 5 Grade C, and No. 6 Grade E—for this is a highlight.
Llewelyn does not command quite such prices, with No. 7 at Grade C, and Nos 8 and 9 at Grade B.
No. 10 is a very well-known book, and Grade E–F. T. F. Powys' volume of stories (No. 11) is Grade C–D.
It must be borne in mind that all three brothers published many limited, signed editions—some simultaneously with the trade editions, some preceding them, and some being original press books in their own right. The prices for these, of course, rise accordingly.

PRIESTLEY, J. B.
Born in Yorkshire 1894.
Author of over thirty novels and books of stories, over sixty plays, and over sixty other works, Priestley is still much loved by the English, although collectors are not so enthusiastic now as they have been. Some works of Priestley are always in demand, however, and a selection of these follows.

1. *The Good Companions* (novel) Heinemann 1929; 1st Amer. Harper 1929
2. *Angel Pavement* (novel) Heinemann 1930; 1st Amer. Harper 1930
3. *When We Are Married* (play) Heinemann 1938; 1st Amer. French 1940
4. *Rain Upon Gadshill* (autobiog.) Heinemann 1939; 1st Amer. Harper 1939
5. *Literature and Western Man* (non-fiction) Heinemann 1960; 1st Amer. Harper 1960
6. *The Prince of Pleasure* (non-fiction) Heinemann

1969; 1st Amer. Harper 1969
7. *The Edwardians* (non-fiction) Heinemann 1970; 1st Amer. Harper 1970
8. *Victoria's Heyday* (non-fiction) Heinemann 1972; 1st Amer. Harcourt Brace 1972
9. *The English* (non-fiction) Heinemann 1973; 1st Amer. Viking Press 1973

Nos 1 and 2 are large books with very distinctive d/ws, and Grade B–C, and A–B respectively—though considerably less without d/w. Nos 3, 4 and 5 are Grade A–B, as are the four beautifully illustrated and produced 'history' books (Nos 6–9).

Films:
The Good Companions 20th Century Fox 1933; Associated British 1957
When We Are Married British National 1943
In addition to these, seven other films have been made from Priestley books.

PRITCHETT, V. S.
Born in Suffolk 1900.
Author of about thirty books, Pritchett is noted chiefly for his short stories and his non-fiction works. Below appears a selection.

1. *The Living Novel* (non-fiction) Chatto & Windus 1946; 1st Amer. Reynal 1947
2. *Collected Stories* Chatto & Windus 1956
3. *A Cab at the Door* (autobiog.) Chatto & Windus 1968; 1st Amer. Random House 1968
4. *Midnight Oil* (autobiog.) Chatto & Windus 1971; 1st Amer. Random House 1972

No.1 is Grade B, and the remainder Grade A.

PUZO, Mario
Born in New York 1920.
Author of less than half-a-dozen books, one of which became a frantic best-seller, and was made into a box-office-breaking film. Nonetheless, it is sought after by quite a few.

The Godfather (novel) Putnam 1969; 1st Eng. Heinemann 1969
Grade B.

Film:
The Godfather Paramount 1971

RAINE, Kathleen
Born in London 1908.

1. *Stone and Flower: Poems 1935–43* Nicholson & Watson 1943
2. *Living in Time: Poems* Editions Poetry 1946
3. *The Pythoness and Other Poems* Hamilton 1949; 1st Amer. Farrar Straus 1952
4. *William Blake* (prose) Longman 1951
5. *Selected Poems* Weekend Press NY 1952
6. *The Year One: Poems* Hamilton 1952; 1st Amer. Farrar Straus 1953
7. *Coleridge* (prose) Longman 1953
8. *The Collected Poems of Kathleen Raine* Hamilton 1956; 1st Amer. Random House 1957
9. *Blake and England* (lecture) Heffer 1960; 1st Amer. Folcroft Editions 1974
10. *The Hollow Hill and Other Poems 1960–1964* Hamilton 1965
11. *Defending Ancient Springs* (essays) OUP 1967
12. *The Written Word* (prose) Enitharmon Press 1967
13. *Six Dreams and Other Poems* Enitharmon Press 1968
14. *Ninfa Revisited* (verse) Enitharmon Press 1968
15. *Blake and Tradition* (prose) Princeton 1968; 1st Eng. Routledge 1969
16. *A Question of Poetry* Gilbertson, Devon 1969
17. *The Lost Country* (verse) Dolmen Press/Hamilton 1971
18. *William Blake* (non-fiction) Thames & Hudson 1971
19. *Faces of Day and Night* (autobiog.) Enitharmon Press 1972
20. *Yeats, the Tarot, and the Golden Dawn* Dolmen Press 1972; 1st Amer. Humanities Press 1973
21. *Farewell, Happy Fields* (autobiog.) Hamilton 1973
22. *On a Deserted Shore* (verse) Dolmen Press/Hamilton 1973
23. *Death in Life, Life in Death* (non-fiction) Dolmen Press 1974
24. *Blake and Antiquity* (non-fiction) Princeton 1974
25. *David Jones: Solitary Perfectionist* Golgonooza Press 1974
26. *The Land Unknown* (autobiog.) Hamilton 1975

27. *The Oval Portrait* (verse) Hamilton 1977

No. 1 is Grade D, Nos 2 and 3 Grade C, and all the others Grade B. In addition to the above, Kathleen Raine edited many volumes.

RANSOME, Arthur
Born in Leeds 1884. Died 1967.
Author of a long line of children's books, though it is the first that has endured and has become a classic, though all remain very popular. Quite scarce now, and Grade C–D.

Swallows and Amazons Cape 1930; 1st Amer. Lippincott 1931

Film:
Swallows and Amazons EMI 1973

RAVEN, Simon
Born in London 1927.

1. *The Feathers of Death* (novel) Blond 1959; 1st Amer. Simon & Schuster 1960
2. *Brother Cain* (novel) Blond 1959; 1st Amer. Simon & Schuster 1960
3. *Doctors Wear Scarlet* (novel) Blond 1960; 1st Amer. Simon & Schuster 1961
4. *The English Gentleman* (essay) Blond 1961
Interestingly enough, this was published in America by Simon & Schuster in 1962 as *The Decline of the English Gentleman*.
5. *Close of Play* (novel) Blond 1962
6. *Boys Will Be Boys and Other Essays* Blond 1963
The following ten novels form the *Alms for Oblivion* sequence:
7. *The Rich Pay Late* Blond 1964; 1st Amer. Putnam 1965
8. *Friends in Low Places* Blond 1965; 1st Amer. Putnam 1966
9. *The Sabre Squadron* Blond 1966; 1st Amer. Harper 1967
10. *Fielding Gray* Blond 1967
11. *The Judas Boy* Blond 1968
12. *Places Where They Sing* Blond 1970
13. *Sound the Retreat* Blond 1971
14. *Come Like Shadows* Blond & Briggs 1972
15. *Bring Forth the Body* Blond & Briggs 1974
16. *The Survivors* Blond & Briggs 1976
This completes the sequence

17. *The Fortunes of Fingel* (stories) Blond & Briggs 1976

Blond also published, in 1966, *Royal Foundation and Other Plays*. Raven has written many television and radio plays, though unpublished.
Virtually all the above are within Grade A at the moment, though the recent completion of the sequence might indicate a rise.

Film:
Incense for the Damned Gaumont 1970 (*Doctors Wear Scarlet*)

READ, Herbert
Born in Yorkshire 1893. Died 1968.
Read actually published over 100 books—most of them on art—and a checklist of them may be found in the following valuable work: George Woodcock *Herbert Read: The Stream and the Source* (Faber 1972).
Below are some highlights.

1. *Collected Poems 1913–25* Faber & Gwyer 1926
2. *English Prose Style* (criticism) Bell 1928; 1st Amer. Holt 1928
3. *The Meaning of Art* Faber 1931
4. *Art Now* Faber 1933; 1st Amer. Harcourt Brace 1937
A particularly fine piece of book production, with its bold blue and white graphics on black cloth, handsome sans-serif type, and Jean Cocteau frontis.
5. *Art and Industry* Faber 1934
6. *The Green Child* (novel) Heinemann 1935; 1st Amer. New Directions 1948
7. *Surrealism* (edited by H.R.) Faber 1936
8. *Art and Society* Heinemann 1937; 1st Amer. Macmillan 1937
9. *Education Through Art* Faber 1943; 1st Amer. Pantheon n.d.
10. *Collected Poems* Faber 1946
A revised edition was published by the Horizon Press in 1966.
11. *The Contrary Experience* (autobiog.) Faber 1963; 1st Amer. Horizon Press 1963

Nos 1, 2, 4, 5, 6 and 7 are Grade C. Nos 3 and 8–11 are Grade B.

RHYS, Jean
Born in Dominica, West Indies 1894. British.

1. *The Left Bank and Other Stories* Cape 1927; 1st Amer. Harper 1927
2. *Postures* (novel) Chatto & Windus 1928 Published in USA as *Quartet* by Simon & Schuster in 1929.
3. *After Leaving Mr Mackenzie* (novel) Cape 1931; 1st Amer. Knopf 1931
4. *Voyage in the Dark* (novel) Constable 1934; 1st Amer. Morrow 1935
5. *Good Morning, Midnight* (novel) Constable 1939
6. *Wide Sargasso Sea* (novel) Deutsch 1966; 1st Amer. Norton 1966
7. *Tigers Are Better Looking* (stories) Deutsch 1968; 1st Amer. Harper 1974
8. *Sleep It Off Lady* (stories) Deutsch 1976; 1st Amer. Harper 1976

Although a very small output, a very big reputation. The early 1sts are scarce, and much in demand. No. 1 is Grade K, and Nos 2–5 are Grade F–G. Nos 6 and 7 are Grade B.

RICHARDS, Frank
Pseudonym of Charles Hamilton. Born in Middlesex 1876. Died 1961.
Known chiefly for his stories in *The Magnet* and *The Gem* during the early nineteen hundreds, which he wrote under many pseudonyms—Martin Clifford, Owen Conquest, Hilda Richards—and, of course, Frank Richards. From 1947 until some years after his death a series of Billy Bunter novels were published—his first appearance in book form— and with yellow-spined pictorial d/ws. A list appears below.

The following were published by Skilton:

1. *Billy Bunter of Greyfriars School* 1947
2. *Billy Bunter's Banknote* 1948
3. *Billy Bunter's Barring-Out* 1948
4. *Billy Bunter's Christmas Party* 1949
5. *Billy Bunter in Brazil* 1949
6. *Billy Bunter's Benefit* 1950
7. *Billy Bunter Among the Cannibals* 1950
8. *Billy Bunter's Postal Order* 1951
9. *Billy Bunter Butts In* 1951
10. *Billy Bunter and the Blue Mauritius* 1952

The following were published by Cassell:

11. *Billy Bunter's Beanfeast* 1952
12. *Billy Bunter's Brain-Wave* 1953
13. *Billy Bunter's First Case* 1953
14. *Billy Bunter the Bold* 1954
15. *Bunter Does His Best* 1954
16. *Billy Bunter's Double* 1955
17. *Backing Up Billy Bunter* 1955
18. *Lord Billy Bunter* 1956
19. *The Banishing of Billy Bunter* 1956
20. *Billy Bunter's Bolt* 1957
21. *Billy Bunter Afloat* 1957
22. *Billy Bunter's Bargain* 1958
23. *Billy Bunter the Hiker* 1958
24. *Bunter Out of Bounds* 1959
25. *Bunter Comes for Christmas* 1959
26. *Bunter the Bad Lad* 1960
27. *Bunter Keeps It Dark* 1960
28. *Billy Bunter's Treasure-Hunt* 1961
29. *Billy Bunter at Butlin's* 1961
30. *Bunter the Ventriloquist* 1961
31. *Bunter the Caravanner* 1962
32. *Billy Bunter's Bodyguard* 1962
33. *Big Chief Bunter* 1963
34. *Just Like Bunter* 1963
35. *Bunter the Stowaway* 1964
36. *Thanks to Bunter* 1964
37. *Bunter the Sportsman* 1965
38. *Bunter's Last Fling* 1965

Richards also published:

39. *Bessie Bunter of Cliff House School* Skilton 1949 (pseud. Hilda Richards)
The only Bessie Bunter novel published.
40. *The Autobiography of Frank Richards* Skilton 1952
No. 1 is Grade B, as is No. 40, though the rest should still be Grade A. The price drops considerably in the absence of d/ws. Because librarians seem to see these books only as unfair to the fat child, they have ceased to buy them. Publishers, therefore, have ceased to print them. Aficionados are searching out the 1sts, however, and they are not so common as a few years ago.
See also: W. O. Lofts and D. J. Adley *The World of Frank Richards* (Howard Baker 1975)

ROHMER, Sax

Pseudonym of Arthur Sarsfield Ward. Born in Birmingham 1883. Died 1959.
Creator of the arch-villain Fu Manchu, about whom he centred a long stream of novels. Below are the first, and one of the better known.

1. *The Mystery of Dr Fu Manchu* Methuen 1913
2. *The Bride of Fu Manchu* Cassell 1933
   This was published in America as *Fu Manchu's Bride* by Doubleday in the same year.

No. 1 might be Grade E, though most of the others should be A–B.

Films:
Mysterious Dr Fu Manchu Paramount 1929
Many others were filmed.

ROSENBERG, Isaac

Born in Bristol 1890. Died 1918.
Another casualty of the Great War, Rosenberg was a poet's poet, his work always having been admired by his contemporaries. *Night and Day* (1912), *Youth* (1915), *Moses* (1916) were printed in his lifetime, and are very scarce—all within Grade K–L. The following two works rekindled interest:

1. *Collected Works* Chatto & Windus 1937
2. *Collected Poems* Chatto & Windus 1949; 1st Amer. Schocken 1949

These are Grade E and C, respectively.

ROTH, Philip

Born in New Jersey 1933.
Surprisingly, there is already a bibliography of Roth:
Bernard F. Rodgers *Philip Roth: A Bibliography* (Scarecrow Press 1974)
Below are all his works to date.

1. *Goodbye Columbus* and *Five Short Stories* Houghton Mifflin 1959; 1st Eng. Deutsch 1959
2. *Letting Go* (novel) Random House 1962; 1st Eng. Deutsch 1962

3. *When She Was Good* (novel) Random House 1967; 1st Eng. Cape 1967
4. *Portnoy's Complaint* (novel) Random House 1969; 1st Eng. Cape 1970
5. *Our Gang* (novel) Random House 1971; 1st Eng. Cape 1971
6. *The Breast* (novel) Holt Rinehart 1972; 1st Eng. Cape 1973
7. *The Great American Novel* (novel) Holt Rinehart 1973; 1st Eng. Cape 1973
8. *My Life as a Man* (novel) Holt Rinehart 1974; 1st Eng. Cape 1974
9. *Reading Myself and Others* (prose) Farrar Straus 1975; 1st Eng. Cape 1975

No. 1 is Grade C, Nos 2 and 3 Grade A–B, No. 4—the highlight—Grade B–C, and the remainder Grade A. The English editions are less—the 1st Cape of No. 4, for instance, is well within Grade A.

Films:
Goodbye Columbus Paramount 1969
Portnoy's Complaint Columbia/Warner Bros 1972

RUNYON, Damon

Born in Kansas 1880. Died 1946.
Notable in particular for the following, now Grade C–D.

Guys and Dolls (stories) Stokes 1931; 1st Eng. Jarrolds 1932

Many Runyon stories have been filmed, and drawn from for musicals.

RUSSELL, Bertrand

3rd Earl Russell. Born in Wales 1872. Died 1970.
Russell published over 120 books in his long lifetime, and made contributions to 50 more. The more popular titles appear below, though a checklist of his works may be found in *The New Cambridge Bibliography of English Literature* vol. 4.

1. *Sceptical Essays* Allen & Unwin 1928; 1st Amer. Norton 1928
2. *Marriage and Morals* (philosophy) Allen & Unwin 1929; 1st Amer. Liveright 1929

3. *The Conquest of Happiness* (philosophy) Allen & Unwin 1930; 1st Amer. Liveright 1930
4. *In Praise of Idleness* (philosophy) Allen & Unwin 1935; 1st Amer. Norton 1935
5. *History of Western Philosophy* Allen & Unwin 1945; 1st Amer. Simon & Schuster 1946
6. *Satan in the Suburbs* (stories) Bodley Head 1953; 1st Amer. Simon & Schuster 1953
7. *Nightmares of Eminent Persons* (stories) Bodley Head 1954; 1st Amer. Simon & Schuster 1955
8. *Portraits from Memory* (memoirs) Allen & Unwin 1956; 1st Amer. Simon & Schuster 1956
9. *Fact and Fiction* (miscellany) Allen & Unwin 1961; 1st Amer. Simon & Schuster 1962
10. *Autobiography* (3 vols) Allen & Unwin 1967–9; 1st Amer. Little Brown 1967–9

Prices for Russell are lower than one would think, all the above being Grade B, with the exception of the *Autobiography*, which is Grade C.

SACKVILLE-WEST, Vita
Born in Kent 1892. Died 1962.
Victoria Sackville-West published around sixty books, a checklist of which appears in *The New Cambridge Bibliography of English Literature* vol. 4, and a selection below. There is much material concerning her in Harold Nicolson (her husband) *Diaries and Letters* (3 vols; Collins 1966–68; Atheneum 1966–68).

1. *The Edwardians* (novel) Hogarth Press 1930; 1st Amer. Doubleday 1930
2. *All Passion Spent* (novel) Hogarth Press 1931; 1st Amer. Doubleday 1931
3. *Collected Poems* (vol. 1) Hogarth Press 1933; 1st Amer. Doubleday 1934
   No second volume was ever published.
4. *The Garden* (verse) Joseph 1946; 1st Amer. Doubleday 1946
5. *In Your Garden* (gardening) Joseph 1951
   This was the first of four gardening books, inspired by the legendary Sissinghurst, the other three being *In Your Garden Again, More for Your Garden* and *Even More for Your*

Garden, published by Joseph in 1953, 1955 and 1958, respectively. See also No. 6.
6. *A Joy of Gardening: A Selection for Americans* Harper 1958

Although interest in the Bloomsbury Group and in the Hogarth Press is still very strong, prices have remained reasonable, all the above being Grade B–C.

SAGAN, Françoise
Pseudonym of Françoise Quoirez. Born in France 1935.
Author of several novels, and notable in particular for:

Bonjour Tristesse (novel) Murray 1955; 1st Amer. Smithers 1955
This was previously published in France in 1954.
Not an uncommon book, and Grade A.

Films:
Bonjour Tristesse Columbia 1957
In addition to the above, three other Sagan novels have been filmed.

SANDFORD, Jeremy
Born in England 1934.
Notable in particular for two 'novelized' non-fiction works which first appeared as television plays and made a lasting impression. Prose versions were published in paperback only.

1. *Cathy Come Home* Pan 1967
2. *Edna, the Inebriate Woman* Pan 1971
   Each is Grade A, though they may be elusive.

SAPPER
Pseudonym of Herman Cyril McNeile. Born in England 1888. Died 1937.
His first few books met with indifference, and then came Bulldog Drummond. The character was an almost immediate success, and was featured in a long series of novels—but beware, for the series was continued even after McNeile's death by one Gerard T.

Fairlie, retaining the Sapper pseudonym. Examples of *true* Sapper-Drummond are as follows:

1. *Bulldog Drummond* Hodder 1920
2. *The Return of Bulldog Drummond* Hodder 1932
This was published in America in the same year by Doubleday as *Bulldog Drummond Returns,* doubtless with good reason.

No. 1 is the first appearance of Drummond, and scarce: Grade D. No. 2 is Grade A.

Films:
Five Bulldog Drummond novels were filmed.

SASSOON, Siegfried

Born in London 1886. Died 1967.
Sassoon is particularly difficult to collect seriously, as his first fourteen works were either privately printed, or else published by a small press, as were many subsequent books by him. These cannot be listed here, but a bibliography exists, listing them all in some detail:
Geoffrey Keynes *A Bibliography of Siegfried Sassoon* (Soho Bibliographies, Hart-Davis 1962)
Below are all the commercially published Sassoon titles.

1. *The Old Huntsman* (verse) Heinemann 1917; 1st Amer. Dutton 1917
2. *Counter-Attack* (verse) Heinemann 1918; 1st Amer. Dutton 1918
3. *The War Poems of Siegfried Sassoon* Heinemann 1919
4. *Selected Poems* Heinemann 1925
5. *Satirical Poems* Heinemann 1926; 1st Amer. Viking Press 1926
6. *Nativity* (Ariel Poem) Faber 1927
7. *The Heart's Journey* (verse) Heinemann 1928; 1st Amer. Harper 1929
This was preceded by a limited edition in 1927.
8. *To My Mother* (Ariel Poem) Faber 1928
9. *Memoirs of a Fox-Hunting Man* (novel) Faber 1928; 1st Amer. Coward McCann 1929
This was published anonymously, and 1928

and 1929 also saw a limited edition and an illustrated edition of the work.
10. *Memoirs of an Infantry Officer* (novel) Faber 1930; 1st Amer. Coward McCann 1930
The initial print of this title was 20,000, compared with 1500 for No. 9.
11. *In Sicily* (Ariel Poem) Faber 1930
12. *Poems by Pinchbeck Lyre* Duckworth 1931
13. *To the Red Rose* (Ariel Poem) Faber 1931
14. *Prehistoric Burials* (poem) Knopf 1932
No. 1 of the Borzoi Chap Books.
15. *The Road to Ruin* (verse) Faber 1933
16. *Vigils* (verse) Heinemann 1935; 1st Amer. Viking Press 1936
These trade editions were preceded by a limited edition, a large-paper edition, and a vellum edition.
17. *Sherston's Progress* (novel) Faber 1936
This, with Nos 9 and 10, forms a trilogy.
18. *The Complete Memoirs of George Sherston* Faber 1937; 1st Amer. Doubleday 1937
Contains Nos 9, 10 and 17.
19. *The Old Century* (prose) Faber 1938; 1st Amer. Viking Press 1939
The t/p bears a Gwen Raverat engraving.
20. *Rhymed Ruminations* (verse) Faber 1940; 1st Amer. Viking Press 1941
A private press edition of 75 copies appeared in 1939.
21. *Poems Newly Selected* Faber 1940
22. *The Flower Show Match* (extracts) Faber 1941
23. *The Weald of Youth* (prose) Faber 1942; 1st Amer. Viking Press 1942
The d/w and t/p bears an engraving by Reynolds Stone.
24. *Siegfried's Journey* (prose) Faber 1945; 1st Amer. Viking Press 1946
As above, this too has a Reynolds Stone engraving.
25. *Collected Poems* Faber 1947; 1st Amer. Viking Press 1949
26. *Meredith* (prose) Constable 1948; 1st Amer. Viking Press 1948
27. *Sequences* (verse) Faber 1956; 1st Amer. Viking Press 1957
28. *Collected Poems 1908–1956* Faber 1961

The fourteen privately printed items that

precede No. 1 are scarce, and expensive, though No. 1 is Grade E–F, as is No. 2. No. 3 is Grade G. Nos 4 and 5 are Grade C–D, which is also the Grade for No. 9—if fine, which it almost never is. The Ariel Poems (Nos 6, 8, 11 and 13) are Grade B, in envelope, but all were issued also in a limited, signed edition, and these are Grade E–G. Nos 7, 10, 17, 18, 19, 21, 22, 25 and 28 are Grade B. Nos 12, 14, 15, 16 and 20 are Grade C, and Nos 23, 24, 26 and 27 are Grade A.

SAYERS, Dorothy L.
Born in Oxford 1893. Died 1957.
In her latter years, she veered away from detective fiction, and concentrated more and more on religious and philosophical writings, though it is for the crime fiction she is remembered and collected, and in particular for Lord Peter Wimsey.
Below is the detective fiction.

1. *Whose Body?* Unwin 1923; 1st Amer. Boni & Liveright 1923
2. *Clouds of Witness* Unwin 1926; 1st Amer. Dial Press 1927
3. *Unnatural Death* Benn 1927
   This was published in 1928 by the Dial Press in America as *The Dawson Pedigree*.
4. *Lord Peter Views the Body* (stories) Gollancz 1928; 1st Amer. Brewer 1929
5. *The Unpleasantness at the Bellona Club* Benn 1928; 1st Amer. Brewer 1928
6. *Strong Poison* Gollancz 1930; 1st Amer. Harcourt 1930
7. *The Documents in the Case* Benn 1930; 1st Amer. Brewer 1930 (with Robert Eustace)
8. *The Five Red Herrings* Gollancz 1931
   This was published in the same year in America by Harcourt as *Suspicious Characters*.
9. *Have His Carcase* Gollancz 1932; 1st Amer. Harcourt 1932
10. *Hangman's Holiday* (stories) Gollancz 1933; 1st Amer. Harcourt 1933
11. *Murder Must Advertise* Gollancz 1933; 1st Amer. Harcourt 1933
12. *The Nine Tailors* Gollancz 1934; 1st Amer. Harcourt 1934
13. *Gaudy Night* Gollancz 1935; 1st Amer. Harcourt 1936
14. *Busman's Honeymoon* Gollancz 1937; 1st Amer. Harcourt 1937
15. *In the Teeth of the Evidence* (stories) Gollancz 1940; 1st Amer. Harcourt 1940

A checklist of Sayers work may be found in *The New Cambridge Bibliography of English Literature* vol. 4, and I understand that a full, descriptive bibliography is to be published fairly soon.
Dorothy L. Sayers is among the most popular of all detective writers, and her 1sts have become more and more difficult to acquire, though surprisingly, when they do come up, the prices seem quite reasonable. Nos 1 to 5 would be Grade E for fine copies, and the remainder Grade B–D, depending very much upon condition, for many 1sts are either library-bound, or so well-read as to be of little use to the collector.

Film:
Busman's Holiday MGM 1940 (*Busman's Honeymoon*)

SEARLE, Ronald
Born in Cambridge 1920.
Searle is, of course, an artist. The books he has illustrated are now avidly collected, and among the modern illustrators he is quite as popular as Ardizzone or Sendak. Like it or not, however, it is for the creation of the educational establishment known as St Trinian's that he will be most remembered.

1. *Hurrah for St. Trinian's* Macdonald 1948; 1st Amer. Macdonald 1948
2. *The Terror of St Trinian's* Parrish 1952
   This was written by 'Timothy Shy' (D. B. Wyndham Lewis), who wrote the introduction to No. 1.
   Also very notable are the four volumes constituting the Saga of Nigel Molesworth— not to mention Fotherington-Thomas (hullo cloud, hullo sky). These were written by Geoffrey Willans in an inimitable schoolboy

vernacular, and the Searle drawings are, quite simply, superb.

1. *Down with Skool!* Parrish 1953
   The title note deserves quoting: 'Contanes Full Lowdown on Skools, Swots, Snekes Cads, Prigs Bulies Headmasters Criket Foopball, Dirty Roters Funks, Parents, Masters Wizard Wheezes, Weeds Aple Pie Beds and Various other Chizzes—in fact THE LOT'.
2. *How to be Topp* Parrish 1954
3. *Whizz for Atomms* Parrish 1956
4. *Back in the Jug Agane* Parrish 1959

All of the above may be found within Grade A—and very cheap at the price.

SHAFFER, Peter

Born in Liverpool 1926.
Author of a dozen plays, three novels, and several screenplays—including that for Golding's *Lord of the Flies*. One very recent play, however, is already becoming a classic:

Equus Deutsch 1973; 1st Amer. Atheneum 1974
At the moment, Grade B, but not very easy to find.

SHAW, George Bernard

Born in Dublin 1856. Died 1950.
Much of Shaw's major work was published during the last century, and many of the 1sts are difficult to identify. Incredibly, there is no recent, and therefore complete, bibliography, but merely a few selective checklists and catalogues published in the twenties. *The Cambridge Bibliography of English Literature,* vol. 3 gives an undetailed checklist of titles, and below is a brief selection of outstanding works.

1. *An Unsocial Socialist* (novel) Sonnenschien 1887; 1st Amer. Brentano 1900
2. *The Quintessence of Ibsenism* (prose) Scott 1891; 1st Amer. Brentano 1913
   The American edition is revised.
3. *Widowers' Houses* (play) Henry 1893; 1st Amer. Brentano 1913
4. *Plays Pleasant and Unpleasant* (2 vols) Richards 1898; 1st Amer. Brentano 1919
5. *Three Plays for Puritans* Richards 1901; 1st Amer. Brentano 1906
6. *Man and Superman* (play) Constable 1903; 1st Amer. Brentano 1913
7. *John Bull's Other Island, Major Barbara,* also *How He Lied to Her Husband* (plays) Constable 1907; 1st Amer. Brentano 1907
8. *The Doctor's Dilemma, Getting Married* and *The Shewing Up of Blanco Posnet* (plays) Constable 1911; 1st Amer. Brentano 1913
9. *Androcles and the Lion, Overruled* and *Pygmalion* (plays) Constable 1916; 1st Amer. Brentano 1916
10. *Heartbreak House* and *Playlets of the War* (plays) Constable 1919; 1st Amer. Brentano 1919
11. *Back to Methuselah* (play) Constable 1921; 1st Amer. Brentano 1921
12. *Saint Joan* (play) Constable 1924; 1st Amer. Brentano 1924
13. *The Intelligent Woman's Guide to Socialism and Capitalism* (prose) Constable 1928; 1st Amer. Brentano 1928
14. *The Adventures of the Black Girl in Her Search for God* (essay) Constable 1932; 1st Amer. Brentano 1932
15. *Collected Letters 1874–1897* Reinhardt 1965
16. *Collected Letters 1898–1910* Reinhardt 1972
17. *The Bodley Head Bernard Shaw: Collected Plays with Their Prefaces* Bodley Head 1970–74
    This definitive work is in 7 volumes.

Hundreds of books and articles have been written on Shaw, though probably the most entertaining and valuable are those memoirs by G. K. Chesterton, Frank Harris, Hesketh Pearson and St John Ervine, published over a fifty-year period.
Nos 1–6 are Grade G, Nos 7 and 8 are Grade D–E, Nos 9, 10, 11, 13, 15 and 16 are Grade C, and Nos 12 and 14 are Grade B. No. 17 would be Grade G, the set.
Inscriptions by Shaw escalate the price considerably—at the very least by 100%, but usually by very much more.

Films:
How He Lied to Her Husband British
International 1931
Arms and the Man Gaumont 1932
Pygmalion MGM 1938
Major Barbara Pascal 1941
Caesar and Cleopatra Pascal 1945
Androcles and the Lion RKO 1952
Saint Joan United Artists 1957
The Doctor's Dilemma MGM 1958
The Devil's Disciple United Artists 1959
The Millionairess 20th Century Fox 1960
My Fair lady Warner Bros 1964 (*Pygmalion*)
Great Catherine Warner Bros 1968; Paramount
1973

SILLITOE, Alan
Born in Nottingham 1928.

1. *Without Beer or Bread* (verse) Outpost
   Publications 1957
2. *Saturday Night and Sunday Morning* (novel)
   Allen 1958; 1st Amer. Knopf 1958
3. *The Loneliness of the Long Distance Runner*
   (stories) Allen 1959; 1st Amer. Knopf 1959
4. *The General* (novel) Allen 1960; 1st Amer.
   Knopf 1960
5. *The Rats and Other Poems* Allen 1960
6. *Key to the Door* (novel) Macmillan 1961; 1st
   Amer. Knopf 1961
7. *The Ragman's Daughter* (stories) Allen 1963;
   1st Amer. Knopf 1963
8. *A Falling out of Love and Other Poems* Allen
   1964
9. *The Road to Volgograd* (travel) Allen 1964; 1st
   Amer. Knopf 1964
10. *The Death of William Posters* (novel)
    Macmillan 1965; 1st Amer. Knopf 1965
11. *A Tree on Fire* (novel) Macmillan 1967; 1st
    Amer. Knopf 1967
12. *The City Adventures of Marmalade Jim*
    (juvenile) Macmillan 1967
13. *Guzman Go Home* (stories) Macmillan 1968;
    1st Amer. Doubleday 1968
14. *Love in the Environs of Voronezh* (verse)
    Macmillan 1968; 1st Amer. Doubleday 1968
15. *All Citizens Are Soldiers* (play) Macmillan

1969; 1st Amer. Dufour 1969 (adaptation
with Ruth Fainlight)
16. *A Start in Life* (novel) Allen 1970; 1st Amer.
    Scribner 1971
17. *Travels in Nihilon* (novel) Allen 1971; 1st
    Amer. Scribner 1972
18. *Raw Material* (novel) Allen 1972; 1st Amer.
    Scribner 1973
19. *Men, Women, and Children* (stories) Allen 1973;
    1st Amer. Doubleday 1974
20. *Flame of Life* (novel) Allen 1974
21. *Storm: New Poems* Allen 1974
22. *Mountains and Caverns* (prose) Allen 1975
23. *The Widower's Son* (novel) Allen 1976

The highlights of Sillitoe are Nos 2 and 3,
with No. 2 very scarce indeed and Grade
C–D, whereas No. 3 is relatively common,
and Grade B. No. 1 is scarce, and would be
Grade D. Nos 4–10 are Grade B, and the
remainder Grade A. In addition to this
checklist, Sillitoe has quite recently published
a number of limited editions with private
presses (see Hughes, Ted, No. 28).

Films:
Saturday Night and Sunday Morning British
Lion 1960
The Loneliness of the Long Distance Runner
British Lion 1962
Counterpoint Universal 1968 (*The General*)
The Ragman's Daughter 20th Century Fox 1972
Sillitoe wrote the screenplays for all but
Counterpoint.

SIMENON, Georges
Born in Liège 1903.
Reputedly one of the most prolific authors
ever, Simenon will be remembered for
creating one of our most popular detectives,
Maigret. Although his first novel was
published in 1920, it was not until twelve
years later that the Inspector made his bow.
Since then, novels—albeit short novels—
concerning the Patron have come in a never-
ceasing deluge, each one being eagerly
received by the fans. Prolific indeed is the
man who can announce his retirement, and

still publish two books a year, as has happened in recent years. The very first Maigret appears below, and would be Grade F–G, though the vast majority are within Grades A–B.

The Crime of Inspector Maigret Covici 1932
The first appearance in England was *Introducing Inspector Maigret,* from Hurst & Blackett in 1933.

In addition to the very popular television series, eight Simenon novels have been filmed.

THE SITWELLS

A vast and valuable bibliography of the Sitwells exists, and it is essential for all serious collectors.

Richard Fifoot *A Bibliography of Edith, Osbert and Sacheverell Sitwell* (Soho Bibliographies, Hart-Davis 1963; rev. ed.1971)

Below is a short selection of each author.

SITWELL, Edith
Born in Scarborough 1887. Died 1964.

1. *Poetry and Criticism* (prose) Hogarth Press 1925; 1st Amer. Holt 1926
2. *Rustic Elegies* (verse) Duckworth 1927; 1st Amer. Knopf 1927
3. *Collected Poems* Duckworth 1930
   This was preceded by a signed, limited edition published by Duckworth and in America by Houghton Mifflin.
4. *Bath* (prose) Faber 1932; 1st Amer. Smith 1932
5. *The English Eccentrics* (prose) Faber 1933; 1st Amer. Houghton Mifflin 1933
6. *Victoria of England* (non-fiction) Faber 1936; 1st Amer. Houghton Mifflin 1936
7. *A Poet's Notebook* (prose) Macmillan 1943
8. *Green Song* (verse) Macmillan 1944; 1st Amer. Vanguard Press 1946
9. *Fanfare for Elizabeth* (non-fiction) Macmillan NY 1946; 1st Amer. Macmillan 1946
10. *The Canticle of the Rose* (verse) Macmillan 1949; 1st Amer. Vanguard Press 1949
11. *Taken Care Of* (autobiog.) Hutchinson 1965; 1st Amer. Atheneum 1965

Nos 1 and 6 are Grade B, Nos 2, 3, 4 and 5 are Grade C, and the remainder Grade A.

SITWELL, Osbert
Born in London 1892. Died 1969.

1. *Collected Satires and Poems* Duckworth 1931
2. *Brighton* (prose) Faber 1935; 1st Amer. Houghton Mifflin 1935 (with Margaret Barton)
3. *Left Hand, Right Hand!* (autobiog.) Little Brown 1944; 1st Eng. Macmillan 1945
4. *The Scarlet Tree* (autobiog.) Little Brown 1946; 1st Eng. Macmillan 1946
5. *Great Morning* (autobiog.) Little Brown 1947; 1st Eng. Macmillan 1948
6. *Laughter in the Next Room* (autobiog.) Little Brown 1948; 1st Eng. Macmillan 1949
7. *Noble Essences* (autobiog.) Macmillan 1950; 1st Amer. Little Brown 1950

No. 1 is Grade B–C, and No. 2 is Grade C. The five-volume autobiography is quite easy to find, though many find the final volume elusive. The set is Grade D–E.

SITWELL, Sacheverell
Born in Scarborough 1897.

1. *Southern Baroque Art* Grant Richards 1924; 1st Amer. Knopf 1924
2. *Collected Poems* Duckworth 1936
3. *Conversation Pieces* (art) Batsford 1936; 1st Amer. Scribner 1937
4. *Edinburgh* (prose) Faber 1938; 1st Amer. Houghton Mifflin 1939
5. *British Architects and Craftsmen* Batsford 1945; 1st Amer. Scribner 1946
6. *Journey to the Ends of Time* Vol. 1 Cassell 1959; 1st Amer. Random House 1959 (autobiog.) Vol. 1 only published.

Nos 1, 2 and 4 are Grades B–C, No. 3 Grade C, No. 5 Grade B and No. 6 Grade A.

SMITH, Stevie

Florence Margaret Smith. Born in Hull 1902. Died 1971.

1. *Novel on Yellow Paper* (novel) Cape 1936; 1st Amer. Morrow 1937
2. *A Good Time Was Had by All* (verse) Cape 1937
3. *Over the Frontier* (novel) Cape 1938
4. *Tender Only to One* (verse) Cape 1938
5. *Mother, What Is Man?* (verse) Cape 1942
6. *The Holiday* (novel) Chapman & Hall 1949; 1st Amer. Smithers 1950
7. *Harold's Leap* (verse) Chapman & Hall 1950
8. *Not Waving but Drowning* (verse) Deutsch 1957
9. *Cats in Colour* (photo essay) Batsford 1959
10. *Selected Poems* Longman 1962; 1st Amer. New Directions 1964
11. *The Frog Prince and Other Poems* Longman 1966
12. *Two in One* Longman 1971
    Contains Nos 10 and 11.
13. *Scorpion and Other Poems* Longman 1971
14. *Collected Poems* Lane 1975; 1st Amer. OUP 1976

All her books are uncommon, and all are in demand. No. 1 is Grade E, and Nos 2–5 are Grade D. Nos 6, 7 and 8 are Grade C. Nos 10, 11 and 13 are Grade B, and Nos 9 and 12 are Grade A. No. 14 is Grade B–C, as the published price was £8·50.

SNOW, C. P.

Baron Snow was born in Leicester in 1905. In addition to the eleven-volume sequence below, for which he is best known, Lord Snow has published five other novels, six plays (with his wife, Pamela Hansford Johnson), and about a dozen prose works. There was a bibliography by Bernard Stone in:

Robert Greacen *The World of C. P. Snow* (Scorpion Press 1962)

The sequence, entitled *Strangers and Brothers*, is narrated by the character Lewis Eliot.

1. *Strangers and Brothers* Faber 1940; 1st Amer. Scribner 1960
2. *The Light and the Dark* Faber 1947; 1st Amer. Macmillan 1948
3. *Time of Hope* Faber 1949; 1st Amer. Macmillan 1950
4. *The Masters* Macmillan 1951; 1st Amer. Macmillan 1951
5. *The New Men* Macmillan 1954; 1st Amer. Scribner 1954
6. *Homecomings* Macmillan 1956; 1st Amer. Scribner 1956
   The Scribner edition omitted the 's' in the title.
7. *The Conscience of the Rich* Macmillan 1958; 1st Amer. Scribner 1958
8. *The Affair* Macmillan 1960; 1st Amer. Scribner 1960
9. *Corridors of Power* Macmillan 1964; 1st Amer. Scribner 1964
10. *The Sleep of Reason* Macmillan 1968; 1st Amer. Scribner 1969
11. *Last Things* Macmillan 1970; 1st Amer. Scribner 1970

No. 1 is quite difficult, and Grade C. Nos 2 and 3 are Grade B, and the remainder Grade A.

SOLZHENITSYN, Alexander

Born in Rostov, Russia, 1918.
Collecting Solzhenitsyn is a task fraught with problems and uncertainties unless one decides precisely what the aim is. To acquire the *absolute* 1st editions in each case would be very difficult, unless one had contacts in several countries. Assuming that the English-language editions are of most interest, I list here the English and American details only. Most collectors in England would settle for the complete English 1st editions, and those in the USA, I imagine, would be satisfied with their American counterparts.

1. *One Day in the Life of Ivan Denisovich* Praeger 1963 (trans. Max Hayward and Ronald Hingley)
2. *One Day in the Life of Ivan Denisovich* Dutton

1963; 1st Eng. Gollancz 1963 (trans. Ralph Parker)
Nos 1 and 2 appeared simultaneously.

3. *We Never Make Mistakes: Two Short Novels* University of South Carolina 1963 (trans. Paul W. Blackstock)
4. *The First Circle* Harper Row 1968 (trans. Thomas P. Whitney)
5. *The First Circle* Collins 1968 (trans. Michael Guybon)
6. *Cancer Ward* Bodley Head 1968–69; 1st Amer. Farrar Straus 1969 (trans. Nicholas Bethell and David Burg)
The English ed. is in two vols, the American in one.
7. *The Cancer Ward* Dial Press NY 1968 (trans. Rebecca Frank)
8. *The Love-Girl and the Innocent* (play) Bodley Head 1969; 1st Amer. Farrar Straus 1970 (trans. Nicholas Bethell and David Burg)
9. *Stories and Prose Poems* Bodley Head 1971; 1st Amer. Farrar Straus 1971 (trans. Michael Glenny)
10. *August 1914* Bodley Head 1972; 1st Amer. Farrar Straus 1972 (trans. Michael Glenny)
11. *'One Word of Truth . . .'* Bodley Head 1972; 1st Amer. Farrar Straus 1973 (Nobel Lecture)
12. *Candle in the Wind* (play) University of Minnesota 1973; 1st Eng. Bodley Head/OUP 1973 (trans. Keith Armes)
13. *The Gulag Archipelago* Harper Row 1974; 1st Eng. Collins 1974 (trans. Thomas P. Whitney)
14. *Letter to Soviet Leaders* Index on Censorship 1974; 1st Amer. Harper Row 1974 (trans. Hilary Sternberg)
15. *The Gulag Archipelago* (2) Harper Row 1975; 1st Eng. Collins 1975 (trans. as 13)
16. *From Under the Rubble* (with others) Little Brown 1975; 1st Eng. Collins 1975 (trans. ed. by Michael Scammell)
17. *Lenin in Zurich* Farrar Straus 1976; 1st Eng. Bodley Head 1976 (trans. H. T. Willetts)
18. *Warning to the Western World* Bodley Head/BBC 1976
Published in 1976 in America by Farrar Straus as *Speeches to the Americans*.
19. *The Gulag Archipelago* (3) Harper Row 1976; 1st Eng. Collins 1978 (trans. H. T. Willetts)
20. *Prussian Nights* (poem) Collins/Harvill 1977 (trans. Robert Conquest)

Of the English editions, Nos 5 and 6 are the most elusive, though equally hard to track down once they have been missed are pamphlets such as Nos 11, 14 and 18.
Nos 1, 2, 4, 5 and 6 are Grade C. Nos 7, 8, 10, 11, 13 and 15 are Grade B, and the remainder are Grade A at the moment. All these prices will soon seem very low, however, as these books become more scarce. There has been an almighty flood of material published on Solzhenitsyn over the past decade, though most of it unsatisfactory for one reason or another. The following, however, is a useful, if weighty, tome:
John B. Dunlop, Richard Haugh and Alexis Klimoff (eds) *Aleksandr Solzhenitsyn: Critical Essays and documentary Materials* (Nordland 1973)

Film:
One Day in the Life of Ivan Denisovich Cinerama 1971

SPARK, Muriel
Born in Edinburgh 1918.

1. *Tribute to Wordsworth* (non-fiction) Wingate 1950 (ed. with Derek Stanford)
2. *Child of Light: A Reassessment of Mary Shelley* Tower Bridge 1951
3. *The Fanfarlo and Other Verse* Hand & Flower Press 1952
The 1st issue is red-lettered on buff wrapps.
4. *A Selection of Poems by Emily Bronte* Grey Walls Press 1952 (ed.)
5. *Emily Bronte: Her Life and Work* Owen 1953 (with Derek Stanford)
6. *John Masefield* (non-fiction) Nevill 1953
7. *My Best Mary: The Letters of Mary Shelley* Wingate 1953; 1st Amer. Folcroft Editions 1972 (ed. with Derek Stanford)
8. *The Bronte Letters* (ed.) Nevill 1954
9. *Letters of J. H. Newman* Owen 1957 (ed. with Derek Stanford)
10. *The Comforters* (novel) Macmillan 1957; 1st Amer. Lippincott 1957

11. *Robinson* (novel) Macmillan 1958; 1st Amer. Lippincott 1958
12. *The Go-Away Bird and Other Stories* Macmillan 1958; 1st Amer. Lippincott 1960
13. *Memento Mori* (novel) Macmillan 1959; 1st Amer. Lippincott 1959
14. *The Ballad of Peckham Rye* (novel) Macmillan 1960; 1st Amer. Lippincott 1960
15. *The Bachelors* (novel) Macmillan 1960; 1st Amer. Lippincott 1961
16. *Voices at Play* (stories and plays) Macmillan 1961
17. *The Prime of Miss Jean Brodie* (novel) Macmillan 1961; 1st Amer. Lippincott 1962
18. *Doctors of Philosophy* (play) Macmillan 1963
19. *The Girls of Slender Means* (novel) Macmillan 1963; 1st Amer. Knopf 1963
20. *The Mandelbaum Gate* (novel) Macmillan 1965; 1st Amer. Knopf 1965
21. *Collected Stories* I Macmillan 1967; 1st Amer. Knopf 1968
22. *Collected Poems* I Macmillan 1967
23. *The Public Image* (novel) Macmillan 1968; 1st Amer. Knopf 1968
24. *The Very Fine Clock* (juvenile) Knopf 1968; 1st Eng. Macmillan 1969
25. *The Driver's Seat* (novel) Macmillan 1970; 1st Amer. Knopf 1970
26. *Not to Disturb* (novel) Macmillan 1971; 1st Amer. Viking Press 1972
27. *The Hothouse by the East River* (novel) Macmillan 1972; 1st Amer. Viking Press 1972
28. *The Abbess of Crewe* (novel) Macmillan 1974; 1st Amer. Viking Press 1974
29. *The Takeover* (novel) Macmillan 1976; 1st Amer. Viking Press 1976

Though her novels are her most popular work, it is the earlier works that are the more difficult to acquire. Nos 2 and 3 are Grade D–E, Nos 1, 5, 6, 7, 8 and 10 are Grade C. Nos 4, 9, 11, 12, 13, 14, 15, 16 and 17 are Grade B, and the rest Grade A.

Film:
The Prime of Miss Jean Brodie 20th Century Fox 1969

SPENDER, Stephen
Born in London 1909.

In addition to the verse, plays and fiction listed below, Spender has published about two dozen prose works, and has edited and translated a further two dozen. His autobiography is of importance:
World Within World Hamilton 1951; 1st Amer. Harcourt Brace 1951
Important also are two very recent prose works:
W. H. Auden: A Tribute Weidenfeld & Nicolson 1975; 1st Amer. Macmillan 1975
Eliot Fontana 1975

1. *20 Poems* Blackwell 1930
2. *Poems* Faber 1933; 1st Amer. Random House 1934
3. *Vienna* (verse) Faber 1934 1st Amer. Random House 1935
4. *The Burning Cactus* (stories) Faber 1936; 1st Amer. Random House 1936
5. *Trial of a Judge* (play) Faber 1938; 1st Amer. Random House 1938
6. *The Still Centre* (verse) Faber 1939
7. *Danton's Death* (play) Faber 1939 (adapt. with Goronwy Rees)
8. *Selected Poems* Faber 1940
9. *The Backward Son* (novel) Hogarth Press 1940
10. *Ruins and Visions* (verse) Faber 1942; 1st Amer. Random House 1942
11. *Poems of Dedication* Faber 1946; 1st Amer. Random House 1947
12. *The Edge of Being* (verse) Faber 1949; 1st Amer. Random House 1949
13. *Sirmione Peninsula* (Ariel Poem) Faber 1954
14. *Collected Poems* Faber 1955; 1st Amer. Random House 1955
15. *Engaged in Writing* and *The Fool and the Princess* (stories) Hamilton 1958; 1st Amer. Farrar Straus 1958
16. *Mary Stuart* (play) Faber 1959 (adapt. from Schiller)
17. *Selected Poems* Random House 1964; 1st Eng. Faber 1965
18. *The Generous Days* (verse) Faber 1971; 1st Amer. Random House 1971

No. 1 is extremely scarce, and Grade K or more. No. 2 is also difficult, and Grade D. Nos 3–7 are Grade C, Nos 8, 10, 11, 12, 14 and 15 are Grade B, and the remainder are Grade A, with the exception of No. 9, which is Grade D–E.

STEVENS, Wallace

Born in Pennsylvania 1879. Died 1955. *Wallace Stevens: A Descriptive Bibliography* by J. M. Edelstein (University of Pittsburgh 1973) is essential reference for all serious collectors. A checklist of his major work appears below.

1. *Harmonium* (verse) Knopf 1923
   A revised ed. was published by Knopf in 1931.
2. *Ideas of Order* (verse) Knopf 1936
   This was preceded by a limited, signed ed. from Alcestis in 1935.
3. *The Man with the Blue Guitar and Other Poems* Knopf 1937
4. *Parts of a World* (verse) Ryerson Press 1942
5. *Transport to Summer* (verse) Knopf 1947
6. *The Auroras of Autumn* (verse) Knopf 1950
7. *The Necessary Angel* (essays) Knopf 1951; 1st Eng. Faber 1960
8. *Selected Poems* Faber 1953; 1st Amer. Vintage 1959
9. *Collected Poems* Knopf 1954; 1st Eng. Faber 1955
10. *Opus Posthumous* (verse) Knopf 1957; 1st Eng. Faber 1959
11. *The Letters* Knopf 1966; 1st Eng. Faber 1967
12. *The Palm at the End of the Mind: Selected Poems and a Play* Knopf 1971

Stevens 1sts are scarce, particularly in England. No. 1 would be around Grade N, Nos 2 and 3 Grade E–F, and Nos 4–7 Grade D. Nos 9 and 10 would be Grade C for the American editions, and Nos 8, 11 and 12 are Grade B.

STEWART, J. I. M.

Born in Edinburgh 1906.
As well as the novels and a few prose works under his own name, he publishes a very large number of detective novels under his pseudonym Michael Innes. In all, there have been about fifteen novels and volumes of stories from Stewart, as well as half-a-dozen prose works, and no less than forty from the pen of Innes. Too many to list here, but below are the first five Stewart novels, and the first five Innes.

Michael Innes

1. *Death at the President's Lodging* Gollancz 1936
   This was published in America by Dodd Mead in 1937 as *Seven Suspects*.
2. *Hamlet, Revenge!* Gollancz 1937; 1st Amer. Dodd Mead 1937
3. *Lament for a Maker* Gollancz 1938; 1st Amer. Dodd Mead 1938
4. *Stop Press* Gollancz 1939
   This was published in America by Dodd Mead in 1939 as *The Spider Strikes*.
5. *The Secret Vanguard* Gollancz 1940; 1st Amer. Dodd Mead 1941

J. I. M. Stewart

1. *Mark Lambert's Supper* Gollancz 1954
2. *The Guardians* Gollancz 1955; 1st Amer. Norton 1957
3. *The Use of Riches* Gollancz 1957; 1st Amer. Norton 1957
4. *The Man Who Wrote Detective Stories and Other Stories* Gollancz 1959; 1st Amer. Norton 1959
5. *The Man Who Won the Pools* Gollancz 1961; 1st Amer. Norton 1961

Michael Innes is very much more popular with collectors than J. I. M. Stewart, and Nos 1 and 2 of Innes are Grade D, and Nos 3, 4 and 5 Grade B. All the Stewarts are Grade A.

STOPPARD, Tom

Stoppard is British, though born in Czechoslovakia in 1937. His plays hit Britain in the mid-sixties—*Rosencrantz* causing a huge stir—and he became an instant success—success which has increased with each new production. He has published comparatively little, but collectors would be well advised to acquire all they can—and quickly, for some items are already maddeningly elusive.

1. *Lord Malquist and Mr Moon* (novel) Blond 1966; 1st Amer. Knopf 1968
2. *Rosencrantz and Guildenstern Are Dead* (play) Faber 1967; 1st Amer. Grove Press 1967
3. *The Real Inspector Hound* (play) Faber 1968; 1st Amer. Grove Press 1969
4. *Enter a Free Man* (play) Faber 1968; 1st Amer. Grove Press 1972

   This play has an interesting history, for it was originally televised in 1963 as *A Walk on the Water*, and then a revised version was televised the following year as *The Preservation of George Riley*.
5. *Albert's Bridge* and *If You're Glad I'll Be Frank: Two Plays for Radio* Faber 1969
6. *After Magritte* (play) Faber 1971; 1st Amer. Grove Press 1972
7. *Jumpers* (play) Faber 1972; 1st Amer. Grove Press 1972
8. *Artist Descending a Staircase* and *Where Are They Now?: Two Plays for Radio* Faber 1973
9. *Travesties* (play) Faber 1975; 1st Amer. Grove Press 1975
10. *Dirty Linen* (play) Faber 1976; 1st Amer. Grove Press 1976

The highlight is No. 2, though in future years No. 7 will also feature. No. 1, although now reissued, can be difficult in the 1st, and might now be Grade C. No. 2 is Grade C–D. All the others are Grade B at the moment, but No. 5 went out-of-print very quickly, and is scarce, and No. 6 was published only in wrapps; so a fine copy might be difficult.

STOREY, David
Born in Yorkshire 1933.

1. *This Sporting Life* (novel) Longmans 1960; 1st Amer. Macmillan 1960
2. *Flight into Camden* (novel) Longmans 1961; 1st Amer. Macmillan 1961
3. *Radcliffe* (novel) Longmans 1963; 1st Amer. Coward McCann 1964
4. *The Restoration of Arnold Middleton* (play) Cape 1967
5. *In Celebration* (play) Cape 1969; 1st Amer. Grove Press 1975
6. *The Contractor* (play) Cape 1970; 1st Amer. Random House 1971
7. *Home* (play) Cape 1970; 1st Amer. Random House 1971
8. *The Changing Room* (play) Cape 1972; 1st Amer. Random House 1972
9. *Pasmore* (novel) Longman 1972; 1st Amer. Dutton 1974
10. *A Temporary Life* (novel) Lane 1973; 1st Amer. Dutton 1974
11. *The Farm* (play) Cape 1973
12. *Cromwell* (play) Cape 1973
13. *Life Class* (play) Cape 1975
14. *Saville* (novel) Cape 1976

Storey has also published a book called *Edward* (Lane 1973), which is a short, cautionary tale concerning a bishop 'who found a key but not a lock'. For the addict, but the drawings by Donald Parker are eye-catching.

No. 1 is particularly scarce for a modern novel, and Grade D. Nos 2 and 3 are Grade B, and the rest Grade A.

Film:
This Sporting Life Rank 1962

STORY, Jack Trevor
Born in Hertfordshire 1917.
Story has written many books, though one in particular is of importance to collectors of modern fiction.

Live Now, Pay Later (novel) Secker & Warburg 1963; Penguin 1963
Unusually for the time, this was published simultaneously in hard and paperback. Both editions are hard to come by, though the bound edition would be Grade B, and the Penguin Grade A.

Films:
Live Now, Pay Later Regal 1962
In addition to this, two other Story novels have been filmed.

STOUT, Rex
Born in Indiana 1886. Died 1976.

Creator of Nero Wolfe, Stout published over seventy novels and books of short stories during his long life, not to mention *The Nero Wolfe Cookbook* (Viking Press 1973), which we shan't.
Below is a short selection.

1. *How Like a God* (novel) Vanguard Press 1929; 1st Eng. Mitchell & Kennerley 1931
   This is Stout's first book.
2. *Fer-de-Lance* (novel) Farrar & Rinehart 1934; 1st Eng. Cassell 1935
   This is the first appearance of Nero Wolfe.
3. *The League of Frightened Men* (novel) Farrar & Rinehart 1935; 1st Eng. Cassell 1935
4. *Some Buried Caesar* (novel) Farrar & Rinehart 1939; 1st Eng. Collins 1939

Nos 1 and 2 could reach Grade F, with Nos 3 and 4 at Grade C. The majority of later novels, however, all of which were published by the Viking Press in America and Collins in England, are Grade A–B.

Films:
Meet Nero Wolfe (Fer-de-Lance) Columbia 1936
The League of Frightened Men Columbia 1937

STRACHEY, Lytton
Born in London 1880. Died 1932.

1. *Landmarks in French Literature* Williams & Norgate 1912; 1st Amer. Holt 1912
2. *Eminent Victorians* Chatto & Windus 1918; 1st Amer. Putnam 1918
3. *Queen Victoria* Chatto & Windus 1921; 1st Amer. Harcourt 1921
4. *Books and Characters* Chatto & Windus 1922; 1st Amer. Harcourt 1922
5. *Pope: The Leslie Stephen Lecture* CUP 1925
6. *Elizabeth and Essex* Chatto & Windus 1928; 1st Amer. Harcourt 1928
7. *Portraits in Miniature* Chatto & Windus 1931; 1st Amer. Harcourt 1931
8. *Characters and Commentaries* Chatto & Windus 1933; 1st Amer. Harcourt 1933
9. *Spectatorial Essays* Chatto & Windus 1964; 1st Amer. Harcourt 1965

10. *Ermyntrude and Esmerelda* Blond 1969; 1st Amer. Stein & Day 1969
    This is illustrated by Erté, and has an Intro. by Michael Holroyd.

A volume of letters between Virginia Woolf and Lytton Strachey was published by the Hogarth Press in 1956, though of course the great work on Strachey is
Michael Holroyd *Lytton Strachey* (2 vols; Heinemann 1967–68; Holt 1968)

No. 1 is a very small, fragile item in the Home University Library series, but there are many variant issues, chronicled in Percy Muir *Points* (1931). The 1st issue could be Grade E. No. 2 is Grade D, though all the others are Grade B. The Holroyd biography would now be Grade C.

SYMONS, Julian
Born in London 1912.
Symons has written about forty-five books, about half being crime fiction, the remainder being split between criticism, popular histories, and two very early volumes of verse. Below are the novels and stories.

1. *The Immaterial Murder Case* Gollancz 1945; 1st Amer. Macmillan 1957
2. *A Man Called Jones* Gollancz 1947
3. *Bland Beginning* Gollancz 1949; 1st Amer. Harper 1949
4. *The 31st of February* Gollancz 1950; 1st Amer. Harper 1950
5. *The Broken Penny* Gollancz 1952; 1st Amer. Harper 1953
6. *The Narrowing Circle* Gollancz 1954; 1st Amer. Harper 1954
7. *The Paper Chase* Collins 1956
   This was published as *Bogue's Fortune* in America by Harper in 1957.
8. *The Colour of Murder* Collins 1957; 1st Amer. Harper 1957
9. *The Gigantic Shadow* Collins 1958
   This was published in America by Harper in the same year, with the title *Pipe Dream*.
10. *The Progress of a Crime* Collins 1960; 1st Amer. Harper 1960
11. *Murder, Murder* (stories) Fontana 1961

12. *The Killing of Francie Lake* Collins 1962
    This was published during the same year by
    Harper in America with the title *The Plain Man*.
13. *The End of Solomon Grundy* Collins 1964; 1st
    Amer. Harper 1964
14. *The Belting Inheritance* Collins 1965; 1st Amer.
    Harper 1965
15. *Francis Quarles Investigates* (stories) Panther
    1965
16. *The Julian Symons Omnibus* Collins 1966
    Contains Nos 4, 10 and 13.
17. *The Man Who Killed Himself* Collins 1967; 1st
    Amer. Harper 1967
18. *The Man Whose Dreams Came True* Collins
    1969; 1st Amer. Harper 1969
19. *The Man Who Lost His Wife* Collins 1971; 1st
    Amer. Harper 1971
20. *The Players and the Game* Collins 1972; 1st
    Amer. Harper 1972
21. *The Plot Against Roger Rider* Collins 1973; 1st
    Amer. Harper 1973
22. *A Three Pipe Problem* Collins 1975; 1st Amer.
    Harper 1975

No. 1 is Grade C, Nos 2–6 Grade B, and the
remainder Grade A, but Symons' popularity
with collectors is growing all the time, so
these prices might rise soon.

Film:
The Narrowing Circle Eros 1955

TAYLOR, Elizabeth
Born in Reading, Berkshire, 1912. Died 1976.
Not one of the most collected authors,
though the quality of her work has lately
received more notice. She published fifteen
books, and below are a few of the more
popular.

1. *At Mrs Lippincote's* (novel) Davies 1945; 1st
   Amer. Knopf 1946
2. *Angel* (novel) Davies 1957; 1st Amer. Viking
   Press 1957
3. *Mrs Palfrey at the Claremont* (novel) Chatto &
   Windus 1971; 1st Amer. Viking Press 1971
   No. 1 is her first book, and Grade B–C. The
   others are Grade A.

THOMAS, Dylan
Born in Swansea 1914. Died 1953.
For this, one of the greatest writers, there are
no less than two essential works of bibliography:

J. Alexander Roth *Dylan Thomas: A
Bibliography* (Dent 1956)
Ralph Maud *Dylan Thomas in Print: A
Bibliographical History* (Dent 1970; University
of Pittsburgh, 1970)
Also essential, of course, is the biography:
Constantine FitzGibbon *The Life of Dylan
Thomas* (Dent 1965; Atlantic, Little 1965)
Below is a checklist of his work.

1. *18 Poems* Sunday Referee & The Parton
   Bookshop 1934
   Black cloth, lettered in gold, with grey d/w.
   The second issue is distinguishable in many
   ways, two being the rounded spine, as
   opposed to the flat spine of the first issue, and
   the advert on the verso for slim volumes by
   George Barker, Dylan Thomas and David
   Gascoyne, not present in first issue. The
   spine lettering tends to discoloration on the
   second issue, due to inferior gold. The 1st
   issue is Grade P and over now, though the
   2nd issue is Grade J–K in fine condition.
   A 2nd edition was published by the Fortune
   Press in, it is thought, 1942, the first issue of
   this having red boards, and a yellow d/w.
   Subsequent issues retain the yellow d/w, but
   have various coloured boards. Grade E.
2. *Twenty-Five Poems* Dent 1936
   Grey boards, grey d/w. Grade I.
3. *The Map of Love* (verse and prose) Dent 1939
   Mauve cloth, grey and purple d/w. Three
   subsequent issues exist, the first identifiable
   by its smooth-grained cloth, and gold
   lettering.
4. *The World I Breathe* New Directions 1939
   This American anthology was bound in
   brown, with cream d/w. It contains selections
   from Nos 1, 2 and 3, though two stories
   appear for the first time.
5. *Portrait of the Artist as a Young Dog* Dent
   1940; 1st Amer. New Directions 1940
   English ed. is green cloth with scarlet d/w,
   American ed. is red cloth with cream d/w.

6. *New Poems* New Directions 1943
   Mauve boards in mauve d/w.
7. *Deaths and Entrances* Dent 1946
   $5\frac{1}{2}'' \times 4\frac{1}{2}''$ only. Orange cloth, vermilion d/w.
8. *Selected Writings* New Directions 1946
   Pinkish cloth in pinkish d/w.
9. *Twenty-Six Poems* Dent 1950
   This consisted of 150 signed copies, the first ten on Japanese vellum, the remainder on handmade paper, divided between Dent and New Directions, all printed in Italy.
10. *In Country Sleep* New Directions 1952
    100 signed copies, and 5,000 ordinary copies.
11. *Collected Poems* Dent 1952; 1st Amer. New Directions 1953
    Published simultaneously with the English ed. was a signed, limited issue of 65 copies, 60 for sale.
12. *The Doctor and the Devils* Dent 1953; 1st Amer. New Directions 1953
    The American ed. was printed off from the English 2nd impression.
13. *Under Milk Wood* Dent 1954; 1st Amer. New Directions 1954
14. *Quite Early One Morning* Dent 1954; 1st Amer. New Directions 1954
15. *Conversation About Christmas* New Directions 1954
    2,000 printed for distribution by the publisher.
16. *Adventures in the Skin Trade and Other Stories* New Directions 1955
    The title story was published alone by Putnam in 1955, with a Foreword by Vernon Watkins.
17. *A Prospect of the Sea* Dent 1955
18. *Letters to Vernon Watkins* Faber/Dent 1957; 1st Amer. New Directions 1957
19. *The Beach of Falesa* Stein & Day 1963; 1st Eng. Cape 1964
20. *Twenty Years A-Growing* Dent 1964
21. *Rebecca's Daughters* Triton 1965; 1st Amer. Little Brown 1965
22. *Me and My Bike* McGraw-Hill 1965; 1st Eng. Triton 1965
23. *Selected Letters of Dylan Thomas* Dent 1966; 1st Amer. New Directions 1967
24. *The Notebooks of Dylan Thomas* New Directions 1967
    Published by Dent in 1968 as *Poet in the Making*.
25. *Early Prose Writings* Dent 1971; 1st Amer. New Directions 1972
26. *The Death of the King's Canary* Hutchinson 1976 (with John Davenport)

No. 3 is Grade I–K, No. 4 Grade E–F, No. 5 Grade I, and Nos 6 and 8 Grade E–F. Nos 7 and 11 are Grade F–G. The signed editions of Nos 9 and 10 could reach Grade P, though No. 9 would be much more in demand. The signed issue of No. 11 would be even higher. No. 13 is, of course, his best-known work, and a fine copy in d/w would now be Grade I and over. Nos 12, 14, 16 and 17 are quite easy, and Grade C. No. 15 is naturally scarce, and Grade E–F. The rest are Grade B.

Film:
Under Milk Wood Rank 1971

THOMAS, Edward
Born in London 1878. Died 1917.
About three dozen books of Thomas's prose have been published, along with fifteen volumes of poetry (during his lifetime, and posthumously). He also edited over a dozen books. A checklist of all of these may be found in the following critical work:
William Cooke *Edward Thomas: A Critical Biography* (Faber 1970)
Below is a brief selection.

1. *Oxford* (prose) Black 1903
2. *The Heart of England* (prose) Dent 1906
3. *Richard Jefferies* (biog.) Hutchinson 1909
4. *Celtic Stories* OUP 1911
5. *Collected Poems* Selwyn & Blount 1920
6. *Collected Poems* Faber 1936

Nos 1, 2 and 3 would be Grade D–E, No. 4 Grade D, No. 5 Grade C–D, and No. 6 Grade B–C.

THOMAS, R. S.
Born in Cardiff 1913.

In addition to the checklist following, Thomas has edited five volumes of verse.

1. *The Stones of the Field* (verse) Druid Press 1946
2. *An Acre of Land* (verse) Montgomery Printing Co. 1952
3. *The Minister* (verse) Montgomery Printing Co. 1953
4. *Song at the Year's Turning* (verse) Hart-Davis 1955
5. *Poetry for Supper* (verse) Hart-Davis 1958; 1st Amer. Dufour 1961
6. *Judgement Day* (verse) Poetry Book Society 1960
7. *Tares* (verse) Hart-Davis 1961; 1st Amer. Dufour 1961
8. *The Bread of Truth* (verse) Hart-Davis 1963; 1st Amer. Dufour 1963
9. *Pieta* (verse) Hart-Davis 1966
10. *Not That He Brought Flowers* (verse) Hart-Davis 1968
11. *The Mountains* (verse) Chilmark Press NY 1968
12. *H'm: Poems* Macmillan 1972; 1st Amer. St Martin's Press 1972
13. *Selected Poems: 1946–1968* Hart-Davis 1973; 1st Amer. St Martin's Press 1974
14. *Laboratories of the Spirit* (verse) Macmillan 1975; 1st Amer. St Martin's Press 1976

R. S. Thomas has a very high reputation, and is much sought after by collectors, though not so 'popular' as other poets. His books are very rarely seen in bookshops—in any edition, though of course the 1sts are particularly scarce. Nos 1, 2 and 3 are obviously particularly difficult, and No. 1 would be Grade G–H, Nos 2 and 3 Grade E–F. Nos 4, 5, 6 and 7 are Grade C—No. 7 being a highlight—Nos 8, 9, 10 and 11 are Grade B, and the remainder Grade A.

THURBER, James
Born in Ohio 1894. Died 1961.
One of the foremost American humorists, Thurber was—and still is—known equally for his cartoons, particularly in *The New Yorker*, and for his writings. Below appears a representative selection.

1. *Is Sex Necessary?* Harper 1929; 1st Eng. Heinemann 1930 (with E. B. White)
2. *My Life and Hard Times* (autobiog.) Harper 1933; 1st Eng. Harper 1934
3. *My World, and Welcome to It!* Harcourt Brace 1942; 1st Eng. Hamilton 1942
4. *Men, Women and Dogs* Harcourt Brace 1943; 1st Eng. Hamilton 1945

Very much collected in both America and the British Isles. Nos 1 and 2 would be Grade E in the American editions, and Grade C in the English. Nos 3 and 4 are Grade C for the American, and Grade B for the English editions.

Films:
Rise and Shine 20th Century Fox 1941 (*My Life and Hard Times*)
The Secret Life of Walter Mitty RKO 1949
This last film is adapted from a short story, possibly his most famous work.

TOLKIEN, J. R. R.
Born in Birmingham, England, 1892. Died 1973.

1. *A Middle English Vocabulary* OUP 1922; 1st Amer. OUP 1922
2. *Sir Gawain and the Green Knight* OUP 1925; 1st Amer. OUP 1925 (ed. with E. V. Gordon)
3. *Songs for the Philologists* (verse) privately printed 1936
4. *Beowulf: The Monsters and the Critics* (lecture) OUP 1936; 1st Amer. Folcroft Editions 1972
5. *The Hobbit* (novel) Allen & Unwin 1937; 1st Amer. Houghton Mifflin 1938
6. *Farmer Giles of Ham* (novel) Allen & Unwin 1949; 1st Amer. Houghton Mifflin 1950
7. *The Fellowship of the Ring* (novel) Allen & Unwin 1954; 1st Amer. Houghton Mifflin 1954
8. *The Two Towers* (novel) Allen & Unwin 1954; 1st Amer. Houghton Mifflin 1955
9. *The Return of the King* (novel) Allen & Unwin 1955; 1st Amer. Houghton Mifflin 1956

Nos 7, 8 and 9 form the trilogy *The Lord of the Rings*. Revised editions of these three volumes were published by the same publishers, in 1966 and 1967 respectively.

10. *The Adventures of Tom Bombadil* (verse) Allen & Unwin 1962; 1st Amer. Houghton Mifflin 1963
11. *Tree and Leaf* (essay) Allen & Unwin 1964; 1st Amer. Houghton Mifflin 1965
12. *The Tolkien Reader* Ballantine NY 1966
13. *Smith of Wootton Major* (novelette) Allen & Unwin 1967; 1st Amer. Houghton Mifflin 1967
14. *The Road Goes Ever On* (verse) Houghton Mifflin 1967; 1st Eng. Allen & Unwin 1968 (music by Donald Swann)
15. *Bilbo's Last Song* (poster poem) Houghton Mifflin 1974; 1st Eng. Allen & Unwin 1974
16. *Sir Gawain and the Green Knight, Pearl, and Sir Orfeo* (trans.) Allen & Unwin 1975; 1st Amer. Houghton Mifflin 1975
17. *The Homecoming of Beorhtnoth* (poem) Allen & Unwin 1975
Published together with reprints of Nos 11 and 13.
18. *The Father Christmas Letters* Allen & Unwin 1976; 1st Amer. Houghton Mifflin 1976
19. *The Silmarillion* (novel) Allen & Unwin 1977; 1st Amer. Houghton Mifflin 1977

Along with *Winnie the Pooh* and the *I Ching*, Tolkien became a cult in the sixties, and it shows no signs of slowing down. Everyone, it seems, loves him. The dog-eared fat, yellow-spined paperback of *The Lord of the Rings* protrudes from the most unlikely places, as will the much-vaunted sequel. Collectors love him, certainly; this is reflected in the prices that they are willing to pay. Nos 1, 2, and 4 are scarce, certainly, and Grade G or more, though the appeal of No. 1 to most collectors would be the fact that it is Tolkien's first book, rather than as bedside reading. No. 3 is extremely scarce and desirable, and although I have not heard of a copy sold, it could easily reach Grade L or more, I feel. With No. 5 we reach the highlight. It is very scarce, and I recently witnessed the sale of a rather worn, ex-library

copy for £40. A fine copy would double this price. No. 6 is uncommon, though Grade C. The trilogy is the other highlight, and a fine set in d/ws could be Grade P, though odd volumes would be accordingly cheaper. Nos 10, 11 and 13 are Grade C, Nos 12, 15, 16 and 17 Grade A, and No. 14 Grade B. There has been quite a large amount of critical work published about Tolkien's writings, and no doubt there will be much more. Two of the most useful appear to be: Paul Kocher *Master of Middle Earth: The Fiction of J. R. R. Tolkien* (Houghton Mifflin, US; Thames & Hudson 1972) J. E. A. Tyler *The Tolkien Companion* (Macmillan 1976)

TRAVERS, P. L.
Born in Queensland, Australia, 1906.
Creator of the character Mary Poppins, who featured in a series of books which she wrote for children. Always popular, but possibly now more so than ever, since the film. Below is the first in the series.

Mary Poppins Howe 1934; 1st Amer. Reynal 1934
A difficult book to find, though Grade B–C.

Film:
Mary Poppins Disney 1964

URIS, Leon
Born in Baltimore 1924.
Uris has published eight very well-known novels, most of which may be found easily, and quite cheaply, for he is not a favourite with collectors—perhaps because many bibliophiles, jealously guarding their small remaining shelf-space, tend naturally to shy away from fat novels; or perhaps not. One novel, however seems always to be of interest:

Exodus Doubleday 1958; 1st Eng. Wingate 1959
A fine American copy in d/w might be Grade B, but the English Grade A.

Films:
Exodus United Artists 1960
Three other Uris novels have been filmed.

VIDAL, Gore
Born in West Point, New York, 1925.

1. *Williwaw* (novel) Dutton 1946; 1st Eng. Heinemann 1970
2. *In a Yellow Wood* (novel) Dutton 1947
3. *The City and the Pillar* (novel) Dutton 1948; 1st Eng. Lehmann 1949
   A revised edition was published by Dutton in 1965, and by Heinemann in 1966.
4. *The Season of Comfort* (novel) Dutton 1949
5. *A Search for the King* (novel) Dutton 1950
6. *Dark Green, Bright Red* (novel) Dutton 1950; 1st Eng. Lehmann 1950
7. *The Judgement of Paris* (novel) Dutton 1952; 1st Eng. Heinemann 1953
8. *Death in the Fifth Position* (novel) Dutton 1952; 1st Eng. Heinemann 1954 (pseud. Edgar Box)
9. *Death Before Bedtime* (novel) Dutton 1953; 1st Eng. Heinemann 1954 (pseud. Edgar Box)
10. *Death Likes It Hot* (novel) Dutton 1954; 1st Eng. Heinemann 1955 (pseud. Edgar Box)
11. *Messiah* (novel) Dutton 1954; 1st Eng. Heinemann 1955
12. *A Thirsty Evil: 7 Short Stories* Zero Press NY 1956; 1st Eng. Heinemann 1958
13. *Visit to a Small Planet and Other Television Plays* Little Brown US 1957 (incl. *Barn Burning, Dark Possession, The Death of Billy the Kid, A Sense of Justice, Smoke, Summer Pavilion* and *The Turn of the Screw*)
14. *The Best Man* (play) Little Brown US 1960
15. *Three Plays* Heinemann 1962 (cont. *Visit to a Small Planet, The Best Man, On the March to the Sea*)
16. *Romulus: A New Comedy* Dramatists Play Service 1962
17. *Three: Williwaw, A Thirsty Evil, Julian the Apostate* (novels) NAL 1962
18. *Rocking the Boat* (essays) Little Brown 1962; 1st Eng. Heinemann 1963
19. *Julian* (novel) Little Brown 1964; 1st Eng. Heinemann 1964
20. *Washington D.C.* (novel) Little Brown 1967; 1st Eng. Heinemann 1967
21. *Myra Breckinridge* (novel) Little Brown 1968; 1st Eng. Blond 1968
22. *Weekend* (play) Dramatists Play Service 1968
23. *Reflections Upon a Sinking Ship* (essays) Little Brown 1969; 1st Eng. Heinemann 1969
24. *Two Sisters* (novel) Little Brown 1970; 1st Eng. Heinemann 1970
25. *An Evening with Richard Nixon* (play) Random House 1972
26. *Homage to Daniel Shays: Collected Essays 1952–1972* Random House 1972
    Published in England by Heinemann in 1974 as *Collected Essays 1952–1972*.
27. *Burr* (novel) Random House 1973; 1st Eng. Heinemann 1974
28. *Myron* (novel) Random House 1974; 1st Eng. Heinemann 1975
29. *1876* (novel) Random House 1976; 1st Eng. Heinemann 1976

Critical work: R. L. White *Gore Vidal* (Twayne 1968)
The early works are little-known, and scarce, though Vidal's recent books should be very easy to find. No. 1 is Grade E, Nos 2, 3 and 4 Grade C. Nos 5–10 are Grade B–C, Nos 11, 12 and 13 are Grade B, and the rest Grade A at the moment.

Films:
The Left-Handed Gun Warner Bros 1958 (*The Death of Billy the Kid*)
Visit to a Small Planet Paramount 1959
The Best Man United Artists 1968
Myra Breckinridge 20th Century Fox 1969
Vidal worked on the screenplays of *The Best Man* and (in collaboration) *Myra Breckinridge*; also on several other films, including *Suddenly, Last Summer*.

VONNEGUT, Jnr, Kurt
Born in Indianapolis 1922.
The following work exists on Vonnegut:
Asa B. Pieratt Jnr and Jerome Klinkowitz *Kurt Vonnegut Jnr: A Descriptive Bibliography and Annotated Secondary Checklist* (Shoe String Press, US 1974)

Below is a list of his published work.

1. *Player Piano* (novel) Scribner 1952; 1st Eng. Macmillan 1953
2. *The Sirens of Titan* (novel) Fawcett 1959; 1st Eng. Gollancz 1962
3. *Canary in a Cathouse* (stories) Fawcett 1961
4. *Mother Night* (novel) Fawcett 1961; 1st Eng. Cape 1968
5. *Cat's Cradle* (novel) Holt Rinehart 1963; 1st Eng. Gollancz 1963
6. *God Bless You, Mr Rosewater* (novel) Holt Rinehart 1965; 1st Eng. Cape 1965
7. *Welcome to the Monkey House* (pieces) Delacorte Press 1968
8. *Slaughterhouse-Five* (novel) Delacorte Press 1969; 1st Eng. Cape 1970
9. *Happy Birthday, Wanda June* (play) Delacorte Press 1971; 1st Eng. Cape 1973
10. *Between Time and Timbuctoo* (play) Delacorte Press 1972
11. *Breakfast of Champions* (novel) Delacorte Press 1973; 1st Eng. Cape 1973
12. *Wampeters, Foma, and Granfalloons: Opinions* Delacorte Press 1974; 1st Eng. Cape 1975
13. *Slapstick* (novel) Delacorte Press 1976; 1st Eng. Cape 1976

No. 8 is the highlight, and a fine American copy in d/w would be Grade C, though the English ed. Grade A. No. 1 is Grade D, Nos 2, 3 and 4 are Grade B–C, and the remainder Grade A–B. Correspondingly less for the English editions.

Film:
Slaughterhouse-Five Universal 1972

WAIN, John
Born in Staffordshire 1925.
Wain has published around two dozen books—verse, novels, stories, essays, criticism and biography. He has also edited about a dozen more. Below is a selection.

1. *Hurry On Down* (novel) Secker & Warburg 1953
   This was published in America by Knopf in 1954 as *Born in Captivity*.

2. *Strike the Father Dead* (novel) Macmillan 1962; 1st Amer. St Martin's Press 1962
3. *Sprightly Running: Part of an Autobiography* Macmillan 1962; 1st Amer. St Martin's Press 1963
4. *Samuel Johnson* (biog.) Macmillan 1974; 1st Amer. Viking Press 1975

Nos 1 and 4 are Grade B, and Nos 2 and 3 Grade A.

WALEY, Arthur
Born in London 1889. Died 1966.
One of the very few writers notable for translations. His fine renderings of Chinese and Japanese literature have never been rivalled, and are collected quite avidly. Below appears a selection, including his best-known works, though a full bibliography does exist: Francis A. Johns *A Bibliography of Arthur Waley* (Allen & Unwin 1968)

1. *A Hundred and Seventy Chinese Poems* Constable 1918; 1st Amer. Knopf 1919
2. *The Tale of Genji* Allen & Unwin 1925; 1st Amer. Houghton Mifflin 1925 (by Lady Murasaki)
3. *The Sacred Tree* Allen & Unwin 1926; 1st Amer. Houghton Mifflin 1926 (2nd part of No. 2)
4. *A Wreath of Cloud* Allen & Unwin 1927; 1st Amer. Houghton Mifflin 1927 (3rd part of No. 2)
5. *Blue Trousers* Allen & Unwin 1928; 1st Amer. Houghton Mifflin 1928 (4th part of No. 2)
6. *The Lady of the Boat* Allen & Unwin 1932; 1st Amer. Houghton Mifflin 1932 (vol. 1 of 5th part of No. 2)
7. *The Bridge of Dreams* Allen & Unwin 1933; 1st Amer. Houghton Mifflin 1933 (vol. 2 of 5th part of No. 2)
   Nos 2–7, it will be seen, constitute the entire *Tale of Genji*. The first collected edition was by Houghton Mifflin in 1935, and one month later by Allen & Unwin. The American edition was two volumes, boxed, and the English both one and two volumes.
8. *Monkey* Allen & Unwin 1942; 1st Amer. Day 1943 (by Wu Ch'eng-en)

The d/w and t/p of English ed. by Duncan Grant.

No. 1 is Grade C, and each of the *Genji* volumes is Grade B. The collected edition is Grade C. No. 8 is also Grade C, in the d/w.

WALLACE, Edgar

Born at Greenwich 1875. Died 1932.

Apart from stories and plays, Wallace wrote an estimated 150 novels in twenty-seven years. Mercifully, there is a bibliography, which ought to be acquired if one is considering collecting the entire *œuvre* of this phenomenon. It is confined to British editions only, however. Of all his well-known books, I shall confine myself to recording just one—the most desirable, although not the most rare, for those wanting merely a representation of his work.

The Four Just Men Tallis Press 1905

The true 1st has the £500 reward advert printed on the front of its yellow cover, and not the later coloured illustration. A fold-out frontis. should be present, as well as the all-important competition slip—situated at the back of the book, it is a perforated form intended to be removed, filled in, and sent up by the hopeful owner of the volume. Collectors, therefore, seek copies from the libraries of singularly uncompetitive people. A fine copy with all these points would be Grade E.

Films:

The Secret Four Ealing 1939 (*The Four Just Men*)

In addition to this, nearly forty other Wallace novels have been filmed.

WATERHOUSE, Keith

Born in Yorkshire 1929.

In addition to the list below, Waterhouse published various humorous books in the late fifties and early sixties under various pseudonyms.

1. *The Café Royal: 90 Years of Bohemia* (non-fiction) Hutchinson 1955 (with Guy Deghy)
2. *There Is a Happy Land* (novel) Joseph 1957
3. *Britain's Voice Abroad* (essay) Daily Mirror 1957 (with Paul Cave)
4. *The Future of Television* (essay) Daily Mirror 1958
5. *Billy Liar* (novel) Joseph 1959; 1st Amer. Norton 1960
6. *Billy Liar* (play) Joseph 1960; 1st Amer. Norton 1960 (with Willis Hall)
7. *Celebration* (play) Joseph 1961 (with Willis Hall)
8. *Jubb* (novel) Joseph 1963; 1st Amer. Putnam 1964
9. *England, Our England* (play) Evans 1964 (with Willis Hall)
10. *All Things Bright and Beautiful* (play) Joseph 1963
11. *The Sponge Room* and *Squat Betty* (plays) Evans 1963
12. *Come Laughing Home* (play) Evans 1965
13. *Help Stamp Out Marriage* (play) French NY 1966
    This was published in England by Evans in 1967 as *Say Who You Are*. This play, along with Nos 10, 11 and 12, was written with Willis Hall.
14. *The Bucket Shop* (novel) Joseph 1968
    This was published in America by Putnam in 1969 as *Everything Must Go*.
15. *The Passing of the Third-Floor Buck* Joseph 1974 (*Punch* pieces)
16. *Billy Liar on the Moon* (novel) Joseph 1975; 1st Amer. Putnam 1976
17. *Mondays, Thursdays* (*Daily Mirror* pieces) Joseph 1976

It is the novels that are the most popular, with *Billy Liar* as the highlight and clear favourite. Nos 2 and 5 are Grade C, Nos 6, 8 and 14 Grade B, and the remainder Grade A, though No. 16 will soon rise.

Film: *Billy Liar* Warner Bros 1962

WATKINS, Vernon

Born in South Wales 1906. Died 1967.

1. *Ballad of the Mari Lwyd* (verse) Faber 1941
2. *The Lamp and the Veil* (verse) Faber 1945
3. *The Lady with the Unicorn* (verse) Faber 1948
4. *Selected Poems* New Directions NY 1948
5. *The North Sea* (play) New Directions 1951; 1st Eng. Faber 1955
   This is a translation of Heine's work.
6. *The Death Bell* (verse) Faber 1954; 1st Amer. New Directions 1954
7. *Cypress and Acacia* (verse) Faber 1959; 1st Amer. New Directions 1959
8. *Affinities* (verse) Faber 1962; 1st Amer. New Directions 1963
9. *Selected Poems 1930–1960* Faber 1967; 1st Amer. New Directions 1967
10. *Fidelities* (verse) Faber 1968

An essential work is *Vernon Watkins 1906–1967,* a tribute edited by Leslie Norris, and including contributions by Heath-Stubbs, Larkin, Kathleen Raine and R. S. Thomas, among others (Faber 1970).
Recently, Watkins is quite in favour with collectors, though his works are not common. No. 1 is Grade C, nos 2–7 Grade B, and the remainder Grade A.

WAUGH, Evelyn

Waugh was born in London 1903 and died 1966. He was the son of Arthur (Managing Director of Chapman & Hall), brother of Alec, and father of Auberon. Although all the Waughs are respected writers, Evelyn emerges as the great writer—some say one of the greatest English novelists. He is also, incidentally, the only Waugh to interest collectors. This interest is avid, and growing each year. Below is a checklist of all his works, excluding a few private press items and contributions to other books.

1. *The World to Come: A Poem in Three Cantos* privately printed 1916
2. *PRB: An Essay on the Pre-Raphaelite Brotherhood* privately printed 1926
3. *Decline and Fall* (novel) Chapman & Hall 1928; 1st Amer. Farrar 1929
4. *Rossetti* (biog.) Duckworth 1928; 1st Amer. Dodd 1928
5. *Labels* (travel) Duckworth 1930
   This was published in America in the same year by Farrar as *A Bachelor Abroad.*
6. *Vile Bodies* (novel) Chapman & Hall 1930; 1st Amer. Farrar 1930
7. *Remote People* (travel) Duckworth 1931
   This was published in America in 1932 by Farrar as *They Were Still Dancing.*
8. *Black Mischief* (novel) Chapman & Hall 1932; 1st Amer. Farrar 1932
9. *A Handful of Dust* (novel) Chapman & Hall 1934; 1st Amer. Farrar 1934
10. *Ninety-Two Days* (travel) Duckworth 1934; 1st Amer. Farrar 1934
11. *Edmund Campion* (biog.) Longman 1935; 1st Amer. Sheed 1935
12. *Mr Loveday's Little Outing* (stories) Chapman & Hall 1936; 1st Amer. Little Brown 1936
13. *Waugh in Abyssinia* (travel) Longman 1936; 1st Amer. Farrar 1936
14. *Scoop* (novel) Chapman & Hall 1938; 1st Amer. Little Brown 1938
15. *Robbery Under Law* (travel) Chapman & Hall 1939
    This was published in America in the same year by Little Brown as *Mexico: An Object Lesson.*
16. *Put Out More Flags* (novel) Chapman & Hall 1942; 1st Amer. Little Brown 1942
17. *Work Suspended* (unfinished novel) Chapman & Hall 1942
18. *Brideshead Revisited* (novel) Chapman & Hall 1945; 1st Amer. Little Brown 1945
19. *When the Going Was Good* (travel) Duckworth 1946; 1st Amer. Little Brown 1947
    Selection from Nos 5, 7, 10 and 13.
20. *Scott-King's Modern Europe* (novel) Chapman & Hall 1947; 1st Amer. Little Brown 1949
21. *The Loved One* (novel) Chapman & Hall 1948; 1st Amer. Little Brown 1948
22. *Helena* (novel) Chapman & Hall 1950; 1st Amer. Little Brown 1950
23. *Men at Arms* (novel) Chapman & Hall 1952; 1st Amer. Little Brown 1952
24. *The Holy Places* (essays) Queen Anne Press 1952

This was published in an ordinary edition at fifteen shillings, and in a limited, signed edition at three guineas.

25. *Love Among the Ruins* (novel) Chapman & Hall 1953
26. *Officers and Gentlemen* (novel) Chapman & Hall 1955; 1st Amer. Little Brown 1955
27. *The Ordeal of Gilbert Pinfold* (novel) Chapman & Hall 1957; 1st Amer. Little Brown 1957
28. *Ronald Knox* (biog.) Chapman & Hall 1959; 1st Amer. Little Brown 1960
29. *A Tourist in Africa* (travel) Chapman & Hall 1960; 1st Amer. Little Brown 1960
30. *Unconditional Surrender* (novel) Chapman & Hall 1961

    This was published in America in 1961 by Little Brown as *The End of the Battle*. Together with Nos 23 and 26 it forms the War trilogy.
31. *Basil Seal Rides Again* (novel) Chapman & Hall 1963; 1st Amer. Little Brown 1963
32. *A Little Learning* (autobiog.) Chapman & Hall 1964; 1st Amer. Little Brown 1964
33. *Diaries* Weidenfeld & Nicolson 1976; 1st Amer. Little Brown 1976

    Large parts of this first appeared in the *Observer Colour Magazine* for 25th March 1973, and for the succeeding seven issues. *The Sunday Times* published two more extracts immediately prior to book publication.

Although not definitive, by the author's own admission, the standard biography at the moment is Christopher Sykes *Evelyn Waugh* (Collins 1975).

No. 1, it will be seen, was privately printed when Waugh was thirteen. I can find out nothing about it, but if a copy ever came up, it would fetch untold fortunes. No. 2, also privately printed, does come up from time to time, though it is now Grade L and more. No. 3 is his first and best-known novel, as well as being scarce—particularly in the d/w, designed by Evelyn himself. A fine copy thus could be Grade M. No. 4 is also scarce, and Grade I. From now on, it is generally true that the travel books are more difficult than the novels, and No. 5 is Grade H. Nos 6

and 7 are Grade F, and Nos 8, 9, 10, 11, 12 and 13 are Grade E. Nos 14, 16, 17, 18 and 19 are Grade C, Nos 23, 26, 28, 30, 31 and 32 are Grade B. Nos 20, 21, 22, 25, 27 and 29 are Grade A. No. 15 is Grade D–E, No. 24 is Grade D for the ordinary edition, and Grade I–J for the limited. No. 33 is Grade C.

Films:
The Loved One MGM 1965
Decline and Fall of a Birdwatcher 20th Century Fox 1968 (*Decline and Fall*)

WEBB, Mary

Born in Shropshire 1881. Died 1927.
Author of several novels, though the one publicly praised by Baldwin has remained the favourite. It is scarce, and a fine copy in d/w could be Grade I. Her other books do not approach this figure.

Precious Bane Cape 1924; 1st Amer. Dutton 1926

WELCH, Denton

Born in England 1914(?). Died 1948.

1. *Maiden Voyage* (autobiog.) Routledge 1943; 1st Amer. Fischer 1945
2. *In Youth Is Pleasure* (novel) Routledge 1944; 1st Amer. Fischer 1946
3. *Brave and Cruel* (stories) Hamilton 1948
4. *A Voice Through a Cloud* (novel) Lehmann 1950; 1st Amer. University of Texas 1966
5. *A Last Sheaf* (stories and verse) Lehmann 1951
6. *Journals* Hamilton 1952

No. 1 is Grade D. No. 2 is Grade B–C. The remainder are Grade B.

WELLS, H. G.

Born in Kent 1866. Died 1946.
The following work has been published: Geoffrey H. Wells *The Works of H. G. Wells 1887–1925: A Bibliography, Dictionary, and Subject Index* (Routledge 1926).
A more up-to-date bibliography has been published by the H. G. Wells Society (1968).

Below appears a necessarily brief list of particular highlights.

1. *The Time Machine* (novel) Heinemann 1895; 1st Amer. Holt 1895
The American edition, it is interesting to note, was printed as being by H. S. Wells.
2. *The Invisible Man* (novel) Pearson 1897; 1st Amer. Arnold 1897
3. *The War of the Worlds* (novel) Heinemann 1898; 1st Amer. Harper 1898
4. *The First Men in the Moon* (novel) Newnes 1901; 1st Amer. Bowen-Merrill 1901
This was first published in *The Strand Magazine*.
5. *Kipps* (novel) Macmillan 1905; 1st Amer. Scribner 1905
This was first published in *Pall Mall Magazine*.
6. *The History of Mr Polly* (novel) Nelson 1910; 1st Amer. Nelson 1910

The values of these books are lower than one would think, with No. 1 at Grade I–J, Nos 2, 3 and 4 at Grade E, No. 5 Grade C, and No. 6 Grade B.

Films:
The Invisible Man United Artists 1933
Kipps 20th Century Fox 1941
The History of Mr Polly Two Cities 1949
The War of the Worlds Paramount 1953
The Time Machine MGM 1960
The First Men in the Moon Columbia 1963
Half a Sixpence Paramount 1967 (*Kipps*)
In addition to these, five other Wells novels or stories have been filmed.

WESKER, Arnold
Born in London 1932.
Author of around a dozen plays, and a few other works. Below are his highlights.

1. *Chicken Soup with Barley* (play) Penguin 1959
2. *Roots* (play) Penguin 1959
This was contained in *New English Dramatists*.
3. *I'm Talking About Jerusalem* (play) Penguin 1960

Nos 1, 2 and 3 form the Wesker trilogy.
4. *The Wesker Trilogy* (plays) Cape 1960; 1st Amer. Random House 1961
Contains Nos 1, 2 and 3, for the first time in hardback.
5. *The Kitchen* (play) Penguin 1960
This was contained in *New English Dramatists* 2. An expanded edition was published in 1962 by Cape, and by Random House.
6. *Chips with Everything* (play) Cape 1962; 1st Amer. Random House 1963

Nos 4 and 6 are Grade B, and the others Grade A. It is quite possible, of course, to pick up Nos 1, 2, 3 and 5 very cheaply.

Film:
The Kitchen British Lion 1961

WHEATLEY, Dennis
Born in 1897, Wheatley did not publish a book until 1933, and although today his Black Magic novels are of interest—particularly the earlier ones—prime interest is reserved for the Dossiers. In collaboration with J. G. Links, Wheatley published four of these, beginning with *Murder off Miami* in 1936. They were, quite simply, a totally new and appealing way of presenting a crime story—as a police dossier, complete with typescript pages, facsimile telegrams, notes, postcards, and clues—such as strands of hair, fingerprints, and spent matches; all this was bound in wrapps, and tied with red ribbon. A sealed compartment at the rear could be slit open to reveal the solution to the crime—and, not unnaturally, very few survive with the seal intact! They were published, unbelievably, at 3/6d—or $17\frac{1}{2}$p. Today fine copies are Grade E, and hard to find. Wheatley himself foresaw this, for the rear cover of *Murder off Miami* reads: '*Keep this carefully*. It is a First Edition of the first Crime Story ever presented in this way. Should others follow, it is possible that an undamaged copy of "Murder off Miami" may be of considerable interest one day.'
They are undated, but later impressions announce 'Nth Thousand' on the cover.

The Dossiers:

1. *Murder off Miami* Hutchinson 1936
   This was published in America by Morrow, in the same year, as *File on Bolitho Lane*.
2. *Who Killed Robert Prentice?* Hutchinson 1937
   This was published in America by Greenberg in the same year as *File on Robert Prentice*.
3. *The Mallinsay Massacre* Hutchinson 1938
4. *Herewith the Clues* Hutchinson 1939

Below is a short selection of Wheatley's Black Magic novels.

5. *The Devil Rides Out* Hutchinson 1934
6. *To the Devil—a Daughter* Hutchinson 1953
7. *The Satanist* Hutchinson 1960

No. 5 is scarce, and Grade B–C. No. 6 is Grade B, and No. 7 Grade A.

Films:
The Devil Rides Out Associated British 1971
In addition to this, three further Wheatley novels have been filmed.

WHITE, Patrick
Born in London 1912. Australian.

1. *Happy Valley* (novel) Harrap 1939; 1st Amer. Viking Press 1940
2. *The Living and the Dead* (novel) Routledge 1941; 1st Amer. Viking Press 1941
3. *The Aunt's Story* (novel) Routledge 1948; 1st Amer. Viking Press 1948
4. *The Tree of Man* (novel) Viking Press 1955; 1st Eng. Eyre & Spottiswoode 1956
5. *Voss* (novel) Viking Press 1957; 1st Eng. Eyre & Spottiswoode 1957
6. *Riders in the Chariot* (novel) Viking Press 1961; 1st Eng. Eyre & Spottiswoode 1961
7. *The Burnt Ones* (stories) Viking Press 1964; 1st Eng. Eyre & Spottiswoode 1964
8. *Four Plays* Eyre & Spottiswoode 1965; 1st Amer. Viking Press 1966 (cont. *The Ham Funeral, The Season at Sarsparilla, A Cheery Soul* and *Night on Bald Mountain*)
9. *The Solid Mandala* (novel) Viking Press 1966; 1st Eng. Eyre & Spottiswoode 1966
10. *The Vivisector* (novel) Viking Press 1970; 1st Eng. Cape 1970
11. *The Eye of the Storm* (novel) Cape 1973; 1st Amer. Viking Press 1974
12. *The Cockatoos: Shorter Novels and Stories* Cape 1974; 1st Amer. Viking Press 1975
13. *A Fringe of Leaves* (novel) Cape 1976; 1st Amer. Viking Press 1976

No. 1 was preceded by a slim volume of verse privately printed in Australia (*The Ploughman and Other Poems*, Beacon Press 1935). The following has also been published in Australia:
Jannette Finch *A Bibliography of Patrick White* (Libraries Board 1966)
Patrick White is now quite avidly collected, particularly since he won the Nobel Prize. The early works are very scarce; they come up so rarely, indeed, that it is especially difficult to give price guidelines. No. 1 would very probably be Grade F–G, however, and Nos 2 and 3 Grade C–D. From this point onwards, the books are quite easy to find, though prices are rising discernibly. Nos 4 and 5 are Grade B, and the rest are Grade A at the moment.

WHITE, T. H.
Born in India 1906. Died 1964. British. Author of around two dozen books, as well as several unpublished works. These are listed in Sylvia Townsend Warner's biography *T. H. White* (Cape/Chatto & Windus 1967).
Below is a selection of highlights.

1. *The Sword in the Stone* (novel) Collins 1938; 1st Amer. Putnam 1939
2. *The Witch in the Wood* (novel) Putnam 1939; 1st Eng. Collins 1940
3. *The Ill-Made Knight* (novel) Putnam 1940; 1st Eng. Collins 1941
4. *The Goshawk* (non-fiction) Cape 1951; 1st Amer. Putnam 1952
5. *The Book of Beasts* (trans.) Cape 1954; 1st Amer. Putnam 1955
6. *The Once and Future King* (novels) Collins 1958; 1st Amer. Putnam 1958
   This is the complete Arthurian epic, and

contains No. 1 with two new chapters, No. 2—rewritten, and with the title *The Queen of Air and Darkness*—No. 3, and *The Candle in the Wind*, previously unpublished.

No. 1 is scarce, and Grade D. Nos 2 and 3 are Grade C, No. 4 Grade A, and Nos 5 and 6 Grade B.

Films:
The Sword in the Stone Disney 1963
Camelot Warner Bros 1966 (*The Once and Future King*)

WILDE, Oscar
Born in Dublin 1854. Died 1900.
In 1967, the classic Wilde bibliography was reissued, with a new Introduction by Timothy d'Arch Smith:
Stuart Mason Bibliography of Oscar Wilde (Rota 1967)
This exhaustive work is essential, and describes works in the utmost detail. Here is only a very brief selection, Wilde—strictly speaking—being a nineteenth-century author.

1. *The Happy Prince and Other Tales* Nutt 1888; 1st Amer. Roberts Bros 1888
   Illus. by Walter Crane.
2. *The Picture of Dorian Gray* (novel) Ward Lock 1891; 1st Amer. Ward Lock 1891
3. *Lord Arthur Savile's Crime and Other Stories* Osgood McIlvaine 1891; 1st Amer. Dodd Mead 1891
4. *Salome* (play) Mathews/Lane 1893
   An edition was published in the following year by the same publishers, in English—the 1893 edition being in the original French. The English edition was illustrated by Beardsley.
5. *Lady Windermere's Fan* (play) Mathews/Lane 1893
6. *A Woman of No Importance* (play) Lane 1894
7. *The Ballad of Reading Gaol* Smithers 1898
8. *The Importance of Being Earnest* (play) Smithers 1899; 1st Amer. French n.d.
   The French edition bears the date 1893, though this is incorrect.
9. *An Ideal Husband* (play) Smithers 1899
10. *De Profundis* (prose) Methuen 1905; 1st Amer. Putnam 1905

Many of Wilde's later works were issued in small, limited editions, signed and on Japanese vellum, though sometimes this was simultaneous with, or soon after, a regular edition; the issues, then, are important when discussing price.
No. 1 is Grade P, No. 2 Grade K, Nos 3, 5, 6, 8 and 9 Grade I. No. 4 would be Grade M, though the Beardsley edition would top this at Grade R. No. 7 would be Grade K for the absolute 1st, though the bibliography ought to be consulted for details. No. 10 is Grade E.
The following have been selected from the vast amount of material on Wilde:
Philippe Jullian *Oscar Wilde* (Constable 1969)
Richard Ellmann (ed.) *The Artist as Critic: The Critical Writings of Oscar Wilde* (Allen 1970)
H. Montgomery Hyde *Oscar Wilde* (Eyre Methuen 1976)

Films:
Flesh and Fantasy Universal 1943 (*Lord Arthur Savile's Crime*)
The Canterville Ghost MGM 1944
The Picture of Dorian Gray MGM 1945; Hemdale 1973
An Ideal Husband British Lion 1948
Lady Windermere's Fan 20th Century Fox 1949
The Importance of Being Earnest General 1952

WILLIAMS, Charles
Born in London 1886. Died 1945.
A bibliography is contained in a volume of essays by Williams entitled *The Image of the City*, selected and with a critical intro. by Anne Ridler (OUP 1958).
Below are a few of his forty-five books.

1. *Bacon* (biog.) Barker 1933
2. *Rochester* (biog.) Barker 1935
3. *Queen Elizabeth* (biog.) Duckworth 1936
4. *Witchcraft* (non-fiction) Faber 1941; 1st Amer. Meridian 1959

5. *All Hallows Eve* (novel) Faber 1945; 1st Amer. Cudahy 1948
The American edition contained an Intro. by T. S. Eliot.
6. *Collected Plays* OUP 1963; 1st Amer. OUP 1963
Intro. by John Heath-Stubbs.

Interest in Charles Williams has recently increased, and his books have become even harder to find than ever. Nos 1, 2 and 3 are Grade B–C, No. 4 is Grade D (for the English edition), and No. 5 is Grade C. No. 6 is Grade B.

WILLIAMS, Tennessee
Originally Thomas Lanier Williams. Born in Columbus, Mississippi, 1911.
Author of two novels, six books of short stories, and nearly sixty plays. The highlights appear below.

1. *The Glass Menagerie* (play) Random House 1945; 1st Eng. Lehmann 1948
2. *A Streetcar Named Desire* (play) New Directions 1947; 1st Eng. Lehmann 1949
3. *The Roman Spring of Mrs Stone* (novel) New Directions 1950; 1st Eng. Lehmann 1950
4. *Cat on a Hot Tin Roof* (play) New Directions 1955; 1st Eng. Secker & Warburg 1956
5. *Sweet Bird of Youth* (play) New Directions 1959; 1st Eng. Secker & Warburg 1961
6. *The Milk Train Doesn't Stop Here Anymore* (play) New Directions 1964; 1st Eng. Secker & Warburg 1964

No. 1 is Grade C for the American ed. and Grade B for the English, as are Nos 2 and 3. Nos 4, 5 and 6 are Grade B, and Grade A for the English editions.

Films:
The Glass Menagerie Warner Bros 1950
A Streetcar Named Desire Warner Bros 1951
Cat on a Hot Tin Roof MGM 1958
The Roman Spring of Mrs Stone Warner Bros 1961
Sweet Bird of Youth MGM 1962
Boom Universal 1968 (*The Milk Train Doesn't Stop Here Anymore*)

Williams wrote the screenplays for *The Glass Menagerie* (with Peter Berneis), *A Streetcar Named Desire* (with Oscar Saul) and *Boom*. In addition to these, eight other Williams plays have been filmed.
In 1976, Tennessee Williams' *Memoirs* were published by Doubleday and in England by W. H. Allen.

WILLIAMSON, Henry
Born in Dorset 1895.
Author of over fifty books, mainly novels and short stories concerned with country topics. A selection of his best-known novels appears below.

1. *The Beautiful Years* Collins 1921; 1st Amer. Dutton 1921
2. *Dandelion Days* Collins 1922; 1st Amer. Dutton 1922
3. *The Dream of Fair Women* Collins 1924; 1st Amer. Dutton 1924
4. *The Pathway* Cape 1928; 1st Amer. Dutton 1929
5. *The Star-Born* Faber 1933
Nos 1–5 form the *Flax of Dream* sequence.
6. *Tarka the Otter* Putnam 1927; 1st Amer. Dutton 1928
7. *Salar the Salmon* Faber 1935; 1st Amer. Little Brown 1936

No. 6 is, of course, the highlight, and Grade D–E. No. 1 is Grade C, Nos 2, 3, 4 and 5 Grade B, and No. 7 Grade C.

WILSON, Angus
Born in Sussex 1913.

1 *The Wrong Set and Other Stories* Secker & Warburg 1949; 1st Amer. Morrow 1950
2. *Such Darling Dodos and Other Stories* Secker & Warburg 1950; 1st Amer. Morrow 1951
3. *Emile Zola* (non-fiction) Secker & Warburg 1952; 1st Amer. Morrow 1952
4. *Hemlock and After* (novel) Secker & Warburg 1952; 1st Amer. Viking Press 1952
5. *For Whom the Cloche Tolls* (essay) Methuen 1953 (with Philippe Jullian)

6. *The Mulberry Bush* (play) Secker & Warburg 1956
7. *Anglo-Saxon Attitudes* (novel) Secker & Warburg 1956; 1st Amer. Viking Press 1956
8. *A Bit Off the Map and Other Stories* Secker & Warburg 1957; 1st Amer. Viking Press 1957
9. *The Middle Age of Mrs Eliot* (novel) Secker & Warburg 1958; 1st Amer. Viking Press 1959
10. *The Old Men at the Zoo* (novel) Secker & Warburg 1961; 1st Amer. Viking Press 1961
11. *The Wild Garden: or, Speaking of Writing* (non-fiction) University of California Press 1963; 1st Eng. Secker & Warburg 1963
12. *Tempo: The Impact of Television on the Arts* (non-fiction) Studio Vista 1964; 1st Amer. Dufour 1966
13. *Late Call* (novel) Secker & Warburg 1964; 1st Amer. Viking Press 1965
14. *No Laughing Matter* (novel) Secker & Warburg 1967; 1st Amer. Viking Press 1967
15. *Death Dance: 25 Stories* Viking Press 1969
16. *The World of Charles Dickens* (non-fiction) Secker & Warburg 1970; 1st Amer. Viking Press 1970
17. *As If by Magic* (novel) Secker & Warburg 1973; 1st Amer. Viking Press 1973

Nos 1, 2, 3, 4, 5 and 12 are Grade B, and the remainder Grade A.

WILSON, Colin
Born in Leicester 1931.

1. *The Outsider* (philosophy) Gollancz 1956; 1st Amer. Houghton Mifflin 1956
2. *Religion and the Rebel* (non-fiction) Gollancz 1957; 1st Amer. Houghton Mifflin 1957
3. *The Age of Defeat* (non-fiction) Gollancz 1959
   This was published in America during the same year by Houghton Mifflin as *The Stature of Man.*
4. *Ritual in the Dark* (novel) Gollancz 1960; 1st Amer. Houghton Mifflin 1960
5. *Adrift in Soho* (novel) Gollancz 1961; 1st Amer. Houghton Mifflin 1961
6. *Encyclopedia of Murder* (non-fiction) Barker 1961; 1st Amer. Putnam 1962 (with Patricia Pitman)

7. *The Strength to Dream: Literature and the Imagination* (non-fiction) Gollancz 1962; 1st Amer. Houghton Mifflin 1962
8. *Origins of the Sexual Impulse* (non-fiction) Barker 1963; 1st Amer. Putnam 1963
9. *The World of Violence* (novel) Gollancz 1963
   This was published in America during the same year by Houghton Mifflin as *The Violent World of Hugh Green.*
10. *Man Without a Shadow* (novel) Barker 1963
    This was published in America during the same year by the Dial Press as *The Sex Diary of Gerard Sorme.*
11. *Necessary Doubt* (novel) Barker 1964; 1st Amer. Simon & Schuster 1964
12. *Rasputin and the Fall of the Romanovs* (non-fiction) Barker 1964; 1st Amer. Farrar Straus 1964
13. *Brandy of the Damned: Discoveries of a Musical Eclectic* Baker 1964
    This was published in America in 1966 by Atheneum as *Chords and Discords: Purely Personal Opinions on Music.* A supplemented edition, entitled *Colin Wilson on Music,* was published by Pan in 1967.
14. *Beyond the Outsider: The Philosophy of the Future* Barker 1965; 1st Amer. Houghton Mifflin 1965
15. *Eagle and Earwig* (essay) Baker 1965
16. *The Glass Cage* (novel) Barker 1966; 1st Amer. Random House 1967
17. *Introduction to the New Existentialism* Hutchinson 1966; 1st Amer. Houghton Mifflin 1967
18. *Sex and the Intelligent Teenager* (non-fiction) Arrow 1966
19. *Voyage to a Beginning* (autobiog.) Woolf 1966; 1st Amer. Crown 1969
20. *The Mind Parasites* (novel) Barker 1967; 1st Amer. Arkham House 1967
21. *The Philosopher's Stone* (novel) Barker 1969; 1st Amer. Crown 1971
22. *Bernard Shaw: A Reassessment* (non-fiction) Hutchinson 1969; 1st Amer. Atheneum 1969
23. *A Casebook of Murder* (non-fiction) Frewin 1969; 1st Amer. Cowles 1970
24. *The Killer* (novel) NEL 1970
    This was published in America in the same year by Crown as *Lingard.*

25. *The God of the Labyrinth* (novel) Hart-Davis 1970
    This was published in America in 1971 by NAL as *The Hedonists*.
26. *Strindberg* (play) Calder & Boyars 1970; 1st Amer. Random House 1971
27. *Poetry and Mysticism* (non-fiction) Hutchinson 1970; 1st Amer. City Lights 1970
28. *The Strange Genius of David Lindsay* (non-fiction) Baker 1970 (with E. H. Visiak and J. B. Pick)
29. *The Black Room* (novel) Weidenfeld & Nicolson 1971
30. *The Occult: A History* Hodder & Stoughton 1971; 1st Amer. Random House 1971
31. *New Pathways in Psychology* Gollancz 1972; 1st Amer. Taplinger 1972
32. *Order of Assassins: The Psychology of Murder* (non-fiction) Hart-Davis 1972
33. *L'Amour: The Ways of Love* (non-fiction) Crown NY 1972
34. *Strange Powers* (non-fiction) Latimer 1973; 1st Amer. Random House 1975
35. *Tree by Tolkien* (essay) Covent Garden Press 1973; 1st Amer. Capra Press 1974
36. *Hesse, Reich, Borges* (essays) Village Press 1974; 1st Amer. Leaves of Grass Press 1974
37. *The Schoolgirl Murder Case* (novel) Granada 1974; 1st Amer. Crown 1974
38. *A Book of Booze* (drink) Gollancz 1974
39. *The Craft of the Novel* (non-fiction) Gollancz 1975
40. *The Space Vampires* (novel) Granada 1976; 1st Amer. Putnam 1976

Although many critics remain firm in their view that Colin Wilson never lived up to the promise of his first book—and, indeed, it is true that none other of his books has had equal success—it has become very clear recently that collectors, particularly the younger ones, do not agree. His books come up reasonably frequently, but they tend to be the same few, some remaining very scarce. No. 1 is, of course, the highlight, and those collectors seeking merely a representation of Wilson would be well advised to try and acquire this now, while the price is still reasonable (Grade C–D). The following are Grade B: Nos 2, 3, 4, 5, 6, 7, 8, 9, 10, 11, 12, 13, 19 (signed, limited edition), 22, 35 (limited edition). The remainder are Grade A, but as the number of collectors increases, these prices are bound to rise.

WODEHOUSE, P. G.

Born in Guildford, Surrey, in 1881, Wodehouse is one of the greatest humorists ever, and certainly the finest of the century. During his long life, he published a very large number of books, and these have been very much collected in recent years, especially since his death in 1975, following shortly after his very belated knighthood. A bibliography exists:

David A. Jasen *A Bibliography and Reader's Guide to the First Editions of P. G. Wodehouse* (Barrie & Jenkins 1971).

This is essential reference, though there are one or two omissions—inevitable with a work such as this, I suppose. There is also a very useful checklist contained in *P. G. Wodehouse: Portrait of a Master* (Garnstone Press 1975), by the same author. Of all the books on Wodehouse, however—and there are now about a dozen—the best is still Richard Usborne *Wodehouse at Work* (Jenkins 1961; updated and reissued by Barrie & Jenkins 1976).

Generally speaking, though with exceptions, the rarity of Wodehouse 1sts is in direct relation to their age—the earliest being the most difficult. There follows a checklist as complete as I can make it, with notes on points where necessary.

1. *The Pothunters* (novel) Black 1902; 1st Amer. Macmillan 1924
   This first book is bound in blue, with silver ornament, and not the later pictorial cover. No adverts. Very, very scarce.
2. *A Prefect's Uncle* (novel) Black 1903; 1st Amer. Macmillan 1924
3. *Tales of St. Austin's* (stories) Black 1903; 1st Amer. Macmillan 1923

4. *The Gold Bat* (novel) Black 1904; 1st Amer. Macmillan 1923

5. *William Tell Told Again* Black 1904
This retelling of the classic tale is scarce in any edition, but the 1st may be recognized by the date on the t/p, and the absence of the publisher's address.

6. *The Head of Kay's* (novel) Black 1905; 1st Amer. Macmillan 1922

7. *Love Among the Chickens* (novel) Newnes 1906; 1st Amer. Circle Publishing Co. 1909
A 'Popular Edition' revised and entirely rewritten by the author was reissued by Jenkins in 1921.

8. *The White Feather* (novel) Black 1907; 1st Amer. Macmillan 1922

9. *Not George Washington* (novel) Cassell 1907 (with Herbert Westbrook)

10. *The Globe By the Way Book* Globe 1908
Again written with Herbert Westbrook, this paperback was a compilation of the 'By the Way' columns from the *Globe* Paper.

11. *The Swoop* (novel) Alston Rivers 1909
A pictorially wrapped paperback—see d/w of this book for illustration.

12. *Mike* (novel) Black 1909; 1st Amer. Macmillan 1924
The second part of this novel was reissued as *Enter Psmith* (Black 1935); the whole novel was then revised and reissued in two volumes—*Mike at Wrykyn* and *Mike and Psmith* (Jenkins 1953).

13. *The Intrusion of Jimmy* (novel) Watt US 1910
This was published a few months later in England by Alston Rivers as *A Gentleman of Leisure*. Not to be confused with the Newnes reissue of 1911.

14. *Psmith in the City* (novel) Black 1910

15. *The Prince and Betty* (novel) Watt US 1912

16. *The Prince and Betty* (novel) Mills & Boon 1912
An almost entirely different book to No. 15.

17. *The Little Nugget* (novel) Methuen 1913; 1st Amer. Watt 1914

18. *The Man Upstairs* (stories) Methuen 1914

19. *Something New* (novel) Appleton US 1915
This was published in England during the same year by Methuen as *Something Fresh.*

20. *Psmith Journalist* (novel) Black 1915

Another version of No. 15.

21. *Uneasy Money* (novel) Appleton 1916; 1st Eng. Methuen 1917

22. *Piccadilly Jim* (novel) Dodd Mead 1917; 1st Eng. Jenkins 1918
Wodehouse's first book with Jenkins.

23. *The Man with Two Left Feet* (stories) Methuen 1917; 1st Amer. Burt 1933

24. *My Man Jeeves* (stories) Newnes 1919
The first Jeeves title. This small red volume was issued in Newnes 1/9d Novel Series.

25. *Their Mutual Child* (novel) Boni & Liveright US 1919
This was published in England in 1920 by Jenkins as *The Coming of Bill.*

26. *A Damsel in Distress* (novel) Doran 1919; 1st Eng. Jenkins 1919

27. *The Little Warrior* (novel) Doran 1920
This was published in England in 1921 by Jenkins as *Jill the Reckless.*

28. *Indiscretions of Archie* (stories) Jenkins 1921; 1st Amer. Doran 1921

29. *The Clicking of Cuthbert* (stories) Jenkins 1922
The 1st lists only eight titles on the verso of the half-title. The book was published in America in 1924 by Doran as *Golf Without Tears.*

30. *Three Men and a Maid* (novel) Doran 1922
This was published in England, in a revised form, by Jenkins in 1922 as *The Girl on the Boat.*

31. *The Adventures of Sally* (novel) Jenkins 1922
Dated 1923. The American edition, entitled *Mostly Sally,* was published in 1923 by Doran.

32. *The Inimitable Jeeves* (stories) Jenkins 1923
This must list ten titles on the verso of the half-title. The American edition, entitled simply *Jeeves,* was published in the same year by Doran.

33. *Leave it to Psmith* (novel) Jenkins 1923; 1st Amer. Doran 1924

34. *Ukridge* (stories) Jenkins 1924
Thirteen titles must appear on the verso of the half-title. The book was published in America in 1926 by Doran as *He Rather Enjoyed It* (!)

35. *Bill the Conqueror* (novel) Methuen 1924; 1st Amer. Doran 1925

36. *Carry On, Jeeves* (stories) Jenkins 1925; 1st Amer. Doran 1927
37. *Sam the Sudden* (novel) Methuen 1925
The American edition of this, published by Doran in the same year, was entitled *Sam in the Suburbs*.
38. *The Heart of a Goof* (stories) Jenkins 1926
The American title was *Divots* (Doran 1927).
39. *Hearts and Diamonds* (play adapt.) Prowse 1926 (with Laurie Wylie)
40. *The Play's the Thing* (play adapt.) Brentano's US 1927
41. *The Small Bachelor* (novel) Methuen 1927; 1st Amer. Doran 1927
42. *Meet Mr. Mulliner* (stories) Jenkins 1927; 1st Amer. Doran 1928
43. *Good Morning, Bill* (play) Methuen 1928
44. *Money for Nothing* (novel) Jenkins 1928; 1st Amer. Doran 1928
45. *Mr. Mulliner Speaking* (stories) Jenkins 1929; 1st Amer. Doubleday 1930
46. *Fish Preferred* (novel) Doubleday 1929
The English edition of this, published by Jenkins in the same year, was entitled *Summer Lightning*.
47. *A Damsel in Distress* (play) French 1930 (with Ian Hay)
48. *Baa, Baa, Black Sheep* (play) French 1930 (with Ian Hay)
49. *Very Good, Jeeves* (stories) Doubleday 1930; 1st Eng. Jenkins 1930
50. *Big Money* (novel) Doubleday 1931; 1st Eng. Jenkins 1931
51. *If I Were You* (novel) Doubleday 1931; 1st Eng. Jenkins 1931
52. *Jeeves Omnibus* (anthol.) Jenkins 1931
53. *Leave It to Psmith* (play) French 1932 (with Ian Hay)
54. *Louder and Funnier* (essays) Faber 1932
Wodehouse's only book of humorous essays, and his only book from Faber. Only those copies in yellow cloth, with the Rex Whistler d/w, are the first issue. Sheets were later bound in green for the Faber Library series.
55. *Doctor Sally* (novel) Methuen 1932
56. *Hot Water* (novel) Jenkins 1932; 1st Amer. Doubleday 1932
57. *Nothing but Wodehouse* (anthol.) Doubleday 1932

58. *Mulliner Nights* (stories) Jenkins 1933; 1st Amer. Doubleday 1933
59. *Heavy Weather* (novel) Little Brown 1933; 1st Eng. Jenkins 1933
60. *Candlelight* (play adapt.) French 1934
61. *A Century of Humour* (ed.) Hutchinson 1934
62. *Library of Humour: P. G. Wodehouse* (anthol.) Methuen 1934
63. *Right Ho, Jeeves* (novel) Jenkins 1934
This was published by Little Brown in America, during the same year, as *Brinkley Manor*.
64. *Thank You, Jeeves* (novel) Jenkins 1934; 1st Amer. Little Brown 1934
65. *Enter Psmith* (novel) Black 1935 (see No. 12)
66. *Mulliner Omnibus* (anthol.) Jenkins 1935
67. *Blandings Castle* (stories) Jenkins 1935; 1st Amer. Doubleday 1935
68. *The Luck of the Bodkins* (novel) Jenkins 1935; 1st Amer. Little Brown 1936
69. *Anything Goes* (play) French 1936
70. *Young Men in Spats* (stories) Jenkins 1936; 1st Amer. Doubleday 1936
71. *Laughing Gas* (novel) Jenkins 1936; 1st Amer. Doubleday 1936
72. *The Three Musketeers* (play) Chappell 1937; 1st Amer. Harms 1937 (with Clifford Grey and George Grossmith)
73. *Lord Emsworth and Others* (stories) Jenkins 1937
This was published as *Crime Wave At Blandings* by Doubleday in America, during the same year.
74. *Summer Moonshine* (novel) Doubleday 1937; 1st Eng. Jenkins 1938
75. *The Code of the Woosters* (novel) Doubleday 1938; 1st Eng. Jenkins 1938
76. *Weekend Wodehouse* (anthol.) Jenkins 1939; 1st Amer. Doubleday 1939
77. *Uncle Fred in the Springtime* (novel) Doubleday 1939; 1st Eng. Jenkins 1939
78. *Wodehouse on Golf* (anthol.) Doubleday 1940
79. *Eggs, Beans and Crumpets* (stories) Jenkins 1940; 1st Amer. Doubleday 1940
80. *Quick Service* (novel) Jenkins 1940; 1st Amer. Doubleday 1940
81. *Money in the Bank* (novel) Doubleday 1942; 1st Eng. Jenkins 1946

82. *Joy in the Morning* (novel) Doubleday 1946; 1st Eng. Jenkins 1947

83. *Full Moon* (novel) Doubleday 1947; 1st Eng. Jenkins 1947

84. *Spring Fever* (novel) Doubleday 1948; 1st Eng. Jenkins 1948

85. *Uncle Dynamite* (novel) Jenkins 1948; 1st Amer. Didier 1948

86. *The Best of Wodehouse* (anthol.) Pocket Books US 1949

87. *The Mating Season* (novel) Jenkins 1949; 1st Amer. Didier 1949

88. *Nothing Serious* (stories) Jenkins 1950; 1st Amer. Doubleday 1951

89. *The old Reliable* (novel) Jenkins 1951; 1st Amer. Doubleday 1951

90. *Best of Modern Humor* (ed.) McBride US 1952

91. *The Week-End Book of Humo(u)r* (ed.) Washburn 1952; 1st Eng. Jenkins 1954

92. *Barmy in Wonderland* (novel) Jenkins 1952
This was published by Doubleday in America as *Angel Cake* in 1952.

93. *Pigs Have Wings* (novel) Doubleday 1952; 1st Eng. Jenkins 1952

94. *Mike at Wrykyn* (novel) Jenkins 1953

95. *Mike and Psmith* (novel) Jenkins 1953
For Nos 94 and 95, see No. 12.

96. *Ring for Jeeves* (novel) Jenkins 1953
This was published as *The Return of Jeeves* by Simon & Schuster in America in 1954.

97. *Bring on the Girls* (autobiog.) Simon & Schuster 1953; 1st Eng. Jenkins 1954
Written with Guy Bolton. The English edition was rewritten, and the photographs differ.

98. *Performing Flea* (letters) Jenkins 1953
An extensively revised edition, entitled *Author! Author!,* was published in America by Simon & Schuster in 1962.

99. *Jeeves and the Feudal Spirit* (novel) Jenkins 1954
This was published in America in 1955 by Simon & Schuster as *Bertie Wooster Sees It Through.*

100. *Carry On Jeeves* (play) Evans 1956 (with Guy Bolton)

101. *French Leave* (novel) Jenkins 1956; 1st Amer. Simon & Schuster 1959

102. *America, I Like You* (autobiog.) Simon & Schuster 1956

103. *Over Seventy* (autobiog.) Jenkins 1957
A revised edition of No. 102.

104. *Something Fishy* (novel) Jenkins 1957
This was published in the same year by Simon & Schuster in America as *The Butler Did It.*

105. *Selected Stories by P. G. Wodehouse* Modern Library 1958

106. *Cocktail Time* (novel) Jenkins 1958; 1st Amer. Simon & Schuster 1958

107. *A Few Quick Ones* (stories) Simon & Schuster 1959; 1st Eng. Jenkins 1959

108. *The Most of P. G. Wodehouse* (anthol.) Simon & Schuster 1960

109. *How Right You Are, Jeeves* (novel) Simon & Schuster 1960
This was published during the same year in England by Jenkins as *Jeeves in the Offing.*

110. *The Ice in the Bedroom* (novel) Simon & Schuster 1961; 1st Eng. Jenkins 1961
The English edition lacks the word 'The' in the title.

111. *Service with a Smile* (novel) Simon & Schuster 1961; 1st Eng. Jenkins 1962

112. *Stiff Upper Lip, Jeeves* (novel) Simon & Schuster 1963; 1st Eng. Jenkins 1963

113. *Biffen's Millions* (novel) Simon & Schuster 1964
This was published in England during the same year as *Frozen Assets* (Jenkins).

114. *The Brinkmanship of Galahad Threepwood* (novel) Simon & Schuster 1965
The English title of this book was *Galahad at Blandings* (Jenkins 1965).

115. *Plum Pie* (stories) Jenkins 1966; 1st Amer. Simon & Schuster 1967

116. *A Carnival of Modern Humo(u)r* (ed.) Delacorte 1967; 1st Eng. Jenkins 1968
This, along with Nos 90 and 91, was edited in association with Scott Meredith.

117. *The World of Jeeves* (anthol.) Jenkins 1967

118. *The Purloined Paperweight* (novel) Simon & Schuster 1967
This was published in England in 1967 by Jenkins as *Company for Henry.*

119. *Do Butlers Burgle Banks?* (novel) Simon &

Schuster 1968; 1st Eng. Jenkins 1968

20. *A Pelican at Blandings* (novel) Jenkins 1969
    This was published in America by Simon &
    Schuster in 1970. The title, unbelievably, was
    No Nudes Is Good Nudes.
21. *The Girl in Blue* (novel) Barrie & Jenkins
    1970; 1st Amer. Simon & Schuster 1971
22. *Much Obliged, Jeeves* (novel) Barrie & Jenkins
    1971
    This novel was published to coincide with P.
    G. W.'s ninetieth birthday. In America it had
    the title *Jeeves and the Tie That Binds* (Simon &
    Schuster 1971).
23. *The World of Mr. Mulliner* (anthol.) Barrie &
    Jenkins 1972; 1st Amer. Taplinger 1974
24. *Pearls, Girls, and Monty Bodkin* (novel) Barrie
    & Jenkins 1972
    In America this was called *The Plot That
    Thickened*, and was published by Simon &
    Schuster in 1973.
25. *The Golf Omnibus* (anthol.) Barrie & Jenkins
    1973; 1st Amer. Simon & Schuster 1974
26. *Bachelors Anonymous* (novel) Barrie & Jenkins
    1973; 1st Amer. Simon & Schuster 1974
27. *The World of Psmith* (anthol.) Barrie &
    Jenkins 1974
28. *Aunts Aren't Gentlemen* (novel) Barrie &
    Jenkins 1974
    Published in America as *The Cat-Nappers* by
    Simon & Schuster in 1974.
29. *The World of Ukridge* (anthol.) Barrie &
    Jenkins 1975
30. *The World of Blandings* (anthol.) Barrie &
    Jenkins 1976
31. *Vintage Wodehouse* (anthol.) Barrie & Jenkins
    1977
32. *Uncollected Wodehouse* (anthol.) Barrie &
    Jenkins 1977
33. *Sunset at Blandings* Chatto & Windus 1977
    (posthumous, unfinished novel, ed. Richard
    Usborne)

In addition to the above, Wodehouse wrote
Introductions to about half-a-dozen books,
and wrote new Prefaces to many of the
volumes in the Jenkins 'Autograph Edition'
of his works. Of course, there are also all the
magazine contributions—ranging from the
Strand to *Playboy*—and most notably the boys'

paper *The Captain*, which contains all his
early school stories, before they were put into
book form. Details of these, and of the sheet
music for the many musicals he worked on
with Kern, Gershwin and others, may be
found in the Jasen biography, mentioned
above.

Although valuation for the later titles is a
relatively simple matter, it becomes a near
impossible task when dealing with the pre-
1920 books, for the simple reason that they
come up so rarely that records do not exist.
One thing is certain: there are far more
collectors seeking these early titles than there
are copies available, and after years searching,
the collectors become desperate, and the
dealers possibly a trifle greedy. The prices
are, quite simply, whatever the dealer can get,
and whatever the collector is willing to pay.
Not to leave the situation quite so vague,
however, I submit the following as a guide.
No. 1 would be very cheap at Grade I,
though I am quite sure there are those willing
to pay £100 for it; the first book of such a
prolific master as Plum is, after all, quite
something. Grade K, however, is probably a
fair price. Nos 2, 3, 4, 5 and 6 are Grade I—
always assuming that all illustrations are
present, for they do seem particularly prone
to become detached. Nos 7, 9, 10 and 11 are
particularly scarce, many collectors never
having seen any of them; Nos 9, 10 and 11
were never reprinted in any form, and are
therefore even more desirable. All these
would be Grade K and upwards. Nos 8, 12—
a veritable highlight—13, 14, 17, 18, 19, 20,
21, 22 and 23 are all very difficult, and Grade
E–G. Nos 15, 16 and 24 are even scarcer, and
would be more. No. 24 is a very interesting
item, for although it is the first book
appearance of Jeeves, its format could easily
be mistaken for a cheap reprint—scope for a
bargain.
At this point, they begin to get a bit easier,
though Nos 25, 26, 27, 28, 29, 30, 31 and 32
are Grade C–D. Nos 33–53 inclusive are
Grade B–C, though they would be worth
more if in fine d/ws—always difficult. No. 54

is scarce, and Grade D. Nos 55–60 are Grade C, and No. 61 Grade A—a common book, but very rare in the d/w, which was intended to be cut up for the coupons on the reverse—and it seems that most were. Nos 62–80 are Grade C, the Jeeves titles always commanding slightly more than the others. Nos 81–93 are Grade B, though Nos 94 and 95 are very elusive, and might go slightly higher. Nos 97 and 102 are difficult, and Grade C. Nos 96, 98, 99, 100, 101 and 103–112 are Grade A–B. No. 117 is Grade B, and the remainder Grade A, with the exception of the recent anthologies (Nos 123, 125, 127, 129 and 130) which are Grade B, because of their publication price.
It ought to be remembered that these prices are rising all the time.

Films:
Summer Lightning Dominion 1932
Piccadilly Jim MGM 1936
Thank You, Jeeves 20th Century Fox 1936
A Damsel in Distress RKO 1937
The Girl on the Boat United Artists 1962

According to the bibliography at the rear of Usborne's *Wodehouse at Work*, more than twenty more films were made between the years of 1915 and 1937.

WOOLF, Leonard
Born in London 1880. Died 1969.
Author of a large number of books, the majority being of a political nature. His publishing achievements, with Virginia, in the Hogarth Press, were great, and many collect the entire output of this Press—not an easy task, but aided by the checklist (Hogarth Press 1976). There follows a selection of Woolf's most notable works.

1. *The Village in the Jungle* (novel) Arnold 1913; 1st Amer. Harcourt Brace 1926
2. *The Hotel* (play) Hogarth Press 1939; 1st Amer. Dial Press 1963
3. *Sowing* (autobiog.) Hogarth Press 1960; 1st Amer. Harcourt Brace 1960

4. *Growing* (autobiog.) Hogarth Press 1961; 1st Amer. Harcourt Brace 1962
5. *Beginning Again* (autobiog.) Hogarth Press 1964; 1st Amer. Harcourt Brace 1964
6. *Downhill All the Way* (autobiog.) Hogarth Press 1967; 1st Amer. Harcourt Brace 1967
7. *The Journey Not the Arrival Matters* (autobiog.) Hogarth Press 1969; 1st Amer. Harcourt Brace 1970

No. 1 is very scarce, and Grade F–G. No. 2 is Grade B, as are the five volumes of autobiography (each).

WOOLF, Virginia
Born in London 1882. Died 1941.
The following is essential reference:
B. J. Kirkpatrick *A Bibliography of Virginia Woolf* (Soho Bibliographies, Hart-Davis 1957) Below is a checklist of her published works.

1. *The Voyage Out* (novel) Duckworth 1915; 1st Amer. Doran 1920
2. *Two Stories* Hogarth Press 1917
Cont. *The Mark on the Wall* by Virginia, and *The Three Jews* by Leonard. It is notable for being the very first Hogarth Press publication, printed in an edition of 150 wrappered copies.
3. *Kew Gardens* (story) Hogarth Press 1919
150 copies printed, in wrapps.
4. *Night and Day* (novel) Duckworth 1919; 1st Amer. Doran 1920
5. *Monday or Tuesday* (stories) Hogarth Press 1921; 1st Amer. Harcourt Brace 1921
Woodcuts and cover design by Vanessa Bell.
6. *Jacob's Room* (novel) Hogarth Press 1922; 1st Amer. Harcourt Brace 1923
7. *Mr Bennett and Mrs Brown* (essay) Hogarth Press 1924
No. 1 in the Hogarth Essays series.
8. *The Common Reader* (essays) Hogarth Press 1925; 1st Amer. Harcourt Brace 1925
9. *Mrs Dalloway* (novel) Hogarth Press 1925; 1st Amer. Harcourt Brace 1925
10. *To the Lighthouse* (novel) Hogarth Press 1927; 1st Amer. Harcourt Brace 1927
11. *Orlando: A Biography* (novel) Crosby Gaige

172

NY 1928; 1st Eng. Hogarth Press 1928; 1st trade Amer. Harcourt Brace 1928
The Gaige edition was limited to 861 copies, 800 numbered and signed for sale at $15.

12. *A Room of One's Own* (essay) Fountain Press/Hogarth Press 1929; 1st trade Eng. Hogarth Press 1929; 1st trade Amer. Harcourt Brace 1929
The 1st joint American-English edition was limited to 492 copies, 450 for sale, and each signed.

13. *Street Haunting* (essay) Westgate Press, San Francisco 1930
Limited to 500 signed copies.

14. *On Being Ill* (essay) Hogarth Press 1930
Limited to 250 signed copies.

15. *Beau Brummell* (essay) Rimington & Hooper NY 1930
Limited to 550 signed copies.

16. *The Waves* (novel) Hogarth Press 1931; 1st Amer. Harcourt Brace 1931

17. *A Letter to a Young Poet* (essay) Hogarth Press 1932
No. 8 in the Hogarth Letters series.

18. *The Common Reader: Second Series* (essays) Hogarth Press 1932; 1st Amer. Harcourt Brace 1932

19. *Flush: A Biography* Hogarth Press 1933; 1st Amer. Harcourt Brace 1933

20. *Walter Sickert: A Conversation* (essay) Hogarth Press 1934

21. *The Roger Fry Memorial Exhibition* (address) Bristol 1935
Only 125 copies printed, and none for sale.

22. *The Years* (novel) Hogarth Press 1937; 1st Amer. Harcourt Brace 1937

23. *Three Guineas* (essay) Hogarth Press 1938; 1st Amer. Harcourt Brace 1938

24. *Reviewing* (essay) Hogarth Press 1939
No. 4 in the Hogarth Sixpenny Pamphlets series.

25. *Roger Fry: A Biography* Hogarth Press 1940; 1st Amer. Harcourt Brace 1940

26. *Between the Acts* (novel) Hogarth Press 1941; 1st Amer. Harcourt Brace 1941

27. *The Death of the Moth* (essays) Hogarth Press 1942; 1st Amer. Harcourt Brace 1942

28. *A Haunted House* (stories) Hogarth Press 1943; 1st Amer. Harcourt Brace 1944

29. *The Moment and Other Essays* Hogarth Press 1947; 1st Amer. Harcourt Brace 1948

30. *The Captain's Death Bed* (essays) Hogarth Press 1950; 1st Amer. Harcourt Brace 1950
The American edition actually preceded by one week.

31. *A Writer's Diary* Hogarth Press 1953; 1st Amer. Harcourt Brace 1954

32. *Virginia Woolf & Lytton Strachey: Letters* Hogarth Press 1956; 1st Amer. Harcourt Brace 1956

33. *Granite and Rainbow* (essays) Hogarth Press 1958; 1st Amer. Harcourt Brace 1958

34. *Contemporary Writers* (essays) Hogarth Press 1965; 1st Amer. Harcourt Brace 1966

35. *Nurse Lugton's Golden Thimble* (story) Hogarth Press 1966
With pictures by Duncan Grant.

36. *Mrs Dalloway's Party* (story) Hogarth Press 1973

37. *The Flight of the Mind: The Letters of Virginia Woolf 1888–1912* Hogarth Press 1975; 1st Amer. Harcourt Brace 1975

38. *Moments of Being* (autobiog.) Sussex University Press 1976

39. *The Question of Things Happening: The Letters of Virginia Woolf 1912–1922* Hogarth Press 1976; 1st Amer. Harcourt Brace 1976

40. *Freshwater* (comedy) Hogarth Press 1976

41. *Diaries: 1915–1919* Hogarth Press 1977

42. *Books and Portraits* (essays) Hogarth Press 1977

Nos 37 and 39 are to be followed by four more volumes, to be published at yearly intervals, and other Woolf items seem to be discovered all the time.
A very fine biography has appeared, which is already a classic:
Quentin Bell *Virginia Woolf* (2 vols; Hogarth Press 1972; Harcourt Brace 1974)
Virginia Woolf is very, very popular, and prices are rising all the time—even for the once-common posthumous works. Condition is all important—many rather nasty 1sts are encountered, either read to death, or covered in library stamps. The d/w is also an

important factor here, as most were designed—and very well designed—by Vanessa Bell. The price guide that follows, then, is for very good or fine copies, in d/w where applicable. Prices are always considerably higher for the Hogarth editions, for obvious reasons.

Nos 1, 2 and 3 are scarce, and Grade M–N. No. 4 is Grade I, as are Nos 5, 6, 8, 9 and 10. No. 7 is Grade E, No. 11 is Grade D–E, and No. 12 is Grade G. Nos 13 and 15 would be Grade L, and No. 14 tops Grade P. No. 16 is, of course, a highlight, and Grade K. Nos 18, 20, 23 and 26 are Grade D, and Nos 17, 19, 24, 25, 27, 28, 30, 31, 35, 37 and 39 are Grade C. No. 21 is extremely scarce, and Grade H–I, No. 22 is Grade F, and the remainder Grade B.

WYNDHAM, John

Pseudonym of John Beynon Harris. Born in Birmingham, England, 1903. Died 1969

1. *Foul Play Suspected* (novel) Newnes 1935 (as John Beynon)
2. *The Secret People* (novel) Newnes 1935 (as John Beynon)
3. *Planet Plane* (novel) Newnes 1935 (as John Beynon)
   Reissued by Michael Joseph in 1972 as *Stowaway to Mars.*
4. *The Day of the Triffids* (novel) Joseph 1951; 1st Amer. Doubleday 1951
5. *The Kraken Wakes* (novel) Jopseph 1953
   This was published in America by Ballantine during the same year with the title *Out of the Deeps.*
6. *Jizzle* (stories) Dobson 1954
7. *The Chrysalids* (novel) Joseph 1955
8. *Re-Birth* (stories) Ballantine NY 1955
9. *The Seeds of Time* (stories) Joseph 1956
10. *The Midwich Cuckoos* (novel) Joseph 1957; 1st Amer. Ballantine 1957
11. *The Outward Urge* Joseph 1959 (with L. Parkes)
    Lucas Parkes is another of Wyndham's pseudonyms, apparently used because the author considered the stories to be unlike his usual style.

12. *Trouble with Lichen* (novel) Joseph 1960
13. *Consider Her Ways and Others* (stories) Joseph 1961
    The title story first appeared in *Sometime, Never* (Eyre & Spottiswoode 1956; Ballantine 1956).
14. *The John Wyndham Omnibus* Joseph 1964; 1st Amer. Simon & Schuster 1966
    Contains Nos 4, 5 and 7, the last two appearing in America for the first time.
15. *Chocky* (novel) Joseph 1968
16. *The Man from Beyond* (stories) Joseph 1975

The pre-war novels are very difficult, as are copies of the American pulp magazines for which he was writing at the time, though the fact that they are under the name Beynon might make for a lucky find; otherwise they would be Grade F–G. No. 4 is his highlight, and Grade C–D. Nos 5, 6, 7, 9, 10 and 12 are Grade C, Nos 8, 11, 13 and 14 Grade B, and Nos 15 and 16 Grade A.

Films:
The Village of the Damned MGM 1960 (*The Midwich Cuckoos*)
The Day of the Triffids Rank 1962

YATES, Dornford

Pseudonym of Cecil William Mercer. Born in London 1885. Died 1960.
Author of thirty-four novels, many featuring Berry, and suddenly quite popular with collectors. They are still within Grade A, however. The first Berry was:

Berry & Co. Ward Lock 1921; 1st Amer. Minton 1928

YEATS, W. B.

Born 1865. Died 1939.
Apart from hundreds of books edited by and contributed to by Yeats, the exhaustive bibliography lists over two hundred titles written by him. It is therefore absolutely essential reference for the serious Yeats collector, though the beginner will find a very long, difficult and expensive road ahead of him:

Allan Wade *A Bibliography of the Writings of W. B. Yeats* (Soho Bibliographies, Hart-Davis 1951; 2nd ed. [revised] 1958)
Below appears a necessarily brief selection.

1. *The Wanderings of Oisin* (verse) Kegan Paul Trench 1889; 1st Amer. Cassell 1891
2. *The Countess Kathleen* [*sic*] (legends) Fisher Unwin 1892; 1st Amer. Roberts Bros 1892
3. *The Celtic Twilight* (verse and essays) Lawrence & Bullen 1893; 1st Amer. Macmillan 1894
   Frontispiece by Jack B. Yeats.
4. *The Land of Heart's Desire* (play) Fisher Unwin 1894; 1st Amer. Stone & Kimball 1894
   Title page by Aubrey Beardsley.
5. *Poems* Fisher Unwin 1895; 1st Amer. Copeland & Day 1895
6. *The Poetical Works of William B. Yeats* Vol. I Macmillan 1906; 1st Amer. Macmillan 1906
7. *The Poetical Works of William B. Yeats* Vol. II Macmillan 1907; 1st Amer. Macmillan 1907
8. *The Green Helmet and Other Poems* Cuala Press 1910; 1st Amer. Paget 1911
9. *Later Poems* Macmillan 1922; 1st Amer. Macmillan 1928
10. *The Tower* (verse) Macmillan 1928; 1st Amer. Macmillan 1928
11. *The Collected Poems of W. B. Yeats* Macmillan 1933; 1st Amer. Macmillan 1933
12. *The Collected Plays of W. B. Yeats* Macmillan 1934; 1st Amer. Macmillan 1935
13. *A Vision* (philosophy) Macmillan 1937; 1st Amer. Macmillan 1938
    A book was issued to subscribers only, privately printed, in 1925, with this title, but according to the bibliography, the 1937 edition is virtually a new book.
14. *The Letters of W. B. Yeats* Hart-Davis 1954; 1st Amer. Macmillan 1955
15. *Autobiographies* Macmillan 1955
    A collection of previously published autobiographical writings.

The first issue of No. 1 is very scarce (only 500 printed), and Grade R. Nos 2, 3 and 4 are also extremely rare, No. 2 being Grade Q, and Nos 3 and 4 Grade P. No. 5 is Grade I, as are Nos 6 and 7 (together), 8, 9 and 10. No. 11 is Grade H, with No. 12 possibly slightly lower. No. 13 is Grade E, as against Grade P for the original limited edition, and Nos 14 and 15 are Grade C.

YEVTUSHENKO, Yevgeny
Born in Russia 1933.

1. *Selected Poems* Penguin 1962; 1st Amer. Dutton 1962
2. *A Precocious Autobiography* Dutton 1963; 1st Eng. Collins 1963
3. *The Poetry of Yevgeny Yevtushenko 1963–1965* October House 1965; 1st Eng. Calder 1966
4. *Poetry of Yevtushenko, Pasternak, and Akhmatova* Bradda US 1965
5. *Yevtushenko: Poems* Dutton 1966; 1st Eng. Pergamon 1967
6. *Poems Chosen by the Author* Collins 1966
   Published simply as *Poems* in America by Hill & Wang in 1967.
7. *The Bratsk Station* (verse) Praeger 1967; 1st Eng. Hart-Davis 1967
8. *Red Cats* (verse) City Lights, San Francisco 1967
9. *Stolen Apples* (verse) Doubleday 1971; 1st Eng. Allen 1972
10. *Yevtushenko's Reader* Dutton 1972 (cont. *The Spirit of Elbe, A Precocious Autobiography* and *Poems*)
11. *From Desire to Desire* (verse) Doubleday 1976

None of these is particularly scarce, though the first impression of the Penguin (No. 1) will be elusive, but Grade A nonetheless. Also Grade A are Nos 6, 7, 9, 10 and 11, with the rest Grade B.

DATE DUE

JAN 1 9 1981			
			PRINTED IN U.S.A.